ICWMC 2016

The Twelfth International Conference on Wireless and Mobile Communications

November 13 - 17, 2016

Barcelona, Spain

ICWMC 2016 Editors

Carlos Becker Westphall, University of Santa Catarina, Brazil

Eugen Borcoci, University "Politehnica" Bucharest, Romania

Dragana Krstic, University of Nis, Serbia

David Sanchez, University of Las Palmas de Gran Canaria, Spain

Kasturi Vasudevan, IITK - Indian Institute of Technology Kanpur - IIT Kanpur, India

David Navarro, Ecole Centrale de Lyon, France

Printed from e-media with permission by:

Curran Associates, Inc.
57 Morehouse Lane
Red Hook, NY 12571

Printed by Curran Associates, Inc. (2016)

International Academy, Research, and Industry Association (IARIA)
412 Derby Way
Wilmington, DE 19810

Phone: (408) 893-6407
Fax: (408) 527-6351

petre@iaria.org

Additional copies of this publication are available from:

Curran Associates, Inc.
57 Morehouse Lane
Red Hook, NY 12571 USA
Phone: 845-758-0400
Fax: 845-758-2633
Email: curran@proceedings.com
Web: www.proceedings.com

Table of Contents

ICWMC 2016

Foreword

The Twelfth International Conference on Wireless and Mobile Communications (ICWMC 2016), held between November 13-17, 2016 - Barcelona, Spain, followed on the previous events on advanced wireless technologies, wireless networking, and wireless applications.

ICWMC 2016 addressed wireless related topics concerning integration of latest technological advances to realize mobile and ubiquitous service environments for advanced applications and services in wireless networks. Mobility and wireless, special services and lessons learnt from particular deployment complemented the traditional wireless topics.

We take here the opportunity to warmly thank all the members of the ICWMC 2016 Technical Program Committee, as well as the numerous reviewers. The creation of such a high quality conference program would not have been possible without their involvement. We also kindly thank all the authors who dedicated much of their time and efforts to contribute to ICWMC 2016. We truly believe that, thanks to all these efforts, the final conference program consisted of top quality contributions.

Also, this event could not have been a reality without the support of many individuals, organizations, and sponsors. We are grateful to the members of the ICWMC 2016 organizing committee for their help in handling the logistics and for their work to make this professional meeting a success.

We hope that ICWMC 2016 was a successful international forum for the exchange of ideas and results between academia and industry and for the promotion of progress in the area of wireless and mobile communications.

We are convinced that the participants found the event useful and communications very open. We also hope the attendees enjoyed the charm of Barcelona, Spain.

ICWMC 2016 Chairs:

ICWMC Advisory Committee

Dragana Krstic, University of Nis, Serbia
Magnus Jonsson, Halmstad University, Sweden
Mari Carmen Aguayo Torres, University of Malaga, Spain
Wolfgang Narzt, Johannes Kepler University Linz, Austria
Robert Bestak, CVUT in Prague, Czech Republic
Abdulrahman Yarali, Murray State University, USA

ICWMC Industry/Research Chairs

Christopher Nguyen, Intel Corp., USA
Mohamad Sayed Hassan, Orange Labs (Alten) / Paris - France
Wolfgang Aichmann, Nokia Siemens Networks, Germany

ICWMC 2016

Committee

ICWMC Advisory Committee

Dragana Krstic, University of Nis, Serbia
Magnus Jonsson, Halmstad University, Sweden
Mari Carmen Aguayo Torres, University of Malaga, Spain
Wolfgang Narzt, Johannes Kepler University Linz, Austria
Robert Bestak, CVUT in Prague, Czech Republic
Abdulrahman Yarali, Murray State University, USA

ICWMC Industry/Research Chairs

Christopher Nguyen, Intel Corp., USA
Mohamad Sayed Hassan, Orange Labs (Alten) / Paris - France
Wolfgang Aichmann, Nokia Siemens Networks, Germany
Ahmed Ibrahim, Intel Corporation, Egypt
Daniele Grasso, STMicroelectronics Srl, Italy

ICWMC Publicity Chairs

Siavash Rahimi, McGill University, Canada
Wu-Shiung Feng, Chang Gung University, Taiwan
Claudio Monteiro, IFTO, Brazil
Isaí Michel Lombera, University of California - Santa Barbara, USA

ICWMC 2016 Technical Program Committee

Jemal Abawajy, Deakin University - Victoria, Australia
Mohammed Abdel-Hafez, UAE University-Al-Ain, United Arab Emirates
Seyed Reza Abdollahi, Brunel University - London, UK
Taufik Abrão, State University of Londrina (UEL), Brazil
Ali Abu-El Humos, Jackson State University, USA
Fumiyuki Adachi, Tohoku University, Japan
Afrand Agah, West Chester University of Pennsylvania, USA
Javier M. Aguiar Pérez, Universidad de Valladolid, Spain
Mari Carmen Aguayo-Torres, Universidad de Malaga, Spain
Chang-Jun Ahn, Chiba University, Japan
Aydin Akan, Istanbul University, Turkey
Ahmed Akl, LAAS/CNRS - Toulouse, France
Samir Al-Ghadhban, King Fahd University of Petroleum and Minerals (KFUPM), Saudi Arabia
Hamed Al-Raweshidy, Brunel University - Uxbridge, UK
Alessandro Aldini, University of Urbino "Carlo Bo", Italy

Erick Amador, Intel Mobile Communications, France
Karine Amis, Institut Mines-Telecom/Telecom Bretagne, France
Lidiane Araújo, Federal University of Pernambuco, Brazil
Jose Enrique Armendariz-Inigo, Universidad Publica de Navarra, Spain
Radu Arsinte, Technical University of Cluj-Napoca, Romania
Hakim Badis, University of Paris-Est Marne-la-Vallée, France
Mohammad M. Banat, Jordan University of Science and Technology, Jordan
Alessandro Bazzi, IEIIT-CNR, University of Bologna, Italy
Nsiri Bechir, National Engineering School of Tunis, Tunisia
Carlos Becker Westphall, Federal University of Santa Catarina, Brazil
Mouncef Benmimoune, Université du Québec, Canada
Gilberto Berardinelli, Aalborg University, Denmark
Robert Bestak, Czech Technical University in Prague, Czech Republic
Gennaro Boggia, Polytechnic University of Bari, Italy
Alireza Borhani, University of Agder - Grimstad, Norway
Olivier Bourchet, Orange, France
David Boyle, Imperial College London, UK
Maurizio Bozzi, University of Pavia, Italy
Maria Calderon, University Carlos III of Madrid, Spain
Juan-Carlos Cano, Universidad Politécnica de Valencia, Spain
Vicente Casares-Giner, Universidad Politécnica de Valencia, Spain
Pedro Castillejo Parrilla, Universidad Politécnica de Madrid, Spain
Eddie Chan, Hong Kong University of Science and Technology, Hong Kong
Sammy Chan, City University of Hong Kong, Hong Kong
Ajit Chaturvedi, Indian Institute of Technology Kanpur, India
Abdellah Chehri, University of Ottawa, Canada
Hsing-Lung Chen, National Taiwan University of Science and Technology - Taipei, Taiwan
Yu Chen, Binghamton University, SUNY, USA
Yunfei Chen, University of Warwick - Coventry, UK
Salim Chitroub, University of Science and Technology - Houari Boumediene (USTHB), Algeria
Silviu Ciochina, Universitatea Politehnica din Bucuresti, Romania
Hugo Coll Ferri, Polytechnic University of Valencia, Spain
Ana Collado, Centre Tecnologic de Telecomunicacions de Catalunya (CTTC) - Barcelona, Spain
Nicolae Crisan, Technical University of Cluj-Napoca, Romania
Danco Davcev, University “Ss Cyril and Methodius” - Skopje, Macedonia
Claudio de Castro Monteiro, Federal Institute of Education, Science and Technology of Tocantins, Brazil
Carl James Debono, University of Malta, Malta
Javier Del Ser Lorente, TECNALIA-Telecom - Zamudio (Bizkaia), Spain
Alisa Devlic, Royal Institute of Technology (KTH), Sweden
Karim Djouani, Pretoria, South Africa / University Paris Est-Creteil (UPEC), France
Trung Q. Duong, Blekinge Institute of Technology, Sweden
Alban Duverdier, Centre National d'Etudes Spatiales(CNES), France
Péter Ekler, Budapest University of Technology and Economics, Hungary
Ghaïs El Zein, IETR - INSA Rennes, France
Gianluigi Ferrari, Università di Parma, Italy
Armando Ferro Vázquez, Universidad del País Vasco / Euskal Herriko Unibertsitatea - Bilbao, Spain
Panayotis Fouliras, University of Macedonia, Thessaloniki, Greece
Jane Louie Fresco Zamora, Nara Institute of Science and Technology, Japan

Copyright Information

For your reference, this is the text governing the copyright release for material published by IARIA.

The copyright release is a transfer of publication rights, which allows IARIA and its partners to drive the dissemination of the published material. This allows IARIA to give articles increased visibility via distribution, inclusion in libraries, and arrangements for submission to indexes.

I, the undersigned, declare that the article is original, and that I represent the authors of this article in the copyright release matters. If this work has been done as work-for-hire, I have obtained all necessary clearances to execute a copyright release. I hereby irrevocably transfer exclusive copyright for this material to IARIA. I give IARIA permission or reproduce the work in any media format such as, but not limited to, print, digital, or electronic. I give IARIA permission to distribute the materials without restriction to any institutions or individuals. I give IARIA permission to submit the work for inclusion in article repositories as IARIA sees fit.

I, the undersigned, declare that to the best of my knowledge, the article is does not contain libelous or otherwise unlawful contents or invading the right of privacy or infringing on a proprietary right.

Following the copyright release, any circulated version of the article must bear the copyright notice and any header and footer information that IARIA applies to the published article.

IARIA grants royalty-free permission to the authors to disseminate the work, under the above provisions, for any academic, commercial, or industrial use. IARIA grants royalty-free permission to any individuals or institutions to make the article available electronically, online, or in print.

IARIA acknowledges that rights to any algorithm, process, procedure, apparatus, or articles of manufacture remain with the authors and their employers.

I, the undersigned, understand that IARIA will not be liable, in contract, tort (including, without limitation, negligence), pre-contract or other representations (other than fraudulent misrepresentations) or otherwise in connection with the publication of my work.

Exception to the above is made for work-for-hire performed while employed by the government. In that case, copyright to the material remains with the said government. The rightful owners (authors and government entity) grant unlimited and unrestricted permission to IARIA, IARIA's contractors, and IARIA's partners to further distribute the work.

Distance Measurement System Based on Visible Light Communications and Ultrasound Emitters

R. Rodriguez, J. Rabadan, V. Guerra, J. Rufo, R. Perez-Jimenez
Institute for Technological Development and Innovation on Communications (IDeTIC)
Universityof Las Palmas de Gran Canaria
Las Palmas de G. C., Spain
e-mail: jose.rabadan@ulpgc.es

***Abstract*— Distance estimation is an important task in positioning systems, as it is needed for performing the triangulation process used by location algorithms. Different techniques, such as received signal strength indication (RSSI), time of arrival (ToA), and time difference of arrival (TDoA), can be used to estimate the distance between devices. Cricket indoor positioning systems, designed by MIT, are based on TDoA techniques, and they use a combination of ultrasound and radiofrequency signals. In this paper, a new distance measurement scheme based on Cricket technology, but introducing some modifications, is proposed. In this way, some new advantages are obtained. The radiofrequency signal is substituted by an optical signal, making the system applicable to environments where radio emissions are not suitable. Furthermore, a double-way measurement is also introduced, in order to allow both measurement devices (base station and mobile node) to perform the distance estimation, unlike in Cricket systems, where only one of the devices is able to calculate the distance.**

Keywords-Distance estimation; VLC; time arrival; double measurement.

I. INTRODUCTION

Indoor distance measurement is a challenging problem for many indoor positioning systems, as they make use of location information to offer contextual services [1][2][3]. During the last few years, many different wireless methods based on WiFi, wireless sensor networks, Bluetooth, and Cricket sensors [4] have been suggested. These techniques use specific algorithms to estimate distance from different signal parameters, such as signal strength, and arriving angles or delays. However, these distance-measurement systems either need an additional network infrastructure or have difficulties in obtaining accurate distances because of multipath propagation. Visible Light Communications (VLC) [5][6] takes advantage of the relative high switching speed of LEDs to use the light from lamps not only for lighting but also as a transmission channel. VLC has a set of communication characteristics: low cost, light-speed propagation, and no electromagnetic interference, which reduces some Radio Frequency (RF) technological drawbacks, such as spectrum saturation or interference between systems.

In this paper, a new VLC distance-measurement scheme, based on the Cricket's TDoA paradigm is proposed. It uses an optical signal instead of the Cricket's radiofrequency one in order to avoid the aforementioned radio signal problems. In this way, the system can be used in other environments, such as underwater scenarios, where radiofrequency presents a prohibitively high attenuation. However, optical links require a more complicated alignment, or the use of several optical emitters and receivers. Moreover, by the moment, optical technology presents the lack of broadly accepted and implemented standards, which assure the interoperability between different systems, and only isolated solutions as the one presented in this work are being developed.

On the other hand, the transmission and reception stages have been modified in order to provide distance measurement capability simultaneously to the two devices involved in the process: the base station (or transmitter node in this work) and the mobile node (or receiver node). In Cricket systems, only receiver-node devices are able to estimate distance from the signal emitted by the transmitter node. In the proposed system, the mobile node returns back a new optical signal to the base station, allowing it to perform its own relative distance estimation. As it is needed in traditional Cricket networks, in order to develop a full positioning system, a trilateration structure [7] must be implemented using several of the presented distance meters.

This paper is organized as follows. In Section II, a description of the proposed method for obtaining the distance is presented. Section III presents a proof of concept implemented prototype. In Section IV, a detailed description of the measurements and results are provided. Section V summarizes the obtained conclusions.

II. DISTANCE ESTIMATION METHODS

In this work, VLC and ultrasound links are used in the measurement devices. The optical signals perform the same function than the Radiofrequency ones in Cricket schemes, which is to serve as time reference for measuring the ultrasound signal time delay. The basic scheme of the proposed system is presented in Fig. 1.

As it can be observed, the transmitter node uses an ultrasound transmitter, an optical transmitter and an optical receiver, whilst the receiver node makes use of an ultrasound receiver, an optical receiver and an optical transmitter. In this way, a single acoustic link and two optical links are established. The use of VLC technology is proposed because the aim of this work is to use the illumination fixtures as base stations in indoor positioning systems. Nevertheless, this scheme can be also used with other optical wavelengths (IR e.g.).

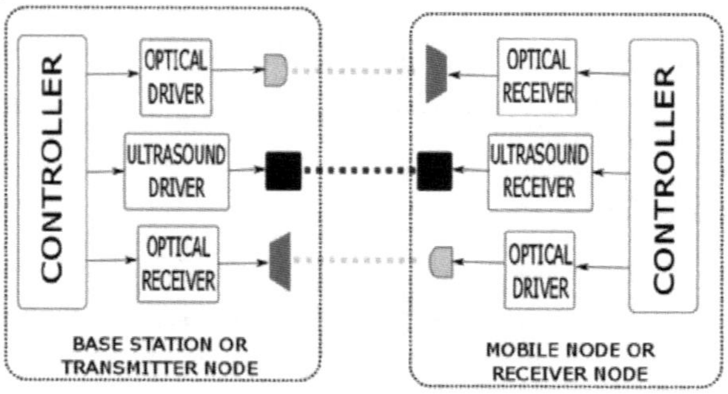

Figure 1. System scheme

In the measurement process, the base station starts sending an optical and an ultrasound signalsynchronously. The mobile node receives the optical signal and waits for the ultrasound signal arrival. As the time for light propagation can be neglected, at least, when compared with acoustic propagation, it can be considered that light is transmitted with zero delay, and the delay between both signals in reaching the receiver node, depends only on the ultrasound propagation. Therefore, the distance from base station to mobile node is proportional to that delay. This procedure is equivalent to the one performed by Cricket systems, except for the use of an optical signal instead of the radiofrequency one for delay reference. In this case, the estimated distance is calculate by (1)

$$D = \frac{t}{\frac{1}{v_S} - \frac{1}{c}} \approx v_S \cdot t \tag{1}$$

Where D is the distance, t is delay time, c is the speed of light and v_S is the speed of sound. Nonetheless, there are several delay sources that must be considered if an accurate result is intended. The main delay sources are the electric-to-acoustic and acoustic-to-electric transduction times in the acoustic interfaces, and the time delay due to the sequential operation of the microcontroller.The delays produced by this sources are solved by means of an adjustment variable. In order to set and synchronize the LED and the ultrasound pulses in the mobile system, an adjustment variable with a value of 250 microseconds has been used.

This value allows adjusting both the time required for ultrasound transducer operation and the runtime delay in the microcontroller. In this way, the delay time between optical and ultrasound pulse is calculated by (2).

$$\Delta\tau_{LED-US} = (T_{\mu C} - T_{ini}) - \Delta\tau_{adj} \tag{2}$$

Where the time between the LED and ultrasound pulses, $\Delta\tau_{LED-US}$, is calculated by subtracting to the measured microseconds by the microcontroller $T_{\mu C}$,the start time measurement T_{ini} , and the adjustment variable $\Delta\tau_{adj}$.

At the instant in which the ultrasound signal is received, the mobile node sends back an optical signal, indicating that the ultrasound signal has reached the mobile node. Neglecting again the optical signal propagation delay, the base station is able to estimate the distance from the delay between its optical and ultrasound transmission and the reception of the optical signal from the mobile node (using again (1)). In this way, we obtain distance estimation capability in both devices, increasing the system flexibility. This proposed modification can be easily introduced in Cricket systems by adding an additional radiofrequency signal transmission. Fig. 2 presents the corresponding chronogram.

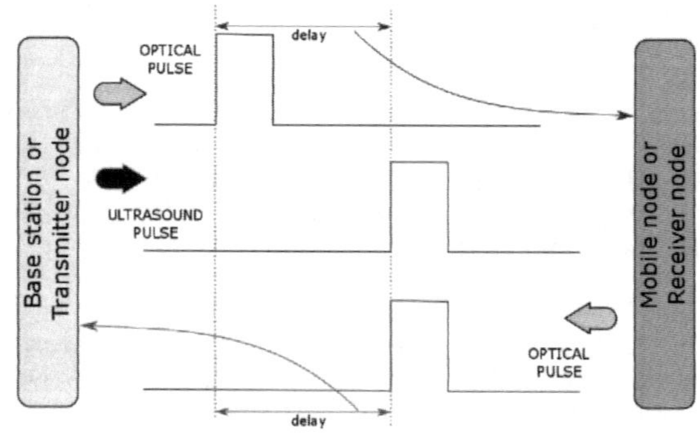

Figure 2. Signals timing for mobile node and base station

It can be seen how the delay values are obtained in the mobile node and in the base station.

III. SYSTEM PROTOTYPE

As a proof of concept, a prototype based on the proposed scheme has been implemented. Fig. 3 depicts the system.

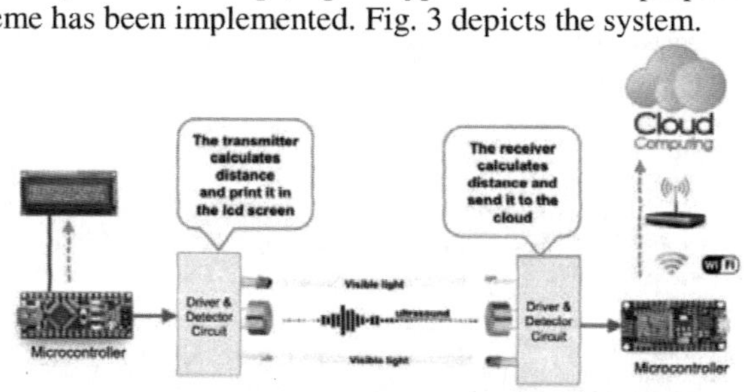

Figure 3. Distance measurement system

This prototype is based on microcontrollers for time measurement and distance calculation. We have used Atmel ATMega328P (Arduino Nano) for base station and NodeMCU (based on ESP8266 chip) for the mobile node. Moreover, the system includes results presentation by means of crystal display (LCD) and a wireless network connection to a cloud server. The measurement process performed by the system is described below

1. The transmitter node sends a light pulse and an ultrasound signal and starts its time counter. Since a MCU is used, both pulses are not sent exactly at the same time and a very small artificial

delay is introduced. This delay presents no jitter and can be easily considered at the receiver side.

2. The optical receiver at the mobile node detects the optical pulse and starts its own time counter. Due to light speed, it can assumed that both time counters start at almost the same time.

3. When the ultrasound signal is detected, the receiver node stops the counter and sends an optical pulse to the transmitter node. In that moment, it can perform the distance calculation from the measured delay. This estimation is stored and published in the web page. Regarding the ultrasound detection, taking into account the behavior of piezoelectric devices, two extra delays due to excitation must be considered. Furthermore, the sound speed is highly affected by temperature, needing the use of a temperature sensor to estimate the local sound speed in order to compensate the propagation-speed error. In order to consider this problem, mobile node includes a temperature sensor and uses this information for calculating the actual sound speed following (3).

$$V_S = 331.5 + 0.60714t\ (m/s) \qquad (3)$$

Where t is the temperature in Celsius degrees.

4. When the transmitter node receives the optical signal, it stops its time counter and proceeds to calculate its relative range. Once more, thanks to light speed, the optical signal can be considered to reach the base station at the same time than the ultrasound signal reach the receiver node. Therefore, both devices obtain the same delay for calculating the distance. Finally, the base station calculates the distance and presents it in the LCD display.

In the next subsections, the devices' main blocks are described and commented.

A. Ultrasound subsystem

The main component of this block is the ultrasound transducer 400ST/R160 from Daventech. This device requires a 40 KHZ signal, which is generated by the microcontroller and a driver circuit, composed mainly by a MAX232 integrated circuit. Fig. 4 shows the emitter's schematic.

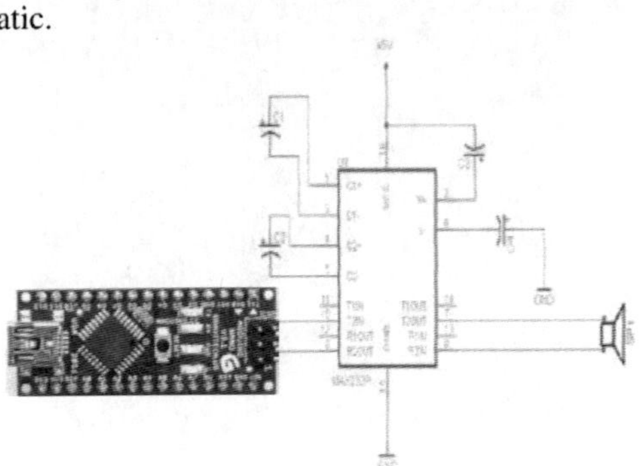

Figure 4. Ultrasound emitter

The ultrasonic wave receiver circuit includes a detector (the same transducer than in the emitter), and a signal amplifier based on CX20106A from Sony, which is connected to the NodeMCU microcontroller, as is shown in Fig. 5.

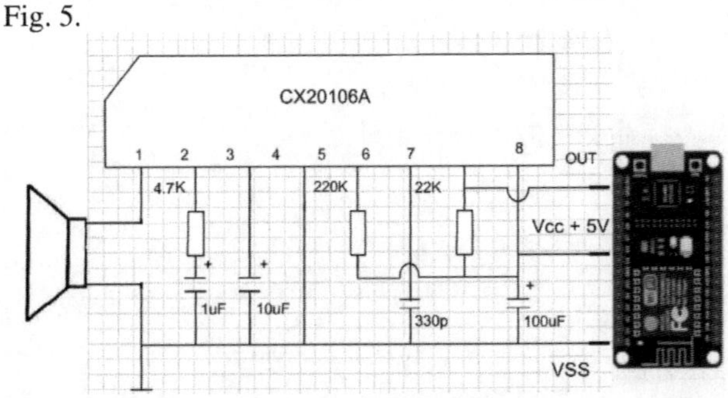

Figure 5. Ultrasound receiver

B. Visible light subsystem

Optical links make use of white LED and phototransistor BPW40 devices as transducers and in this case, simple current drivers and amplified receivers have been implemented.Since the system is a proof of concept, low-gain schemes have been used. Nevertheless, the use of integrated high-gain amplification circuits would improve the performance of a commercial device. Fig. 6 shows the emitter and receiver circuits used in this prototype.

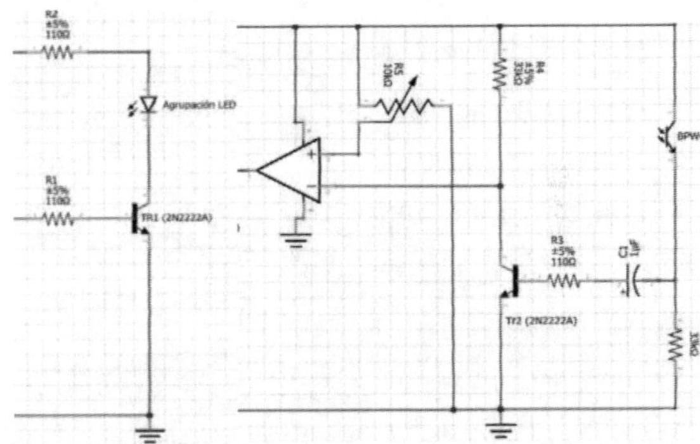

Figure 6. Optical emitter and receiver schemes

Fig. 7 and 8 present the circuits corresponding to the base station system and the mobile node system. As it was explained before, both devices have optical emitter and receiver blocks, whilst the ultrasound block is different: is a transmitter in the base station and a receiver in the mobile node.

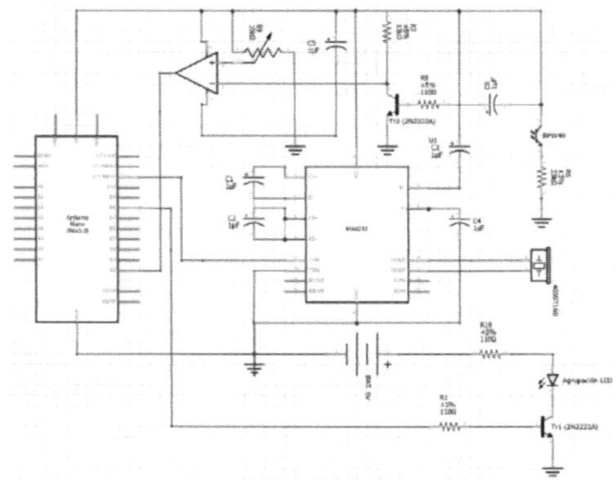

Figure 7. Base station scheme

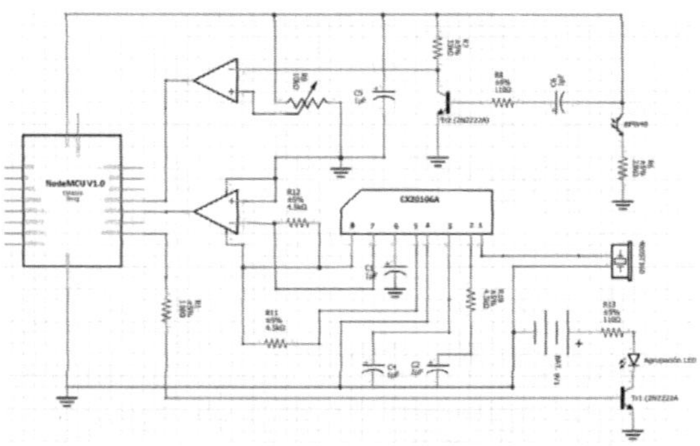

Figure 8. Mobile node scheme

Finally, an actual picture of base station and mobile node is shown in Fig. 9.

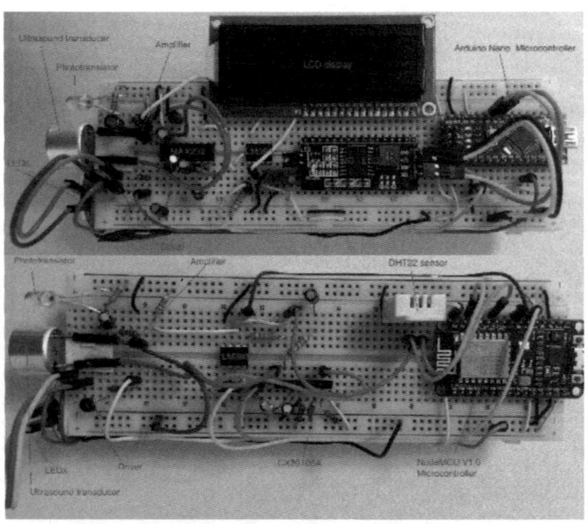

Figure 9. Base station and mobile node scheme

Where it can be appreciated the actual dimmensions and circuitry conplexity of the implemented prototypes.

IV. RESULTS

In this section, experimental results of the implemented proposed system are presented. First, some signals which are used in the process, such as the emitted and received ultrasound signal and the pulse generated for the microcontroller, can be shown in Fig. 10.

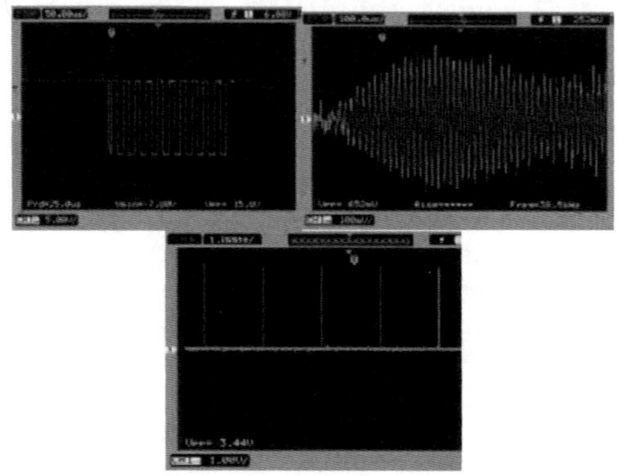

Figure 10. Ultrasound driving signal (left), received ultrasound signal (right) and detected (down) signals.

Note that the received ultrasonic signal is affected by severe multipath distortion. However, since this block acts only as a power indicator, multipath only introduces a delay (which can be estimated and considered in the distance calculation). Furthermore, the received signal is amplified and passed through an open-loop comparator, generating a pulse to serve as input to the microcontroller. Regarding the optical part of the system, the emitted and received pulses are depicted in Fig. 11.

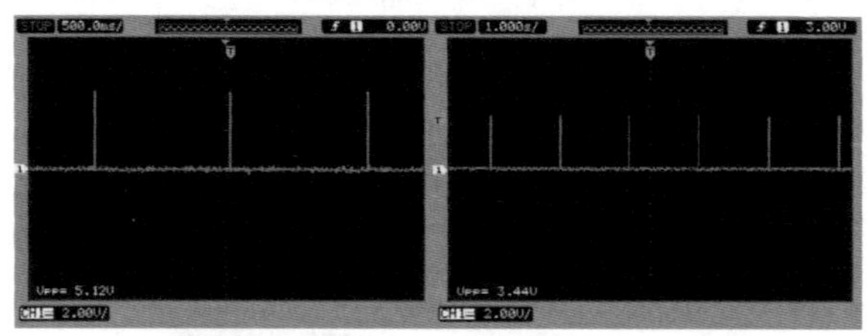

Figure 11. Optical emitted (left) and detected (right) signals.

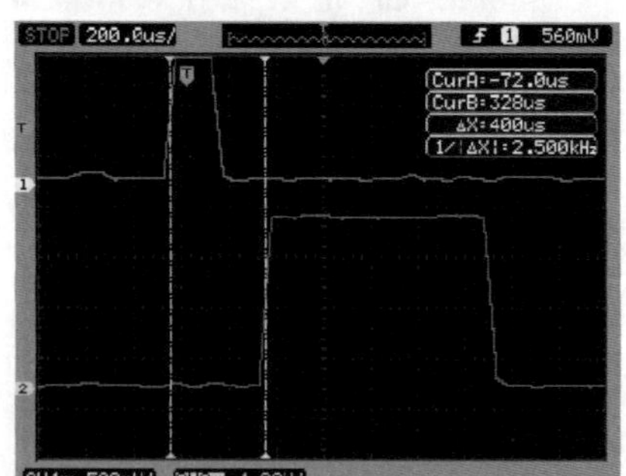

Figure 12. Optical (yellow) and Ultrasound (green) received pulses.

An example of delay measurement is presented in Fig. 12, where the optical and ultrasound pulses received by the mobile nodecan be observed.A delay between signals of ΔX= 400 µs is observed. Introducing it in (1), along with the sound speed (0.0343 cm/s), results in an estimated distance of 13.72 cm. Theseresults suggest an interesting high accuracy of the system, since the distance between terminals was set to 14 cm.

In order to test the system performance, different distances were tried. Fig. 13 compares the obtained results in the base station and mobile devicewith the real value.

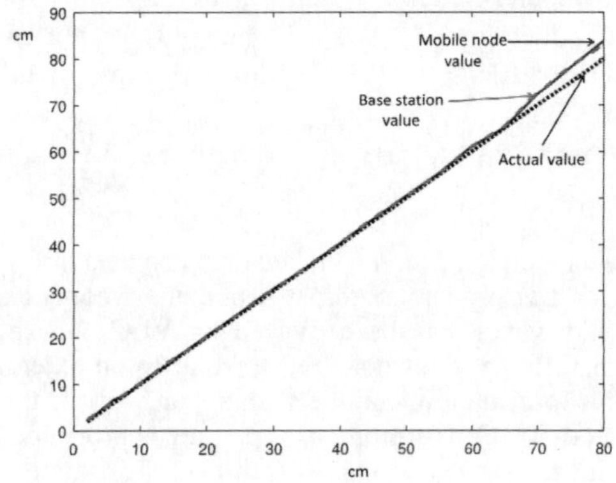

Figure 13. Measured distance values

Finally, Fig. 14 shows the measurement error in both devices.

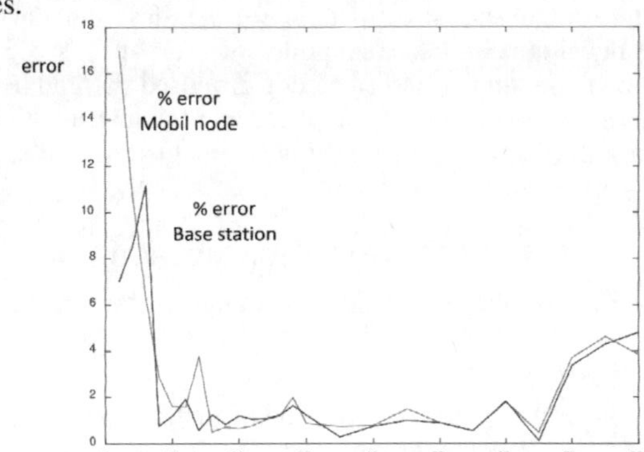

Figure 14. Measures error in base station (left) and mobile node (right).

It can be observed that the error remains below 2% except at the measurement limits of the system, where it is dramatically increased due to low signal strength (long distance) or due to the limited processing speed of the CPU (short distance).

V. CONCLUSIONS

In this work, a new VLC distance-measurement scheme, based on TDoA has been proposed. It is based on Cricket technology but introducing some modifications, which provide several advantages. The main change consists of the substitution of the cricket radiofrequency signal by an optical one.

In this way, the system can be used in new environments not suitable for radiofrequency technology, such as underwater scenarios, where radiofrequency suffers a prohibitively high attenuation.

On the other hand, in the proposed system, the mobile node returns back a new optical signal to the base station for it to perform its own distance estimation. Therefore, the proposed system provides distance measurement capability to both devices involved in the process: the base station and the mobile node. In Cricket systems, only one of the devices is able to calculate the distance, from the signals (radio and ultrasound) emitted by the other. Nevertheless, this technique can be easily incorporated to Cricket modules, just including a new radiofrequency signal.

As a proof of concept, a basic prototype has been implemented. It consists on a base station, which generates optical and ultrasound signals, and a mobile node, which provides the optical signal to the base station. While this prototype has some limitation, such as its short range, results probe that both system devices are able to calculate the distance between them, with similar accuracy (about 2% of error). Therefore, with this implementation, the accuracy and feasibility of the proposed technique is demonstrated.

ACKNOWLEGMENT

This work was supported in part by the Spanish Research National Plan (ARIES Project Ref. TEC2013-47682-C2-1).

REFERENCES

[1] A. Awad, T. Frunzke, and F. Dressler, "Adaptive Distance Estimation and Localization in WSN using RSSI Measures,", Proceedings of 10th Euromicro Conference on Digital System Design Architectures, Methods and Tools (DSD 2007), pp. 471–478, Aug. 2007.

[2] G. Del Campo-Jimenez, J. M. Perandones, and F. J. Lopez-Hernandez, "A VLC-based beacon location system for mobile applications", Proceedings of IEEE International Conference on Localization and GNSS (ICL-GNSS), pp. 1-4, Jun. 2013.

[3] H. Kim, D. Kim, S. Yang, Y. Son, and S. Han, "An indoor visible light communication positioning system using a RF carrier allocation technique", IEEE Journal of Lightwave Technology, vol.31 n°.1, pp. 134-144, Jan. 2013.

[4] N. B. Priyantha, A. Chakraborty, and H. Balakrishnan, "The Cricket Location-Support system", Proceedings of 6th ACM MOBICOM, pp. 266-274, Aug. 2000.

[5] F. Delgado, I. Quintana, J. Rufo; J. Rabadan, C. Quintana, and R. Perez-Jimenez, "Design and Implementation of an Ethernet-VLC Interface for Broadcast Transmissions", IEEE Communications Letters, vol. 14 n°12, pp. 1089–1091, Oct. 2010.

[6] Y. Tanaka, T. Komine, S. Haruyama, and M. Nakagawa, "Indoor Visible Light Transmission System Utilizing White LED Lights", IEICE Transactions on Communications, vol. E86-B, n°. 8, pp. 2440-2454, Aug. 2003

[7] D. E. Manolakis, "Efficient solution and performance analysis of 3-D position estimation by trilateration", IEEE Transactions on Aerospace and Electronic Systems, vol. 32, n°. 4, pp. 1239–1248, Oct 1996.

Time Synchronization Method Using Visible Light Communication for Smartphone Localization

Takayuki Akiyama
Department of Informatics
SOKENDAI
(The Graduate University for Advanced Studies)
Tokyo, Japan
Email: tak@nii.ac.jp

Masanori Sugimoto
Department of Computer Science
School of Engineering
Hokkaido University
Sapporo, Japan
Email: sugi@ist.hokudai.ac.jp

Hiromichi Hashizume
Information Systems Architecture
Science Research Division
National Institute of Informatics
Tokyo, Japan
Email: has@nii.ac.jp

***Abstract*—We describe a time synchronization technique based on visible light communication (VLC). The precision of time synchronization is the key factor for localization based on time of arrival. Hence, we have proposed the *SyncSync* method using a modulated light-emitting diode (LED) light and a smartphone video camera, which enables time-of-arrival localization by measuring the time of flight of sound waves. This method gives better results than those of time-difference-of-arrival localization. However, we had to use a dedicated light synchronization device for our method. VLC is becoming a popular application of smartphones. If VLC demodulation could be used for time synchronization in acoustic localization, VLC and indoor localization could be integrated into a single application. In this paper, we examine the feasibility of using VLC codes for localization time synchronization. Experimental results show a time synchronization precision equivalent to 1.0 cm for an airborne acoustic wave. This is sufficiently precise for practical applications.**

Keywords*–*Time synchronization; Visible light communication; Acoustic localization; ToA measurement; Smartphone.

I. Introduction

Smart devices are being increasingly used for services in which geographical location is an important factor. Numerous location-aware applications have been developed for the popular mobile operating systems and the development costs are low. The key to many of these applications is the rich assortment of smartphone sensors, such as global navigation satellite system or global positioning system (GNSS/GPS) receivers, accelerometers, gravity sensors, and gyroscopes.

In a previous study [1], we introduced an indoor 3D localization system for smartphones. We used the smartphone's microphone to detect acoustic signals and its video camera for time synchronization between sender nodes and the smartphone. We conducted time-of-arrival (ToA) measurements based on the time synchronization, and this offered better performance than did time-difference-of-arrival (TDoA). In our ToA measurements, the standard deviations were less than 10 mm, whereas for TDoA they were 10 mm to 100 mm. In the worst cases, the positioning calculations diverged.

Here, we report our new time synchronization technique based on visible light communication (VLC) [2]. Our experimental results show that the performance of VLC-based synchronization is comparable to that of dedicated systems. As VLC becomes more prevalent for mobile devices, our method will become useful for both communication and localization.

Many of the parameters that are needed for localization, such as transmitter coordinates and the frequencies used for acoustic waves, can be conveyed by VLC. Hence, the application software does not need to refer to an external database for this information, and the system can work without network connectivity. Furthermore, user privacy is protected because no individual user is announced to others. These are some of the advantages of the proposed method.

Our motivation is to realize localization with this scheme. We have verified the concept of the proposed method and found some issues with it. Here, we describe the status of the development. The remainder of the paper is organized as follows. Section II describes our proposed method. Section III presents the results of an experimental investigation of our method. Finally, Section IV gives conclusions and suggestions for future work.

II. Proposed Method

We describe the proposed method in this section.

A. System Overview

We aim to realize ToA-based acoustic localization that uses VLC for time synchronization. We use a transmitter module that consists of loudspeakers and an LED. The loudspeakers emit short bursts of sound simultaneously, which are registered by a smartphone. The smartphone then calculates the time of flight (ToF) of each burst, and determines its position using ToA-based multilateration. The LED is modulated for VLC, the carrier wave of which is synchronized to the emitted bursts. In the demodulation process, the VLC carrier signal is extracted and used to estimate the emission time; this is the time synchronization of the system. The ToF is the time between burst emission and reception.

B. LED Modulation

Many of the video cameras that are now available use complementary metal-oxide-semiconductor (CMOS) image sensors. An image sensor is a 2D array of photodiodes that record a meshed image as electrical charges. Because most CMOS image sensors read out the horizontal lines of the array one by one, the reconstructed image consists of lines acquired sequentially. This is known as the *rolling shutter* effect, and is exploited by many VLC systems [3][4].

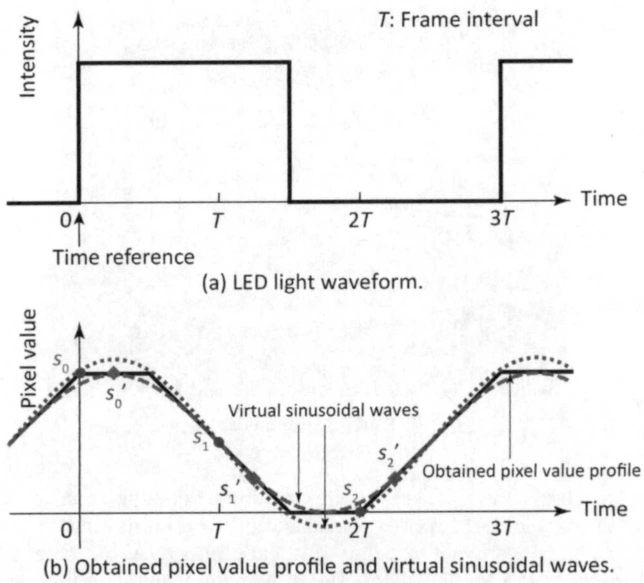

Figure 1. LED light waveform, obtained pixel value profile, and virtual sinusoidal waves.

In a previous study [5], we modulated an LED with a square wave whose frequency was exactly half the frame rate of the video camera. Capturing the modulated light by a CMOS image sensor, we observed a gradation pattern in the obtained image. By assuming that the exposure time was the video-frame period, the profile of the pattern in the shutter-scanning direction becomes part of a triangle wave. We detected either the top or bottom of the profile and used it as a reference point for time synchronization.

We now consider the case in which the modulation frequency of the square wave is one third of the video frame rate (Fig. 1 (a)). The interval of integration of the square wave is the exposure time of the video camera, and the rolling shutter works as a sliding window function. Applying the window function for three consecutive frames (i.e., the period of the LED modulation), we obtain the pixel value profile shown in Fig. 1 (b). This can be approximated as a sinusoidal wave whose phase denotes when the LED is turned on or off.

C. Three-point Demodulation Method

We use the smartphone camera to capture a video of the illuminated LED. In each frame, the group of pixels that contains the LED is regarded as the region of interest (RoI). The *triad* $\boldsymbol{s} = (s_0, s_1, s_2)^{\mathrm{T}}$ is the set of mean RoI pixel values for three consecutive frames. It is used to detect a complex sinusoidal wave

$$f(\theta) = Ae^{j\theta} + Be^{-j\theta} + C, \tag{1}$$

where θ denotes the phase of the sinusoidal wave, A and B express its amplitude, C is the constant component of the wave, and $j = \sqrt{-1}$. Note that the unknown values of A, B, and C are complex. Assigning $\theta = 0$, $2/3\pi$ and $4/3\pi$ in (1), we get a matrix equation

$$\begin{pmatrix} s_0 \\ s_1 \\ s_2 \end{pmatrix} = \begin{pmatrix} f(0) \\ f(\frac{2}{3}\pi) \\ f(\frac{4}{3}\pi) \end{pmatrix} = \begin{pmatrix} 1 & 1 & 1 \\ \omega & \omega^2 & 1 \\ \omega^2 & \omega & 1 \end{pmatrix} \begin{pmatrix} A \\ B \\ C \end{pmatrix} = M \begin{pmatrix} A \\ B \\ C \end{pmatrix}, \tag{2}$$

where

$$\omega = \frac{-1 + j\sqrt{3}}{2},$$
$$\omega^2 = \bar{\omega} = \frac{-1 - j\sqrt{3}}{2},$$
$$M = \begin{pmatrix} 1 & 1 & 1 \\ \omega & \omega^2 & 1 \\ \omega^2 & \omega & 1 \end{pmatrix}.$$

Here, $\bar{\cdot}$ denotes the complex conjugate, and ω, ω^2, and $\omega^3 = 1$ are the three cube roots of 1. We can solve (2) as

$$\begin{pmatrix} A \\ B \\ C \end{pmatrix} = \frac{1}{3} \begin{pmatrix} 1 & \omega^2 & \omega \\ 1 & \omega & \omega^2 \\ 1 & 1 & 1 \end{pmatrix} \begin{pmatrix} s_1 \\ s_2 \\ s_3 \end{pmatrix} = \frac{1}{3} M^* \begin{pmatrix} s_1 \\ s_2 \\ s_3 \end{pmatrix}. \tag{3}$$

Here, M^* is the conjugate transpose of M.

Because $\boldsymbol{s}$ is a vector whose components are real, $B = \bar{A}$ holds. Then, (1) can be written as

$$f(\theta) = a\cos(\theta + b) + c, \tag{4}$$

where the unknowns a, b, and c are real numbers that satisfy

$$a = 2|A|,$$
$$b = \arg A,$$
$$c = C. \tag{5}$$

The sinusoidal function (4) is not the original square wave that modulated the LED, but it corresponds to it uniquely. Therefore, we refer to (4) as the *virtual sinusoidal wave*.

We set the time reference as the rising edge of the original square wave. Because the LED modulation and the exposure time of the video camera are not synchronized, the time at which the RoI pixel values are sampled varies in each measurement. Two examples of triads, $\boldsymbol{s} = (s_0, s_1, s_2)^{\mathrm{T}}$ and $\boldsymbol{s'} = (s'_0, s'_1, s'_2)^{\mathrm{T}}$, are shown in Fig. 1 (b). Although each triad yields a different sinusoidal wave, we can determine the time reference by using (4) in each case.

D. VLC with Three-point Demodulation Method

We modulate the LED with six square wave patterns. They have the same frequency, amplitude, and mean, but their initial phases are separated by $2/3\pi$. This is a phase-shift keying (PSK) scheme that uses six symbols. The constellation diagram is shown in Fig. 2.

As explained above, a pixel value is the result of integrating the LED output during an exposure. If the exposure time spans the boundary of the LED's lighting pattern, the integration of this term is not suitable for demodulation. To avoid this situation, we introduce a *guard frame* that is similar to the guard interval [6] used in telecommunications. Appended to the original frame, a guard frame is the same lighting pattern as the first frame of the original pattern. Accordingly, the signal length of a symbol becomes four times that of the frame duration. This method ensures that we can select three consecutive frames from a video sequence that have the correct integral values of the original waveform. Fig. 3 shows the waveform for symbol "5", whose phase is $-1/3\pi$.

III. EXPERIMENT

We explain an experiment of the proposed method.

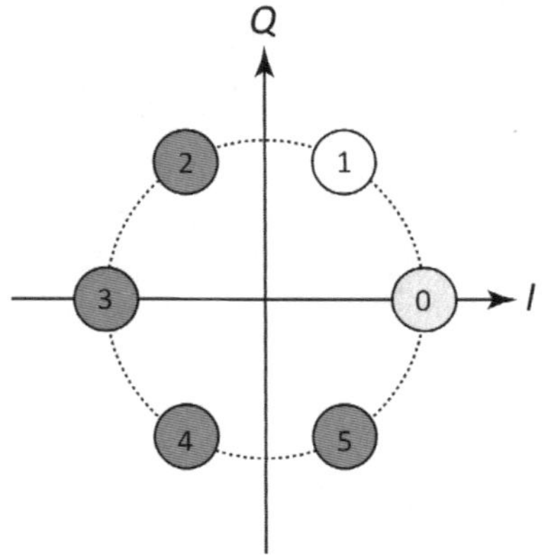

Figure 2. Constellation diagram for 6-PSK.

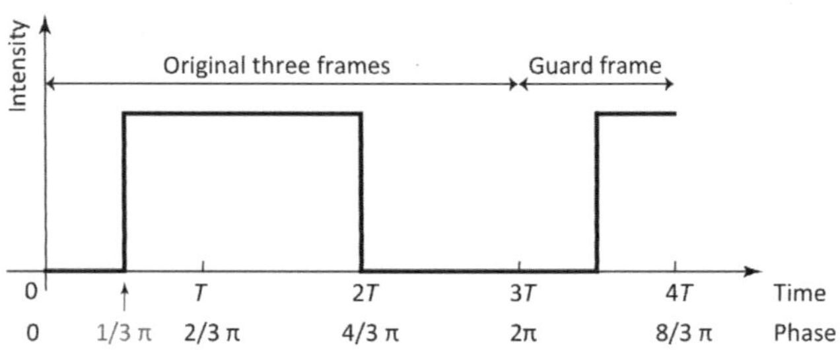

Figure 3. Waveform of symbol "5".

A. Experimental Setup

We conducted an experiment to evaluate the feasibility of the proposed method. Fig. 4 shows a diagram of the experimental system. In the transmitter, an LED floodlight is placed behind a circular translucent window (20 cm in diameter) to emit the modulated light (Fig. 5). The LED floodlight consisted of 56 red LEDs (OS5RKA5111A, Opto-Supply; dominant wavelength: 624 nm). The waveform signal of the LED modulation was generated by an arbitrary function generator (AFG3102, Tektronix). This signal drove a lab-built voltage-to-current converter that supplied electric current to the LED floodlight.

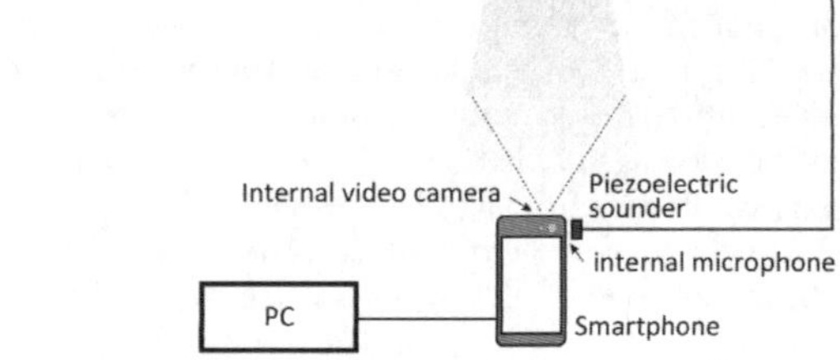

Figure 4. Experimental system.

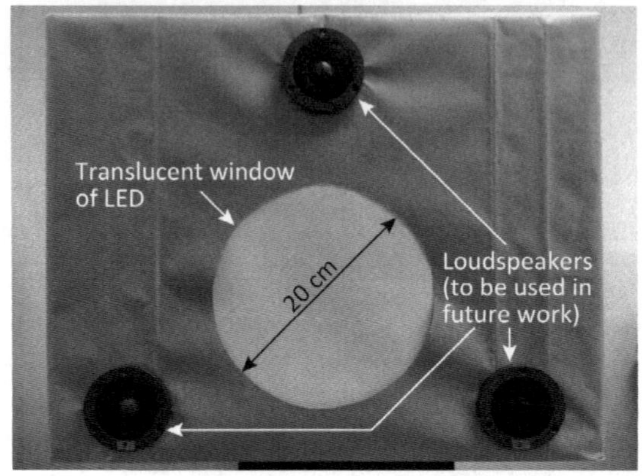

Figure 5. Transmitter.

Three loudspeakers were mounted on the transmitter (Fig. 5) for the purpose of acoustic localization in future work, but they were not used in this experiment. A piezoelectric sounder (PKM13EPYH4000-A0, Murata Manufacturing) was attached directly to the smartphone microphone to evaluate the performance of the smartphone's audio signal processing. Acoustic waves were emitted in 4 ms bursts through the sounder at the beginning of each LED modulation cycle. The phase accordance method [7] was used to determine the precise time of signal reception.

A smartphone (iPhone 6s Plus, Apple) was mounted on a tripod at a distance of 1.0 m, 1.5 m, or 2.0 m from the LED to capture video images. We developed a video-capture application to allow the smartphone to record the pixel values of two RoIs (RoI1 and RoI2). Because they were separated in the shutter-scanning direction, the detected phases of RoI1 and RoI2 were different. The frame rate of the video camera was 60 fps. Although demodulation could be processed with the video-capture application, the recorded pixel values were sent as logging messages and analyzed offline by a personal computer (PC) to evaluate the performance statistically. Timestamps of the video frames were extracted from the sampling buffer of the smartphone through its application programming interface.

Audio signals captured by the smartphone's microphone were recorded alongside the video images as MPEG-4 files that were transferred to the PC. The audio sampling rate was 48.0 ksps. Timestamps of the audio buffer were also extracted and recorded for analysis.

The LED's modulating signal was generated as follows. The signal consisted of a preamble and a payload. The preamble was used to detect the existence of a signal and to find the top frame of a triad. It comprised 12 "0" symbols of the 6-PSK. For the payload, we sent the text message "HELLO, WORLD". Each character in the message was converted to a 6-bit binary code and divided into three 2-bit pieces that were assigned to the symbols "2"–"5". The symbol "1" was not used for data transmission but its existence was used as an integrity check on the receiver side. The payload of the transmission had 36 symbols, meaning that the total length of the signal was 48 symbols. As each symbol occupied four video frames, the duration of the signal was 3.2 s. The signal was transmitted repeatedly, and the video capture duration was 30 s for each measurement.

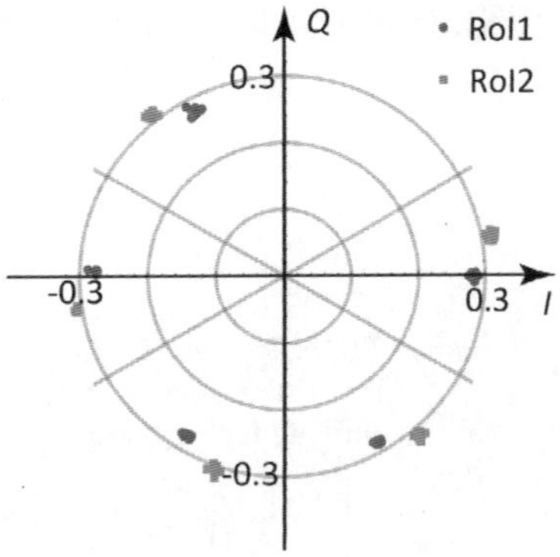

Figure 6. Constellation diagram of the results.

B. Performance of VLC Demodulation and Time Synchronization

The pixel values captured by the smartphone application were demodulated on a PC. We assume a sequence of pixel values $p_i(i = 1, 2, 3, \dots)$ in an RoI. We can make a series of triads as $t_1 = (p_1, p_2, p_3), t_2 = (p_2, p_3, p_4), t_3 = (p_3, p_4, p_5), t_4 = (p_4, p_5, p_6), \dots$. As mentioned before, there is a *right* triad that does not span two symbols in $t_1 \dots t_4$. A right triad appears every four triads. Triads in the preamble are used to select the correct sequence of triads in the payload.

A typical constellation diagram of the results is shown in Fig. 6. Here, the plotting plane is rotated so that the mean phase of RoI1's preamble becomes zero. It can be seen that the symbols are definitely separated, which means that the message was perfectly demodulated. The phase difference between RoI1 and RoI2 is due to the scanning speed of the rolling shutter. Using this speed and the phase of RoI1 or RoI2, we can estimate the phase of the first scanning line of the image buffer (Fig. 7).

When the smartphone was 2.0 m from the LED, the standard deviation of the regression was 0.015 rad, which is equivalent to 4.1 cm for an airborne acoustic wave. We use the standard error here to evaluate the precision of the estimated phase. Within 1 s (i.e., using at least 15 triads), the standard error of the regression becomes 1.1 cm for an airborne acoustic wave. With separations of 1.5 m and 1.0 m, the standard errors are 1.0 cm and 1.7 cm, respectively. The relationship between the separation and the precision, including analysis of the signal-to-noise ratio, should be investigated in detail in future work. Even though our previous study, which used a dedicated modulating waveform, showed a better standard error of 0.17 mm, the proposed system is sufficiently precise and is also applicable to VLC.

The timestamp of the image buffer and the time offset derived from the phase of the first line yield the reference time relative to the buffer's time. The precision of this reference time depends on the timing clock of the video camera. The standard deviation was 1.5 µs in this experiment.

C. Performance of Audio Signal Detection

We extracted the acoustic bursts from the video files and determined their positions on the audio track. The audio buffer size of the smartphone was 4,096 bytes and the timestamp of each buffer was recorded in a logging message. The emission time of each burst was calculated from the timestamp of the buffer to which the burst belonged and from the relative position of the burst in the buffer. The precision of the burst interval was 2 µs to 7 µs.

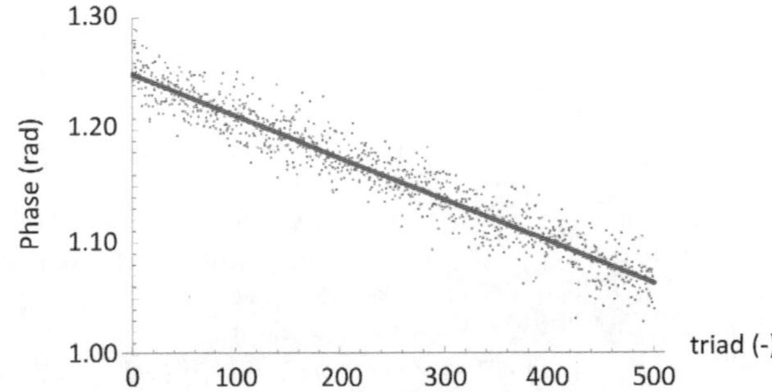

Figure 7. Estimated phase of the triad.

D. Alignment of Video and Audio Signals

We compared the time references obtained from the video images and audio bursts. Although they should have had the same time, a difference was observed. We intend to investigate this phenomenon in future work.

IV. Conclusion and Future Work

We have confirmed the feasibility of time synchronization using VLC. We successfully transmitted short messages and were able to obtain time references with practicable precision. The audio signals were also detected precisely. However, we were unable to align the video and audio tracks on the time axis. We intend to resolve this issue in order to perform ToA-based acoustic localization using VLC time synchronization.

Acknowledgment

This work was supported by JSPS KAKENHI Grant Number 26280036.

References

[1] T. Akiyama, M. Sugimoto, and H. Hashizume, "Syncsync: Time-of-arrival based localization method using light-synchronized acoustic waves for smartphones," in Indoor Positioning and Indoor Navigation (IPIN), 2015 International Conference on, pp. 1–9, Oct 2015.

[2] C. Danakis, M. Afgani, G. Povey, I. Underwood, and H. Haas, "Using a CMOS camera sensor for visible light communication," in 2012 IEEE Globecom Workshops, pp. 1244–1248. IEEE, Dec. 2012.

[3] O. Ait-Aider, N. Andreff, J. Lavest, and P. Martinet, "Exploiting Rolling Shutter Distortions for Simultaneous Object Pose and Velocity Computation Using a Single View," in Fourth IEEE International Conference on Computer Vision Systems (ICVS'06), pp. 35–35. IEEE, 2006.

[4] G. Lepage, J. Bogaerts, and G. Meynants, "Time-Delay-Integration Architectures in CMOS Image Sensors," IEEE Transactions on Electron Devices, vol. 56, no. 11, pp. 2524–2533, Nov. 2009.

[5] T. Akiyama, M. Sugimoto, and H. Hashizume, "Light-synchronized acoustic toa measurement system for mobile smart nodes," in Indoor Positioning and Indoor Navigation (IPIN), 2014 International Conference on, pp. 749–752, Busan, Korea, 2014.

[6] H. Liu and G. Li, OFDM Fundamentals. John Wiley & Sons, Inc., 2006, pp. 13–30. [Online]. Available: http://dx.doi.org/10.1002/0471757195.ch2

[7] H. Hashizume, A. Kaneko, Y. Sugano, K. Yatani, and M. Sugimoto, "Fast and accurate positioning technique using ultrasonic phase accordance method," in Proceedings of IEEE Region 10 Conference (TENCON2005), pp. 1–6, Melbourne, Australia, 2005.

Analysis of Real and Complex Modes of Grounded Slab with the Transverse Resonance Method

Riham Borghol
University of Tunis El Manar, National Engineering School of Tunis, LR99ES21 Lab. Sys' Com, ENIT
Tunis, Tunisia
e-mail: borgholriham@gmail.com

Aguili taoufik
University of Tunis El Manar, National Engineering School of Tunis, LR99ES21 Lab. Sys' Com, ENIT
Tunis, Tunisia
e-mail: Taoufik.aguili@gmail.com

***Abstract*— In this work, we focus our attention on dispersion characteristics of Transverse Electric (TE) and Transverse Magnetic (TM) surface modes, leaky modes and volume modes of double-positive grounded slab. We have analyzed the dispersion using the Transverse Resonance Method (TRM). The simple method represents the boundary conditions of the grounded slab by an equivalent circuit. It reveals that this structure, though it contains several types, just the ordinary type exists for surface modes and just the improper type exists for leaky modes. Numerical results illustrate the properties and the existence conditions for these modes.**

Keywords*— Grounded SLAB; surface modes; volume modes; leaky modes; Transverse Resonance Method.

I. INTRODUCTION

A few years ago, the miniaturization of antennas leads to the appearance of new modes which are the surface modes. These modes have received considerable attention in the scientific community. Surface modes are used in different fields for many applications, such as the surface Radar [1], the surface wave filters [2], the surface plasmons for biodetection[3] as well as the seismic imaging with surface wave [2]. In electromagnetic, these modes can approach the antenna elements and this rapprochement generates the coupling phenomenon. Therefore, they provide a new way to miniaturization [4]. Surface modes exist at a discontinuity interface between two different mediums. At this interface, leaky modes can also exist. Usually, leaky modes are excited when perturbing a surface mode or a guided mode propagating in an open waveguide with proper periodic corrugations or modifications [5]. These Leaky modes propagate faster than the speed of the light and, at the same time, they leak energy along the interface. Leaky modes are used for applications in the millimeter-wave ranges.

Based on the modal analysis for double-positive grounded slab, the present authors have revealed that only surface and leaky modes can exist for TE and TM polarization [6][7],but they did not demonstrated the existence of volume mode which is identified as the magnetostatic wave. Volume mode is characterized by the limited field to structure and no energy is lost from it.

In this work, we investigate the propagation of real modes (i.e., surface, volume) [8][9] and complex modes (i.e., leaky) [5][10] supported by a slab placed on a perfectly conducting ground plane (grounded slab). In Section 2, we will present the other existing works and we will compare them with our work. In Section 3, we will analyse the dispersion characteristics of TE and TM modes based on a general method called the Tranverse Resonance Method (TRM) [11][12]. In Section 4, we will discuss the results obtained from the MATLAB simulations. In Section 5, we will conclude this paper.

II. STATE OF THE ART

In 2003, Paolo Baccarelli has worked on the propagation of surface waves in a particular structure double-negative metamaterial grounded slab [8]. In 2004, the same author has presented the dispersion and radiation properties of leaky waves on the same structure [7]. He has demonstrated that leaky waves of only the proper type exist in double-negative grounded slab, while proper or improper leaky waves exist in single negative grounded slab. Paolo Baccarelli has investigated in his work only the dispersion of surface and leaky modes on single- and double-negative grounded slabs.

Our work focuses on the dispersion of surface, volume and leaky modes in double-positive grounded slab. In literature, there are many techniques through which we can realize this analysis such as the analytical technique dyadic Green's function [13][14] which can be estimated to complex forms depending on how the material is described macroscopically. Another technique is postulating fields on one side of the discontinuity and using Snel's law of reflection and refraction [15]. In our study, we use The TRM. This approach allows deriving the dispersion properties of real and complex modes for open structure in a simple way. It is also useful to describe the open structure with an equivalent circuit parameters as admittance or reflection coefficient. This circuit model permits to find in a simple way the dispersion equation for the two polarizations TE and TM. The resolution of these two equations permits to know the modes in this structure and their existence conditions.

III. ANALYSIS

Let us consider a grounded slab characterized by a lossless dielectric medium of height d and relative constitutive parameters ε_r and $\mu_r = \mu_0$. It is infinite along the two directions x and z, as shown in Fig.1.

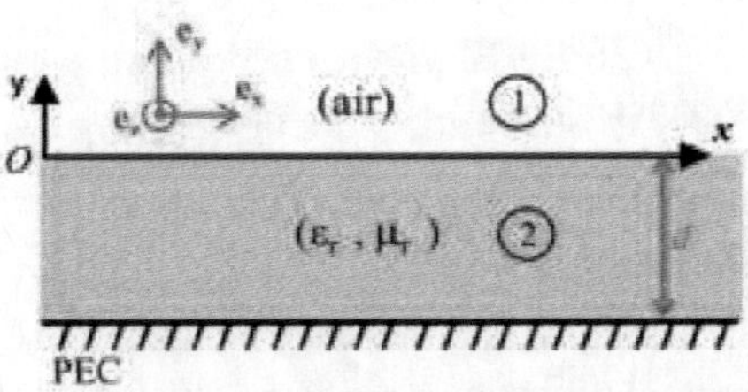

Figure 1. Schematic illustration of infinity grounded slab. The dielectric slab is characterized by a relative permittivity ε_r and permeability μ_r.

Taking into consideration the assumption that no variation along the x direction and that the electromagnetic field depends on time and the longitudinal coordinate as $e^{-j(\omega t + k_z z)}$, the real and complex modes can be separated into two polarizations TE modes with $E_y = E_z = 0$ and TM modes with $H_y = H_z = 0$. The field related to such structure can be travel in an equivalent transmission line model illustrated in Fig. 2. This model describes the transverse discontinuity with equivalent network parameters to simplify the resolution of the Maxwell equations using the TRM.

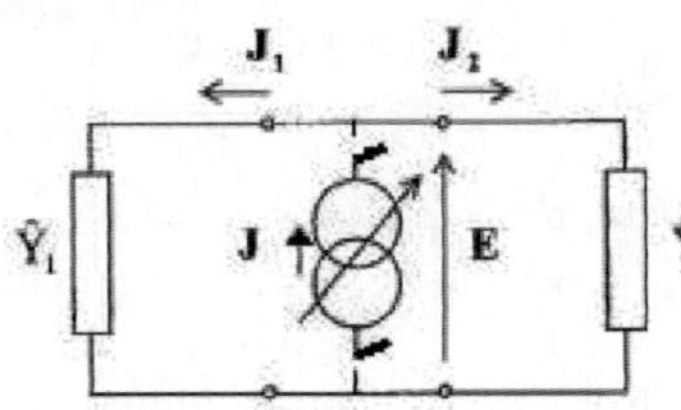

Figure 2. Equivalent circuit used to illustrate the transverse Resonance Method.

The symbolic representation of the two homogeneous media (air, dielectric) separated by the discontinuity plan (xoz) is given by two equivalent admittances Y_1 and Y_2. The equivalent admittance $Y_2(k_z, k_0)$ of the dielectric slab is a function of the transverse propagation constant k_z and the free space propagation constant k_0. Consequently, it is then possible to find the dispersion equation by using the univalent circuit. The variable j, which is a virtual current source, is zero at the discontinuity plan. It is equivalent to an open circuit. E is a dual grader [14].

According to Kirchhoff's current and Ohm's law, we deduce :

$$(Y_1 + Y_2) = 0 \tag{1}$$

Where $Y_1 = y_{1M}^{\alpha}$ and $Y_2 = y_{2M}^{\alpha} \coth(k_{y2} d)$.

$\alpha = TE, TM$ indicate the polarization supported by the structure. The expression of the relevant characteristic admittances for the two polarizations areas are the following [15]:

$$y_{1M}^{TE} = \frac{k_{y1}}{j\omega\mu_0} \tag{2}$$

$$y_{1M}^{TM} = \frac{j\omega\varepsilon_0}{k_{y1}} \tag{3}$$

$$y_{2M}^{TE} = \frac{k_{y2}}{j\omega\mu_0} \tag{4}$$

$$y_{2M}^{TM} = \frac{j\omega\varepsilon_0\varepsilon_r}{k_{y2}} \tag{5}$$

Where k_{y1} and k_{y2} are the transverse wavenumbers.

The use of the equivalent circuit model allows us to derive the dispersion relation of the structure for TE and TM modes:

TE:

$$k_{y2}\coth(k_{y2} d) + k_{y1} = 0 \tag{6}$$

TM:

$$k_{y2}\, th(k_{y2} d) + k_{y1}\, \varepsilon_r = 0 \tag{7}$$

The resolution of these two equations gives the transverse propagation constant k_z of real and complex modes. The real modes propagate in z direction with a real propagation constant $k_z = \beta_z$ and the complex modes propagate with a complex propagation constant $k_z = \beta_z - j\alpha_z$ [16].

A. Surface Modes

1) TM Polarization

In the TM polarization, the magnetic fields can be written in the two regions as:

$$\begin{cases} H_{x1} = C_1 e^{-jk_z z} e^{-k_{y1} y} \\ H_{x2} = C_1 e^{-jk_z z} \cosh(k_{y2}(y+d)) \end{cases} \tag{8}$$

Surface mode propagates without radiation along the structure. There is no attenuation of the wave along z since the dielectric slab is lossless. Therefore, the propagations constant k_z is real ($k_z = \beta_z$). This mode is characterized by a field that is exponential in the air and that is confined above the interface between the two media [17]. So, the wave number k_{y1} is real $k_{y1} = \beta_{y1}$ while β_{y1} is positive.By applying the difference between the two wave equations, we obtain the result equation:

$$k_{y2}^2 - \beta_{y1}^2 = -k_0^2(\varepsilon_r - 1) \quad (9)$$

Since $\varepsilon_r > 1$ and β_{y1} is a positive real, the wavenumber k_{y2} can be real or purely imaginary. In case k_{y2} is real, the dispersion equation can be written as:

$$\varepsilon_r \beta_{y1} = -\beta_{y2} th(\beta_{y2} d) \quad (10)$$

This equation implies that $\varepsilon_r < 0$ but it is not compatible with $\varepsilon_r > 1$. Therefore, the wave number k_{y2} is purely imaginary. At this condition, these surface modes can be obtained graphically by finding the intersection between two equations that are written as:

$$\begin{cases} \varepsilon_r \beta_{y1} = \alpha_{y2} \tan(\alpha_{y2} d) \\ \beta_{y1}^2 + \alpha_{y2}^2 = k_0^2(\varepsilon_r - 1) \end{cases} \quad (11)$$

The first equation corresponds to the tangent function. The second one corresponds to a circle with center (0,0) and radius a, where $a = k_0 d\sqrt{\varepsilon_r - 1}$. We will present in Fig.3.

2) TE Polarization

In the TE polarization, the electric fields can be written in the two regions as:

$$\begin{cases} E_{x1} = C_1 e^{-jk_z z} e^{-k_{y1} y} \\ E_{x2} = C_1 e^{-jk_z z} \sinh(k_{y2}(y + d)) \end{cases} \quad (12)$$

In this case, the dispersion equations can be written as:

$$\begin{cases} \beta_{y1} = -\alpha_{y2} \cot(\alpha_{y2} d) \\ \beta_{y1}^2 + \alpha_{y2}^2 = k_0^2(\varepsilon_r - 1) \end{cases} \quad (13)$$

As for the TM polarization, the intersection of these two equations allows us to find the surface modes which are supported in this structure. This intersection will be shown in Fig. 4.

B. *Volume Modes*

Volume modes propagate in the two media of this structure without radiation along the longitudinal z direction, and with a real propagation constant $k_z = \beta_z$. The magnetic field in the TM polarization is represented by these equations in the two regions:

$$\begin{cases} H_{x1} = C_1 e^{-jk_z z} e^{-jk_{y1} y} \\ H_{x2} = C_1 e^{-jk_z z} \cosh(k_{y2}(y + d)) \end{cases} \quad (14)$$

The difference between the two wave equations allows us to obtain this equation:

$$k_{y2}^2 + \beta_{y1}^2 = -k_0^2(\varepsilon_r - 1) \quad (15)$$

We imply that the wave number of the slab k_{y2} is purely imaginary. Therefore, we can write these two equations:

$$\begin{cases} \varepsilon_r \beta_{y1} = \alpha_{y2} \tan(\alpha_{y2} d) \\ \beta_{y1}^2 - \alpha_{y2}^2 = -k_0^2(\varepsilon_r - 1) \end{cases} \quad (16)$$

In order to find volume modes, we trace these two equations in the landmark ($\alpha_{y2} d/\pi, \beta_{y1} d/\pi$) for a height d=1.5cm and a relative permittivity ε_r.

In TE polarization, the electric field is written in the two regions by the two equations:

$$\begin{cases} E_{x1} = C_1 e^{-jk_z z} e^{-jk_{y1} y} \\ E_{x2} = C_1 e^{-jk_z z} \sinh(k_{y2}(y + d)) \end{cases} \quad (17)$$

Volume mode is characterized by a real wavenumber $k_{y1} = \beta_{y1}$ and a purely imaginary wavenumber $k_{y2} = -j\alpha_{y2}$. It is represented by the intersection of the two equations which are written as:

$$\begin{cases} \beta_{y1} = -\alpha_{y2} \cot(\alpha_{y2} d) \\ \beta_{y1}^2 - \alpha_{y2}^2 = -k_0^2(\varepsilon_r - 1) \end{cases} \quad (18)$$

The first equation corresponds to cotangent function. The second one corresponds to a circle with center (0,0) and radius a, where $a = k_0 d\sqrt{\varepsilon_r - 1}$.

C. *Leaky Modes*

The leaky mode propagates with radiation along the z direction [10]. It can radiate either forward or backward with a complex propagation constant $k_z = \beta_z - j\alpha_z$. The leaky mode is characterized by two complex wave numbers k_{y1} and k_{y2}.

In a conventional dielectric ($\varepsilon_r > 0$), the leaky mode is improper modes. But in a dielectric of a negative permittivity, the leaky mode is proper mode [4]. As a conclusion, in the studied structure only complex improper modes may exist, while complex proper modes are forbidden.

In case TE polarization, the dispersion equation can be written as:

$$W = -Z\coth(Z) \qquad (19)$$

Where: $W = k_{y1}d = u - jv$ and $Z = k_{y2}d = x - jy$

By taking into consideration that $k_{y2}^2 + k_{y1}^2 = -k_0^2(\varepsilon_r - 1)$, we obtain the two equations:

$$\begin{cases} \cosh(2x)\cos(2y)(x^2 - y^2) - 2xy\sinh(2x)\sin(2y) = -a^2 \\ \sinh(2x)\sin(2y)(y^2 - x^2) - 2xy\cosh(2x)\cos(2y) = 0 \end{cases} \qquad (20)$$

The solutions of this system illustrate the leaky mode for the grounded slab with relative permittivity $\varepsilon_r = 2.2$ and a height d=1.5cm.

IV. Numerical Results and Discussion

There are two kinds of surface modes, ordinary surface modes and surface plasmon [4]. According to our analysis, we conclude that only the trapped surface modes can exist in our structure because $k_0 < \beta_z < k_0\sqrt{\varepsilon_r}$. However, the existence of surface plasmon is conditioned by $\beta_z > k_0\sqrt{\varepsilon_r}$. It can be present in other structures like surface plasmon waveguides and plasma slabs. The ordinary surface mode is illustrated in Fig. 3 by a red cross, which represents the intersection of the tangent function and the circle whose center (0,0) and radius a for TM polarization.

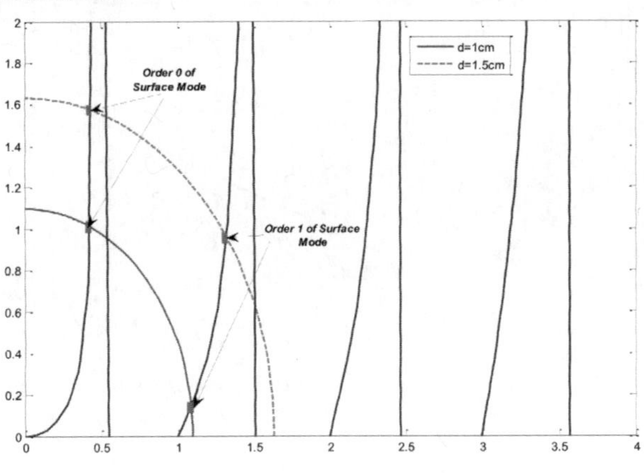

Figure 3. Location of TM surface modes for grounded slab with $\varepsilon_r = 2.2$. The green circle corresponds to d=1cm and the pink circle to d= 1.5cm.

For TE polarization, ordinary surface mode is illustrated in Fig. 4 by a red cross, which represents the intersection of the cotangent function and the circle whose center (0, 0) and radius a.

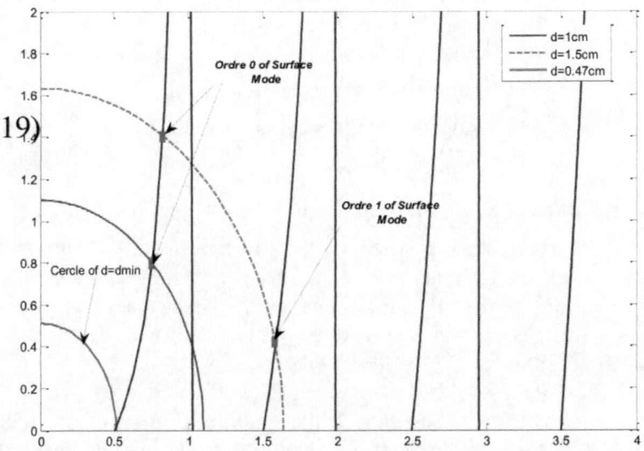

Figure 4. Location of TE surface modes for grounded slab with $\varepsilon_r = 2.2$ for three values of heigth d = 0.74cm (red circle),d=1cm (green circle) and d=1.5cm (pink circle).

When we increase the height d and the dielectric permittivity ε_r, the number of surface modes supported by this structure increases for both polarizations. This number is equal to n+1 with n as a natural number satisfying the relation $n - 1 \leq a/\pi \leq n$ [4].

In TE polarization, surface modes cannot exist below the limit value of radius a which is equal to 0.74cm. The red circle in Fig. 4 represents the limiting case.

Fig. 5 shows the dispersion characteristics of the surface mode for TM and TE polarizations supported by a grounded slab with relative permittivity $\varepsilon_r = 2.2$, permeability $\mu_r = \mu_0 = 1$ and height $d = 1.5cm$.

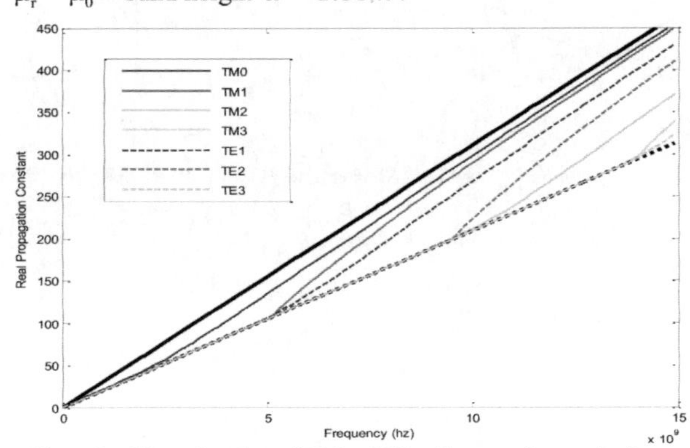

Figure 5. Dispersion plots of TM and TE ordinary surface modes for grounded slab showing the real propagation constant (β) versus the operating frequency (f). The dielectric slab is characterized by $\varepsilon_r = 2.2$, $\mu_r = \mu_0 = 1$ and d = 1.5cm.

One of the dispersion characteristics of grounded slab is that the cutoff of the principal mode TM $_0$ of surface mode does exist, as shown in Fig. 5. But, in case $\mu_r \neq 1$, the TM $_0$surface modes cutoff is suppressed.

The cutoff frequency of each guided modes of higher-order is also shown in Fig. 5 for TM and TE polarizations. The cutoff frequency is the lowest frequency of guided propagation at which $\beta_z = K_0$ [18]. For higher-order modes, when the frequency is increased, the propagation constant approaches to $K_0\sqrt{\varepsilon_r}$ but it cannot exceed this value ($K_0\sqrt{\varepsilon_r}$). This limit is the upper limit of ordinary surface modes, whereas, the lower limit is k_0. This means that the ordinary surface modes are slow. When the relative permittivity of slab is increased, the propagation constant decreases and the lost power is confined near the slab region.

In Fig. 6 and Fig. 7, the graphic location of the second kind of real modes, i.e., volume mode are represented in TM and TE. Volume mode is represented by a red cross which is the intersection of two curves. The first curve represents the tangent function for TM polarization and cotangent for TE polarization while the second curve represents the hyperbola function.

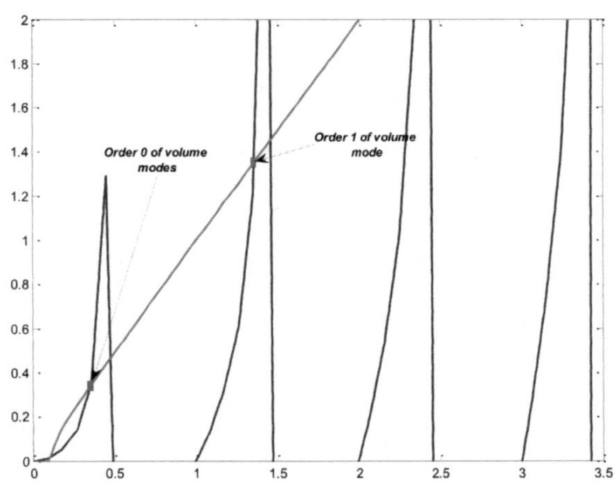

Figure 6. Location of TM volume modes for grounded slab of height d=1.5cm with $\varepsilon_r = 2.2$ and $\mu_r = \mu_0 = 1$.

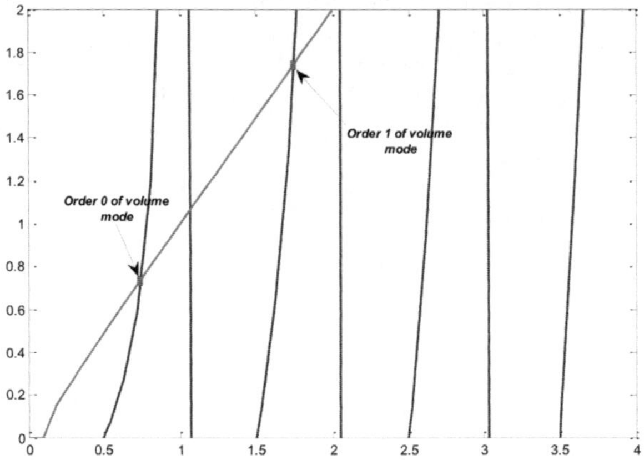

Figure 7. Location of TE volume modes for grounded slab of height d=1.5cm with $\varepsilon_r = 2.2$ and $\mu_r = \mu_0 = 1$.

We can see that when we increase the height d of the structure, the number of the volume mode decreases for the two polarizations, and the principal mode TM_0 can be suppressed. This number equal to m-1, when m is a natural number satisfying the relation $m-1 \leq a/\pi \leq m$.

In Fig. 8, the dispersion characteristics of volume mode (for the real propagation constant versus frequency) are represented in TM and TE polarizations for the grounded slab structure with $\varepsilon_r = 2.2$ and $\mu_r = \mu_0 = 1$.

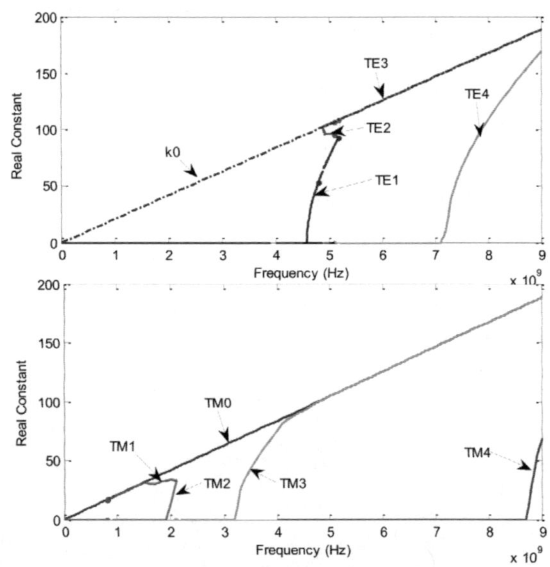

Figure 8. Dispersion plots of TE and TM volume modes for grounded slab of heigth d = 1.5cm with a relative permitivity $\varepsilon_r = 2.2$.

Through Fig. 8, we observe that the real propagation constant cannot exceed the propagation constant in free space (i.e., $\beta_z > K_0$). Thus, the volume mode for both polarizations exists in the grounded slab structure. The representation of Fig. 8 shows that the dispersion curve of first mode of higher-order TM_1 tends, on the one hand, towards the fundamental mode TM_0 in low frequencies, and disappears, on the other hand, when the frequency $f = 2.1GHz$. The dispersion curve of the third mode of higher-order TM_3 tends toward that of the principal mode TM_0 of volume mode in high frequencies. In polarization TE, there is no fundamental mode. The mode of higher-order TE_2 appears at the same frequency of TE_3 where f= 4.89GHz and disappears at the same frequency of TE_1 where f=5.18GHz.

In grounded slab with positive permittivity and permeability, just one type of the complex mode exists, which is the improper mode [7]. The dispersion characteristics of these modes are represented in Fig. 9. The dielectric slab is characterized by height d=1.5cm, $\varepsilon_r = 2.2$ $\mu_r = \mu_0 = 1$ and height d = 1.5cm.

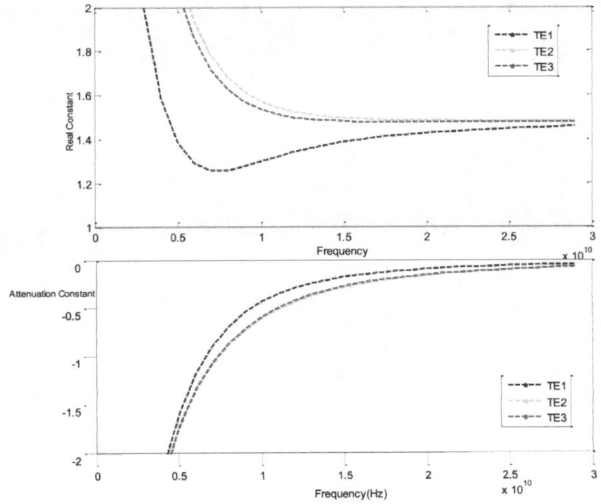

Figure 9. Dispersion curves of normalized real and attenuation constants of TE leaky modes for grounded dielectric slab .

We can see that leaky modes exist in the grounded slab when $\beta_z > K_0$. When the frequency is lower than the first cutoff frequency of the surface mode $f_{c1} = 4.4GHz$, all complex modes exist with very high normalized β_z and α_z. When the frequency increases, the normalized real constants $(0,0)$ decrease rapidly within a very narrow frequency range and remain constant at $\sqrt{\varepsilon_r}$. However, the normalized attenuation constants α_z/k_0 increase rapidly and remain constant at zero. Leaky mode is characterized by an order mode n. The minimum of n for leaky mode must be equal to the maximum of this order mode for surface mode [4].

V. CONCLUSIONS

In this paper, we investigate the dispersion characteristics and existence conditions of real and complex TE and TM modes. These modes are separated by the nature of the propagation constant. Surface mode is characterized by $k_0 < \beta_z < k_0\sqrt{\varepsilon_r}$, volume mode is characterized by $\beta_z < k_0 < k_0\sqrt{\varepsilon_r}$ and leaky mode is characterized by $\beta_z > K_0$. We observe that only the improper type of the leaky mode and only ordinary type of the surface mode occur in the double-positive grounded slab. The analysis are achieved by a simple method which is the TRM.

REFERENCES

[1] A. Baussard and S. Grosdidier, 'D'etection de cibles par radar HFSW :utilisation des curvelets et des ondelettes continues', Laboratoire EI-ENSIETA.

[2] V. Laude, 'Acoustique physique-physical acoustics', Institut FEMTO-ST.

[3] J. Picaud, 'Biodétection par résonance des plasmons de surface localisés', decembre 2009.

[4] O. Balosso,'Introduction des Ondes de surface dans un Modèle Adapté de Faisceaux Gaussiens pour le Traitement du Couplage Antenne-Structure', thèse, université Toulouse 3 Paul Sabatier pp. 1-41, 2014.

[5] A. Alu, F. Bilotti, N. Engheta and L. Vegni, 'Subwavelength Planar Leaky-Wave Components With Metamaterial Bilayers',IEEE Trans. Antennas Propag., vol. 55, no. 3,March 2007.

[6] K. Y. Kim, Young Ki Cho and Heung-Sik Tae,'Guided Mode Propagations of Grounded Double-Positive and Double-Negative Metamaterial Slabs with Arbitary Material Indexes', May 2006.

[7] P. Baccarelli, P. Burghignoli, F. Frezza, A. Galli , P. Lampariello, G. Lovat and S. Paulotto,'The nature of radiation from leaky waves on single-and double-negative metamaterial grounded slabs', IEEE MTT-S Digest, 2004..

[8] P. Baccarelli, P. Burghignoli, G. Lovat and S. Paulotto, 'Surface-wave Suppression in a Double-Negative Metamaterial Grounded Slab', 2003.

[9] V. H. Mok and L. E. Davis, 'Electromagnetic Surface Waves in Mixed Media', Munich 2003.

[10] P. Baccarelli, P. Burghignoli, F. Frezza, A. Galli, P. Lampariello, G. Lovat and S. Paulotto, 'Effects of Leaky-Wave Propagation in Metamaterial Grounded Slabs Excited by a Dipole Source', IEEE Trans. Micro. Teoey Tech, vol. 53, no. 1, January 2005.

[11] H. Aubert, H. Baudrand, 'L'electromagnetisme par les schemas équivalents', pp. 22-p34.

[12] N. Raveu, O. Pigaglio, 'Résolution de problémes hautes fréquences par les schémas équivalents', pp. 32-48

[13] S. B. Fonseca and A. J. Giarola, 'Surface wave excitation of microstrip disk antennas', IEEE Trans. Antennas Propag, vol 12, no. 10, pp. 426-429, 1984.

[14] D. G. Duffy, 'Green's Function with Applications', Boca Raton: Chapman and Hall/CRC, 2001.

[15] S. J. Orfanidis, 'Electromagnetic Waves and Antennas', ch. 7, pp. 238-272, Piscataway: E-Book, 2008

[16] T. Tamir and A. A. Oliner, 'Guided complex Waves', Prog. IEEE, vol. 110, no. 2, pp.310-334, Feb 1963.

[17] D. M. Pozar,'Microwave Engineering', New York: John Wiley and Sons, 2004.

[18] K. Y. Kim, Young Ki Cho and Heung-Sik Tae,'Guided Mode Propagations of Grounded Double-Positive and Double-Negative Metamaterial Slabs with Arbitary Material Indexes', Journal of the Korean Physical Society, vol. 49, no. 2, August 2006, pp. 577-587.

Application of Mobile Technology in Delivery Process of Postal Operator

Juraj Vaculík
AIDC lab, Faulty of operation and economy of transport and communication, University of Zilina
Zilina, Slovakia
email: juraj.vaculik@fpedas.uniza.sk

Marián Chladný
AIDC lab, Faulty of operation and economy of transport and communication, University of Zilina
Zilina, Slovakia
email: chladny@fpedas.uniza.sk

Abstract—**This paper focuses on the possibility of implementing Radio Frequency Identification (RFID) technology in logistic processes with a focus on the final phase of delivery to the addressee. Via SMS, the addressee is informed that he will receive a delivery, and our intention is that the sender is also notified by SMS when the consignee is taken over. The intention of our work is to improve the postal services using modern technology.**

Keywords-RFID Technology; Mobile Services; Postal Operators; Process of Delivery

I. Introduction

It is important for people to be informed - to obtain and receive information when they need it and on what interest them. In the current era of information technology, it is not a problem to obtain needed information and also to provide them. In our research, we focused on the new technology in the postal sectors and on the final phase of delivery. The proposed solution of delivery (a letter or parcel) is by using RFID technology that gives an identifier to each shipment - tag by which it is possible to track the shipment. In reality, it means that the recipient is informed about the coming consignment via SMS in advance. Moreover, when the delivery is completed, the sender receives the confirmation.

Although the possibility of notification via SMS is not new, in our research, we strive for interoperability between different technologies. One technology may not be sufficient, but the correct application of specific technologies can bring the desired value added. In our case, we focus on combination of RFID technology and mobile communication in postal processes.

Presently, one of the challenges in SMS notifications is that only the recipient of the consignment is being informed of the status of delivery - SMS is a tool for one way notification only. Our aim is to apply this technology throughout the processing chain, from point to point. This way, sender as well as recipient is being updated on the status of delivery or the delivery can be optimized in advance (e.g., receiving the information from recipient about being out of town for next three days).

At present, the provision of added value to customers and the use of advanced innovative technologies can be considered as the greatest competitive advantage, especially when the companies engaged in the logistics, do not only sell products (e.g., delivery from one place to another), but they also provide the related services (e.g., notification on delivery status, insurance, etc.). Therefore, it is necessary to use modern technology which not only saves time when handling goods, but also improves the processes of serving the end customers.

The main objective of our research was to confirm the assumed interoperability in laboratory environment. In Section II, we shortly discuss the usability of RFID technology in practice. The possibilities of SMS communication is being discussed in Section III. Finally, in Section IV, we describe the proposed solution of implementation of these technologies in the present postal processes.

II. Technology Background

RFID identifier, by which the shipment can be monitored, is assigned to each consignment. It is one of the key components used in providing information to the recipient and sender via SMS. Another key component is of course SMS server that arranges the whole communication.

The advantage of RFID system is that it can be used in environments where the humidity, temperature, dust or vibrations are preventing the use of bar codes.

RFID system consists of two basic parts: readers and RFID identifiers (carriers of information). The identifiers can be active (containing power supply, e.g., battery) or passive. The reader is the crucial component of the RFID system. Depending on the particular application, it may be stationary or mobile. Readers in RFID systems have two functions. The first is to broadcast the RF signal and the other is to receive information from the RFID identifiers. This information is sent to the superior information system, where it is then processed. The broadcasted RF signal has two functions as well. The first is to ensure detection of an RFID identifier. This function is similar for passive and active systems. The second function is important in systems using passive chips. In these cases, the magnetic field created by the reader is used to obtain the energy necessary to send the signal from the RFID tags back to reader. Return signal is modulated by the information that is stored in it. Some systems used in stores for guarding the goods by Electronic Article Surveillance (EAS) operate in a manner very similar to RFID, although the information is bistable (on/off).

Complex systems can process additional information obtained from RFID tags, such as temperature, position, etc. In order to store additional information, RFID tag needs to be equipped with supplementary circuits granting the mentioned operations (e.g., temperature sensor). The role of the RFID identifier is that when it comes within range of the reader, it sends identification. More complex identifiers are able to process significantly larger amount of information. Each identifier is composed of an antenna, transceiver and transponder. At Ultra high frequency (UHF) technology, antenna takes the largest part of the RFID identifier. With higher frequency band, the size of the antenna decreases. The role of the antenna is to receive and transmit the signals. When receiving a signal, antenna has double role. One role is to generate energy to power the identifier and the second role is to process the code which is used by tag in communication between the identifier and the reader. Transceiver unit is a device containing transmitter and receiver that share common circuits. The unit, complemented by the received signal, will create the energy necessary for the operation of the entire RFID identifier.

III. Possibilities of SMS Communication

This section talks about possibility to communicate through SMS server (Ozeki) and its connection to RFID middleware.

A. *Ozeki SMS Server*

In our laboratory for Automatic Identification and Data Capture (AIDC lab), we operate with Ozeki SMS Server. Ozeki Informatics Ltd. is a leading supplier of software for mobile messages. It offers a program easy to use and rich portfolio of telecommunications products for businesses and organizations. The company is actively working on providing further innovations that increase productivity. Using a Global System for Mobile Communications (GSM), modem and SMS Internet protocol (IP) technologies, products enhance productivity, flexibility, and provide significant advantages for professionals to create mobile communications services. The server offers two core modules:

- **Short Message Service Point to Point** (SMS-PP) - one SMS can contain up to 160 characters. Newer phones allow sending longer messages, but the sender's phone breaks up the longer message to short parts and receiving phone merges them into one again. Message is sent between two or multi phones or applications.
- (SMS-CB) **Short Message Service Cell Broadcast** - these messages use the Cell Broadcast channels. They are used, for example, for weather forecasts, local news, and traffic situation or for determining the actual position. Message is sent to all phones in a given area that are turned on and CB is set to the appropriate channel. The maximum length of message is 93 characters.

In the following part, we discuss the possibilities of the first module (SMS-CB):

- **GSM modem** is the core of GSM / General Packet Radio System (GPRS) Modem Connection (Fig. 1) that allows to use the mobile phone or wireless modem connected to the PC (using the data cable) to send and receive SMS messages. Mobile phone or modem must contain Subscriber Identification Module (SIM) cards, which can be bought from any GSM service provider.

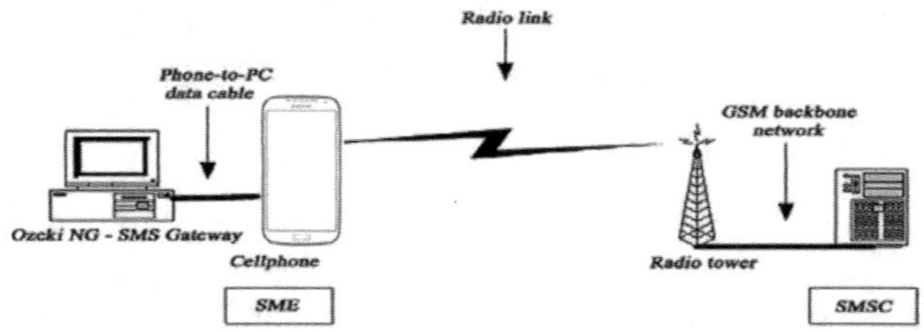

Figure 1. Configuration of GSM modem

- **IP SMS** (Fig. 2) consists of protocols Computer Interface to Message Distribution (CIMD2) Connection (), SMPP Connection (Short Message Peer to Peer), UCP Connection Universal Computer Protocol / External Machine Interface (UCP / EMI) (Fig. 3). These protocols can be used to connect the computer directly to the Short Message Service Centre (SMSC) GSM service provider. This way, SMS messages can be sent and received via the Internet or private IP network.

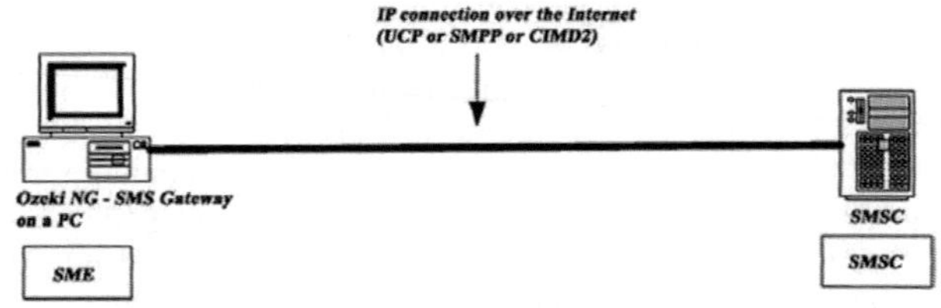

Figure 2. IP SMS connection

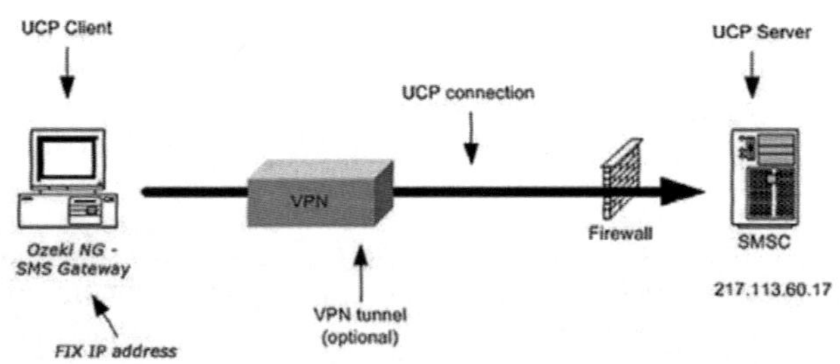

Figure 3. UCP connection

- **Pull Interface Connection** - Short Message Peer-to-Peer (SMPP) Push / Pull a special connection that implements Unstructured Supplementary Service Data (USSD) push / pull communication protocol-based Comviva FLARES. This protocol can be used to connect the standard SMPP.
- **HTTP Connection Server** (HyperText Transfer Protocol Server) - enables service providers to use the HTTP protocol for the transmission of messages coming into operation. This technology is often used

in premium rated SMS services (Fig. 4). This connection can also be used as "virtual phone" for the purposes of software development.

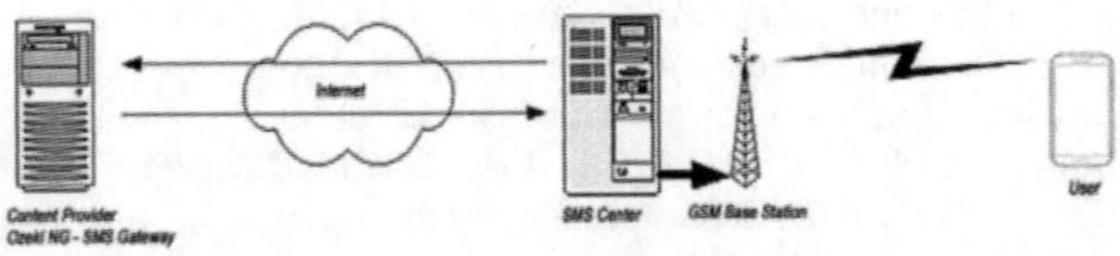

Figure 4. Architecture of premium value services

- **Simple Mail Transfer Protocol (SMTP) Connection** - Connecting the SMTP lets the user to send SMS messages via e-mail. Email connection for SMS is available with many mobile operators and IP based multichannel GSM gateway.
- **Simple Network Paging Protocol (SNPP) Connection (Paging)** - This protocol allows the user to send messages to pagers via the Internet.

B. RFID middleware Aton mobile platform

RFID middleware Aton uses a tool to send SMS. In this section, we show how both programs, Aton mobile platform (AMP) and Ozeki SMS server, have to be configured in order to mutually communicate and send SMS at the desired time. The graphical model of RFID information processing is stated in Fig. 5.

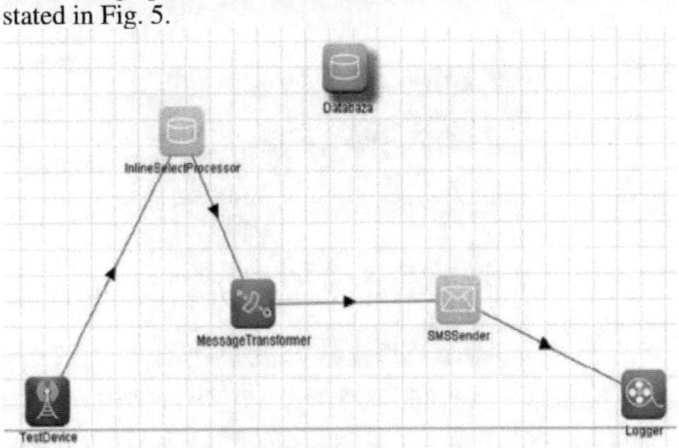

Figure 5. The basic structure of the proposed application

The aim of the solution is the implementation of RFID technology in logistics processes with a focus on final processing of postal consignments. We focus on informing the sender and recipient on the status of the delivery. Via SMS, the addressee is informed that he will receive a delivery, and our intention is that the sender is also notified by SMS when the consignee is taken over.

It is necessary to configure RFID middleware Aton and server Ozeki in the adequate way in order to send an SMS at the right time.

Basic components of our proposed application are:

- **TestDevice** - detection gateway scanned tag passes through,
- **Database** - a set of tables where data is stored,
- **InlineSelectProcessor** - processor to access and read data from the database,
- **MessageTransformer** - processor which is used to transform the input message for the correct output,
- **SMSSender** - processor for sending SMS,
- **Logger** - processor that ensures the creation of output and logging data.

The configuration parameters of SMSSender processor (Fig. 6) are set as:

- **default.sender** – OZEKI (name of service)
- **smpp.password** – abc123
- **smpp.server – address of server**
- **smpp-username** – admin
- **sms.char.maxlength** – 0 (without limit)

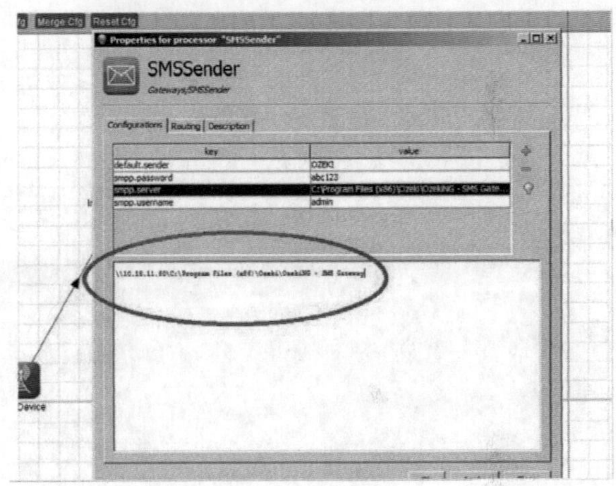

Figure 6. Settings of SMSSender processor

Admin username and password 'abc123' is standardly preset in the software Ozeki. According to the needs, the user can change this information. For security reasons, Ozeki Company Ltd. recommends to change the name and password immediately after software setup. The possibility of smpp.server defines the path where the software Ozeki is available, for example:

\\10.15.11.80\\Ozeki\OzekiNG - SMS Gateway.

Form of message AMP sends to Ozeki

<message>
<from>mobile number**</from>**
<to>
<address>number of addressee</address>
<address>number of sender</address>
</to>
<body>
text of message
</body>
</message>

Mobile number must be entered with international prefix (e.g., +421 905 555 555).

Form of message to be sent to addressee:

<message>
<from>+421915879503</from>
<to><address>+421911870113</address></to>
<body> Dear Customer. You received the shipment no. 1234, it will be delivered to your address tomorrow. For another method of service call hotline xxx
</body>
</message>

Form of message to be sent to the sender once the delivery is taken over by addressee:

<message>
<from>+421915879503</from>
<to><address>+4219114753278</address></to>
<body> Dear Customer. The shipment no. 1234 you sent on xx.yy.2016 has successfully seen delivered to the addressee.
</body>
</message>

C. Technical components

We have used a GSM modem Siemens MC35 which consists of an external GSM antenna, RS232 serial cable, SIM card and the AC adapter (Fig. 7).

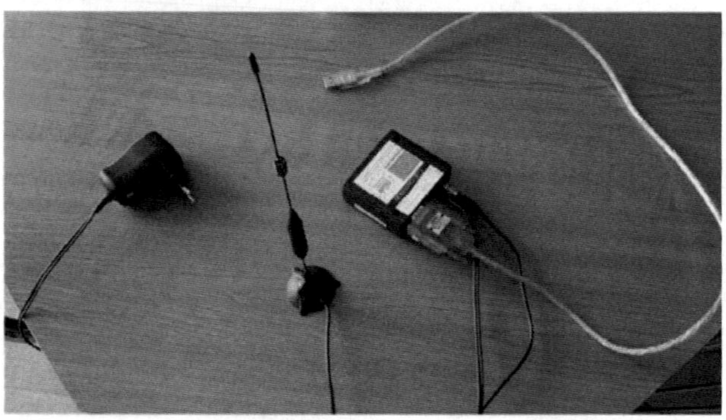

Figure 7. Parts of GSM modem

After installing the necessary Ozeki software, NG SMS Gateway is being installed (Fig. 8).

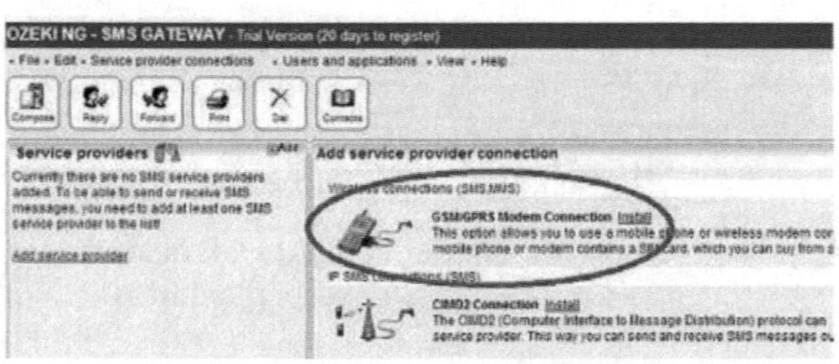

Figure 8. Module of Ozeki system

After installing a particular module, it is necessary to configure the modem before the first connection. Once the Ozeki program is open, user will automatically find the necessary hardware installed on the computer.

Fig. 9 shows Ozeki server detecting hardware on serial port COM3 (standard for this kind of modem connection). In next step, the software correctly retrieves the necessary parameters for connection. Consequently, it is necessary to set SMS center operator (we used the company Orange Slovakia, Inc.), operator number (+421 905 303 303) and mobile number of the SIM card (+421 915 879 503). Then, there is the possibility to set the modem name, in our case, we have chosen GSMModem0.

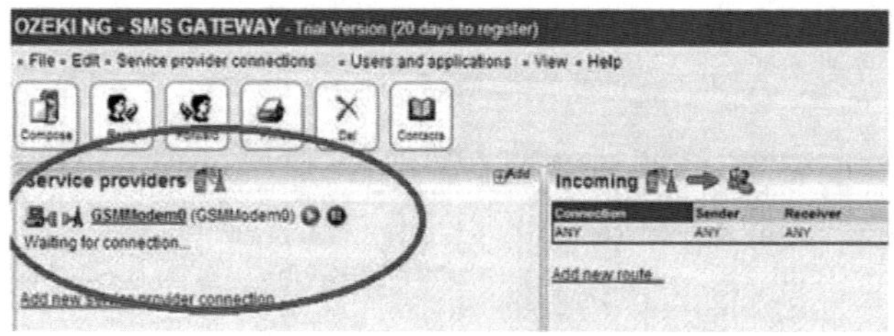

Figure 9. Name of GSM modem

Once the configuration is completed, the creation of the actual SMS is enabled by choosing “Compose” option from menu. In the first selection field, we select the text type of SMS (not multimedia SMS, etc.), the mobile number of recipient and finally the actual text of message. When SMS system Ozeki is connected to the middleware AMP, the above described steps are redundant as the text of SMS will be imported directly from AMP. The picture of test SMS is visible in Fig. 10.

Figure 10. A demonstrative example of SMS messages

As per Ozeki system configuration, each SMS is stored in database of sent SMS. (Fig. 11).

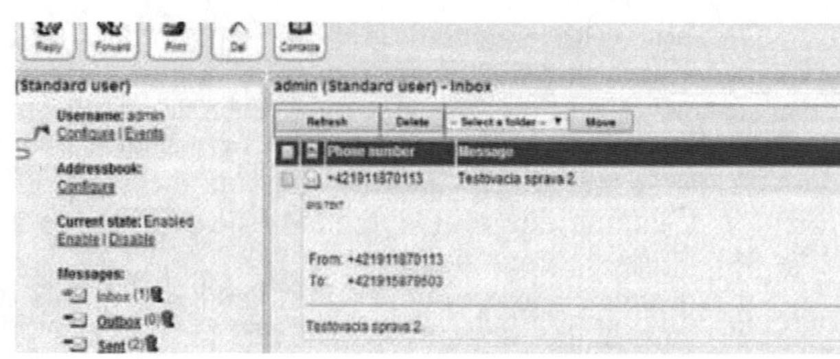

Figure 11. Database record of sent SMS

IV. DESIGN OF MAIL DELIVERY PROCESS

The following part describes the proposed process of mail delivery using RIFD technology with an emphasis on informing the recipient of the consignment via SMS, as well as the sender. The whole process of sending the confirmation SMS to the sender is triggered by the initial SMS message sent to the addressee (first database record about the consignment) and the actual final delivery. In case the consignment is not delivered directly to the recipient, but it needs to be e.g., picked up in person on post office, the system generates SMS informing the recipient about this fact.

If the consignment is being delivered directly to the address of the recipient, the sender is informed about the successful delivery by the SMS message shown in Fig 12.

Figure 12. Confirmation message about successful delivery generated by Ozeki system

As stated, there are different ways of making the delivery (via the postman, courier, in person pick up on the post office, etc.). In our designed process, the confirmation report (text differs by the way of actual delivery) is sent in form of SMS to the sender. This terminates the whole process of delivery.

Example of processing and delivery of consignment using RFID technology and mobile network services that we have proposed and tested in our laboratory is pictured in Fig. 13:

1. Submission of shipment - The sender brings consignment to the delivery office in order to send it the recipient.
2. Expedition of shipment – Except of standard information (name of the recipient, address,..), the shipment must contain the phone number of both, the recipient and the sender; at this point, the consignment is equipped by RFID tag carrying data that will be recognized by AMP middleware.
3. Transportation by postal courses - at the beginning of transportation, RFID tag is scanned and information is inserted to the database together with the time and date of scanning and code number of the actual postal course.
4. Delivery of shipments – delivery to target post office; RFID tag is scanned and database is updated; the necessary information is sent to Ozeki system.
5. SMS message to recipient - Ozeki sends SMS message to the recipient; the system automatically sends SMS messages to all the addressees about the arrival of shipment to distribution center.
6. Optional feedback of recipient – the recipient can inform the post office of being e.g. out of town so that the date and time of delivery is adjusted.
7. Delivery to the recipient – Delivery of the consignment to the recipient (to particular address, by picking up the consignment at the post office, etc.)
8. SMS message to sender - confirmation message about successful delivery is sent to sender.

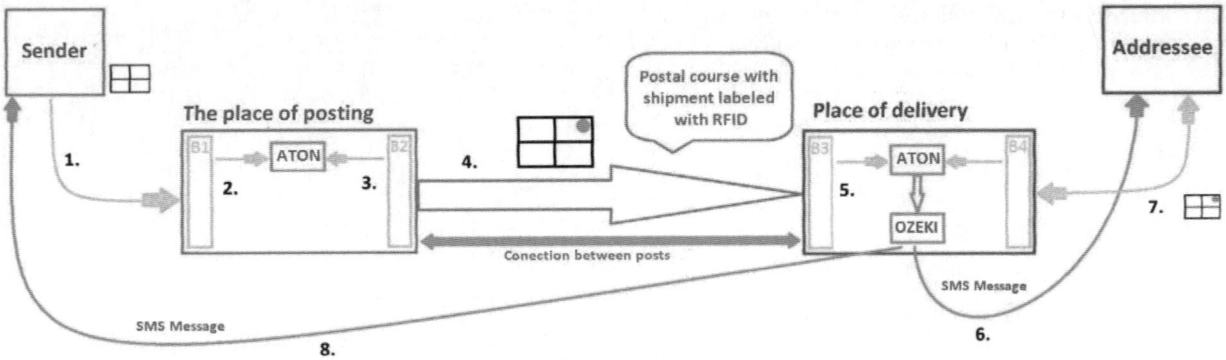

Figure 13. Example of proposed process and delivery of consignment

V. Conclusion

The current trend is to be constantly informed about everything that takes place around us. An enterprise, engaged in postal services, can improve its services and grant the access to more information for its customers by using the necessary technology. This is an advantage that will help to succeed in the competition for the end customer over the others competitors.

We suggest the model of using RFID technology in the postal services. Our intention is that the recipient and the sender receive a text message with the shipment status. This can be arranged for any consignment in question. In our case, we opted for recommended letters or parcels that have been equipped with RFID identifier – a tag. The position of the shipment is not only tracked, but our designed system can also provide reports and send information via SMS. Addressee receives the message at the time when the consignment reaches the distribution center, so that the recipient can choose the method of the delivery. Sender is informed about the successful delivery once the shipment is taken over.

Our proposed solution is the combination of RFID technology and mobile communication granted via Ozeki system. This combination has been proven as the most suitable during tests in our laboratory environment. RFID tag is the key element of our solution as it carries the essential information needed for future processing. Because of this, every consignment needs to be equipped by RFID tag. Additional information can be included if needed (name, address, telephone number); otherwise this information is accessible in the database.

Although we are aware of the financial cost of the proposed solution, the level of value added makes the investment very attractive. They key features are the improvement of information flow, improvement of customer service, the possibility of immediate feedback and last but not least, it can contribute to the significant delivery time reduction.

The process we propose needs to be perceived as only the beginning of future research. It is possible to develop solutions such as mobile applications for smartphones used for communication with postal operator, to generate new services such as Just-in-Place (sending the coordinates of the current position) or delivery within the specified time and many more. It would be possible to add a workaround for sharing the feedback (for example to determine the quality of the service or the satisfaction of users). However, these are solutions which we are working are the subjects of our future research.

Acknowledgment

E!7592 AUTOEPCIS - RFID Technology in Logistic Networks of Automotive Industry.

References

[1] D. Friedlos: Royal Mail posts RFID tags to monitor deliveries. [online]. [quoted 6.3.2010]. Available on Internet: <http://www.computing.co.uk/computing/ news/2161216/royal-mail-posts-rfid-tags>.

[2] S. L. Garfinkel RFID Security and Privacy. [online]. [quoted 27.3.2010]. Available on Internet: <http://www.oecd.org/dataoecd-/18/53/35473108.pdf>.

[3] R. Haq RFID technology in the postal sector. [online]. [quoted 6.3.2010]. Available on Internet: <www.arabian-supplychain.com/article-2619-rfid_technology_in_the_postal_-sector/>.

[4] M. Chladny: Applications of RFID technology in logistics of postal operators, diploma thesis, University of Zilina, 2014

[5] J. Tengler: System for receiving and delivery with the use of RFID technology and mobile network services, disertation thesis, University of Zilina, 2013

[6] R. Wessel: Swiss Post Deliveres RFID to Its Parcel Centers, Transportation Hubs. [online]. [quoted 6.3.2010]. Available on Internet: <http://www.rfidjournal.com/ article/articleview/-4270/1/1>.Slovak post, a.s. [online]. [quoted 2014] available on Internet

[7] Wordwide support OZEKI. [online] [quoted 2014] Available on Internet.

[8] OZEKI Informatics Ltd. [online]. [quoted 2014] Available on Internet

[9] J. Vaculík and J. Tengler: Analysis of the process of identification of mail and making them more effective in terms of transport. IPoCC. Pardubice 2010. P.303 -308, ISBN 978-80-86530-68-0.

[10] J. Vaculík and I. Michálek: RFID middleware and web postal services, Future role of postal services in the face of new market conditions and communication technologies. Pardubice: University of Pardubice, 2008, p.152 - 157, ISBN, 978-80-7395-144-3.

Modeling and Performance Analysis of a Converged Network

Jihad Qaddour,
Dept. Information Technology
Illinois State University
Normal, IL, USA
Email: jqaddou@ilstu.edu

Yesh Polishetty
Dept. Information Technology
Illinois State University
Normal, IL, USA
Email: ypolish@ilstu.edu

***Abstract*—Moving from the existing independent infrastructure to integrate shared environment (converged network) will reduce the infrastructure maintenance cost, which we use for performance analysis. This paper addresses a converged network performance analysis based on OPNET simulations. Efficiency metrics, response times, transit time, throughput and transfer delay for different transaction routes in a converged network are evaluated. Various rounds of testing have been conducted using Single User Testing and Load Performance Testing to collect performance metrics to identify architecture bottlenecks. Based on performance analysis, we observed some poor performance as well as more delays in the response times to reach TC servers. We concluded that the response times between a client and TC servers violated the Service Level Agreement. This Paper identifies that most delays were contributed mainly by processing times of TC servers in a converged network.**

Keywords-Preformance Analysis; Convergence; Response times; OPNET; Modeling.

I. INTRODUCTION

When a request is sent from the Trusted Zone in an organization, it passes through several layers. One of the problems is to identify where the bottleneck of the performance of the application is. Figure 1 shows the application architecture, which includes vendor, sales client, admin users, different servers at different tiers, and multiple firewalls to secure the network. Moreover, we show the response times, that will be measured, between the users and different server's zones. The server layer's zones include Mule Servers, TC servers, web servers, and database servers. For sending request transactions from a client to different servers, we use OPNET for modeling the architecture of the network and simulation to calculate different performance metrics, such as transit times, response times, throughput, and others. With the help of these performance metrics, we can analyze the performance of each transaction and compare the result to identify any performance issues, delay violations, and the Bottleneck in the architecture to be resolved [1]. According to Liu [3], application problems can be detected in the earlier stages of the life cycle of the application before converging into the shared environment. OPNET accelerates troubleshooting by rapidly pin pointing the root cause. It ensures application Service Level Agreement (SLA) and the compliance. Using OPNET simulation, we can identify problems related to application performance at different tier levels as well the transit time delays between different applications regardless of its web/windows-based infrastructure [2].

For the application to be converged and move from existing infrastructure to the shared infrastructure using OPNET Simulation, the bottlenecks can be identified, and ways to improve the performance can be analyzed and optimized. This helps the organization move the infrastructure easily, maintain the consistency, and provides redundancy within the available space [5]. According to [3], OPNET tools are used to monitor application performance live in production and to test the environments. Consequently, the application can be easily monitored and maintained to achieve the organization requirements and attain the SLA. Using OPNET modeling and simulation tools, we will collect performance metrics (response times, transit times, throughput, and others) to analyze the performance of the network. We will run two different testing methods: Single User Testing and Load Performance Testing, using three different transactions (Dashboard, URL, and submit requests) to identify the architecture's bottleneck.

The remainder of the paper is organized as follows: In section II, we present a detailed discussion on all the components of the converged network; Section III describes network application testing where we use two different testing methods; Section IV discusses the OPNET, which was the simulation tool we used for performance analysis and modeling; Section V presents our finding, analysis discussion, and solution to enhance the converged network performance; and Section VI is the conclusion, where we identified the architecture bottleneck and proposed solutions.

II. COMPONENTS INVOLVED

In this section, we will introduce the components that are involved in the testing: users, different servers, and details about application infrastructure.

a. Users

All users are sending various transactions from different computers, which are known as 'clients' to reach different servers for different business applications. For this testing we are using three different transactions from a client to servers, at different tiers using different connections to be able to compare the results between each tier and identify the performance delays of the application.

b. TC Server

TC server provides organization with secure supported and extended Java application server based, which is fully compatible with Apache Tomcat. Many companies are attracted by the performance and the convergence benefits of using the TC server. TC servers allow for easy installation. When there are any changes in the infrastructure of the application, there will be minimal security risks observed. These risks can be mitigated easily after installing into the shared environment [4].

c. Mule Server

A Mule server is an enterprise service bus, which is used to transfer a request from one server to another. It can be served as a security layer, and using a Mule server can improve the performance of the application as well. The time spent on a Mule server is very short compared to the time spent on the application and web servers [5].

d. Web Servers

Dedicated Web servers are used to extend the security and improve reliability. Web servers can be customized based on the infrastructure and different user requirements [3].

e. Application Infrastructure

Figure 1 explains the application architecture. Network Single User Testing and Load Performance Testing will be conducted using this model and then different results for different testing will be recorded.

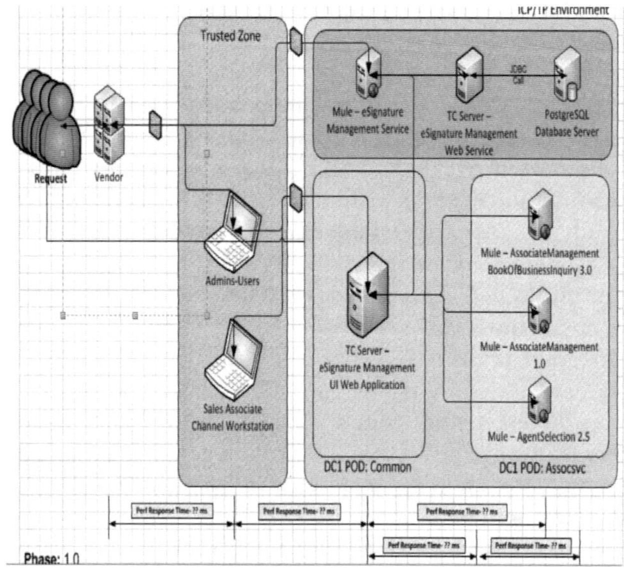

Figure 1. Application Infrastructure

III. NETWORK APPLICATION TESTING

Two different tests were conducted in this paper: The Load Performance Testing and Single User Testing.

a. Load Performance Testing (LPT)

In this testing, we send multiple requests to the application and we use LPT tools and OPNET to collect different performance metrics (such as response time, transit time, and throughput for performance analysis of the application and network behaviors). The main objective of LPT is to find out where the application breaks, so that the new convergence can be constructed based on the size the application that can stand. Through this testing, we find out the transit times between clients and all servers at different layers of the application. This helps us to calculate the total delays and the break point of the application to stay connected. Based on the testing results, we use the performance metrics as an input to building convergence in the shared environment [2].

Figure 2 shows object-by-object and different components performance. The red color shows the delay in getting a response. The yellow color indicates the object is processing the request. Finally, the green color indicates the response times. As we can conclude from this test, the red color is very high, which indicates that getting the response takes much longer times. Therefore, this identifies that the delay getting the response is the architecture bottlenecks. A solution for this needs to be investigated, including the replacement of slower devices by faster ones.

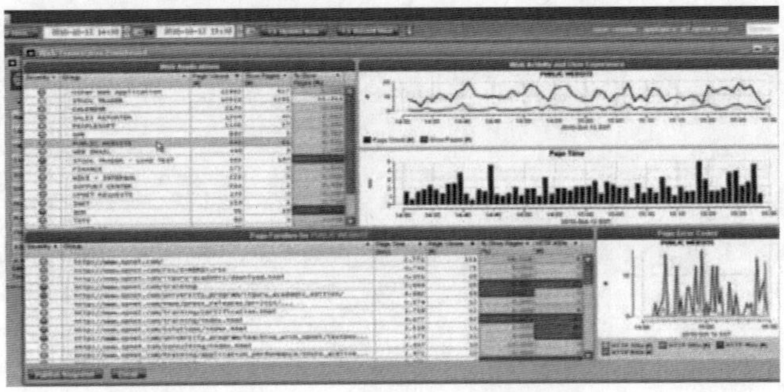

Figure 2. Load Testing Performance

b. Single User Testing (SUT)

SUT determines the most accurate time for the layers in the application. It also determines the firewall response times and the throughput for the application. This is fast and simple testing compared to the LPT. This testing was used as a smoke testing before conducting the actual LPT [5].

Performing SUT will give the high level information of the application behavior. Using various tools, we can collect metrics during SUT like routing information of requests, response time between two hosts, wait-time, first time to connect, connection time, compression information for each resource, and number and size of requests between each user action [4].

Data collected in SUT can be used to evaluate the application performance during early stages of development, which may greatly resolve most of the performance bottlenecks. Response time and throughput for each component or transaction can be measured and analyzed to find out the possible root cause for delays and bottlenecks in the application to fix the problem [5].

IV. TOOL USED

OPNET Network tool is used for simulation, network application performance, and to set the application model. OPNET is an event based network simulation tool. Using OPNET, we can conduct different simulation testing to analyze and optimize the performance of hardware and application software of the network. OPNET delivers high definition application performance with the dashboards. Figure 3 shows the Dashboard for an application. This shows various business logics/applications and the related application performance. The green and red colors indicate the status of the application performance when the applications are up and running during the run time environment [4].

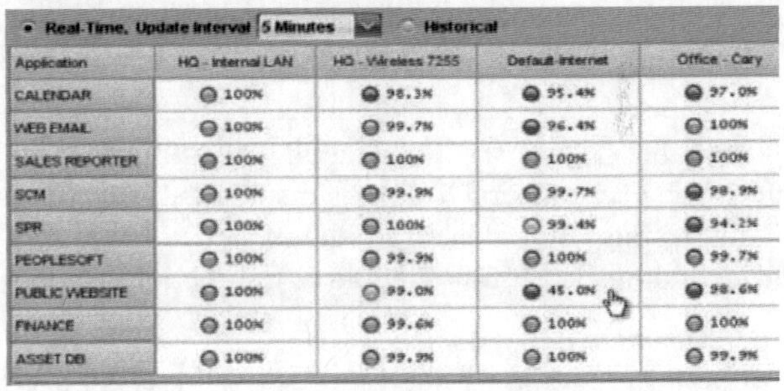

Figure 3. OPNET Dashboard

Using OPNET, the overall application performance can be observed and calculated (such as response times, transit times, and throughput for each tier). In addition, the spikes in the application inside the webserver or database server can be identified as well as the reason for these spikes. OPNET simulation shows that the application is degraded with too many requests simultaneously. We can also measure many performance metrics such as memory performance, throughput, response times, and transit times, which help to optimize them and analyze the performance of different hardware and applications [5].

V. DISCUSSION AND ANALYSIS

In this section, we present detailed discussion and analysis. We will discuss the application transactions, which observed during different process transactions of testing. Moreover, we will analyze different connections between all components and discuss the testing results to identify the problems.

a. Observations

Figure 1 shows the application architecture, which was used for sending requests and collecting different performance metrics to do performance analyzing and optimization. We sent requests manually, then we observed three different transactions as follow: Transaction 1 was Launch Dashboard without cache. Transaction 2 was Launch Create URL without cache, and Transaction 3 was Submit Request without cache.

TABLE 1. TRANSACTION DETAILS

Transaction Name	Response Times	Throughput
Launch Dashboard	4.2 seconds	336.3kb
Launch URL	883.9 milliseconds	107.7kb
Submit Request	3.9 seconds	136.7kb

In Table 1, we show the application transactions that have been observed during different transactions of this testing. We also show the response times and throughput information of the three transactions.

b. Deep Dive Analysis

Plotting the previous three transactions (Dashboard, URL, and Submit Request launches) versus response times shows that transaction 1 (launch Dashboard without cache) is taking the longest time (4.2 seconds), while the second transaction (launch URL) takes the least time, less than 1s. In Figure 4, we plotted the three transactions versus response times. This result shows that this was due to the increase in connections between different components. The minimum transaction as can be seen in the above table was the URL, which we recommended to all the users to use instead of the other two methods.

As a result, the application performance using Dashboard and Submit Request were the most degraded and took much longer times. Moreover, the (SLA) was defined by the organization to be less than 4 seconds, which means all the transactions should be returned in less than 4 seconds. The shorter the response times, the more effective the result. If we compare the result in Figure 4 to SLA, we conclude that the first transaction (Dashboard) does not meet the requirement (4.2 s > 4.0 s), which is 200 milliseconds more than the business requirement. In the third transaction (sending request) the transaction time barley met the SLA requirement. Therefore, the application performances in these two transactions were degraded. Consequently, a solution is needed, such as replacing some existing hardware with faster alternatives, and improved software.

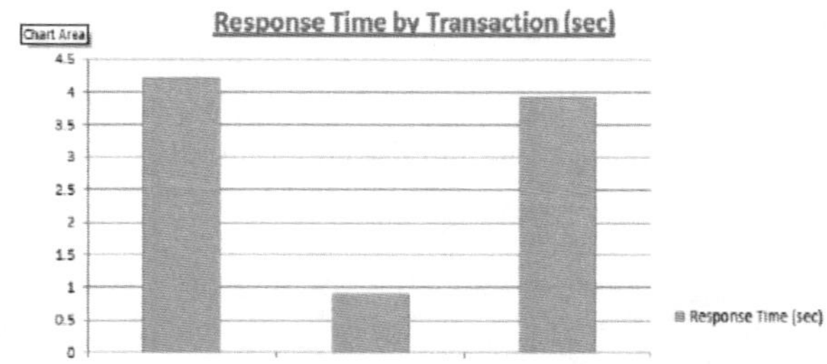

Figure 4. Response Time Graph

TABLE 2. TIER LEVEL DETAILST

Tier for Launch Dashboard	Latency Observed (milliseconds)
Client to Application Central Server	13.2 milliseconds
Client to Open Am Server	13.2 milliseconds
Application central server to TC server	3.9 seconds
Application central server to Environment Server	273 milliseconds
Application central server to Application east server (Bloomington)	0

In Table 2, we show the latency between a client and different servers at different tiers. Using OPNET, we calculated the times between a client and different servers at different tiers. We observed that the request from Bloomington, Illinois for the central server has no latency delay. On the other hand, when the request is sent from a central server to any other area servers, the network latency delay is around 13.2 milliseconds. But the key bottleneck is identified when a request sent from a central server to a TC server: the response time is taking around 3.9 seconds. This delay time is very long, which means the request spent most of the time processing the TC server.

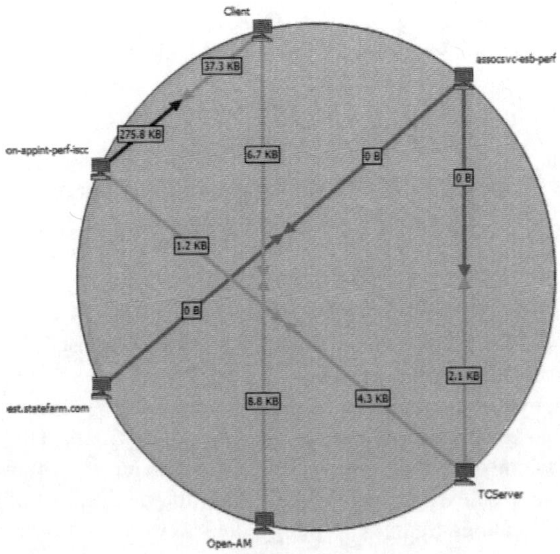

Figure 5. Multi Transaction Report

In Figure 5, we show the transaction report response times and other performance metrics during the testing process of the application. We run the above three transactions (Dashboard, URL, and Submit Request) again for several testing periods. The testing would initially start as SUT to make sure that the application is properly designed. Then the LPT would run several times by sending a sequence of requests at a time to check the application performance, which means more load is put in the architecture. LPT was performed to replicate the exact scenario of the application in the new environment, which will be used by many other services. This is called the shared environment. The outcome of this testing was similar to the previous testing, which result that the most time spent was in the TC server layer. This confirms that, while running a full load in the architecture, we have the same result. Most time was spent in processing, within the TC server. As a solution, changing TC server with a faster one will shorten the process time and delay would be shorter.

VI. CONCLUSION

Using OPNET modeling and simulation, we collected performance metrics (response times, transit times, throughput, and others) to analyze the performance of the network. We run two different testing: SUT and LPT, using three different transactions (Dashboard, URL, and Submit Request). After running these tests several times, we conclude that the architecture bottleneck was identified to be the processing time in the TC server layer, which is causing most delays. Moreover, the delay is violating the SLA (equals 4s), which means all the transactions times should be returned in in less than 4 seconds. For future work, we recommend a full investigation of the solutions to this problem. One solution could be replacing the TC server with a faster one. Another solution might be limiting the connections times between the application's units to improve the performance of the applications and reduce the cost of the infrastructure. Such solutions can be investigated in an another paper.

REFERENCES

[1] X. Chang, "Network simulations with OPNET," Proceedings of the 31st conference on Winter simulation, Simulation a bridge to the Future, Volume 1, pp. 307-314.

[2] C. Zhu, O. W. Yang, J. Aweya, M. Ouellette, and D. Y. Montuno, "A comparison of active queue management algorithms using the OPNET Modeler," IEEE Communications Magazine 40, pp. 158-167, June 2002.

[3] K. Salah and A. Alkhoraidly, "An OPNET-based simulation approach for deploying VoIP," International Journal of Network Management 16, pp. 159-183, March 2006.

[4] M. S. Hasan, H. Yu, A. Carrington, and T. C. Yang, "Co-simulation of wireless networked control systems over mobile ad hoc network using SIMULINK and OPNET," IET Communications 3, pp.1297-1310, 2009.

[5] M. Young, P. Leys, J. Potemans, B. Van den Broeck, J. Theunis, E. Van Lil, and A. Van de Capelle, "Use of the raw packet generator in OPNET," OPNETWORK 2002 Handbook, Mill Valley, CA University Science, 2002.

[6] Q. Duan, "Modeling and delay analysis for converged network-cloud service provisioning systems," Computing, Networking and Communications (ICNC), January 2013.

The Secrecy Capacity of the Semi-deterministic Wiretap Channel with Three State Information

Mustafa El-Halabi
Department of Computer and Communications Engineering
American University of Science & Technology
Beirut, Lebanon
Email: mhalabi@aust.edu.lb

***Abstract*—Exploiting the channel state knowledge can play a fundamental role in improving security, hence a wiretap channel model with distinct channel state information is considered. In particular, it is assumed that the channel between the transmitter, the legitimate receiver and the eavesdropper is a function of three different states. One of the states is an unknown state, the second one is known to the legitimate receiver and the third state is non-causally known to the encoder. For this setting, a secrecy rate is shown to be achieved using a coding scheme based on structured binning in conjunction with a time-sharing argument. The secrecy capacity for this model is established for the specific case when the legitimate receiver's observation is a deterministic function of the the channel input and the states.**

***Index Terms*—Wiretap channel, state information, secrecy capacity, random binning, time-sharing.**

I. Introduction

In the race towards setting and defining the grounds for 5G wireless networks, information-theoretic security is steering lot of attention in recent years as a major player to safeguard data confidentiality. The 5G heterogeneous networks and the massive MIMO architecture call for a new security paradigm which is less dependent on secret key exchange; a problem with an order of complexity that increases with the ubiquity of the network [1].

Shannon in [2] introduced the channel state information to information theoretic models, wherein he considered the channel state to be a side information which is causally known to the transmitter. In [3], the side information was considered to be non-causally known to the transmitter and the capacity for the corresponding channel was obtained using a Gel'fand-Pinsker (GP) binning scheme.

In the context of information-theoretic security, there has been many attempts to investigate the role of state information on the secrecy performance of wiretap channels. A transmitter is attempting to send a confidential message to a designated receiver, through a channel governed by a certain state sequence, while a wiretapper is getting hold of the encoded message as a result of the openness nature of the communication channel. In [4], *Chen & Vinck* considered the problem of wiretap channel where the transition probability depends on a state sequence non-causally known to the encoder, and the wiretapper's signal is a degraded version of the legitimate receiver's signal. The achieved secrecy rate was based on a *double-binning* scheme; a synthesis of the *wiretap codes* used in [5], [6] for wiretap channels and the GP coding used in [3]. Interestingly, looking into the Gaussian model, it was shown that secrecy rate can actually be enhanced in the presence of known side information [4]. In [7],*Chia & El-Gamal* studied the problem of wiretap channel with causal side information, where an achievable secrecy rate was obtained using block Markov coding, Shannon strategy, and key generation from common state information.

In this paper, we propose a variant of the wiretap channel with state information problem. In our model, the signal received by the legitimate receiver depends on two state sequences S_1 and S_2, such that S_1 is non-causally known to the transmitter and S_2 is known to the receiver, while the signal received by the wiretapper depends on one unknown state sequence S_3. A model where the wiretap channel depends on two-sided state sequences was addressed in [8], where a rate-equivocation region was established using a time-sharing argument, whereas the assumption of the wiretapper's signal being affected by an unknown state sequence was treated in [9]. In this sense, our model can be viewed as a generalization of the previous two models and provides more insight on the impact of different kinds of side information on secure communication. In addition, we propose an upper bound on the secrecy capacity of the wiretap channel with three state information, and show that the secrecy rate achieved by our coding scheme matches the upper bound for the case when the legitimate receiver is a deterministic function of the channel input and the states.

The paper is organized as follows. Section II reviews the capacity of the channel with two-sided state information and the capacity for the corresponding deterministic channel. Section III introduces the problem and present the model. Section V presents the coding scheme and the achieved secrecy rate for the wiretap channel with three state information. Section IV derives an upper bound on the secrecy capacity. Section VI proves the secrecy capacity of the semi-deterministic model. Section VII summarizes the main results and the contribution of the paper.

II. Channel With Two-Sided State Information

In this section we review the building block for our model, which is the channel with two-sided state information introduced in [10], and derive the capacity for the corresponding

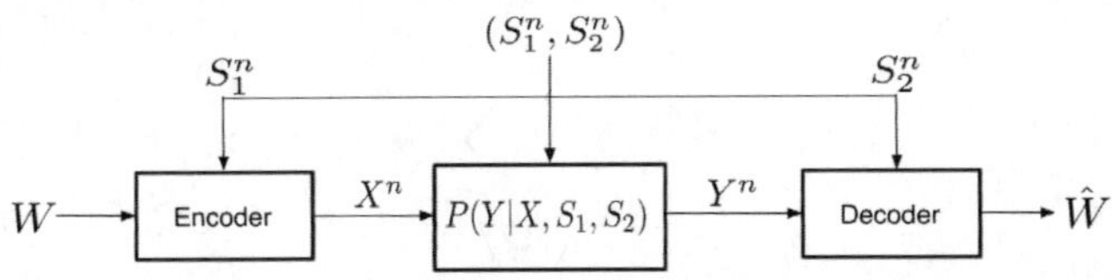

Figure 1. Channel with two-sided state information; S_1 non-causally known to the encoder, state S_2 known to the decoder.

deterministic channel. The conditional probability distribution depends on two correlated channel states S_1 and S_2 with joint probability distribution $p(s_1, s_2)$; the state S_1 is non-causally known to the receiver and the state S_2 is known to the receiver. See Figure. 1.

The capacity of this channel was obtained by *Cover et.al* in [10] and we restate the result in the following theorem.

Theorem 1. *The capacity C of the memoryless channel $p(y|x, s_1, s_2)$, with channel state S_1 non-causally known at the encoder as side information and channel state S_2 known to the decoder, is given by*

$$C = \max_{p(u,x|s_1)} [I(U; Y, S_2) - I(U; S_1)]\,. \tag{1}$$

where U is an auxiliary random variable verifying the following Markov chain: $U \to (X, S_1) \to (Y, S_2)$.

Proof: See proof in [10]. ∎

We now characterize the capacity of the *deterministic* channel with two-sided states. In this case the channel output is a deterministic (bivariate) function of the channel input X and the channel states S_1 and S_2:

$$Y = f(X, S_1, S_2) \quad \textit{with probability 1} \tag{2}$$

Theorem 2. *The capacity of the deterministic channel with two-sided states is given by*

$$C = \max_{p(x|s_1)} H(Y|S_1, S_2) \tag{3}$$

Proof: Upper bound. An upper bound on the channel capacity for the model represented in Figure. 1, corresponds to the capacity of the channel where the states S_1 and S_2 are both fed to the encoder and the decoder. The capacity of this channel is given in [10, Corollary. 1] by $\max_{p(x|s_1,s_2)} I(X; Y|S_1, S_2)$. Hence, an upper bound on the capacity of the deterministic channel is

$$\begin{aligned} C &\leq \max_{p(x|s_1)} I(X; Y|S_1, S_2) \\ &= \max_{p(x|s_1)} [H(Y|S_1, S_2) - H(Y|X, S_1, S_2)] \\ &= \max_{p(x|s_1)} H(Y|S_1, S_2) \end{aligned} \tag{4}$$

where (4) is due to (2).

Lower bound. As the channel output is a deterministic function of (X, S_1, S_2), we can choose $U = (Y, S_2)$ and substitute back in (1). This gives the following lower bound on the capacity of the deterministic channel

$$\begin{aligned} C &\geq \max_{p(x|s_1)} [I(Y, S_2; Y, S_2) - I(Y, S_2; S_1)] \\ &= \max_{p(x|s_1)} H(Y, S_2|S_1) \\ &= \max_{p(x|s_1)} [H(S_2|S_1) + H(Y|S_1, S_2)] \\ &= \max_{p(x|s_1)} H(Y|S_1, S_2) \end{aligned} \tag{5}$$

where (5) is obtained by choosing S_1 and S_2 to be fully correlated. The matching between the upper bound and the lower bound proves the theorem. ∎

III. Problem Formulation and System Model

Consider the discrete-time memoryless wiretap channel shown in Figure. 2. The transmitter wishes to send a message W from a message set $\mathcal{M}$ reliably to the legitimate receiver, while keeping it perfectly secured from an eavesdropper. The transition probability of the main channel and the wiretap channel depends on three state sequences S_1^n, S_2^n and S_3^n, with values in a finite set $(\mathcal{S}_1, \mathcal{S}_2, \mathcal{S}_3)$. The state sequence S_1^n is non-causally known at the encoder, while S_2^n is known to the legitimate receiver and S_3^n is unknown.

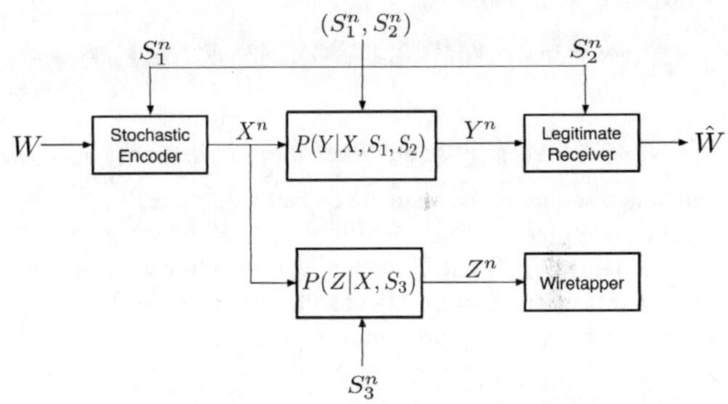

Figure 2. Wiretap channel with three channel state information; S_1 non-causally known to the encoder, state S_2 known to the legitimate receiver and state S_3 unknown to the wiretap channel

Using S_1^n, the encoder maps W to an $n - tuple$ channel input $X^n \in \mathcal{X}^n$ and sends it over the main channel and the wiretap channel. The main channel depends on the transition probability $p(y^n|x^n, s_1^n, s_2^n)$, with $Y^n \in \mathcal{Y}^n$ being the legitimate receiver observation. The wiretap channel depends on the transition probability $p(z^n|x^n, s_3^n)$, with $Z^n \in \mathcal{Z}^n$ being the wiretapper's observation. The channels are memoryless,i.e.,

$$\begin{aligned} p(y^n|x^n, s_1^n, s_2^n) &= \Pi_{i=1}^n p(y_i|x_i, s_{1i}, s_{2i}) \\ p(z^n|x^n, s_3^n) &= \Pi_{i=1}^n p(z_i|x_i, s_{3i}) \end{aligned}$$

We assume at different instances (S_1, S_2, S_3) to be independent identically distributed (i.i.d) random variables with joint probability distribution $p(s_1, s_2, s_3)$. The legitimate receiver aims at recovering $\hat{W}$; its estimate of the transmitted message, based on the received signal Y^n. The average decoding error probability is defined as $P_e^{(n)} = \frac{1}{|\mathcal{M}|}\sum_{t=1}^{|\mathcal{M}|} Pr\{W \neq \hat{W}|W = t\}$. A secrecy rate R_s is achievable if there exists a sequence of length n code, such that the average error probability at the intended receiver and the leakage rate $\frac{1}{n}I(W;Z^n)$ between the message W and the the received signal Z^n, both approach zero as $n \to \infty$. The secrecy capacity is defined as the supremum of all achievable rates.

It is important to note that the considered formulation is a special instant of the general problem where all sorts of state information could affect the communication between the receiver and transmitter.

IV. Upper Bound

We start by deriving an upper bound on the secrecy capacity for the model shown in Figure. 2. The upper bound will prove to be equal to the secrecy capacity for the semi-deterministic model in Section VI.

Proposition 1. *The secrecy capacity C_s of the discrete memoryless wiretap channel with three state information $p(y,z|x,s_1,s_2,s_3)$ with channel state S_1 non-causally known at the transmitter as side information, S_2 known to the legitimate receiver, and S_3 unknown to the wiretapper, can be bounded from above as*

$$C_s \leq \max_{p(x|s_1)} \min\{I(X;Y|S_1,S_2,S_3), I(X,S_1,S_3;Y,S_2|Z)\}. \tag{6}$$

Proof: We start by noting that $\max_{p(x|s_1)} I(X;Y|S_1,S_2,S_3)$ is an upper bound on the Shannon capacity of the legitimate receiver channel by creating a fictitious channel which gives the channel states S_1, S_2 and S_3 to the legitimate receiver as well as to the transmitter and uses the result from [10, Corollary. 1]. On the other hand, the term $\max_{p(x|s_1)} I(X,S_1,S_3;Y,S_2|Z)$ is an upper bound on the secrecy capacity of the wiretap channel, as it allows the channel state S_1, known to the transmitter, and the channel state S_3 to encode the transmitted message W, thus getting three encoded copies of the message instead of one (i.e.,*fully action-dependent state* [11]), and also by giving the signal received by the wiretapper Z to the legitimate receiver through a fictitious channel (i.e., Sato-like upper bound [12]). In order to move the maximization outside of the minimization, we need to recur to a single-letterization technique introduced in [13], which we apply as follows: By Fano's inequality, any achievable secrecy rate R_s must satisfy

$$\begin{aligned}
n(R_s - \epsilon_n)& \\
&\leq I(W;Y^n)\\
&\leq I(W;Y^n,S_1^n,S_2^n,S_3^n)\\
&\leq I(X^n;Y^n|S_1^n,S_2^n,S_3^n)\\
&= H(Y^n|S_1^n,S_2^n,S_3^n) - H(Y^n|X^n,S_1^n,S_2^n,S_3^n)\\
&= H(Y^n|S_1^n,S_2^n,S_3^n) - \sum_{i=1}^{n} H(Y_i|X_i,S_{1i},S_{2i},S_{3i})\\
&\leq \sum_{i=1}^{n} H(Y_i|S_{1i},S_{2i},,S_{3i}) - \sum_{i=1}^{n} H(Y_i|X_i,S_{1i},S_{2i},S_{3i})\\
&= n[H(Y_Q|S_{1Q},S_{2Q},S_{3Q},Q)\\
&\quad -H(Y_Q|X_Q,S_{1Q},S_{2Q},S_{3Q},Q)]\\
&\leq n[H(Y_Q|S_{1Q},S_{2Q},S_{3Q}) - H(Y_Q|X_Q,S_{1Q},S_{2Q},S_{3Q})]\\
&= n\cdot I(X_Q;Y_Q|S_{1Q},S_{2Q},S_{3Q})
\end{aligned}$$

where $\epsilon_n \to 0$ in the limit as $n \to \infty$, and Q is a standard time-sharing variable. Similarly, for any achievable secrecy rate R_s we have

$$\begin{aligned}
n(R_s - \epsilon_n)& \\
&\leq I(W;Y^n) - I(W;Z^n)\\
&\leq I(W;Y^n,Z^n) - I(W;Z^n)\\
&= I(W;Y^n|Z^n)\\
&\leq I(X^n,S_1^n,S_3^n;Y^n,S_2^n|Z^n)\\
&= H(Y^n,S_2^n|Z^n) - H(Y^n,S_2^n|X^n,S_1^n,S_3^n,Z^n)\\
&= H(Y^n,S_2^n|Z^n) - \sum_{i=1}^{n} H(Y_i,S_{2i}|X_i,S_{1i},S_{3i},Z_i)\\
&\leq \sum_{i=1}^{n} H(Y_i,S_{2i}|Z_i) - \sum_{i=1}^{n} H(Y_i,,S_{2i}|X_i,S_{1i},S_{3i},Z_i)\\
&= n[H(Y_Q,S_{2Q}|Z_Q,Q) - H(Y_Q,S_{2Q}|X_Q,S_{1Q},S_{3Q},Z_Q,Q)]\\
&\leq n[H(Y_Q,S_{2Q}|Z_Q) - H(Y_Q,S_{2Q}|X_Q,S_{1Q},S_{3Q},Z_Q)]\\
&= n\cdot I(X_Q,S_{1Q},S_{3Q};Y_Q,S_{2Q}|Z_Q).
\end{aligned}$$

Note that the channel states are memoryless, so S_{1Q}, S_{2Q} and S_{3Q} have the same distribution as $S_{j,i}$ for any $i = 1,\ldots,n$ and $j = 1,2,3$. The channel is also memoryless, so the conditional distribution of (Y_Q,Z_Q) given $(X_Q,S_{1Q},S_{2Q},S_{3Q})$ is given by the channel transition probability $p(y|x,s_1,s_2)$ and $p(z|x,s_3)$. Letting $X_Q = X$, $S_{1Q} = S_1$, $S_{2Q} = S_2$, $S_{3Q} = S_3$, $Y_Q = Y_1$, $Z_Q = Z$, and $n \to \infty$ completes the proof. ■

V. Achievable Secrecy Rate

The following theorem presents an achievable rate R_s for our model.

Theorem 3. *An achievable rate for the* wiretap channel with three states information *is*

$$R_s = \max_{p(u,x|s_1)} I(U;Y,S_2) - \max\{I(U;S_1,S_3), I(U;Z)\} \tag{7}$$

where U is an auxiliary random variable such that $U \to (X,S_1,S_2,S_3) \to (Y,Z)$.

Proof: We fix $p_U(u), p_{X|U,S_1}(x|u,s_1)$ and $\epsilon_1,\epsilon_2,\epsilon_3 > 0$. Let $R_s \doteq I(U;Y,S_2) - \max\{I(U;S_1,S_3), I(U;Z)\} - \epsilon_1 - \epsilon_3$ and $R \doteq \max\{I(U;S_1,S_3), I(U;Z)\} - I(U;Z) + \epsilon_3 + \epsilon_2$.

Codebook: Generate $2^{I(U;Y,S_2)-\epsilon_1}$ identically independent sequences u^n, each according to $p(\mathbf{u}) = \Pi_{i=1}^{n} p(u_i)$. We distribute the u^n sequences randomly into 2^{nR_s} bins, indexed by $m \in \{1,...,M = 2^{nR_s}\}$. Now each bins has

$2^{n[\max\{I(U;S_1,S_3),I(U;Z)\}+\epsilon_3]}$. Further we randomly distribute the sequences in each bin into 2^{nR} subbing, indexed by $j \in \{1,...,J = 2^{nR}\}$. Thus each subbing has $2^{n[I(U;Z)-\epsilon_2]}$.

Encoding: To send message m, the transmitter looks into the m-th bin and select a $u^n(m)$ such that $u^n(m)$ and the interfering sequence s_1^n are jointly typical; $(u^n(m), s_1^n) \in T_\epsilon^n(p_{US_1})$. If there are more than one pair, then we randomly select one. We generate the channel input x^n according to the mapping $p_{x^n|u^n,s_1^n}(X|U, S_1)$.

Decoding: The decoder chooses m so that $(u^n(m), s_2^n, y^n) \in T_\epsilon^n(p_{US_2Y})$ if such m exists and is unique; otherwise, an error is declared.

Performance Analysis: We start by analyzing the error probability. There are three types of errors relating to encoding and decoding:

1) $\mathcal{E}_1$: error event corresponding to encoding; given the message bin m and the state sequence s_1^n, there is no jointly typical $(u^n(m), s_1^n)$ in bin m.
2) $\mathcal{E}_2$: error event corresponding to decoding; given the received sequence y^n and the state sequence s_2^n, there is no $u^n(m)$ such that $(u^n(m), y^n, s_2^n)$ is jointly typical.
3) $\mathcal{E}_3$: error event corresponding to decoding; given the received sequence y^n and the state sequence s_2^n, there is $u^n(m')$ such that $(u^n(m'), y^n, s_2^n)$ is jointly typical, where $m' \neq m$.

Without loss of generality, we assume that message $m = 1$ was sent. Since the probability that $(u^n(m), s_1^n)$ is jointly typical is larger than $(1-\epsilon)2^{-nI(U;S_1)}$, and that there are $2^{n[\max\{I(U;S_1,S_3),I(U;Z)\}+\epsilon_3]}$ sequences per bin, we have the following

$$\begin{aligned}
&Pr(E_1)\\
&\leq [1-(1-\epsilon)2^{-N[I(U;S_1)+3\epsilon]}]^{n[\max\{I(U;S_1,S_3),I(U;Z)\}+\epsilon_3]}\\
&\leq exp\{-(1-\epsilon)2^{-N[I(U;S_1)+3\epsilon]}\}^{n[\max\{I(U;S_1,S_3),I(U;Z)\}+\epsilon_3]}\\
&= exp\{-(1-\epsilon)2^{n[\max\{I(U;S_1,S_3),I(U;Z)\}-I(U;S_1)+\epsilon_3-3\epsilon]}\}\\
&\leq \delta_\epsilon^{(1)}(n)
\end{aligned}$$

Having the Markov chain: $U \to (X, S_1, S_2, S_3) \to (Y, Z)$, we then have $U \to (X, S_1) \to (Y, S_2)$. Hence, if $(u^n(m), x^n, s_1^n)$ is jointly typical, then $(u^n(m), x^n, s_1^n, s_2^n, y^n)$ is jointly typical. As a result,

$$Pr(E_2) \leq \delta_\epsilon^{(2)}(n)$$

Denoting by E_3' the event that we can find a $u^n(m')$ $(m' \neq m)$ which is jointly typical with y^n, then

$$\begin{aligned}
Pr(E_3) &\leq Pr\{E_3'\}\\
&\leq \sum_{u^n \neq u^n(m)} 2^{-n[I(U;Y)]-3\epsilon}\\
&= \left(2^{n[I(U;Y,S_2)-\epsilon_1]}-1\right)2^{-n[I(U;Y)-3\epsilon]}\\
&\leq 2^{n[I(U;Y,S_2)-I(U:Y)-\epsilon_1+3\epsilon]}\\
&\leq \delta_\epsilon^{(3)}(n)
\end{aligned}$$

By the union bound on these three probabilities of error, the average probability of error $P_e^n \to 0$ as $n \to \infty$ This concludes the proof of reliability. Now we turn into verifying the secrecy performance of our code, through the calculation of the leakage rate between the transmitted message W and the received signal Z^n.

$$\begin{aligned}
&I(W;Z^n)\\
&= H(W) - H(W|Z^n)\\
&= H(W) - H(W,Z^n) + H(Z^n)\\
&= H(W) - H(W,J,Z^n) + H(J|W,Z^n) + H(Z^n)\\
&= H(W) - H(W,J,Z^n,U^n) + H(U^n|W,J,Z^n)\\
&\quad +H(J|W,Z^n) + H(Z^n)\\
&= H(W) - H(W,J|Z^n,U^n) - H(U^n,Z^n)\\
&\quad +H(U^n|W,J,Z^n) + H(J|W,Z^n) + H(Z^n)\\
&\overset{a}{\leq} \log|\mathcal{M}| - H(U^n|Z^n) + H(U^n|W,J,Z^n)\\
&\quad +H(J|W,Z^n)\\
&\overset{b}{\leq} \log|\mathcal{M}| - H(U^n|Z^n) + H(U^n|W,J,Z^n)\\
&\quad +\log|\mathcal{J}| + H(U^n|Y^n,S_2^n)\\
&= nR_s - H(U^n|Z^n) + H(U^n|W,J,Z^n)\\
&\quad +n[\max\{I(U;S_1,S_3);I(U;Z)\} - I(U;Z)]\\
&\quad +n(\epsilon_2+\epsilon_3) + H(U^n|Y^n,S_2^n)\\
&\overset{c}{=} nR_s - n[I(U;Y,S_2) - I(U;Z)]\\
&\quad +H(U^n|W,J,Z^n) + n\max\{I(U;S_1,S_3);I(U;Z)\}\\
&\quad -nI(U;Z) + n(\epsilon_3+\epsilon_2)\\
&= n(\epsilon_3+\epsilon_2) + H(U^n|W,J,Z^n)\\
&\overset{d}{\leq} n(\epsilon_3+\epsilon_2) + h(\bar{p}) + n\bar{p}[I(U;Z) - \epsilon_2]
\end{aligned} \tag{8}$$

where,

(a) follows from $H(W) \leq \log|\mathcal{M}|$ and $H(W,J|Z^n,U^n) = 0$.
(b) follows from $H(J|W,Z^n) \leq H(J) \leq \log|\mathcal{J}|$ and $H(U^n|Y^n,S_2^n)) \geq 0$.
(c) follows from $I(U^n|Y^n,S_2^n) = nI(U|Y,S_2)$ and $I(U^n;Z^n) = nI(U;Z)$.
(d) follows from applying Fano's inequality to the wiretap channel whose input is U^n in the codebook consisting of the subbin j in bin m.

Applying the common random channel coding argument to (8), $\bar{p} \to 0$ as $n \to \infty$, hence

$$\lim_{n\to\infty} \frac{1}{n} I(W;Z^n) \to 0 \tag{9}$$

This concludes the achievability proof for our coding scheme. ∎

VI. Semi-Deterministic Wiretap Channel with Three State Information

In this section we characterize the secrecy capacity of the *semi-deterministic* wiretap channel with three states, for the case where legitimate receiver output is a deterministic (bivariate) function of the channel input X and the channel states S_1 and S_2:

$$Y = f(X, S_1, S_2) \quad \textit{with probability 1} \tag{10}$$

For the *semi-deterministic* model, the lower bound (7) and the upper bound (6) coincide, leading to a *precise* characterization of the secrecy capacity. The result is summarized in the following theorem.

Theorem 4. *The secrecy capacity of the* semi-deterministic wiretap channel with three states *is given by:*

$$C_s = \max_{p(x|s_1)} \min\{H(Y|S_1, S_2, S_3), H(Y, S_2|Z)\} \tag{11}$$

Proof: As the legitimate receiver output is a deterministic function of the channel input X and the channel states S_1 and S_2, and we have the following Markov chain $U \to (X, S_1, S_2, S_3) \to (Y, Z)$, we can let the auxiliary random variable $U = (Y, S_2)$.By substituting back in (7), we get the following

$$\begin{aligned} I(U; Y, S_2) &- I(U; S_1, S_3) \\ &= H(Y, S_2) - H(Y, S_2|Y, S_2) - H(Y, S_2) \quad (12) \\ +H(Y, S_2&|S_1, S_3) \\ &= H(Y, S_2|S_1, S_3) \\ &= H(S_2|S_1, S_3) + H(Y|S_1, S_2, S_3) \\ &= H(Y|S_1, S_2, S_3) \quad (13) \end{aligned}$$

where (13) is obtained by choosing the channel states to be fully correlated.Similarly,

$$I(U; Y, S_2) - I(U; Z) = H(Y, S_2|Z)$$

Thus

$$C_s \geq \max_{p(x|s_1)} \min\{H(Y|S_1, S_2, S_3), H(Y, S_2|Z)\}$$

The converse part of the theorem follows from the upper bound (6) and the fact that Y is a deterministic function of (X, S_1, S_2), so we have

$$\begin{aligned} I(X; Y|S_1, , S_2, S_3) &= H(Y|S_1, S_2, S_3) - \\ & \quad H(Y|X, S_1, S_2, S_3) \\ &= H(Y|S_1, S_2, S_3) \end{aligned}$$

and

$$\begin{aligned} I(X, S_1, S_3; Y, S_2|Z) &= H(Y, S_2|Z) - H(Y, S_2|X, S_1, S_2, Z) \\ &= H(Y, S_2|Z). \end{aligned}$$

This completes the proof of the theorem. ■

VII. Conclusion

For a number of channels, the conditional probability distribution is affected by certain channel state information. The state information could be available to the transmitter, or to the receiver or not available to either one of them. Also, the state information could be causally-known or non-causally known. This motivated the inspection of a special instant of the general problem, where the conditional probability distribution at the channel's output depends on three state information; one of unknown nature, another always available at the receiver as side information, and a third state non-causally known at the encoder. The paper suggests the use of a structured-binning scheme along with a time sharing argument to achieve a certain secrecy rate, which meets the upper bound and the achieves the secrecy capacity under the assumption that the channel is semi-deterministic. It is conjectured that this scheme can be used under any other assumptions on the nature and the number of state information affecting the conditional probability distribution of the channel. The author aims at tacking the same scenario under the assumption of constrained stochastic encoding, wherein the encoder is generating pseudo-randomness which is limited rather than being unlimited.

References

[1] N. Yang, L. Wang, G. Geraci, and M. El kashlan, "Safeguarding 5G wireless communication networks using physical layer security," *IEEE Communication Magazine*, vol. IT-53, no. 4, pp. 20–27, April 2015.

[2] C. E. Shannon, "Channels with side information at the transmitter," *J. Res. Devel.*, vol. 2, pp. 289-293, 1958.

[3] S. I. Gel'fand and M. S. Pinsker, "Coding for channel with random parameters," *Probl. Contr. Inf. Theory*, vol. 9, no. 1, pp. 19–31, 1980.

[4] Y. Chen and A. J. H. Vinck, "Wiretap channel with side information," *IEEE Trans. Inf. Theory*, vol. 54, no. 1, pp. 395–402, Jan. 2008.

[5] A. D. Wyner, "The wire-tap channel," *Bell Sys. Tech. Journal*, vol. 54, no. 8, pp. 1355–1387, Oct. 1975.

[6] I. Csiszár and J. Körner, "Broadcast channels with confidential messages," *IEEE Trans. Inf. Theory*, vol. IT-24, no. 3, pp. 339–348, May 1978.

[7] Y. K. Chia and A. El Gamal, "3-receiver broadcast channel with common and confidential messages," *Proc. IEEE Int. Symp. Inf. Theory*, Seoul, Korea, July 2009, pp. 1849–1853.

[8] W. Liu and B. Chen, "Wiretap channel with two-sided state information," in *Proc. 41st Asilomar Conference on Signals, Systems and Computers*, Pacific Grove, CA, pp. 893–897, Nov. 2007.

[9] H. G. Bafghi, B. Seyfe, M. Mirmohseni and M. R. Aref, "On the achievable rate region of a new Gaussian wiretap channel with side information," in *Information Theory Workshop (ITW)*, Lauzanne, Switzerland, pp. 657–661, Sept. 2012.

[10] T. .M. Cover and M. Chiang, "Duality between channel capacity and rate distortion with two-sided state information," *IEEE Trans. Inf. Theory*, vol. IT-48, no. 6, pp. 1629–1638, June 2002.

[11] T. Weissman, "Capacity of channels with action-dependent states," *IEEE Trans. Inf. Theory*, vol. 56, no. 11, pp. 5396–5411, Nov. 2010.

[12] H. Sato,"An outer bound to the capacity region of broadcast channels," *IEEE Trans. Inf. Theory*, vol. 24, pp. 374–77, May 1978.

[13] F. M. J. Willems, "An information theoretic approach to information embedding," in *Proc. 21st Symp. Inf. Theory Benelux*, Wassenaar, The Netherlands, May 2000, pp. 255–260.

GNSS Jamming Nulling Scheme using Jamming-Free Subspaces

Inone Joo, Sanghyuk Choi and Cheonsig Sin
Satellite Navigation and Radar Research Section
Electronics and Telecommunications Research Institute(ETRI)
Daejeon, Korea
e-mail: inone@etri.re.kr

***Abstract*—In this paper, Global Navigation Satellite System (GNSS) jamming nulling scheme using jamming-free subspaces is presented to overcome the jamming attack. It is based on the adaptive beamforming using array antennas. The eigenvalue decomposition (EVD) of the covariance matrix is used for separation between the jamming subspaces and the others. The proposed scheme determines the array weights by the jamming-free subspaces, which are composed of all subspaces except all jamming subspaces. The simulation results demonstrate that the proposed scheme nulls the jamming signal and receives all Global Position System (GPS) signal under the jamming environment.**

Keywords- GNSS; GPS; Jamming; Nulling; beamforming; subspaces.

I. INTRODUCTION

Even though GNSS is most widely used in many applications for position, velocity, and precise time (PNT), it is easily vulnerable to the jamming. As GPS jammers are purchased for about $30 over the online, GPS jamming events could be more often happened. It is known that a 1 watt jammer can disturb GPS coarse/acquisition (C/A) code acquisition up to 63 km and C/A code tracking up to 32 km [1]. North Korea has repeatedly jammed GPS signals in South Korea during 6 days from March 31, 2016 to April 5. It was reported that 1,786 base stations for mobile telecommunication, 962 airplanes and 694 ships in South Korea experienced GPS disruptions. As many critical applications are still being dependent on absolute and accurate position or time by GNSS receiver, the GNSS jamming making the GNSS receiver malfunctioned is very critical threat to those applications using GNSS system. In order to overcome the jamming attack, the anti-jamming technique is needed. The spatial nulling scheme using array antennas has been considered as an effective technique. So, in this paper, the GNSS jamming nulling scheme based on array antennas is presented using jamming-free subspaces, which are composed of all subspaces except all jamming subspaces. The eigenvalue decomposition (EVD) of covariance matrix is used for separation between the jamming subspaces and the others. The simulation results demonstrate that the proposed scheme nulls the jamming signal and receives GPS signal under the jamming environment. Sect. II describes the proposed scheme based on the signal model. In Sect. III, we present the simulation results of GNSS jamming nulling scheme. Finally, the conclusion is drawn in Sect. IV.

II. GNSS JAMMING NULLING SCHEME

A. Signal model

Firstly, we consider the signal model including GNSS signals, jamming signals, and noise. Assuming that M-element array antenna with half-wavelength spacing, the samples vector $\mathbf{x}(n)$ after down-conversion and analog-to-digital conversion can be expressed as

$$\mathbf{x}(n) = \mathbf{s}(n) + \mathbf{J}(n) + \mathbf{v}(n) \tag{1}$$

where $\mathbf{s}(n)$ and $\mathbf{J}(n)$ denotes the GNSS signal vector and the jamming signal vector respectively and $\mathbf{v}(n)$ is the additive white Gaussian noise vector.

Let $z(n) = \mathbf{w}^H\mathbf{x}(n)$ be the output data of the beamformer where $\mathbf{w}$ is beamforming weight vector. Then, covariance is given by

$$E\{z(n)z^H(n)\} = \mathbf{w}^H E\{\mathbf{x}(n)\mathbf{x}^H(n)\}\mathbf{w} \tag{2}$$

where $\mathbf{R} = E\{\mathbf{x}(n)\mathbf{x}^H(n)\}$ denotes the covariance matrix.

B. Proposed scheme

Fig. 1 shows the block diagram of the proposed scheme. As GNSS signals use the spread spectrum scheme, they have a spreading gain against jamming. Therefore, the power of jamming, which is vulnerable to GNSS signals is considerably higher than that of GNSS signal. Accordingly, after performing the EVD of the covariance matrix $\mathbf{R}$, we can collect the jammer-free subspaces. The EVD of the covariance matrix $\mathbf{R}$ yields

$$\mathbf{R} \cong [\mathbf{U}_\mathbf{J}\ \mathbf{U}_\mathbf{JF}]\begin{bmatrix}\Lambda_\mathbf{J} & 0\\ 0 & \Lambda_\mathbf{JF}\end{bmatrix}\begin{bmatrix}\mathbf{U}_\mathbf{J}^\mathbf{H}\\ \mathbf{U}_\mathbf{JF}^\mathbf{H}\end{bmatrix} \tag{3}$$

where $\mathbf{U}_\mathbf{J}$ and $\mathbf{U}_\mathbf{JF}$ denotes the eigenvector of the jamming subspaces with equivalent power of $\Lambda_\mathbf{J}$ and the jamming-free subspaces with equivalent power of $\Lambda_\mathbf{JF}$

The number of the jamming subspaces is determined by the minimum description length (MDL) or Akaike Information Criterion (AIC) [2]. Lastly, the beamforming array weighting vector $\mathbf{w}$ is calculated by the Linearly Constrained Minimum Variance (LCMV) beamformer [3]

$$\mathbf{w} = \mathbf{R}^{-1}\mathbf{C}(\mathbf{C}^H\mathbf{R}^{-1}\mathbf{C})^{-1}\mathbf{f} \tag{4}$$

where $\mathbf{C}$ is the constraint matrix composed of the jamming-free subspaces and $\mathbf{f} = [1 \ \ \ldots \ \ 1]^T$

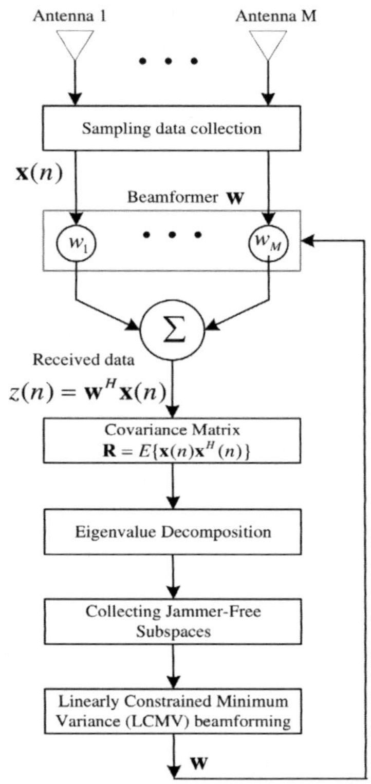

Figure 1. Block diagram of the proposed scheme.

III. SIMULATION RESULTS

The uniform circular array (UCA) consisting of M=10 sensors with half-wavelength spacing is used. A GPS satellite (PRN#12) and a jammer are located at (elevation 30º, azimuth 100º) and (elevation 50º, azimuth 200º). The 2046 samples are used in one millisecond. The signal type and the power of jamming are used as the continuous wave (CW) in GPS L1 frequency with JSR=30dB. Fig. 2 shows that the proposed scheme is able to null the jamming signals.

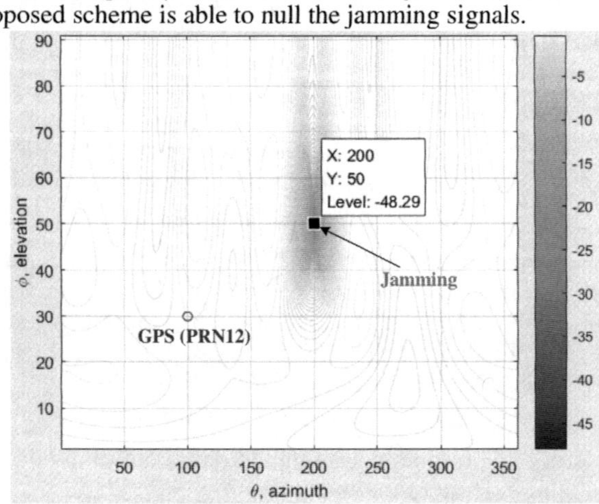

Figure 2. Block diagram of the proposed scheme.

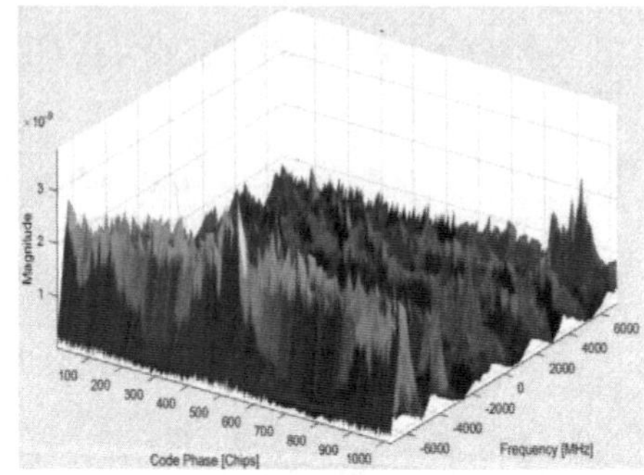

Figure 3. CAF using the received signal

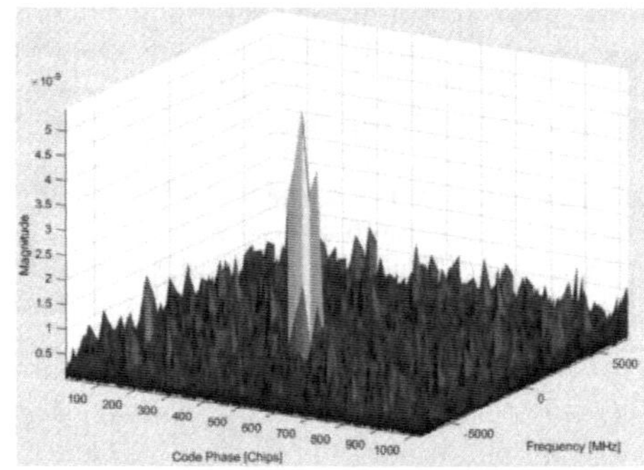

Figure 4. CAF after the proposed nulling scheme

Fig. 3 shows the cross ambiguity function (CAF) of GPS signal (PRN 12) using the received signal, which are incident on each element of array antenna. It is observed form Fig. 4 that GPS signal (PRN 12) is acquired successfully after the proposed nulling scheme.

IV. CONCLUSION

The GNSS jamming nulling scheme based on array antennas was proposed using jamming-free subspaces. The EVD of covariance matrix is used for separation between the jamming subspaces and the others. The simulation results showed that the proposed scheme nulls the jamming signal and receives GPS signal under the jamming environment (JSR=30dB). Also, it was demonstrated that GPS signal (PRN 12) was successfully acquired after the proposed nulling scheme.

ACKNOWLEDGMENT

This work was supported by ICT R&D program of MSIP/IITP. [2014-044-052-001, Development of Verification Platform Technologies for GNSS Signal Interference].

REFERENCES

[1] G. D. Rash, "GPS jamming in a laboratory environment", Department of Defense, 2012.

[2] H. L. Van Trees, Optimum Array Processing. Part IV of Detection, Estimation, and Modulation Theory, Wiley-. Interscience, 2002.

[3] B. D. Van Veen and K. M. Buckley, "Beamforming: A versatile approach to spatial filtering," IEEE ASSP Mag., pp. 4-24, Apr. 1988.

On the Impact of Residual Inter-Subchannel Interference for the Single-Carrier Block Transmission

Ming-Xian Chang and Tzy-Yu Wu

Institute of Computer and Communication Engineering and Department of Electrical Engineering
National Cheng-Kung University, Taiwan E-mail: mxc@eembox.ee.ncku.edu.tw; q36021397@mail.ncku.edu.tw

***Abstract*—In the fast time-varying channel, there exists interference among subchannels for the orthogonal frequency-division multiplexing (OFDM) system. The problem of inter-subchannel interference (ICI) also appears in the single-carrier (SC) block transmission with frequency-domain equalization (FDE). There are several ICI reduction algorithms for the OFDM system, and some of these algorithms can be applied in the SC-FDE system. On the other hand, unlike the scenario of carrier-frequency offset, the ICI caused by the time-varying mobile channel cannot be completely removed, and the residual ICI exists after the ICI reduction. In this paper, we analyze the effect of residual ICI. We show that the impacts of the residual ICI on the OFDM system and the SC-FDE system are quite different. For the SC-FDE system, the residual ICI incurs the "error rising" when we detect the time-domain symbols after the frequency-domain equalization. The error-rising effect is worse than the error-floor effect. To avoid the error-rising effect caused by the residual ICI, one can apply the maximum-likelihood (ML) detection, or its complexity-reduced schemes, like the K-Best algorithm. The simulation results verify our analysis.**

***Keywords*— OFDM, ICI, SC-FDE**

I. INTRODUCTION

In modern wireless communications, the orthogonal frequency-division multiplexing (OFDM) system is widely applied for its low-complexity frequency-domain equalization (FDE) in the multipath fading channel. The intersymbol interference (ISI) can be removed with a proper cyclic prefix (CP). On the other hand, one can also implement the single-carrier (SC) block transmission with FDE by adding a CP ahead of each transmitted block of symbols. Compared with traditional SC systems, the SC-FDE system attains higher spectral efficiency. The SC-FDE system also avoids the effect of high peak-to-average power ratio (PAPR) in the OFDM system.

In the high-mobility channel, both the OFDM system and the SC block transmission suffer the inter-subchannel interference (ICI). Compared with the ICI caused by the carrier-frequency offset, the ICI caused by the channel mobility is more difficult to handle. Since for the high-mobility channel, the received signal is composed of the components from different angles around the receiver, and these components have different Doppler frequency shifts. Among the ICI cancellation or reduction algorithms [1]-[9] for the OFDM system, the ICI self-reduction algorithms [3][4][6][7][9] are of much lower complexity, and the ICI reduction is independent of the signal-to-noise ratio (SNR). We can also apply some of these algorithms for the SC block transmission in the high-mobility channel. The algorithm in [6] extends periodically the time-domain (TD) signal to add the diversity of FD symbols, and the receiver makes efficient combination of the diversity to reduce the ICI. The algorithm of [9] further provides more efficient combining coefficients to improve the performance. Both the algorithms in [6][9] can be directly applied in the SC block transmission.

Since we cannot completely remove the ICI incurred by the fast time-varying mobile channel, there exits residual ICI after the ICI reduction in the receiver. However, as we will show in this paper, the impacts of the residual ICI on the OFDM and on the SC-FDE systems are quite different. For the OFDM system, the residual ICI on a subchannel only affects the FD symbols on this subchannel. If the fading of a subchannel at some time slot is deep, then the residual ICI may lead to incorrect detection of the symbol on this subchannel, but it does not affect the detection of symbols on other subchannels. However, for the SC-FDE system, the transmitted symbols are in time domain. When the fading of a subchannel is deep, the residual ICI in this subchannel may be enhanced in the process of FD equalization, and this enhanced interference affects all TD symbols after the IFFT. By analysis we show that the residual ICI leads to the "error-rising" effect on the error rate when the SNR increases for the SC-FDE system. The simulation results also verify our analysis. We can apply the maximum-likelihood (ML) detection or its complexity-reduced algorithms, such that the error-rising effect can be removed, as shown by the simulation. In our simulation, we apply an efficient ICI self-reduction algorithm that is a modified version of the algorithm in [9]. Instead of taking direct periodical extension the original symbols as both [6] and [9], the algorithm first reduces the number of symbols within a block, followed by the periodical extension to the original block size.

The rest of this paper is organized as follows. Section II introduces the signal model. The effect of residual ICI is analyzed in Section III. In Section IV, we discuss the use of ML detection and the related complexity-reduced schemes. Some simulation results are shown Section V. Finally, Section VI concludes this paper.

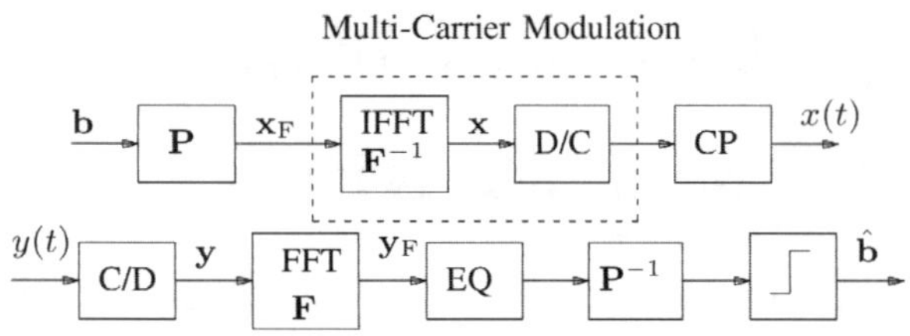

Fig. 1. The transceiver in the precoded OFDM system.

Notation: In this paper, we use bold lower-case letters and bold upper-case letters to denote vectors and matrices, respectively. For example, the identity matrix is denoted by **I**. The transpose and Hermitian transpose of a vector or matrix are denoted by $(\cdot)^T$ and $(\cdot)^H$, respectively. We define the fast Fourier transform (FFT) matrix $\mathbf{F}$ of size N as $[\mathbf{F}]_{km} \triangleq \frac{1}{N}e^{-i2\pi\frac{km}{N}}$, $0 \le k, m < N$, and therefore its inverse is $\mathbf{F}^{-1} = N\mathbf{F}^H$.

II. SIGNAL MODEL

Fig. 1 shows a precoded OFDM (POFDM) system. A block of transmitted symbols is denoted by

$$\mathbf{b} = (x_0, x_1, \ldots, x_{N-1})^T \tag{1}$$

where N is the block size. When we set $\mathbf{P} = \mathbf{I}$, we have the typical OFDM system; while for $\mathbf{P} = \mathbf{F}$, it is the SC block transmission system and $\mathbf{x} = \mathbf{b}$. The associated baseband signal can be expressed as

$$x(t) = \sum_{k=0}^{N-1} x_k\, g\left(t - k\frac{T}{N}\right), \quad -T_g \le t < T, \tag{2}$$

where T denotes the original duration of transmitting a block of symbols in (1), and T_g is the duration of guard interval. In (2), we denote by $g(t)$ the associated periodic pulse [10] with the period T. The period of $g(t)$ is T, and during $(-T_g, 0)$ we transmit the periodic extension of $g(t)$ (or CP). The ideal interpolation pulse $g(t)$ in (2) can implement the exact multi-carrier modulation when combined with the IFFT [10].

At the receiver, after removing the CP, we can write the received signal as

$$y(t) = \sum_{\ell=0}^{L_p-1} h^{(\ell)}(t)\, x(t - \tau^{(\ell)}) + w(t) \tag{3}$$

for $0 \le t < T$, where L_p is the number of paths, and we denote by $h^{(\ell)}(t)$ and $\tau^{(\ell)}$ the channel impulse response and delay, respectively, of the ℓth path. In (3), the noise component of $y(t)$ is denoted by $w(t)$. We assume that $\tau^{(\ell)} \le T_g$ for $0 \le \ell < L_p$, such that there is no ISI.

The received signal $y(t)$ is sampled at t=kT/N for $0 \le k < N$, and these N samples are denoted by $\mathbf{y} = (y_0, y_1, \ldots, y_{N-1})^T$, where $y_k = y(kT/N)$. Then $\mathbf{y}$ is transformed into frequency domain by the FFT for equalization. The FFT of $\mathbf{y}$ is denoted by $\mathbf{y}_F = (Y_0, Y_1, \ldots, Y_{N-1})^T$. We can write Y_m as

$$Y_m = H_{m,m}X_m + \sum_{\substack{m'=0\\ m'\neq m}}^{N-1} H_{m,m'}X_{m'} + W_m \tag{4}$$

for $0 \le m < N$. In (4), we observe that on the mth subchannel, there exists interference from other subchannels, due to time variation of the multipath channel. The interference from the m'th subchannel on the mth subchannel depends on $H_{m,m'}$, which can be expressed as

$$H_{m,m'} = \frac{1}{N}\sum_{\ell=1}^{L_p-1} e^{-j2\pi\frac{m'}{T}\tau_\ell} \sum_{k=0}^{N-1} h_k^{(\ell)} e^{-j2\pi\frac{(m-m')k}{N}} \tag{5}$$

for $0 \le m, m' < N$, where $h_k^{(\ell)} = h^{(\ell)}(kT/N)$, and W_m's are the noise components of Y_m's. For time-invariant or slowly time-varying channels, each $h_k^{(\ell)}$ is constant during $0 \le k < N$, or $h_k^{(\ell)} = h^{(\ell)}$, which is independent of k. In this scenario, by (5) we observe that $H_{m,m'}$'s are zero for $m \neq m'$, since

$$\sum_{k=0}^{N-1} h_k^{(\ell)} e^{-j2\pi\frac{(m-m')k}{N}} = h^{(\ell)} \sum_{k=0}^{N-1} e^{-j2\pi\frac{(m-m')k}{N}} = 0 \tag{6}$$

if $m \neq m'$, and there is no ICI in (4).

In the above, for the SC-FDE system, although the transmitted symbols are in time domain, it also suffers the effect of ICI. For the typical OFDM system, in which one can readily apply either the block type or the comb type pilot schemes in Fig. 2 for the CR estimation. However, for the SC block transmission, one can only readily apply the block type pilot arrangement. Since the transmitted symbols in (1) are in time domain, if we apply the comb type pilot scheme, then when inserting FD pilot symbols, we need to increase the sizes of $\mathbf{x}_F$, $\mathbf{x}$, $\mathbf{y}$, and $\mathbf{y}_F$ in Fig. 1. Then we also need to increase the sizes of $\mathbf{F}^{-1}$ for IFFT in the transmitter and $\mathbf{F}$ for FFT in the receiver. This makes $\mathbf{P}$ and $\mathbf{F}$ have different sizes.

On the other hand, for the block type pilot arrangement, consider a group of FD symbols along time slots in the process of joint CR estimation, as indicated by the red line in Fig 2(a). If we apply the ICI self-reduction schemes in [6][9], the TD periodic extension increases the relative time variation of channel along time slots, and degrades the performance of CR estimation. Therefore, we also give a modified ICI self-reduction algorithm in Appendix A based on [9]. For this modified algorithm, we do not apply direct TD periodic extension, and the block duration is the same as the original block duration.

III. THE RESIDUAL ICI

One can apply some ICI reduction algorithms to reduce the effect of ICI. However, unlike the case of carrier-frequency offset, we cannot completely remove the ICI in the time-varying multipath channel. Therefore, there exists residual ICI after the ICI reduction. We can express the signal after the ICI reduction as

$$\hat{Y}_m = H_m X_m + I_{\text{res},m} + W_m, \quad 0 \le m < M, \tag{7}$$

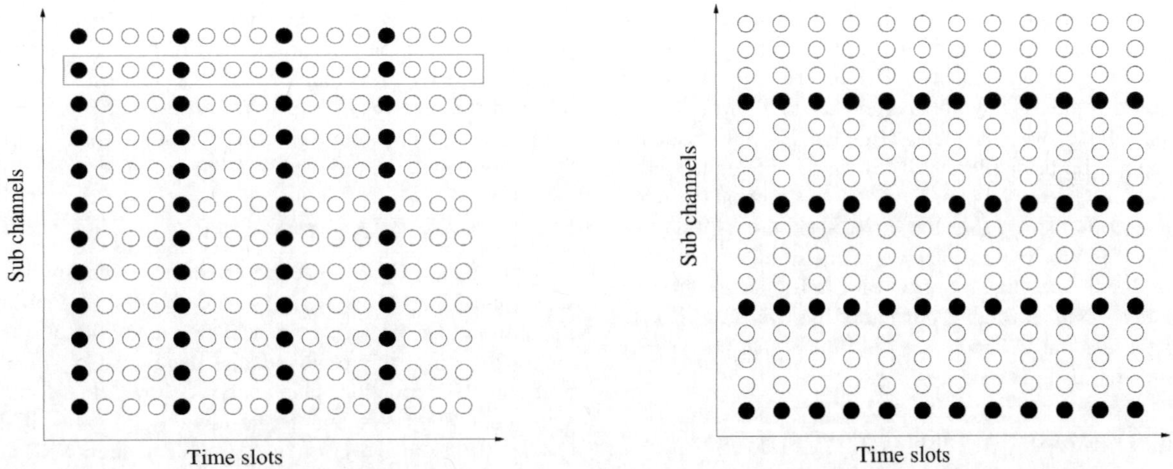

(a) Block type pilot arrangement.

(b) Comb type pilot arrangement.

Fig. 2. Two types of pilot arrangement, where the solid circles denote the pilot symbols.

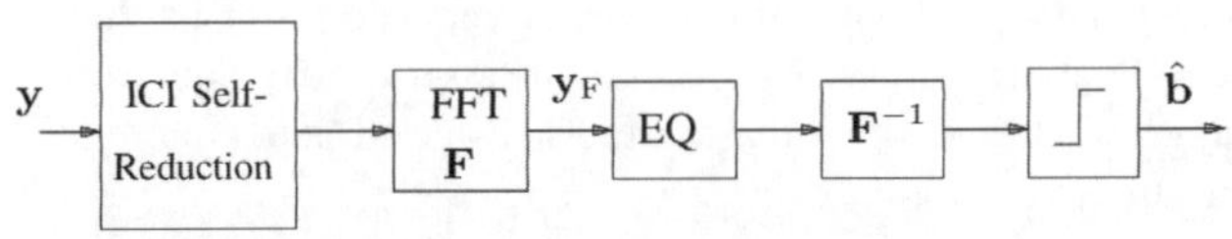

Fig. 3. The receiver with an ICI self-reduction algorithm and FD equalization.

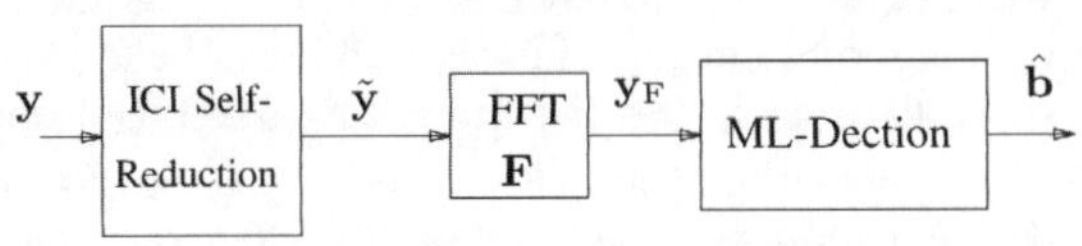

Fig. 4. The receiver with an ICI self-reduction algorithm and ML detection.

where $I_{\mathrm{res},m}$ denotes the residual ICI on the mth subchannel. The expression of $I_{\mathrm{res},m}$ depends on the ICI reduction algorithm. In general, the power of each $I_{\mathrm{res},m}$ is proportional to the power of transmitted symbols.

A. Detection Based on the MMSE Principle

We first consider the signal model without ICI, and write (7) as

$$\hat{Y}_m = H_m X_m + W_m, \qquad 0 \le m < M, \tag{8}$$

For the OFDM system, if we have the estimate of H_m, we can detect X_m simply by making hard decision on the equalized signal,

$$\frac{\hat{Y}_m}{H_m} = X_m + \frac{W_m}{H_m}, \qquad 0 \le m < M. \tag{9}$$

For the SC block transmission, however, since the symbols are in time domain, we need to further take the IFFT of (9). For the scenario of deep fading, or $|H_m| \ll 1$ for some m, the detection in (9) incurs the noise enhancement, which results in a large $\left|\frac{W_m}{H_m}\right|$. The noise enhancement may cause large interference on other TD symbols after the IFFT. Therefore, for the SC block transmission, we need to modify (9) as

$$\frac{\hat{Y}_m}{H_m + 1/\gamma_s} = \frac{H_m}{H_m + 1/\gamma_s} X_m + \frac{W_m}{H_m + 1/\gamma_s} \tag{10}$$

where $\gamma_s = (2\sigma_X^2)/(2\sigma_W^2)$ for the quaternary phase-shift keying (QPSK) modulation. The equalization in (10) is based on the minimum mean-squares error (MMSE) principle. Compared with (9), the item $1/\gamma_s$ can mitigate the effect of noise enhancement when deep fading $|H_m| \ll 1$ occurs, since $\frac{W_m}{H_m + 1/\gamma_s} \le \frac{W_m}{1/\gamma_s}$. For the OFDM system, on the other hand, the noise enhancement in (9) does not affect the symbols on other subchannels, and we can simply apply (9) for equalization.

B. The Effect of Residual ICI

In (10), we consider the scenario that there is no ICI. When the ICI exists, after the ICI reduction, there exits residual ICI on each subchannel, since the ICI cannot be completely removed in the time-varying multipath fading channel. Substituting (7) for $\hat{Y}_m$ in (10), we have

$$\frac{\hat{Y}_m}{H_m + 1/\gamma_s} = \frac{H_m}{H_m + 1/\gamma_s} X_m + \frac{W_m + I_{\mathrm{res},m}}{H_m + 1/\gamma_s} \tag{11}$$

for the QPSK modulation and $\gamma_s = \frac{2\sigma_X^2}{2\sigma_W^2}$. When $|H_m| \ll 1$ (deep fading on the mth subchannel), we can approximate the second term of (11) as

$$\frac{W_m + I_{\mathrm{res},m}}{H_m + \frac{2\sigma_W^2}{2\sigma_X^2}} \approx \frac{2\sigma_X^2}{2\sigma_W^2}(I_{\mathrm{res},m} + W_m). \tag{12}$$

Since the power of residual ICI, $I_{\mathrm{res},m}$, is proportional to the signal power, or $2\sigma_X^2$. At high SNR, or $|W_m| \ll 1$, we can further approximate (12) as

$$\frac{2\sigma_X^2}{2\sigma_W^2} I_{\mathrm{res},m} \tag{13}$$

which increases with SNR more than linearly. For the OFDM system, this only affects the detection of the transmitted symbol X_m on the mth subchannel. However, for the SC block transmission, because the transmitted symbols are in time domain, the enhanced ICI in (12) will affect the detection of other TD symbols after the IFFT of (11).

In the above, we show that after the ICI self-reduction, if we apply the principle of MMSE in the FD equalization, the residual ICI may be enhanced at some subchannel which is under deep fading, and this affects all the TD symbols after the IFFT for the SC block transmission. We will show by simulation that the bit-error rate (BER) rises with the increasing SNR at high SNR, and this verifies that the enhanced residual ICI increases with the signal power more than linearly, as (13) indicates.

IV. Maximum-Likelihood Detection

To avoid the effect of "error-rising" caused by the residual ICI when the receiver applies the MMSE FD equalization after the ICI reduction, one can resort to the ML detection or the associated complexity-reduced suboptimal schemes. Referring to Fig. 1, we can write $\mathbf{y}_\mathrm{F}$ as

$$\mathbf{y}_\mathrm{F} = \mathbf{H}\mathbf{x}_\mathrm{F} + \mathbf{w}_\mathrm{F} \tag{14}$$

where $\mathbf{H}$ is a diagonal matrix that represents the FD channel responses, and $\mathbf{w}_\mathrm{F}$ is the vector of noise plus residual ICI. Note that in (14), we assume $\mathbf{H}$ is a diagonal matrix after the ICI reduction. Since $\mathbf{x}_\mathrm{F} = \mathbf{F}\mathbf{x}$, we can write (14) as

$$\mathbf{y}_\mathrm{F} = \mathbf{H}\mathbf{F}\mathbf{x} + \mathbf{w}_\mathrm{F}. \tag{15}$$

For the SC block transmission, after the ICI self-reduction, as indicated in Fig 4, the ML detection of the transmitted vector of symbols $\mathbf{x}$ is given by

$$\hat{\mathbf{x}} = \arg\min_{\mathbf{x}} \|\mathbf{y}_\mathrm{F} - \mathbf{H}\mathbf{F}\mathbf{x}\|^2. \tag{16}$$

Although by the exhaustive search of all possible possible $\mathbf{x}$ and calculating the associated norm $\|\mathbf{y}_\mathrm{F} - \mathbf{H}\mathbf{F}\mathbf{x}\|^2$, we can determine the ML estimate of $\mathbf{x}$ by finding the minimum norm in (16), the exhaustive search and calculation leads to much high complexity that grows exponentially with the length of $\mathbf{x}$. We can resort to the sphere decoding (SD) algorithm, which can efficiently implement the ML detection, or the corresponding complexity-reduced suboptimal schemes, like the K-Best algorithm. Note that in (16), we do not have explicit equalization process, and this avoids the enhancement of residual ICI and the associated error-rising effect, as we will show in Section V.

V. Simulation Results

In Fig. 5 and Fig. 6, we consider the detection of an SC-FDE system. The size of a block is 64, and there are 64 virtual subchannels in frequency domain. We apply an modified ICI self-reduction algorithm given in Appendix A, which we propose based on the algorithm in [9]. In Fig. 5, the system is equalized in frequency domain with the MMSE principle. We observe the error-rising effect, as indicated by the analysis in Section III-B. The performance also degrades with the increased values of normalized Doppler frequency $f_d T_s$, where f_d is the maximum Doppler frequency shift and T_s is the block duration. In Fig. 6, the detection is implemented by the suboptimal K-best algorithm based on (16) and the receiver in Fig. 4. We observe in Fig. 6 that the error rising effect is removed, and with the K-Best algorithm, the performance is improved with the increased values of k.

VI. Conclusion

In this paper, we analyze the effect of residual ICI in the detection of SC-FDE system. For the time-varying multipath channel, unlike the case of carrier-frequency offset, the ICI cannot be completely removed, and there exists residual ICI after the ICI reduction. Our analysis shows that compared with the OFDM system, the residual ICI in the SC-FDE system results in the error-rising effect at high SNR if we apply the MMSE FD equalization. The error-rising effect is more unwanted than the error-floor effect. On the other hand, we can alternatively apply the ML detection that can be efficiently implemented by the SD algorithm, or the corresponding suboptimal complexity-reduced schemes, like the K-Best algorithm. The simulation results verify the error-rising effect, and show that by the ML-based detection, one can effectively remove the error-rising effect.

Appendix A
An ICI Self-Reduction Algorithm

Now we give an improved ICI self-reduction algorithm based on the algorithm in [9]. This algorithm can be applied in the SC-FDE system. We set $\mathbf{P} = \mathbf{F}$ and this leads to $\mathbf{x} = \mathbf{b}$ for the transmitter in Fig. 1. As [7] indicates, for the ICI reduction in the high-mobility channel, unlike the scenario of carrier-frequency offset, we need to reduce the transmission throughput. Unlike the algorithm in [9], which directly apply periodical extension on the original block $(x_0, x_1, \dots x_{N-1})^T$, we first reduce the block size to $M < N$, where $M \geq N/2$. The transmitted symbols within a block are $x_0, x_1, \dots x_{M-1}$. Denoted by

$$\mathbf{x} = (x_0, x_1, \dots x_{M-1}, x_0, \dots, x_{N-M-1})^T \tag{A.1}$$

then $\mathbf{x}$ contains the periodic extension of $x_0, x_1, \dots x_{M-1}$. The output of the D/C converter

$$x(t) = \sum_{m=0}^{M-1} X_m e^{i2\pi \frac{m}{T'} t} \tag{A.2}$$

for $-T_g \leq t < T$. In (A.2), note $x(t)$ is a periodic signal whose period is $T' = \frac{M}{N}T$, and $\{X_m\}_{m=0}^{M-1}$ are the FFT of $\{x_k\}_{k=0}^{M-1}$. Compared with (2), we notice that the signal in (A.2) does not extend the original signal duration T.

We can express the received signal as (3), in which $x(t)$ is now given in (A.2). The received signal $y(t)$ is then sampled at $t = k\frac{T}{N} = k\frac{T'}{M}$, $0 \leq k < N$, and the samples are denoted by $y_0, y_1, \dots, y_{N-1}$, where $y_k = y(k\frac{T}{N})$. We can pass these samples y_k's through the following FFT,

$$Y_m^{(d)} \triangleq \frac{1}{M} \sum_{k=0}^{M-1} y_{k+d} e^{-i2\pi \frac{mk}{M}} \tag{A.3}$$

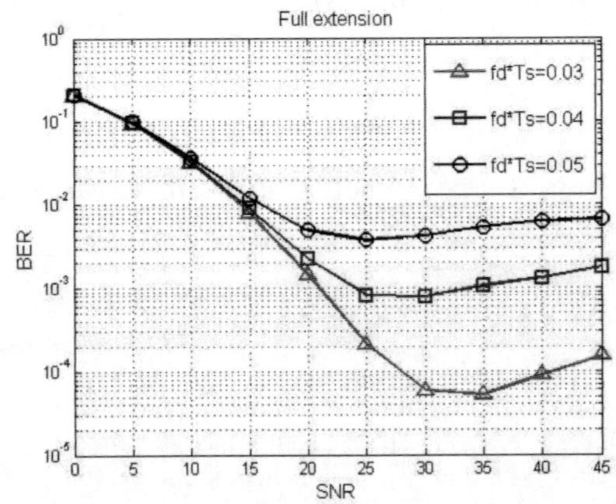

Fig. 5. A SC block transmission system with FD MMSE equalization.

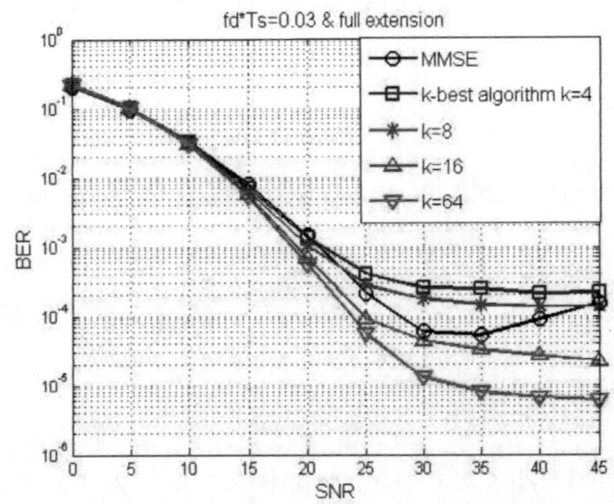

Fig. 6. A SC block transmission system and the detection is based on the K-Best algorithm.

for $0 \leq d \leq N-M$, $0 \leq m < M$. We can write $Y_m^{(d)}$ as

$$Y_m^{(d)} = H_{m,m}^{(d)}(X_m e^{i2\pi\frac{md}{M}}) + \sum_{\substack{m'=0\\m'\neq m}}^{M-1} H_{m,m'}^{(d)}(X_{m'}e^{i2\pi\frac{m'd}{M}}) + W_m^{(d)} \tag{A.4}$$

where

$$H_{m,m'}^{(d)} = \frac{1}{M}\sum_{\ell=0}^{L_p-1} e^{-i2\pi\frac{m'}{T'}\tau^{(\ell)}} \sum_{k=0}^{M-1} h_{k+d}^{(\ell)} e^{-i2\pi\frac{(m-m')k}{M}} \tag{A.5}$$

for $0 \leq m, m' < M$, and

$$W_m^{(d)} = \frac{1}{M}\sum_{k=0}^{M-1} w_{k+d} e^{-i2\pi\frac{mk}{M}}. \tag{A.6}$$

The receiver combines $Y_m^{(d)}$'s into

$$\hat{Y}_m = \frac{1}{N-M}\sum_{d=0}^{N-M-1} u_d Y_m^{(d)} e^{-i2\pi\frac{md}{M}} \tag{A.7}$$

for $0 \leq m < M$, and the combining weights are

$$u_d = \begin{cases} (2M-N+2)/2, & \text{if } d=0 \text{ or } N-M-1,\\ 1, & \text{elsewhere.}\end{cases} \tag{A.8}$$

When $M = N/2$, note $u_d = 1$ for $0 \leq d < N-M$.

However, the operations in (A.3) and (A.7) need $(N-M+2)$ FFT's. We can implement an equivalent low-complexity algorithm by substituting (A.3) into (A.7), and with some manipulation, we can further write (A.7) as

$$\hat{Y}_m = \frac{1}{M}\sum_{q=0}^{M-1} \tilde{y}_q e^{-i2\pi\frac{mq}{M}} \tag{A.9}$$

where

$$\tilde{y}_q = \begin{cases} \left(\sum_{k=0}^{q} u_k\right) y_q + \left(1 - \sum_{k=0}^{q} u_k\right) y_{q+M}, & 0 \leq q < N-M,\\ y_q, & N-M \leq q < N,\end{cases} \tag{A.10}$$

for $0 \leq q < M$. Therefore, we can obtain $\hat{Y}_m$'s by taking only one FFT on $\tilde{y}_q$'s, and $\tilde{y}_q$'s are just the linear combination of y_k's by (A.10). Following the operation in Fig. 4, the ICI self-reduction transforms $\mathbf{y}$ into $\tilde{\mathbf{y}}$ based on (A.10), followed by the FFT of $\tilde{\mathbf{y}}$ in (A.9).

REFERENCES

[1] W. G. Jeon, K. H. Chang, and Y. S. Cho, "An equalization technique for orthogonal frequency-division multiplexing systems in time-variant multipath channels," *IEEE Trans. Commun.*, vol. 47, pp. 27-32, Apr. 1999.

[2] Y.-S. Choi, P. J. Voltz, and F. A. Cassara, "On channel estimation and data detection for multicarrier signals in fast and selective Rayleigh fading channels," *IEEE Trans. Commun.*, vol. 49, pp. 1375-1387, Aug. 2001.

[3] Y. Zhao and S.-G. Häggman, "Intercarrier Interference Self-Cancellation Scheme for OFDM Mobile Communication Systems," *IEEE Trans. Commun.*, vol. 48, pp. 1185-1191, Jul. 2001.

[4] A. Seyedi and G. J. Saulnier, "General ICI self-cancellation scheme for OFDM systems," *IEEE Trans. Veh. Technol.*, vol. 54, pp. 198-210 Jan. 2004.

[5] A. Gorokhov and J.-P. Linnartz, "Robust OFDM receiver for dispersive time-varying channels: equalization and channel acquisition," *IEEE Trans. Commun.*, vo. 52, pp. 572-583, Apr. 2004.

[6] M.-X. Chang, "A novel algorithm of inter-subchannel interference self-cancellation for OFDM systems," *IEEE Trans. Wireless Commun.*, vol. 6, pp. 2881-2893, Aug. 2007.

[7] J. Ma, P. V. Orlik, J. Zhang, and Y. Li, "Reduced-rate OFDM transmission for inter-subchannel interference self-cancellation over high-mobility fading channels," *IEEE Trans. Wireless Commun.*, vol. 11, pp. 2013-2023, Jun. 2012.

[8] X. Li, S. Member, S. Hong, V. D. Chakravarthy, M. Temple, and Z. Wu, "Intercarrier interference immune single carrier OFDM via magnitude-keyed modulation for high speed aerial vehicle communication," *IEEE Trans. Commun.*, vol. 61, pp. 658-668, Feb. 2012.

[9] C.-Y Ma, S.-W. Liu, and C.-C. Huang, "Low-complexity ICI suppression methods utilizing cyclic prefix for OFDM systems in high-mobility fading channels," *IEEE Trans. Veh. Technol.*, vol. 63, pp. 718-730, Feb. 2014.

[10] M.-X. Chang, "Realizable Ideal D/C and C/D conversions for bandlimited periodic signals and characteristics of single-carrier block transmission," in *IEEE Trans. Signal Process.*, vol. 59, pp. 1670-1682, Apr. 2011.

An Architecture for Self-protection in Internet of Things

Ruan de A. C. Mello, Admilson de R. L. Ribeiro, Fernando M. de Almeida, Edward D. Moreno
Department of Computing
Federal University Sergipe UFS
São Cristóvão, Brazil
E-mails: ruanmello@gmail.com, admilson@ufs.br, fernando.m.al.91@gmail.com, edwdavid@gmail.com

***Abstract*—To make the Internet of Things a more receptive environment and well regarded by everyone, it is important to invest in security. The devices involved in the Internet of things environment have limited computational resources and expose the network to many threats. With the use of an architecture to be able to detect, classify and mitigate the effects of these threats, it is possible to create a safer environment. This paper proposes a security architecture for the Internet of Things, considering the limited computational resources of the environment in question. This Architecture uses the Dendritic Cells Algorithm (DCA) combined with a neural network to detect attacks and use the White List to ignore the malicious nodes in the network.**

Keywords–Internet of Things; Autonomic Computing; Self-Protection.

I. INTRODUCTION

Next ages of computing will tend to be beyond the traditional work environment. The Internet of Things (IoT) is a recent paradigm that makes part of this new age and its main goal is to create the possibility of communication between people and things and also between things without the need of human intervention [1].

Atzori et al. [2] calls attention to the impact of the fast advance of IoT and the great challenges that follow such as the interoperability between devices, the limited computational resources and especially the security. According to Roman et al. [3] the Internet and the users are under constant attacks, but there are many business models that try to provide the ethical and safe use of the Internet. The IoT environment is considered more vulnerable than the conventional Internet [2]. This occurs because when the wireless network has many nodes, it becomes easier for both physical and logical attacks, since it is not possible to apply one complex security mechanism due to lack of computational resources. There are many malicious models and many others will emerge associated with this environment. The challenge is to prevent the growth of such models or at least to minimize their impact.

Dobson [4] highlights the relevance of the autonomic characteristics, considering the growing amount of devices interconnected in the IoT environment. In 2011, the number of connected devices already exceeded the real number of people around the world and it is estimated that in 2020 this number will reach 24 billion.

The Vice President - Senior of International Business Machines (IBM), Paul Horn, introduced in March 2001, for the first time the use of the term Autonomic Computing [5]. Horn deliberately chose a term with a biological connotation trying to compare in this manifesto the need of self-management in complex systems aimed to reduce the burden on system administrators with the way that the autonomic nervous system regulates the heart beat and body temperature [5]. Thus, the conscious brain will be released from the burden of dealing with these and many other functions that can be considered low-level, but vital for your functioning. In this manifesto, he presented the four properties of self-management: self-configuring, self-optimizing, self-healing and self-protection.

Our work completes the architecture proposed by Almeida et al. [6] addressing the self-protection on the IoT. The proposed architecture consists of five modules. The tasks are distributed among the modules in order to share the responsibilities. By dividing responsibilities between modules, it makes easier to design self-protection systems for the IoT environment. This Architecture uses the dendritic cell algorithm (DCA) combined with a Multilayer Perceptron Neural Network with Limited Weights (MLPLW) to detect attacks in the network. The MLPLW can learn non-linear patterns during the execution, making the attack detection more efficient. In case of attack on the network of IoT, the architecture proposed will discover the type of attack and minimize the damage.

The remainder of this document has seven sections: Section II presents five common types of attacks to the IoT environment that will come to be mitigated with the proposed architecture; Section III introduces some aspects of autonomic computing and presents the autonomic loop MAPE-K; Section IV presents the Dendritic Cells Algorithm; Section V describes the architecture proposed; Section VI presents two related works to Internet security and the system of self-protection; Section VII presents the initial results; Section VIII concludes the paper.

II. ATTACKS IN INTERNET OF THINGS

According to Atzori [2] the characteristics of IoT (low power, limited energy and limited resources) expose the network to many threats. Most of them attack the limited power of the sensors. In other cases these threats modified or deleted some data. Following this section, we will discuss some of the latest and more common attacks on the environment of the IoT and wireless sensor networks [7].

1) Sinkhole: In a Sinkhole attack, the attacker tries to attract all the traffic from neighboring nodes [8]. So, practically, the attacker node listens to all data transmitted from neighboring nodes. Only this attack does not cause too much damage in the network, but together with another type of attack (Selective Forward or Black Hole), can become very powerful.

2) Selective forward: In a Selective Forward attack, the attacker node receives the transmission packets, but refuses to transmit some of them and drops those that it refused to transmit. The attacker must choose which packets to discard according to some standard such as size, destination or origin [9]. In this case, only the packets released by the attacker node can be freely transmitted.

3) Black Hole: In a Black Hole attack, the attacker node receives the transmission packets and drops all packets received, regardless of type, size, origin or destination [9].

4) Flooding: There are vulnerabilities related to the exhaustion memory. One manner to take advantage of this vulnerability is when an opponent sends too many requests trying to connect to the victim, every request makes the victim allocate the resources in an attempt to maintain the connection [10]. Thus, to prevent the total resource depletion is necessary to limit the number of connections. However, this solution also prevents valid nodes to create a connection with the victim, causing problems such as queuing [10].

5) Hello Flood: The attack Hello Flood uses a device with a powerful signal to regularly send some messages; that way, the network is left in a state of confusion [7]. In order to find ad-hoc networks, many protocols use Hello Messages for discovering neighbor nodes and automatically create a network. With the Hello Flood attack, an attacker can use a device with high transmission power to convince every other node in the network that the attacker is its neighbor, but these nodes are far away from the attacker. In this case the power consumption of sensors is significantly increased, because of protocols that depend on exchange information between neighbor nodes for topology maintenance or flow control [7].

Previously, we saw some of the most common attacks on IoT networks and in the next topics will be analyzed the possible strategies to end or to mitigate the damage caused by them.

To stop the damages caused by attacks on a network, first it is necessary to detect these attacks, using an intrusion detection system (IDS). An IDS analyzes network activity and attempts to detect any unusual behavior that may affect the integrity of the network. Based on information provided by IDS, strategies are created to cope the attacks. For example:

- To mitigate Sinkhole - If the geographical locations of the nodes of RPL DODAG are known, the effect of Sinkhole attacks can be mitigated by the use of flow control, making sure, that the messages are traveling to the correct destination. The RPL protocol also supports multiple instances DODAG offering alternative routes to the root DODAG [11].
- To mitigate Hello Flood - A simple solution to this attack, it is perform a bidirectional check for each message "HELLO" [12]. If there is no recognition, the path is assumed to be bad and a different route is chosen. If geographical locations of the nodes of RPL DODAG are known, all packets received from a node that is far beyond of the common network node transmission capacity can be dropped.
- To mitigate Selective Forward - An effective countermeasure against Selective Forward attacks is to ensure that the attacker cannot distinguish the different type of packets, forcing the attacker to send all or none packets [13].

Raza et al. [14] said that the most efficient and fastest way to stop the damage of routing attacks is isolate the malicious node. Some forms to ignore the attacker node were studied. These forms are:

- The Black List: After identifying the nodes and find the attackers, it will be created a list and all the malicious nodes will be added in order to exclude them from the possible routes of traffic data. To ignore the attacker, it will be done a verification in the Black List excluding all nodes found of the typical RPL DODAG that have a root and multiple nodes.
- The Gray List: After identifying the nodes and find the attacker, it will be created a list. The suspicious attacker node will be added to this list with the intention of excluding it from the possible routes of traffic data, for a predetermined time. After the end of the predetermined time the suspicious attacker node is deleted from the list. In this way, if have any doubt about the identification of the attacker node, the node may re-join the network. To ignore the suspicious attacker nodes, when create the routing, it will be done a verification in the Gray List excluding all nodes found of the typical RPL DODAG that have a root and multiple nodes.
- The White List: As in the example of the Black List, it will be created a list after identifying the nodes and find the attacker node. But this time will be added into the White List only the valid nodes and all malicious nodes will be excluded. This way will have a verification stating which nodes are valid and must belong to a typical RPL DODAG with a root and several nodes.

III. AUTONOMIC COMPUTING

The initiative of autonomic computing proposed by IBM, is based on the human nervous system [4]. The idea is, as the body's mechanisms that have functions with self-management and do not demand any conscious act such as heartbeat or intestinal activity, a computer system creates mechanisms that will also allow it to have a self-management [4].

According to the manifest proposed by IBM in 2001, there are four self-managing properties: self-configuration, self-healing, self-optimizing and self-protection [5].

- Self-Configuration Through self-configuring autonomic system will be installed and set up to attend the high level predetermined policies according to user intentions.
- Self-Healing Through this property it is possible for autonomic systems detect, diagnose and repair local problems resulting from bugs or failures in software and hardware.
- Self-Optimization The property of self-optimization is present on systems that can perform some change, proactively, to improve the performance and quality of service.

- Self-Protection The self-protection property is present in the systems that can defend themselves from malicious attacks and unauthorized changes. The autonomic system with self-protection is used to prevent and anticipate security breaches.

Dobson [4] say that self-management mechanisms in the autonomic computing are not independent entities. For example, the success of an attack against the system, requires actions of self-healing, self-configuration and self-optimization initially to ensure, that the system will have a trusted operation. After that, the self-protection would have responsibility for dealing with similar attacks in the future.

A. MAPE-K Autonomic Loop

The MAPE-K loop was presented by IBM as a reference model. Composed of five modules that can be seen in Fig. 1, the MAPEK-K Loop is intended to distribute the tasks of each element of the autonomic computing [5]. The modules that build the MAPE-K Loop are, respectively, monitoring, analysis, planning, execution and knowledge.

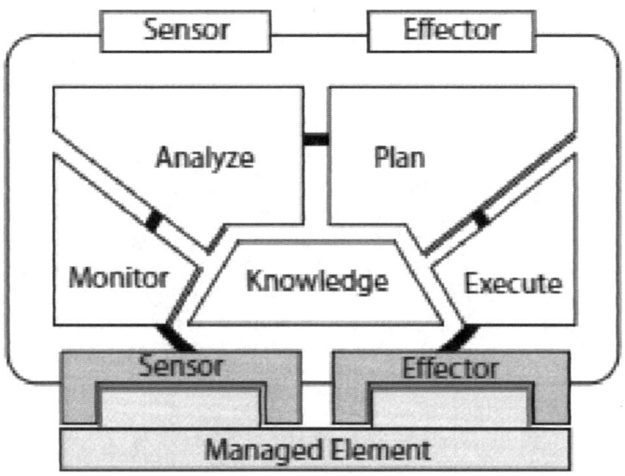

Figure 1. Mape-K Autonomic Control Loop [15].

- The Monitoring module uses sensors to collect data from the managed element, which could be a software or hardware resource, or an autonomic manager itself.
- The Analysis module provides mechanisms to interpret the collected data from the monitoring phase and predict future situations.
- The Planning module builds the necessary actions to achieve the goals.
- The Execution module uses effects to make changes on managed elements.
- The Knowledge module is in charge of keeping relevant data in the memory to accelerate decision making.

IV. DENDRITIC CELL ALGORITHM

The Dendritic Cell Algorithm (DCA) was introduced by Greensmith [16] and is inspired by the Danger Theory regarding the human Immune System. The main elements of DCA are Dendritic Cells (DC), the lymph node and antigens. The DC input signals are signs of danger, safe signals, PAMP signals, signs of inflammation. The DC output signals are: migration signal (costimulatory Molecules-CSM), semi-mature signal and mature signal.

Iteratively, the antigens are presented to DC. All signals increment the migration signal indicating when the dendritic cells will migrate to the lymph node and being processed. The danger signs and PAMP increment the mature signal of the DC while the safe signal increments the semi-mature signal of the DC. The sign of inflammation potentiates the growth of all signals.

When DC reaches the migration threshold is sent to the lymph node, and DC will be labeled how mature if the mature signal is greater than semi-mature or semi-mature otherwise. When the lymph node has a number of DCs, the antigens anomaly index is calculated, the Mature Context Antigen Value (MCAV) from the equation (1) where M is the number of mature DCs and SM the number of semi- mature DCs.

$$MCAV = \frac{M}{(SM + M)} \quad (1)$$

If MCAV has a value greater than the threshold, the DCA detects the presence of an intruder.

V. SELF-PROTECTION ARCHITECTURE

The Self-protection architecture for the IoT proposed in this work has five modules (Monitoring, Analysis, Planning, Executing and Knowledge) and was based on the MAPE-K loop. It is important to remember that the main contribution of this work is the implementation of the missing modules (Planning and Execution). This way, we will be completing the architecture proposed by Almeida et al. [6].

The monitoring and analysis modules are responsible, respectively, for collecting through the sensors, some information of the network that will be analyzed to measure the possibility of being associated with an attack. These two modules are present in the network nodes and in the border router (6BR). The planning and execution modules will be responsible, respectively, for identifying the attacker, the type of attack and to mitigate the damage in the network. The information listed as relevant data for analysis, planning and execution is: type of transport protocol, type of application protocol, time of communication, number of messages sent, number of messages effectively sent and number of messages received.

In Fig. 2, we can see that the border node (6BR) will have all components. This occurs because the 6BR has sensing and also for being the main element of the network. The components of the monitoring module and a part of the analysis module components are present in the network nodes that have the self-protection system. The components of the planning and execution modules are present only in 6BR, but the need to distribute them among the other network nodes can be considered. The five modules present in the architecture will be described more clearly in the following subsections.

1) Monitoring Phase: The components responsible for the monitoring phase are present in all network nodes, especially in 6BR. At this stage, the network information and the nodes are monitored. Some important information collected during the sensing to future analysis is: number of successfully sent

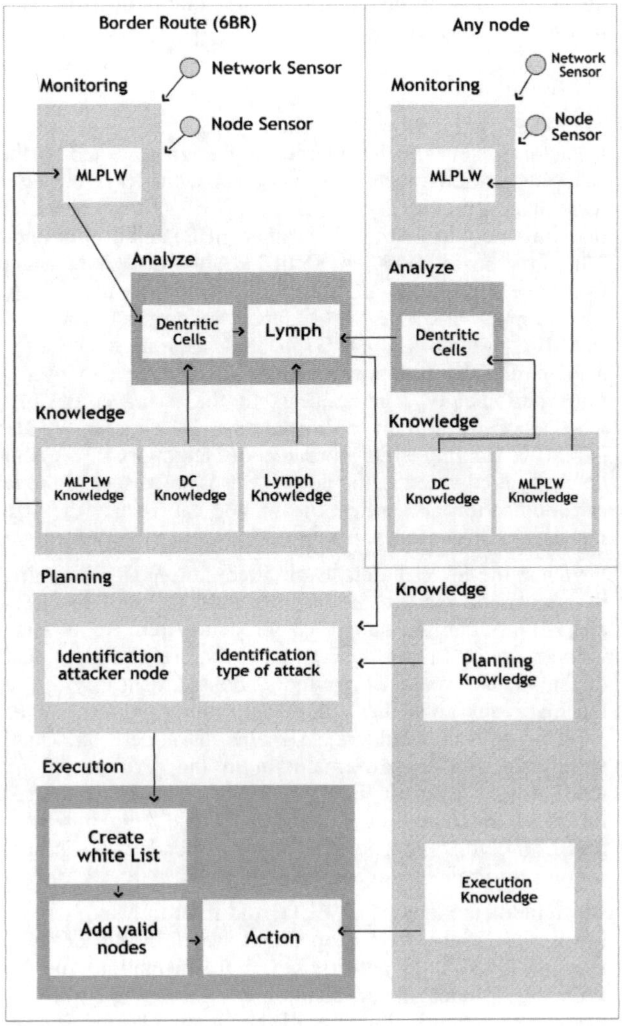

Figure 2. Self-Protection Architecture.

packets, number of sent packets, number of lost packets and the information about routing in DODAG tree. The main component of the monitoring phase, in this architecture proposed, is the Multiplier Perceptron Neural Network with Limited Weights (MLPLW), that can learn non-linear patterns during the execution. The MLPLW in this architecture is used to predict what information received indicates a problem in the node or in the network, for example, the MLPLW can predict the decrease of successfully sent packets from the packet sender address, if the training is enough. The prediction of the MLPLW is sent to the Analysis phase, to the Dendritic Cell Algorithm.

2) Analysis Phase: The component responsible for analysis phase uses the Dendritic Cell Algorithm (DCA), which is inspired by the danger theory of the human immune system. This algorithm has a high distributive potential and a low false positive rate. The DCA is used to analyze the results received from the MLPLW and determine if an attack is happening. The Dendritic Cells collect information from the MLPLW and migrates to the Lymph when the cell becomes mature or semi-mature. The Lymph receives mature and semi-mature dendritic cells and determine if the system is in danger. This information indicates an attack or not and, if there is an attack, it is sent to the Planning phase.

3) Planning Phase: The component responsible for the planning phase needs confirmation that really exist the presence of attack on the network, otherwise it becomes obsolete. Because the main objective is to find out what type of attack occurred on the network and to identify the attacker node through the information acquired by the analysis module. Thus, the execution module will decide the most appropriate action to be taken to mitigate the damage caused by the attack. The type of attack will be classified according to the following set of options: route selection group, packets control group and exhaustion attack group.

Through the obtained results, it is possible to differentiate the type of attack occurred. For example:

- If an attack belongs to the route selection group (Sinkhole), it will be taken into account the flow of messages in the legitimate nodes and in the attackers nodes. In this case, it will be needed to evaluate the influence of attackers in the choice of a better route. For this, it is necessary to compare the flow of messages from legitimate nodes regarding to the attackers nodes, through a medium and total number of messages.
- If an attack that belongs to the packet control group, which includes messages disposal (Black Hole and Selective Forward), it will be taken into account the number of messages sent, messages effectively sent and messages received.
- If an attack that belongs to an exhaustion attack group (Hello Flood and Flooding), it will be taken into account the number of packets sent by the attacker node, which is intended to send a huge number of messages to overload the system.

4) Execution Phase: The component responsible for the execution phase should mitigate or stop the damage caused by the attacks occurred on the network. The type of attack and the identification of the attacker node will be information that will influence in the choice of the predetermined action to mitigate or stop the damage in the network. These two important information will be provided by the Planning Phase. The reason to find out the attacker node is, trying to isolate as quickly as possible and create a new route, thus, avoid further damage to the network. The type of attack will be among one of the three groups mentioned above. According to the group selected there will be a specific action to solve the problem, because at each type of attack causes different types of damage on the network.

The first action to be taken by the components of the execution module, since the attack was detected, it is to ignore the malicious node. To perform this action it is important to be made the identification of network nodes, legitimate and malicious. Raza et al. [14] say that it is necessary to be careful with the way of identifying nodes. If possible it should be avoided the identification by IP address or MAC address, because they can be easily falsified. After making the identification of the nodes, some ways to ignore the attacker node were studied. Three ways to isolate the malicious node were analyzed before choosing the most convenient. The three ways are: Black List, Gray List and White List.

The way chosen was the White List, because the maintenance of this list is simple. This way, all valid nodes will recalculate their rank in the RPL protocol (DODAG). To recalculate the rank of all valid nodes, it will be necessary to ignore the DODAG Information Object (DIO) of all nodes with higher rank than theirs and of nodes that are not present in the White List. Thus, for a stranger node join in the network, it should be reported as safe and added in the White List.

5) Knowledge Phase: The components of knowledge phase will be responsible for keeping all the knowledge acquired by the system. Knowledge about the planning and execution modules will be at 6BR. The information kept by the Knowledge Module will be used to facilitate and accelerate the discover of the type of attack, the attacker node and the action to be taken to protect the network.

VI. RELATED WORK

The related works listed in this paper not only detect the attack, but also tries to mitigate the damage caused by the attacker. The related works will be described more clearly in the following subsections.

A. CAD

In [9], the authors describe how they developed a way to detect, identify the attacker node and classify the attack in a Wireless Mesh Networks (Wireless Mesh Networks - WMNs). They considered a special case of denial of service (DoS), known as Selective Forward, where the attacker node behaving maliciously pushing forward only a subset of the packets that received but discards the others.

While most studies about Selective Forward focuses on attack detection assuming a wireless channel, error free, the authors Shila et al. [9] considered more interesting the challenging scenario where the fall of the package may be due to an attack or normal loss events, such as the collision of access to the medium or bad quality of the channel.

Specifically, they developed an algorithm that can effectively distinguish the Selective Forward from the packet losses occurring in normal loss events. The developed algorithm is called CAD (Channel Aware Detection) and is based on two strategies, channel estimation and traffic monitoring. If the loss rate monitored in certain jumps exceeds the normal rate of estimated loss, the nodes involved will be identified as attackers. In addition, they perform analytical studies to determine the optimal detection thresholds that minimize the sum of false alarm and missed detection probabilities.

The traffic control procedure works basically that way, each intermediate node, monitors along the path the behavior of the neighbors. Given a path determined by the routing protocol, the CAD sends messages along the way to probe, to detect possible attacks. In the event of a positive detection, CAD, then triggers the underlying routing protocol to activate a process for finding out a new route.

CAD design was used by Network Simulator NS2 Berkeley (v2.29) for simulations. By the end of the simulation, using the CAD algorithm, the results showed that, in the presence of normal loss events or without, CAD can detect and classify the attack, increase the packet delivery rate in the network and finding out attacker nodes.

B. SVELT

SVELT, name given by authors, Raza et al. [14] to Intrusion Detector System for the Internet of Things projected by them, is applied in 6LoWPAN networks that use the RPL routing protocol. The approach of SVELTE is distributed and centralized, inserting modules in the edge router (6BR) and network nodes. The three main modules SVELTE are 6LoWPAN Mapper, Component Detector Intruder and distributed mini - firewall. The Mapper 6LoWPAN (6Mapper) reconstructs the routing tree RPL protocol (DODAG) in 6BR, each network node has a client for the 6Mapper. To rebuild the tree DODAG, you must periodically send requests to the 6Mapper customers, who respond to their corresponding information: NodeID, ParentID, Neighbor IDs and ranks of Neighbors IDs. It should be considered whether the network uses some form of reliable communication authentication, so you can reduce the size of requests and responses.

Once the SVELT detects an attack, the goal is to mitigate its effects and remove the intruder from the network, Raza et al. [14] say that the simplest approach to remove an attacker is to ignore it. Taking this approach requires the identification of the attacker node. The authors adopted, as a way to ignore the malicious node the White List, which would include all valid nodes and would reject malicious nodes. This method is reliable and easy to maintain in the presence of many attackers. As a result, in SVELTE a white list is used. The informed location of the nodes will also help mitigate the SVELTE Sybil and CloneID attacks intended to disrupt the routing information forging identities.

Implementations of SVELTE and mini-firewall were made in ContikiOS, the code is open and available. Raza et al. [14] used the ContikiOS and its RPL implementations of 6LoWPAN and IP stack. The evaluation was made empirically using Cooja, the network simulator of the ContikiOS, measuring the rate of detection, true positives and false positives for each experiment.

The authors concluded that the SVELTE is very effective for Sinkhole and Selective Forward attacks on a network with fewer losses. When the network has more losses, the system has better results when the RPL network becomes stable. Getting rates close to 90% on a network with losses when the RPL network stabilizes and results close to 100% on a network without loss. As for energy consumption, SVELTE solution consumes 30% more energy than using only the RPL. As the consumption of memory, 6Mapper client has 1414 bytes of overhead, the Firewall client has 246 bytes, 6Mapper server varies with the number of nodes and neighbors: 3580 bytes for one node and one neighboring, 3846 bytes into 8 nodes and 1 neighbor, 4152 bytes into 16 nodes and 1 neighbor and 4724 bytes into 16 nodes and 8 neighbors.

C. Comparison of Related Work

The SVELTE, as the authors claim, is the first IDS (Intrusion Detector System) for the IoT. The work presented has a huge contribution to design an IDS with the characteristics of a network for IoT, considering the technologies used in the communications stack, such as 6LoWPAN and RPL routing protocol. However its approach does not have autonomic characteristics for auto protect the network from further attacks, only the determined attack on the network project level.

TABLE I. COMPARISON OF RELATED WORK.

Qualities	*SVELT*	*CAD*	*Architecture proposal*
Designed for IoT	X	-	X
Autonomicity	-	X	X
Mitigate SinkHole	X	X	X
Mitigate Selective Foward	X	X	X
Mitigate BlackHole	X	X	X
Mitigate Flooding	-	-	X
Mitigate Hello Flood	-	-	X

Like the SVELT, CAD not only detects the attack, but also tries to mitigate the damage caused by the attacker. The CAD is directed to the WMNs and can differentiate between losses occurring in the normal events of a legitimate attack Selective Forward efficiently. In Table 1, we present the differences between the related works and the proposed architecture.

VII. RESULTS

The initial results of this research are about the technique used in the monitoring phase. The chosen technique for the first efforts is an ANN (Artificial Neural Network), a MLPLW based on the neural network with limited precision weights [17].

The MLPLW implemented has 10 neurons in the hidden layer and each weight is represented by a byte. The training technique of the MLPLW is the QBPSS (Quantized Back-Propagation Step-by-Step) [17], a modified version of Back-Propagation for neural network with limited weights.

TABLE II. MEMORY CONSUMPTION.

Resource	*MLP*	*MLPLW*	*MLPLW with training*
ROM Memory	214 bytes	354 bytes	1716 bytes
RAM Memory	3360 bytes	420 bytes	420 bytes

The KDD99 dataset it is widely used in Intrusion Detection Systems. Thus, KDD99 dataset was used with our MLPLW ANN implementation with a stream based training [18]. Each input is used once and the accuracy and false positive rates were measured every thousand inputs. After the first thousand inputs, the MLPLW achieved 97,65% accuracy, but oscillated until the thirty-fourth thousand input. The oscillation of the accuracy rate of the MLPLW is depicted in Fig. 3.

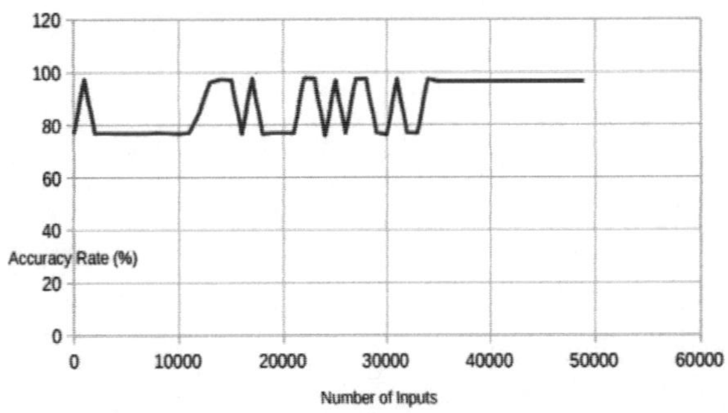

Figure 3. Accuracy rate of MLPLW.

As our proposed architecture shall be used in the Internet of Things context, the used techniques should be in accordance to the use of resources. It is possible to see in Table II, that the MLPLW have a small impact in memory utilization in an ARM Cortex-M3 with 512 KB of Persistent memory and 64 KB of Volatile memory.

VIII. CONCLUSION

The completion of this proposal will help provide a self-protection mechanism for IoT networks, facilitate detection and the classification of possible attacks on smart devices, mitigate the damage of the attacks suffered ensuring better performance and increase the confidence of users when using devices connected to IoT network.

The architecture proposed deals with five different attacks (Sinkhole, Selective forward, Black Hole, Flooding and Hello Flood) bearing in mind the memory consumption and energy due to a lack of resource of the available devices in the IoT environment. This Architecture uses the Dendritic Cell Algorithm combined with a neural network (MLPLW) to detect attacks and use the White List to ignore the malicious nodes in the network.

The MLPLW implemented shows that the monitor phase of the proposed architecture can use less than 1% of the memory of the embedded system and still have a high accuracy rate.

For future work, there will be the implementation of the proposed architecture to validate it. The performance of the system should be evaluated to verify if the proposed architecture has better results than related work. New attacks and new technologies will emerge, and then the work in question may be extended becoming increasingly complete.

ACKNOWLEDGMENT

This work was supported by CAPES and FAPITEC/SE

REFERENCES

[1] J. Gubbi, R. Buyya, S. Marusic, and M. Palaniswami, "Internet of things (iot): A vision, architectural elements, and future directions," Future Generation Computer Systems, vol. 29, September 2013, pp. 1645–1660, doi:10.1016/j.future.2013.01.010.

[2] L. Atzori, A. Iera, and G. Morabito, "The internet of things: A survey," Computer networks, vol. 54, October 2010, pp. 2787–2805, doi:10.1016/j.comnet.2010.05.010.

[3] R. Roman, P. Najera, and J. Lopez, "Securing the internet of things," Computer, vol. 44, September 2011, pp. 51–58, doi:10.1109/MC.2011.291.

[4] S. Dobson, R. Sterritt, P. Nixon, and M. Hinchey, "Fulfilling the vision of autonomic computing," IEEE Computer, January 2010, doi:10.1109/MC.2010.14.

[5] J. O. Kephart and D. M. Chess, "The vision of autonomic computing," Computer, vol. 36, January 2003, pp. 41–50, doi:10.1109/MC.2003.1160055.

[6] F. M. de Almeida, A. d. R. L. Ribeiro, and E. D. Moreno, "An architecture for self-healing in internet of things," UBICOMM 2015, July 2015, p. 89.

[7] D. Martins and H. Guyennet, "Wireless sensor network attacks and security mechanisms: A short survey," in Network-Based Information Systems (NBiS), 2010 13th International Conference on. IEEE, November 2010, pp. 313–320, doi:10.1109/NBiS.2010.11.

[8] P. Goyal, S. Batra, and A. Singh, "A literature review of security attack in mobile ad-hoc networks," International Journal of Computer Applications, vol. 9, November 2010, pp. 11–15.

[9] D. M. Shila, Y. Cheng, and T. Anjali, "Mitigating selective forwarding attacks with a channel-aware approach in wmns," Wireless Communications, IEEE Transactions on, vol. 9, May 2010, pp. 1661–1675, doi:10.1109/TWC.2010.05.090700.

[10] A. D. Wood and J. A. Stankovic, "Denial of service in sensor networks," Computer, vol. 35, December 2002, pp. 54–62, doi:10.1109/MC.2002.1039518.

[11] T. Heer, O. Garcia-Morchon, R. Hummen, S. L. Keoh, S. S. Kumar, and K. Wehrle, "Security challenges in the ip-based internet of things," Wireless Personal Communications, vol. 61, September 2011, pp. 527–542, doi:10.1007/s11277-011-0385-5.

[12] C. Karlof and D. Wagner, "Secure routing in wireless sensor networks: Attacks and countermeasures," Ad hoc networks, vol. 1, September 2003, pp. 293–315.

[13] L. Wallgren, S. Raza, and T. Voigt, "Routing attacks and countermeasures in the rpl-based internet of things," International Journal of Distributed Sensor Networks, vol. 2013, June 2013.

[14] S. Raza, L. Wallgren, and T. Voigt, "Svelte: Real-time intrusion detection in the internet of things," Ad hoc networks, vol. 11, November 2013, pp. 2661–2674.

[15] D. Weyns, S. Malek, and J. Andersson, "Forms: a formal reference model for self-adaptation," in Proceedings of the 7th international conference on Autonomic computing. ACM, June 2010, pp. 205–214, doi:10.1145/1809049.1809078.

[16] J. Greensmith, U. Aickelin, and S. Cayzer, "Introducing dendritic cells as a novel immune-inspired algorithm for anomaly detection," in Artificial Immune Systems. Springer, August 2005, pp. 153–167, doi:10.1007/11536444_12.

[17] J. Bao, Y. Chen, and J. Yu, "An optimized discrete neural network in embedded systems for road recognition," Engineering Applications of Artificial Intelligence, vol. 25, June 2012, pp. 775–782.

[18] A. Carvalho, K. FACELI, A. LORENA, and J. GAMA, "Inteligência artificial–uma abordagem de aprendizado de máquina," Rio de Janeiro: LTC, 2011.

System-Level Simulation for the Dependability Improvement of UHF RFID Systems

Vincent Beroulle, Oum-El-Keir Aktouf, David Hély
Univ. Grenoble Alpes, LCIS
F-26000, Valence, France
e-mail: firstname.lastname@lcis.grenoble-inp.fr

Abstract— **The SafeRFID project targets the improvement of Ultra High Frequency Radio Frequency Identification (UHF RFID) system dependability using system level simulation and emulation. RFID systems are based on low cost components (tags) more and more often used in critical applications and running in harsh environments (railway, aeronautic, food production, product manufacturing). Defects can have different origins (1) hardware failures, (2) medium perturbations (electromagnetic interferences), or (3) software bugs. The main goals of this project are (1) to develop hardware and software validation environments to validate and evaluate methods for detecting and diagnosing defects within RFID systems, (2) to develop new middleware services to improve the performances of RFID systems in presence of defects and (3) to develop robust tag architectures. This paper sums up all these complementary solutions which have been validated thanks to system level simulation and emulation and which have been integrated in a global dependable UHF RFID system. The results of this work are (1) the design of a robust middleware and of (2) a hardware tag and (3) the evaluation of the dependability of such global RFID systems thanks to system level simulation and emulation.**

Keywords*— *RFID; system level simulation; dependability; middleware; tag architectures

I. INTRODUCTION

In critical domains, RFID system errors can have catastrophic consequences in terms of human safety whereas in high quality applications, they can have economic consequences for product quality, manufacturing costs, etc. Monitoring RFID systems, which are based on low cost and uncertain components, is thus a must in order to perform on-line detection of failures. These failures can result from hardware malfunctions (aging effects are particularly sensitive to harsh environments), medium disturbances (for example, electromagnetic bursts), or software bugs. For example, these failures can be due to a broken or a misplaced antenna, RF interferences, low signal strength, middleware dysfunctions, etc. Therefore, the main goal of the SafeRFID project is to propose a global strategy for the simulation of RFID system in order to develop and evaluate the on-line detection and diagnosis of defects in UHF RFID systems in order to enhance the RFID systems dependability.

The objectives of existing RFID middlewares are especially to manage various data sources in RFID systems and process large amount of raw data. Some of them also provide error fixing mechanisms such as WinRFID [5]. Other RFID middlewares focus on a reliable integration of RFID technology into existing applications (SunRFID [6], FlexRFID [7]). Fault-tolerance is taken into account in the RFID middleware [8] by detecting abnormal behavior of the system. However in these middleware no low level information (physical information) coming from each reader measurements are mixed with the high level information gathered by the numerous readers in the system.

The classical RFID system on-line monitoring methods are based on reader performances monitoring. In fact, to detect component or environment failures and defects, many performance parameters of the reader can be observed. The classical performance parameters observed are the Average Tag Traffic Volume (ATTV) and the Read Errors to Total Reads (RETR) [4]. ATTV allows determining unusual tag traffic which is a symptom of a faulty system. For instance, if between 8:00am and 11:00am a reader usually reads 100 tags/hour every day and if one day, during the same period, the same reader reads only 50 tags/hour, then it can be assumed that a failure or a disturbance has occurred. The second parameter RETR consists of counting erroneous reads over the total read attempts (correct and faulty) of a specific reader. High RETR means there is probably a problem. The evolution of this RETR can also be analyzed. These methods can also be used as final optimization approaches during RFID system deployment.

In order to validate RFID systems during design phases, several RFID simulators have been proposed in the literature [2][3][11], but none of them focuses on the RFID systems dependability evaluation. These simulators allow simulating the communication protocol between the tags and readers or the interactions between the readers and middleware. Thus, designers generally use these simulators to perform a functional verification of their systems. For instance, Rifidi [1] only fits with RFID system deployment issues; fault simulation with Rifidi would be unrealistic. RFIDSim [3] is a complete RFID simulator; nevertheless its main goal is to evaluate RFID protocols and tag hardware characteristics are not modelled.

This paper gathers the results of the SafeRFID project. This project integrates in the same RFID system complementary and multi-level solutions for improving the system dependability. These solutions target the improvement (1) of the tags hardware architecture, (2) of the readers fault detection capability and (3) of the middleware for multi-readers RFID systems fault diagnosis. In this context, our three main results are: (1) two new validation environments, a simulator and a FPGA-based emulation platform allowing hardware and software RFID systems co-design and fault simulation; (2) new on-line test and diagnostic services for RFID middleware, and (3) a new tag robust architecture.

The next sections of this article are organized as described in the following. In Section II, two new RFID validation environments are described. The first one is a system level simulator which is capable of performing fault injection. The second one is an emulation platform (based on FPGA), which is also capable of both performing hardware fault injections and monitoring its internal signals. Section III presents two test and diagnosis methods, which have been implemented and validated thanks to these simulators or emulators. This section also describes the robust tag architecture developed within the SafeRFID project. Section V includes the conclusions of the article.

II. VALIDATION ENVIRONMENTS

This section describes the two validation environments which have been developed for the purposes of the SafeRFID project. These two environments allow (1) the validation of software and hardware RFID components and (2) RFID system robustness thanks to fault injection. The first validation environment is a complete RFID System Level Simulator. The second one is a RFID emulation platform allowing modelling and evaluating tag IC digital architecture into actual RFID Systems. These two validation environments are compliant with the RFID UHF EPC Class 1 Gen 2 standard.

A. *SERFID Simulator: a virtual validation environment*

"Simulation and Evaluation of RFID Systems" (SERFID) is a UHF RFID systems simulator. It permits to evaluate RFID systems robustness thanks to fault simulation. It models the whole RFID system including the numerous hardware tags and readers and their electromagnetic environment. An Ethernet interface is plugged to the simulator so that SERFID can be controlled by a distributed middleware, as real readers usually are. Thus, SERFID allows validating and optimizing middleware implementation. Fig. 1 illustrates a SERFID high level view containing several readers and tags.

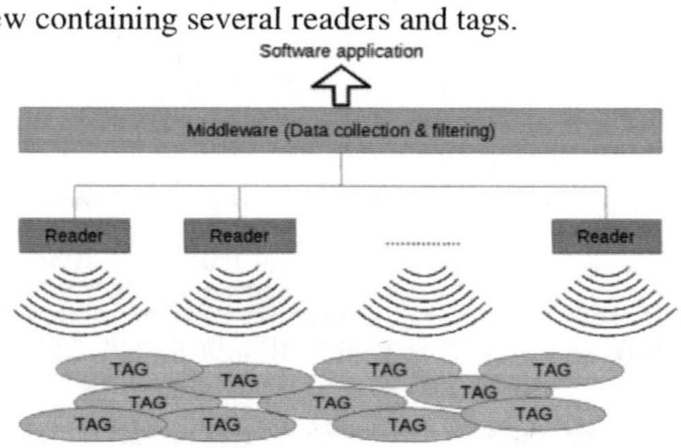

Figure 1. SERFID high level view model with several readers and tags

SERFID has been developed using the C++ SystemC library, which is adapted to both hardware and software components modeling. SERFID models the communication links between each tag and reader using high level functional models (Timed Transaction Level Model). The communication links between tags and readers have been divided into 2 parts. This distinction allows the injection of global defects affecting all the tags and readers and the injection of local defects affecting only one tag/reader couple. For example, the fault injection allows parametric variations on the Bit-Error-Rate (BER) of the global or local communication links. More details on this simulator are given in [9].

B. *RFIM: an emulation platform*

In order to evaluate tag digital baseband architectures, simulation is limited, since this requires low level (at least register transfer) time accurate simulation. Emulation is then an appropriate tool in order to evaluate tag digital baseband architectures taking into account the whole RFID system. FPGA emulation provides three major advantages over simulation: (1) proof of compliance with the standard protocol, as we will use an RFID reader known to be compliant with this standard, (2) simulation time reduction and (3) in-circuit emulation. In-circuit emulation provides also the opportunity to inject errors within the tag to evaluate its effects within the tag and the system. This emulator aims at emulating all type of errors which can occur within the digital baseband in order to provide a tool for robustness evaluation and countermeasure validation. This emulator also allows monitoring the internal tag behavior which helps to understand fault propagation within the design. Moreover, the proposed monitoring system included into the emulator provides a convenient and powerful tool to analyze system behaviors. The emulator embeds a fault injection mechanism to validate the dependability of the IC. Errors are explicitly induced by the deliberate introduction (injection) of faults into the system. An emulation platform, the so called RFIM (RFID Fault injection and Monitoring) with fault injection capability has then been described in [10]. This FPGA based emulator is made of an UHF RFID tag with on chip faults injection mechanism.

As shown in Fig. 2, the RFIM platform is divided into eight modules: monitoring interface, fault injector, activation of injection, event detector, golden and instrumented faulty tags, register comparator and embedded microprocessor. The embedded microprocessor controls all the platform modules and then permits to perform on-line tag monitoring and to play on-line fault attacks. The processor allows the on-line capture of data in the two tag basebands for analyzing the RFID communication. The interface monitoring is a mechanism that transports the internal register values from the tag basebands to the microprocessor. This monitoring interface block uses a First-In-First-Out (FIFO) memory in order to compensate the latency of the microprocessor for outputting register values. Faults are only injected in the faulty tag. The golden tag, which is always fault free served as a reference. The register comparator compares all the internal registers of the golden and the faulty tags. This comparison helps the embedded processor to detect and to localize faults and errors in the faulty tags.

Our prototype has been validated into real RFID environment. It allows both observing and controlling the internal tag parameters and data. Thanks to these capabilities, the emulator can help designers to evaluate different digital IC architectures.

This evaluation concerns, on one hand, the validation of the tag robustness against environmental aggressions and, on the other hand, the validation of the tag security against human attacks. These validations can be performed into real RFID system, using commercial readers and other commercial tags.

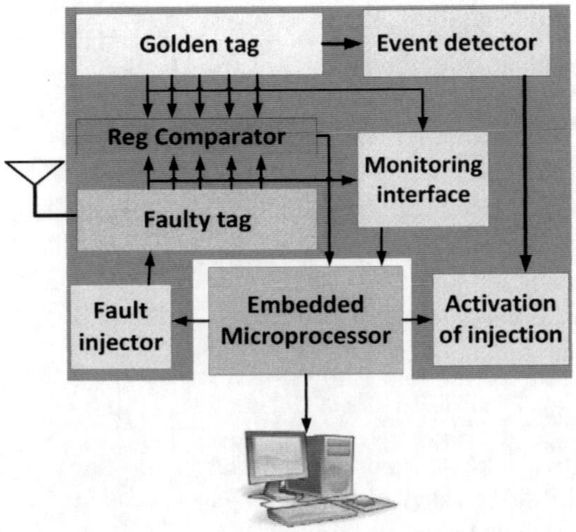

Figure 2. RFIM platform for faults injection and monitoring

This allows quick and accurate validation taking into account all the complex physical effects involved into RFID systems. The spying capabilities of the emulator gives us an opportunity to study some types of attacks on RFID system, to detect malicious hardware, which disturbs the security of this technology and to design and to validate solutions for robust and secure architectures.

III. TEST AND DIAGNOSIS METHODS AND TAG ROBUSTNESS ENHANCEMENT

This section describes the three main approaches which have been proposed by the SafeRFID project in order to improve UHF RFID system dependability. Each approach is embedded on a specific part of the RFID system: the reader, the middleware and the tag digital architecture.

A. *Profile test method*

The Profile test method is inspired by classical monitoring techniques (ATTV, RETR), which are based on reader performances monitoring. This method, as the classical monitoring methods are, is nonintrusive. In this method, we propose to measure and compare individual tags performance indicators rather than a single global average parameter. To do this, we define a new performance metric - called read rate profile – individually involving all the tags of the population rather than an average value computed for the same population.

The initialization of our monitoring method requires computing the statistical parameters of the fault free inventory read rate profiles. Let us first explain what these inventory read rate profiles are. Each tags inventory leads to a specific inventory read rate profile, which is the ordered read rate curve of the entire tag population. The '-'curve in Fig. 3 represents the inventory profile of a fault free inventory occurrence. Then, from all these initial inventory profiles, an average read rate profile is computed. This average profile is represented by the bold curve in Fig. 3. The second step for the initialization of our approach consists in computing a threshold for the failure detection. This threshold, called limit profile, is represented by the '+'curve in Fig. 3. An inventory profile with one or more tag read rates under this limit implies that the RFID system is considered faulty. The '•'curve in Fig. 3 illustrates a faulty inventory profile with several points under the limit. The limit profile is computed using the average profile and the standard deviation of each ordered tags. Details on this test approach are given in [11] [12] [13].

B. *SafeRFID-MW: a middleware for On-Line Testing and Diagnostic*

The proposed Profile testing method, as well as most existing test methods (RETR, ATTV, etc.), operates mainly at the reader level. These local results are not capitalized for global processing of errors at the whole system level. Consequently, in case of distributed RFID systems based on several readers, there are no means to determine the whole system state. In our work, this issue has been solved by developing a special RFID middleware that integrates not only testing operations at the level of each reader, but also diagnosis processes at the middleware level. Our middleware called SafeRFID-MW implements a diagnosis algorithm called RFID_Diag_Algo. This algorithm uses the basic idea of probabilistic diagnosis developed in the work of Fussel and Rangarajan [14] on multiprocessor systems. Nevertheless, the fault model, as well as the diagnosis operations has been largely adapted to the RFID constraints. RFID_Diag_Algo algorithm performs three steps: i) reader partitioning in groups according to some criteria issued by the application (i.e., which readers, read the same groups of tags), ii) read rate result comparison in a way that ensures a consensus on faulty components, whether readers or tags, iii) evaluation of the diagnosis accuracy by applying a new probabilistic model suitable to such systems. Details of this algorithm are presented in [15][16].

Although Low Level Reader Protocol (LLRP) is a complete communication protocol that allows notifying communication errors between the middleware and the readers, the LLRP protocol cannot detect failures due to reader misconfigurations or some runtime conditions. It can neither determine error causes. Therefore, it is not suitable as it for use in applications where demands for dependability are critical, especially as the tag-reader interface is very sensitive to external perturbations and may present a random behavior. In the SafeRFID project, the LLRP protocol has been extended to take into account errors [17].

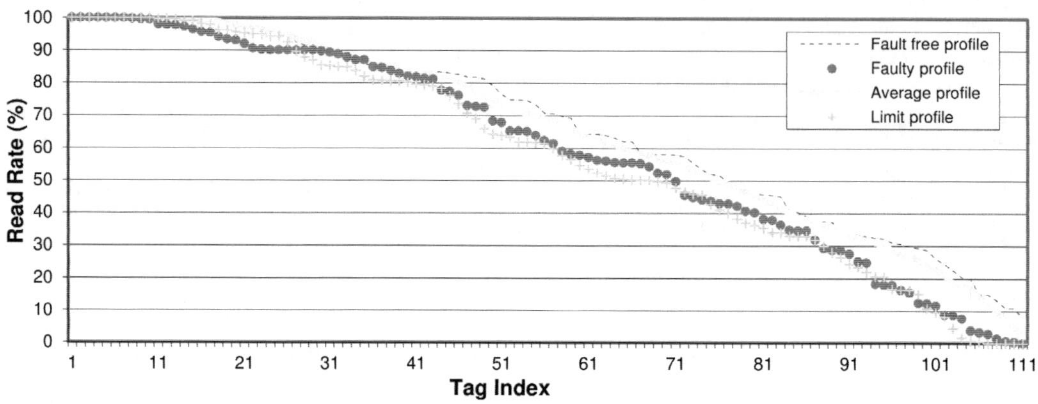

Figure 3. Average, limit, fault free and faulty inventory profiles

A prototype of the SafeRFID-MW has been developed using the Java language. Different implementations of the probabilistic diagnosis have been analyzed, and we have shown which one is better according to the running environment and the objectives of the end user [17].

C. Tag Robustness Enhancement

Thanks to RFIM, the most sensitive parts of the tag digital baseband architecture have been identified through fault injection campaigns. The fault injection campaigns consist in measuring for a given period the number of times the tag is detected by a reader while faults are injected in a part under analysis. This experiment has also been done when several tags are in front of the reader in order to evaluate the faulty tag effects on other tags. The experiments have been carried out on all registers of the digital baseband in order to identify the most sensitive ones. Experimental results [19] show that only a few registers dramatically decrease the system performance (i.e., the tag read rate). Fig. 4 hereafter gives the influence of the fault injection on the number of times the tag has been successfully identified. Light gray gives the value in case no faults are injected; dark gray gives the resulting number in case faults have been injected within the parameters given in horizontal axis.

At a first glance, we can see that all parameters are not equally sensitive. While some faulty parameters reduce the number of times the tag has been identified from 4500 to less than 500, other ones have a very limited influence on the tag response. This can be explained by the role played by the parameter during an inventory round, and the refreshment rate of the value during the same round.

We have proposed in a first approach to use hardware redundancy to decrease the fault effects. A Triple Modular Redundancy (TMR) has been applied on the most sensitive registers identified thanks to the fault injection campaigns. Since the tag digital baseband architecture is powered wirelessly and has a limited resource, the TMR was chosen to protect the most sensitive registers only. Moreover such registers are very small which makes the cost acceptable. As shown in Fig. 5, the TMR [4] technique consists on the triplication of the target component to protect.

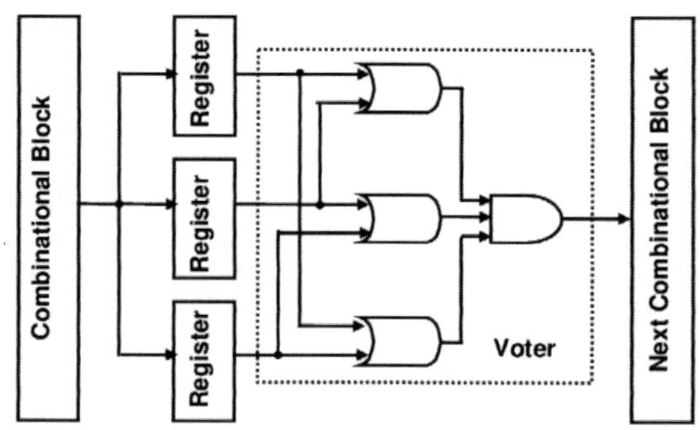

Figure 5. Triple Modular Redundancy Protection

The three resulting outputs from triplication are connected to a voter block that compares the three received data and elects that of majority. If one of the three components fails or suffers a direct SEU. TMR technique implies an area increase of the redundant part of more than 200% due to the component triplication. It also needs a voter that is implemented just with some OR and AND gates for each bit of the triplicated component. We have experimentally noted that the use of this TMR, improves the read rate in the presence of faults into sensitive registers. The proposed protection only adds 30 flip-flops to the whole circuit. TMR although expensive is in this case an acceptable method since thanks to the fault injection campaigns the most sensitive elements have been identified in a real RFID context, limiting the TMR use to only a few bits.

We have also proposed and validated a complementary approach allowing fault detection and diagnosis. This approach consists in adding hardware checkers into the tag circuit. Some of these checkers are provided by the synthesizable assertions available in the Open Verification Library library (OVL) and others are designed to monitor tag finite state machine transitions. The faults detected by the checkers are counted and saved within the tag memory.

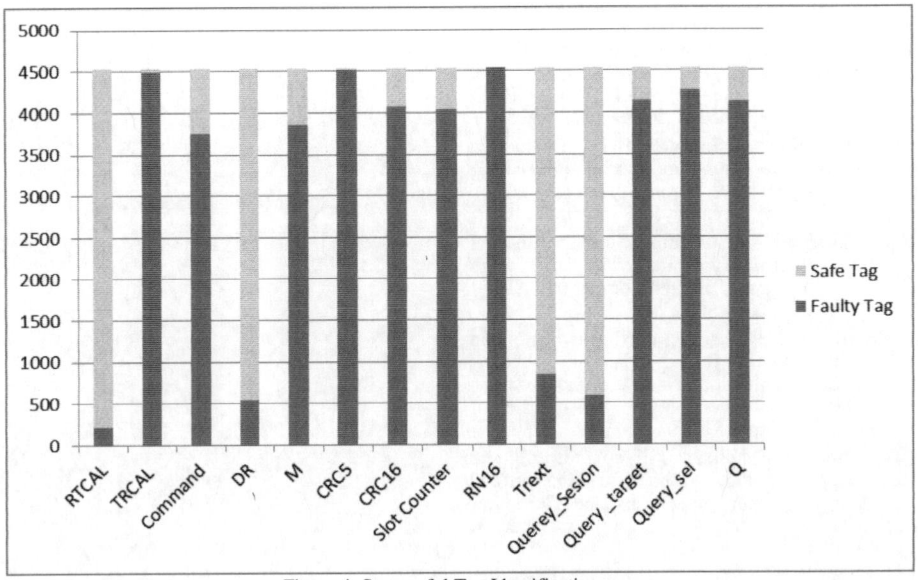

Figure 4. Successful Tag Identifications

Then, a user can read this information through the RFID reader and thereafter acquire diagnosis information. This approach has been implemented and evaluated on RFIM. Details on these robust architectures are given in [19] [11].

IV. CONCLUSION AND FUTURE WORK

The SafeRFID project addresses the dependability issues in RFID systems. The proposed framework considers both hardware and software components as well as analog and digital aspects of RFID systems. Three main layers have been identified: the hardware layer with tags and readers, the communication layer represented by the LLRP protocol and the software layer including the RFID middleware. The main results of this work are: (1) the development of a fault simulator (SERFID) and of an FPGA based emulator (RFIM) that allows fault injection and test method evaluations, (2) the design and implementation of a robust LLRP-compliant RFID middleware prototype that provides fault detection and diagnosis new services, and (3) the development of a tag robust architecture with self-diagnosis capability.

ACKNOWLEDGMENT

This work has been supported by the French National Research Agency project “SafeRFID” [ANR 2010 JCJC 0305 01]

REFERENCES

[1] C. E. Palazzi, A. Ceriali, and M. Dal Monte, “RFID Emulation in Rifidi Environment”, in Proc. of the International Symposium on Ubiquitous Computing (UCS'09), Beijing, China, Aug 2009.

[2] C. Angerer, R. Langwieser, “ Flexible evaluation of RFID system parameters using rapid prototyping”, RFID, 2009 IEEE International Conference on Digital Object Identifier: 10.1109/RFID.2009.4911188 Publication Year: 2009 , Page(s): 42 – 47

[3] C. Floerkemeier, S. Sarma, “RFIDSim—A Physical and Logical Layer "Simulation Engine for Passive RFID “ Automation Science and Engineering, IEEE Transactions on Volume: 6 , Issue: 1 Digital Object Identifier: 10.1109/TASE.2008.2007929 Publication Year: 2009 , Page(s): 33 – 43

[4] F. Thornton, “How to Cheat at Deploying and Securing RFID”, Syngress Publishing ©2007, ISBN 1597492302 9781597492300

[5] R. Shorey et al., Mobile, Wireless and Sensor Networks : Technology, Applications and Future Directions, Chapter “WinRFID – A middleware for the enablement of Radio Frequency Identification (RFID) based Applications” B. S. Prabhu et al., John Wiley and Sons Inc., 2006.

[6] Sun Microsystems, Inc., "Sun Java™ System RFID Software 3.0 Administration Guide," February 2006.

[7] A. Sengupta, S. Z. Schiller, “FlexRFID: A design, development and deployment framework for RFID-based business applications”, Information Systems Frontiers, vol. 12, n° 5, pp. 551-562, November 2010

[8] N. Ahmed, “Reliable Framework for Unreliable RFID Devices” 8th IEEE International Conference on Pervasive Computing and Communications Workshops (PERCOM Workshops), Mannheim, 2010

[9] G. Fritz, V. Beroulle, O-E-K. Aktouf, and D. Hély, “SystemC Modeling of RFID Systems for Robustness Analysis”, 19th International Conference on Software, Telecommunications and Computer Networks IEEE SoftCOM 2011Split - Hvar - Dubrovnik, September 15 – 17, 2011, IEEE Catalog Number: CFP1187A-CDR; ISBN 978-953-290-027-9

[10] O. Abdelmalek, D. Hély, and V. Beroulle “Fault Tolerance Evaluation of RFID Tags”, in IEEE Latin America Test Workshop (LATW 2014), Fortaleza, Brésil, 13-16 March 2014

[11] G. Fritz, V. Beroulle, O. Aktouf, M. D. Nguyen, and D. Hély, “RFID System On-line Testing Based on the Evaluation of the Tags Read-Error-Rate”, Journal of Electronic Testing: Volume 27, Issue 3 (2011), Page 267-276, (DOI: 10.1007/s10836-010-5191-6).

[12] G. Fritz, B. Maaloul, V. Beroulle, O-E-K. Aktouf, and D. Hély, "Read rate profile monitoring for defect detection in RFID Systems", IEEE International Conference on RFID-Technologies and Applications (RFID-TA 2011), , pp. 89-94, Sitges, Barcelona, Spain, on September 15-16, 2011, IEEE catalog number: CFP11RFT-CDR ; ISBN: 978-1-4577-0026-2

[13] G. Fritz, V. Beroulle, O-E-K. Aktouf, and D. Hély, "Evaluation of a new RFID system performance monitoring approach", Design, Automation & Test in Europe, (DATE 2012), interactive presentation, Dresden, Gremany, 12-16 march 2012

[14] D. Fussell, S. Rangarajan, "Probabilistic diagnosis of multiprocessor systems with arbitrary connectivity", IEEE 19th International Symposium on Fault-Tolerant Computing, FTCS-19. Digest of Papers., Chicago, IL, pp. 560-565, 1989.

[15] R. Kheddam, O. Aktouf, and I. Parissis, "Saferfid-mw: Safe and Fault-Tolerant rfid Middleware", R. Kheddam, O. Aktouf, I. Parissis, Journal of Communications Software and Systems (jcomms), Special issue on rfid Technologies and Internet of Things, Vol. 9, n° 1, mars 2013, pp. 57-73.

[16] R. Kheddam, O. Aktouf and I. Parissis, "On-line monitoring and diagnosis of rfid readers and tags", 20th ieee International Conference on Software, Telecommunications and Computer Networks (softcom 2012), Split, Croatia, 11-13 september 2012, pp. 1-9.

[17] R. Kheddam, O. Aktouf and I. Parissis, "An extended llrp model for rfid system test and diagnosis", 8th Workshop on Advances in Model Based Testing (a-most 2012) dans le cadre de 5th ieee International Conference on Software Testing, Verification and Validation. Montreal, Canada, 17-21 april 2012, pp. 529-538.

[18] R. Kheddam, O. Aktouf, I. Parissis and S. Boughazi, " Monitoring of rfid Failures Resulting from llrp Misconfigurations", 21st ieee International Conference on Software, Telecommunications and Computer Networks (softcom 2013), Split, Croatia, septembrer 2013, pp. 1-6.

[19] O. Abdelmalek, D. Hély, and V. Beroulle "Emulation of Faults Injection on UHF Transponders", in 17th IEEE Symposium on Design and Diagnosis of Electronic Circuit and System (DDECS 2014), Warsaw, Poland, 23-25 April 2014

[20] I. Mezzah et al., "Assertion based on-line fault detection applied on UHF RFID tag", 8th IEEE International Design & Test Symposium 2013, Maroc (2013)

Energy Management of a Set of Sensor Nodes at Application Level using the LINC Middleware

Olesia Mokrenko

Air Liquide Medical Systems
Parc de haute technologie,
6 rue Georges Besse,
F-92182 Antony, France
Email: olesia.mokrenko@airliquide.com

Suzanne Lesecq, Maria Isabel Vergara-Gallego

Univ. of Grenoble Alpes
CEA, LETI, MINATEC Campus
17 rue des Martyrs,
F-38054 Cedex 9, France
Email: FirstName.LastName@cea.fr

Abstract—**Optimization of the energy consumption of sensor networks is traditionally performed either at the sensor node level or at the network level. However, more energy savings can be obtained if the application that makes use of the sensor nodes is considered. In order to achieve such extra energy gains, control theory can be applied. This paper summarizes control strategies implemented to minimize the energy consumption of a set of sensor nodes, while ensuring the application Quality of Service (QoS), this latter being mainly expressed with a minimum number of samples that must be available at the application level at each sampling time. With the Control strategies proposed, the sensor network lifetime is increased compared to the case without control strategy at application level. The control strategies have been implemented and evaluated on a real testbed composed of heterogeneous sensor nodes, and using the LINC middleware for node coordination.**

Keywords–Energy management; control strategy; middleware.

I. Introduction

Sensor Networks, and especially their wireless version (WSNs), have been a hot research topic for the last decades [1]. The optimization of energy consumption, in particular when the nodes are powered by batteries, is mandatory if the goal is to deploy sensor nodes that will run autonomously for years, without battery changes. This goal can be achieved if the power consumption is drastically decreased at all the "system" levels, from the sensor node itself to the communication protocols, but also at the application level.

At sensor node level, several improvements already exist, ranging from the design of novel radio technologies [2] to microcontroller architectures [3], and energy management methodologies [4]. Many approaches have been proposed at the different layers of the communication stack to increase the network lifetime [5]. They mainly minimize the node active period using duty cycle, optimize routing protocols, and reduce the quantity of transmitted data. However, the WSN lifetime can be extended if the energy consumption is reduced not only at the node level but also at a more global level, i.e. including the applications running on top of the WSN.

A trade-off between performance (or application QoS) and energy consumption must be found. A promising solution to reach this trade-off is to rely on Control Theory. From a model of the system (here a WSN system), possibly taking into account constrains, Control Theory can ensure the application QoS while minimizing the energy consumption of the whole WSN. This control objective can be naturally expressed as an optimization problem. The associated control law will then require a bit of information from the nodes and protocol layers (e.g., energy consumption of the nodes, remaining energy in the batteries of the nodes, the work each node has to perform) in order to manage the nodes and the whole system. To our knowledge, most of the work relying on Control Theory for the minimization of energy consumption in WSNs are related to managing the transmission power of the sensor nodes. These mechanisms are applied at the node level, where no knowledge regarding the global state of the network is required. Moreover, the application constraints are not taken into account. Note that [5] reviews various energy conservation schemes but none of them seems grounded in control theory. [6] proposes a classification of power control mechanisms in WSN, based on Control Theory and actually related to power control protocols only. The present paper details the implementation, on a real test-bed, of power control strategies at application level based on Model Predictive Control (MPC) and on a Hybrid Dynamical System (HDS) approach. The objective of both strategies is to minimize the energy consumption of the whole WSN while the application QoS is fulfilled. This problem is naturally expressed as an optimization one with constraints, which boils down to MPC. However, the system to be controlled (i.e., the WSN) is hybrid, with evolution of the battery charge driven by differential equations while the state of the sensor nodes is discrete (e.g., on, off, sleep modes). Therefore, a HDS approach is also a good candidate for the WSN power control. For the selected test-bed, the MPC strategy described in [7],[8], doubles the WSN lifetime when compared to the implementation without control at application level. Theoretical details regarding the HDS strategy can be found in [9]. Preliminary results show that, in simulation, the lifetime is extended by a factor slightly smaller than 2, which is logical due to the sub-optimal solution provided by the HDS approach.

The main goals here are to describe how the gap between theory and implementation has been closed, and demonstrate and validate the theoretical results. Thus, the control strategies will not be described in details, and the reader can refer to [7],[8],[9] for details regarding the control approaches. Two communication technologies are deployed on the test-bed, leading to a heterogeneous network. This shows that the proposed strategies are independent from the communication technologies. The implementation is based the LINC [10] coordination middleware. Thanks to its resource-based approach and transactional guaranties, LINC makes it possible for the global controller to take decisions according to the current state of the sensor nodes, and to force the WSN to behave as expected at the application level.

The paper is organized as follows. Section II presents a description of the sensor network considered and the proposed application. Section III describes how the network has been implemented and integrated with the power controllers (MPC and HDS) at application level. Section IV summarizes the implementation results. Finally, Section V discuses the related works and Section VI summarizes the main findings and gives future work directions.

II. System description

Consider a WSN that has been deployed to monitor environmental parameters in a given zone in a building. The parameters typically monitored are the temperature, the CO_2 and humidity levels. The sensor readings are sent by the sensor nodes to a sink node that will basically interact with building appliances, e.g., the heating system or the air conditioning units. Actually, measurements are collected to feed the Building Automation Systems that will control the temperature or the ventilation in the given zone. These correspond indeed to the application level. The present work deals with the collection of enough measurements for the application to perform its task (e.g., temperature control, ventilation control) adequately. To reach a nominal behavior at the application level, a given application Quality of Service (QoS) must be reached. Here, the application QoS refers to the minimum amount of information required for the correct functionality of the application. It is defined with the sampling frequency of the nodes and the quantity and quality of sensor readings.

In the present work, the sensor nodes are supposed to be densely deployed in the zone, leading to information redundancy. Thus, the minimum number of nodes needed to ensure the application QoS is smaller than the total number of nodes deployed. It is therefore possible to switch off some nodes, leading to energy savings and network lifetime extension. Moreover, a node can be replaced by another one when, for instance, the first one runs out of energy.

The sensor nodes may differ from:

- *the available energy:* sensor nodes are powered by batteries with possibly harvesting systems to harvest energy. As a consequence, the nodes can have different available energy;
- *the energy consumption:* to read a given environmental parameter, the sensor nodes may require different energy budgets, depending on their hardware;
- *heterogeneity:* sensor nodes can be heterogeneous regarding communication protocol, data format and/or hardware characteristics.

As a consequence, the choice of the active nodes at a given instant of time is not straightforward. Moreover, nodes may become *Unreachable*) without notice. This disconnection may be caused by energy shortage, communication troubles, or hardware failures. Nodes may also "re-enter" the network when they leave the *Unreachable* state if the *Unreachable* condition is no more valid. As multiple hardware platforms and communication protocols can be deployed, it is necessary to rely on a middleware layer to support heterogeneity. Such a layer abstracts the controller from the communication protocols, data formats, or other low level matters.

Fig. 1 illustrates the data collection system, split in four levels: I) the *sensor nodes*, II) the *communication infrastructure*, III) the *data collection and synchronisation* level and IV) the *Controller*. These levels are now detailed.

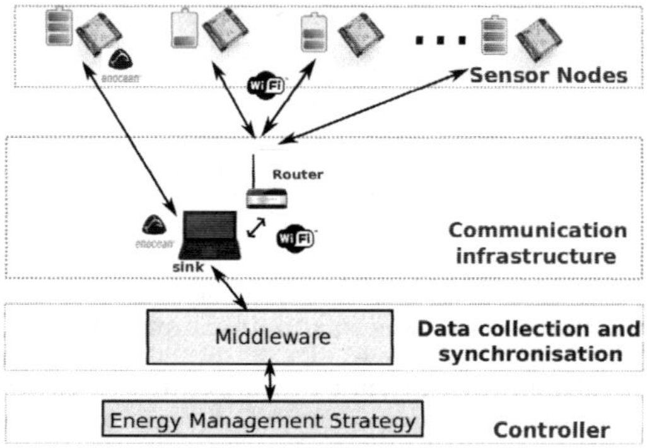

Figure 1. WSN System levels

A. Sensor nodes

Sensor nodes are usually split in four main parts, namely, computation, communication, sensing and power supply [11]. For each node, different power modes are defined, corresponding to a combination of the state for each unit in the node. The energy consumption of the node in a given power mode is given in the node datasheet provided by the manufacturer. The activity of the sensor nodes (i.e., sensing, computing, communication) is usually "duty cycled": the node periodically wakes-up, senses environmental parameters, processes and transmits these data, and finally enters the sleep mode (i.e., all units are disabled, waiting for a timer event). The node consumption is related to the duty cycle.

The energy management strategies implemented here assign a *functioning mode* to each *Reachable* node. Each functioning mode is defined by a given period for the sensing and communication tasks. Hence, all nodes in the network are duty cycled, and their energy consumption depends on their duty cycle for communication and sensing. Basically, the controller (that implement either the MPC of a HDS approach) combines information received from the nodes regarding their remaining energy and the application QoS requirements, to decide the most suitable functioning mode for each *Reachable* node.

Information regarding the remaining energy of the nodes is sent on a periodic basis to the controller. Thus, a minimum communication duty cycle is required for the proper functionality of the controller. Note that the remaining energy must be estimated because it cannot be measured directly.

B. Communication architecture

In order to exchange data between the nodes and the sink, a communication topology is chosen. Here, a star topology is considered and the sensor nodes communicate directly with the sink through a router. Hence, the controller can choose to increase the communication period of one node, without affecting the communication with the other ones.

Note that a cluster-tree topology can be easily implemented. For this topology, the cluster coordinators are responsible for forwarding information from nodes in the cluster. Thus, coordinators are duty cycled and synchronized with the associated nodes for data reception and forwarding. Hence, to communicate with all the associated nodes, the wake-up (or communication) period of the coordinator must be at most the shortest communication period of all the associated nodes. Therefore, the controller can change the functioning mode of all end-nodes in the network. The functioning mode of the coordinators are then set accordingly. Besides, further parameters have to be taken into account by the controller. For example, the number of hops required to send a packet to the sink, which is proportional to the communication energy cost, must be considered. All these factors can be easily integrated in the controller. Nodes must inform their role in the network (coordinator or end node) and the number of hops to the sink. The controller will take into account all these aspects when control decisions are provided, as in the star topology case.

More complex topologies, such as mesh networks, require the controller to know the current topology and routing information, which is highly dynamic. Indeed, the controller cannot arbitrarily change the functioning mode of the nodes because it can break the routing and topology maintenance mechanisms. Thus, the integration with a mesh network requires extra extension of our control strategies.

C. Data collection and synchronization

This third layer is in charge of data collection and synchronization of the sensor nodes. It calls the controller when its mandatory inputs are "ready". These tasks are achieved through the LINC [10] coordination middleware.

LINC uses an associative memory [12] implemented as a distributed set of bags. This offers a decoupling in space and time between data producers (here, the sensor nodes) and data consumers (here, the controller). LINC has been successfully used in various application domains. It currently supports around 30 communication technologies. The associative memory also provides an abstraction layer to present all the measurements in the same format to the controller.

To ensure the expected application QoS, the sensor nodes communicate with the sink at a given time period (depending on their functioning mode) that depends on the application domain. Between two communication instants, the external timer of the sensor node is activated according to the desired period. Then, the nodes enter the sleep state, waiting for a timer interrupt. However, the node oscillators may experience drift over time. Therefore, if the clocks are not re-synchronized, some nodes may wake up outside of the time-window accepted by the sink. Moreover, if they wake up too early, their measurements will be outdated when used by the controller. If they wake up too late, the controller will not take their readings into account as the nodes will be considered *Unreachable*.

To avoid synchronization issues, LINC ensures that the clocks of the nodes are synchronized, with a synchronization frame periodically exchanged. The synchronization period depends on the type of oscillators being implemented in the nodes (the more precise the oscillator, the longer the synchronization period). This parameter can be determined empirically or according to the characteristics of the nodes. The synchronization procedure is completely independent from the controller. Thus, this latter does not need to take care of synchronization burden. It only processes the measurements currently received from the *Reachable* nodes.

The time/space decoupling and the abstraction offered by LINC have been particularly useful here. Indeed, it is straightforward to ensure that the latest measurements are available in the associative memory. The measurements are simply added to a dedicated bag whenever this is required (sampling/ synchronization periods). The controller is called when the current state of the nodes is known. The LINC application waits during a configurable time period to receive information from nodes. If no information is received after this time, the node is considered *Unreachable*.

D. Control design

The controller is based either on a Model Predictive Control (MPC) or on a HDS approach. Details on these strategies are provided in [7],[8],[9] and will not be reported here.

The energy consumption of each node during a sampling period depends on the functioning mode that is assigned by the controller. To increase the network lifetime (i.e., the time the network can ensure the application QoS), the controller must choose the functioning mode of each mode (which corresponds to the "control value") in order minimize the energy consumption of the whole set of nodes while the application QoS is met. This objective is indeed an optimization problem that can be solved using Model Predictive Control. Actually, at each control sampling time, MPC minimizes a given cost function (possibly under constraints) over a control horizon in order to fix the control values. Due to the discrete nature of the functioning mode (on, of, sleep, unreachable), the optimization problem is a Mixed Integer Quadratic Programming (MIQP) one, the optimization variables being both boolean values (control value) and positive real values (available energy in the node battery) with bounds. Moreover, a set of constraints must be taken into account. The first subset is related to the remaining energy in the batteries that must be strictly positive to avoid battery damages (lower bound). Moreover, the remaining energy cannot be infinite and a maximum value cannot be exceeded. The second subset of constraints expresses that each node can be in a unique functioning mode. The last subset expresses the application QoS. The reader can refer to [7] where theoretical details are provided.

The control objectives can also be achieved using a Hybrid Dynamic System approach. Actually, the system under control is hybrid *per se*: the remaining energy in the node battery is conducted by differential equations while the functioning modes are discrete values. Moreover, a given node will experience "jumps" from one mode to another one, depending

TABLE I. POWER CONSUMPTION OF FLYPORT PLATFORM AND ENOCEAN TRANSCEIVER (Supply Voltage 3.3 V) [13], [14]

Mode	Power	Remarks
Wi-Fi connected	162, 70 mA	MCU *on* / Wi-Fi *on*, connected to access point
Wi-Fi not connected	39, 75mA	MCU *on* / Wi-Fi *on* but not connected
EnOcean *Rx*	61.21 mA	No Wi-Fi
EnOcean *Tx*	52.21 mA	No Wi-Fi
Hibernate	28,21 mA	MCU *on* and Wi-Fi *off*
Sleep	1,44 mA	MCU *off* and Wi-Fi *off*

on the controller decisions. This will modify the differential equation that models the node energy consumption. The reader can refer to [9] where theoretical details are provided.

Both controllers have been first designed in the Matlab environment, and evaluated in simulations. The numerical values used in simulation (e.g., maximum energy in the node batteries, energy consumption in each functioning mode) have been extracted from datasheets [13]. Then, the controllers have been written in python, and optimized to reach an efficient implementation in terms of computational time.

III. Implementation Description

The main objective of this work was to validate the theoretical and simulation results obtained with the energy management strategy at application level, on a real test-bed. This latter is now described, along with the data collection approach.

A. Test-bed description

The hardware test-bed consists of one sink, one router, and 6 sensor nodes spread over a given zone. The sensor nodes are the *Openpicus* Flyport Wi-Fi 802.11g [13] with either Wi-Fi or EnOCean TCM-310 [14] transceivers, leading to a heterogeneous network. Table I summarizes the power consumption of the Flyport platform. The *Openpicus* Flyport Wi-Fi 802.11g platforms embed a Microchip PIC 16-bits processor with a Wi-Fi radio module and ready-to-use protocol stacks. *Openpicus* provides a FreeRTOS-based framework implementing the CSMA-CA MAC protocol and the TCP transport protocol. Applications are written as FreeRTOS tasks.

When using Wi-Fi, *Openpicus* nodes form an infrastructure topology: they connect to one access point or router. This latter forwards all the received packets from/towards the sink. For the EnOcean protocol, an EnOcean transceiver is connected to the GPIOs of the Openpicus platform. This transceiver exhibits very low-power serial communication, that permits the exchange of very short frames. The EnOcean node communicates directly with the sink, this latter making use of an EnOcean USB dongle module.

B. Functioning mode definition

Two functioning modes and an *Unreachable* state are defined for each node, for both the Wi-Fi and the EnOcean transceiver:

- in *Mode 1* (*Active*), both the communication and sensing tasks are activated periodically. The sensing period is equal to the communication duty cycle $T_s = 1min$;
- in *Mode 2* (*Standby*), the node sensing unit is disabled. The node wakes-up periodically, as requested by the controller, to report to the sink its battery state-of-charge and to receive its functioning mode for the next period of time as computed by the controller. The communication period of a node in this mode is equal to the controller period $T_c = 1hour$;
- nodes enter the *Unreachable* state when they are unable to communicate with the sink due to network issues, hardware damage, or lack of energy.

When a node transmits a frame to the sink (e.g., sensed value, available energy) it waits for an answer. The answer can be an acknowledgement, a resynchronisation frame, or a command frame asking the node to change its functioning mode.

C. Application QoS

The application QoS is expressed as the minimum number of measurements that must be provided by the WSN to the application at each control sampling time. It is related to the *mission* that must be performed by the controller.

In the scenario implemented, d_1 nodes must be assigned to the *Active* mode in order to meet the mission. The mission can also change dynamically, i.e., depending on a time schedule or on external events. This dynamic feature permits following the needs of the application over time. In the present setup, we consider that during working hours, $d_1 = 3$ nodes must be in *Mode 1* while during the night periods d_1 is equal to 1.

The lifetime of the WSN is defined as the period of time during which the mission can be fulfilled. This corresponds to the time when the number of reachable nodes becomes smaller than the minimum number of required active nodes d_1.

D. Data collection

To collect data from the sensor nodes, the nodes must be encapsulated in LINC. This is made easy using the PUTUTU framework [15] that provides generic LINC objects to speed up integration of sensor and actuator technologies. Fig. 2 illustrates the LINC application put in place. The application is composed of three LINC objects all running in the sink:

- the *openpicus_wifi_object* acts as a TCP server that listens for connections from Wi-Fi nodes. It stores measurements and battery information sent by these nodes;
- the *openpicus_enocean_object* opens a serial connection with the EnOcean dongle to communicate with the EnOcean nodes. It stores the measurements and battery information sent by these nodes;
- the *controller_object* collects information about the battery status of all reachable nodes (from the two other objects). It periodically calls the controller to get the new functioning mode for each node. The updates are propagated to the `openpicus_wifi_object` and the `openpicus_enocean_object` that send the new functioning mode to each node if it has changed.

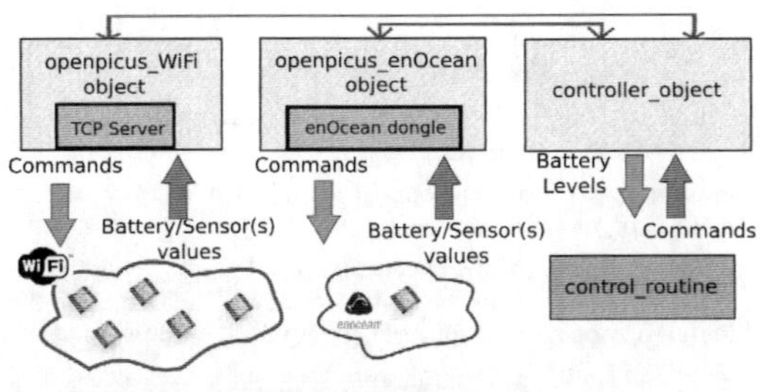

Figure 2. LINC Application for integration

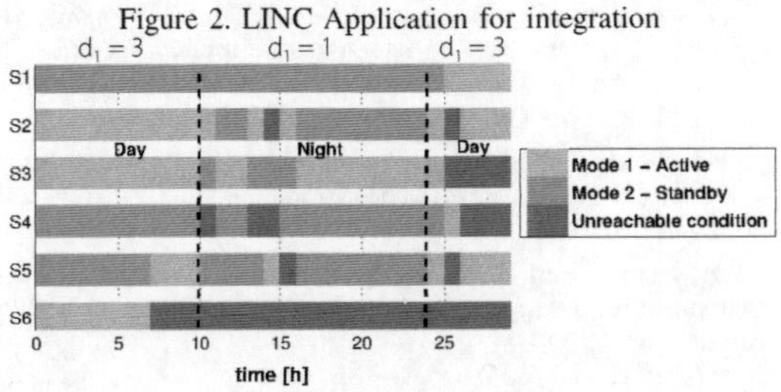

Figure 3. Functioning mode of each sensor node vs. time. Example with MPC strategy

The first time the nodes communicate with the sink, their clock is synchronized with the sink clock and keep synchronized according to the synchronization period. This latter can be adjusted dynamically. Empirical experiments have shown that a synchronization period of approx. $6hours$ is appropriate for this implementation. This synchronization period leads to a maximum clock drift of a couple of seconds, which is acceptable given the dynamics of the application.

IV. Experimental Results

An experiment of 30 $hours$ duration was run to evaluate both power control strategies at application level. The experiments started at $T_0 = 8\ a.m.$ S6 is the EnOCean node, the other ones being Wi-Fi. During working hours (resp. night period), 3 (resp. 1) sensors must be *Active*. Fig. 3 shows the functioning modes of the sensor nodes during the experiment when the MPC strategy is implemented. As can be seen, the mission is fulfilled during all the experiment duration. It can be observed that S6 became *Unreachable* after 6 hours, when its battery reached the minimum energy level. S4 was disconnected twice from the network at time10 hours during 1 hour, and at time 14 hours during 2 hours. The disconnection is due to radio channel perturbations. The same phenomenon happens with nodes 2 and 5. When a node falls in the *Unreachable* state, it is no longer taken into account by the controller. When the controller receives again information related to the remaining energy of this sensor node, it adds the node again in the set of nodes to be controlled. Note that the nodes do not possess "wake-up-on-event" capability. Therefore, if an active node becomes unreachable during a control period T_c, the controller will switches a node from mode 2 to mode 1 when T_c is elapsed. This means that we may experience periods of time no longer than T_c when the mission is not strictly speaking fulfilled. If the nodes could be woken up at any time by an external mechanism, before the end of the duty cycle, this issue would be solved.

In the present scenario, harvesting systems are not integrated in the sensor nodes. When available, they can help a node re-enter the "game" when it has regained enough energy to communicate and be placed by the controller in the *Active* or *Standby* mode.

TABLE II. SCALABILITY OF THE MPC AND HDS APPROACHES

Number of nodes	6	18	54
MPC Computational Time $[sec]$	0.051	0.052	0.053
HDS Computational Time $[sec]$	0.004	0.043	0.375

Using the MPC (resp. HDS) approach, the lifetime is increased up to $36,7\%$ (resp. 30.8%) when compared to the "basic" control. This latter corresponds to the situation where only the mission is considered, without any concern regarding energy consumption.

The scalability of the MPC (when a MILP solver is used) and HDS approaches has been analyzes. Table II shows the controller computational time obtained in the Matlab environment (on an Intel Xeon Processor E5620 with 12MB of cache, 2.50 GHz) for 6, 18 and 54 sensor nodes. Notice that the HDS computational time becomes higher that the MPC one due to state space explosion.

V. Related Work

To the authors' knowledge, most of research works related to power management in WSN focus on the protocol stack [5], [6] or on the node hardware optimization. The application needs are seldom taken into account in the energy/power management strategies [16]. This latter proposes a Dynamic Power Management (DPM) strategy at node level that takes into account application constraints to keep the sensor node, as much as possible, in sleep or idle mode without losing the real time responsiveness of the application. The DPM strategy is based on a hybrid automaton. It is implemented within the node. Its main advantage compared to our approach is that the control strategy is fully distributed. However, the DPM strategy does not have knowledge of the WSN state and of the changes in the application needs. Moreover, having the DPM strategy embedded within the node induces overconsumption. Note that there is no real implementation of the DPM strategy proposed in [16]. The present paper relies on a middleware layer to apply the control approach. The controller collects information from the nodes and it can fix some parameters (e.g., the functioning mode of each node). Middlewares and frameworks have been previously proposed with similar purposes. PyFUNS [17] is a framework that modifies network parameters according to the application. In PyFUNS, applications are written as python scripts. Then, the framework calibrates the network for energy efficiency. However, it is suitable only for nodes running the ContikiOS. The architecture described here may support any operating system and communication stack thanks to LINC. MILAN [18] is a middleware that continuously controls the network functionality according to the application demands. The implementation of such mechanism is very complex given the huge number of parameters that must be taken into account. Moreover, it seems difficult to integrate a control strategy with MILAN where several assumptions are made on the WSN behaviour. Other coordination middlewares, also using associative memory, have been used for WSN, such as Agimone [19], TeenyLIME [20] or Agilla [21]. However, they do not offer the same properties as LINC (e.g., distributed transactions, support of many protocols and integration frameworks). Moreover, these works focus on developing applications.

VI. Conclusions

This paper presents the implementation of control strategies (MPC and HDS) for global energy management of a WSN. The implementation uses the LINC coordination middleware. The different aspects taken into account for the proper implementation, such as data collection and synchronisation, are described Experimental results on a star topology are reported. The functioning mode of each reacheable node is set according to decisions taken by the global controller whose objective is to minimize the energy consumption of the whole set of sensor nodes while ensuring the application Quality of Service. Simulation results show that the control strategies are scalable. The control approach is based on Model Predictive Control. This permits to add new constraints or control objectives if needed. LINC has been used in various application domains (e.g., smart buildings, smart cities or smart parking). Hence the proposed approach may be extended to other application domains.

Future work directions include the implementation of the control strategy on a WSN with a more complex topology, such as mesh networks. Such implementation will require a deeper knowledge about the network status, i.e., routing information and current topology.

Acknowledgment

This work has been partly funded by the Artemis ARROWHEAD nb332987 and the H2020 TOPAs nb676760 projects.

References

[1] J. Yick, B. Mukherjee, and D. Ghosal, "Wireless sensor network survey," Computer Networks, vol. 52, no. 12, 2008, pp. 2292 – 2330.

[2] F. D. Hutu, A. Khoumeri, G. Villemaud, and J.-M. Gorce, "A new wake-up radio architecture for wireless sensor networks," EURASIP Journal on Wireless Communications and Networking, Oct. 2014, p. 177.

[3] M. Hempstead, M. J. Lyons, D. M. Brooks, and G.-Y. Wei, "Survey of hardware systems for wireless sensor networks." J. Low Power Electronics, 2008, pp. 11–20.

[4] Y. Akgul et al., "Power management through dvfs and dynamic body biasing in fd-soi circuits," in Proceedings of the 51st Annual Design Automation Conference. ACM, 2014, pp. 1–6.

[5] G. Anastasi, M. Conti, M. D. Francesco, and A. Passarella, "Energy conservation in wireless sensor networks: A survey," Ad Hoc Networks, vol. 7, 2009, pp. 537 – 568.

[6] N. Pantazis and D. Vergados, "A survey on power control issues in wireless sensor networks," IEEE Communications Surveys, vol. 9, 2007, pp. 86 – 107.

[7] O. Mokrenko et al., "Dynamic power management in a wireless sensor network using predictive control," in 40th Annual Conference of the IEEE Industrial Electronics Society, 2014.

[8] Mokrenko et al., "Design and implementation of a predictive control strategy for power management of a wireless sensor network," in IEEE European Control Conference, 2015.

[9] O. Mokrenko, C. Albea, L. Zaccarian, and S. Lesecq, "Feedback scheduling of sensor network activity using hybrid dynamical system approach," in 54th IEEE Conference on Decision and Control, 2015.

[10] M. Louvel and F. Pacull, "Linc: A compact yet powerful coordination environment," in Coordination Models and Languages, ser. Lecture Notes in Computer Science. Springer, 2014, pp. 83–98.

[11] I. F. Akyildiz, W. Su, Y. Sankarasubramaniam, and E. Cayirci, "Wireless sensor networks: a survey," Computer networks, 2002, pp. 393–422.

[12] N. Carriero and D. Gelernter, "Linda in context," Commun. ACM, vol. 32, 1989, pp. 444–458.

[13] openpicus, "http://www.openpicus.com, 2015." [Online]. Available: http://www.openpicus.com

[14] enocean, "www.enocean.com." [Online]. Available: www.enocean.com/en/enocean_modules/tcm-310/

[15] F. Pacull et al., "Self-organisation for building automation systems: Middleware linc as an integration tool," in IECON 2013-39th Annual Conference on IEEE Industrial Electronics Society. Vienna, Austria: IEEE, 2013, pp. 7726–7732.

[16] R. Passos, C. Coelho, A. Loureiro, and R. Mini, "Dynamic power management in wireless sensor networks: An application-driven approach," in Second Annual Conference on Wireless On-demand Network Systems and Services (WONS'05), pp. 109–118.

[17] S. Bocchino, S. Fedor, and M. Petracca, "Pyfuns: A python framework for ubiquitous networked sensors," in Wireless Sensor Networks. Springer, 2015, pp. 1–18.

[18] W. B. Heinzelman, A. L. Murphy, H. S. Carvalho, M. Perillo et al., "Middleware to support sensor network applications," Network, IEEE, vol. 18, no. 1, 2004, pp. 6–14.

[19] G. Hackmann, C.-L. Fok, G.-C. Roman, and C. Lu, "Agimone: Middleware support for seamless integration of sensor and ip networks," in Distributed Computing in Sensor Systems. Springer, 2006, pp. 101–118.

[20] P. Costa, L. Mottola, A. L. Murphy, and G. P. Picco, "Teenylime: transiently shared tuple space middleware for wireless sensor networks," in Proceedings of the international workshop on Middleware for sensor networks. ACM, 2006, pp. 43–48.

[21] Fok, Chien-Liang and Roman, Gruia-Catalin and Lu, Chenyang, "Agilla: A mobile agent middleware for self-adaptive wireless sensor networks," ACM Transactions on Autonomous and Adaptive Systems (TAAS), vol. 4, no. 3, 2009, p. 16.

Validating a Wireless Protocol Implementation at Binary Level through Simulation Using High Level Description of Protocol Properties in Light Esterel

Calypso Barnes*†, François Verdier†, Alain Pegatoquet†, Daniel Gaffé†, Jean-Marie Cottin*
*Électricité de France R&D, Chatou, France
Email: first_name.last_name@edf.fr
†Université Côte d'Azur, CNRS, LEAT, France
Email: first_name.last_name@unice.fr

***Abstract*—The development and debugging of a wireless protocol are complex tasks that many face in the industry and academia. This paper aims at facilitating those tasks by proposing a simulation framework that is capable of verifying and validating a protocol stack at binary level. This simulation framework is based on the co-simulation of QEMU and SystemC, which are interfaced through TLMu. An observer module was developed to analyze the traffic in the simulated network, which contains protocol properties modeled in Light Esterel to check that the frame exchanges comply with the protocol properties, in order to validate the protocol implementation.We describe the development of the simulation framework and its node models capable of executing the protocol's binary stack. We then explain the modeling of protocol properties in Light Esterel and their insertion in the simulation framework. Finally, we test the OCARI protocol for wireless sensor networks in the simulation framework.**

Keywords*-*Network Simulation; Co-Simulation; Protocol Verification; Wireless Sensor Networks; Embedded Software

I. INTRODUCTION

Wireless Sensor Networks (WSN) are an expanding technology employed in a wide and growing variety of applications. To communicate, they use a set of rules and conventions called protocol. Developing, debugging and deploying wireless sensor network protocols are complex tasks, especially when these protocols are aimed at applications requiring a high reliability, such as medical or industrial applications [1]. In such applications, a lost packet, a missed alarm or a sensor blocked due to interrupts can potentially lead to devastating consequences. That is why all wireless protocols, especially the ones aimed at more critical applications, have to be extensively tested and validated before they can be industrialized. While testing and debugging of WSN protocols heavily rely on testbeds, this phase can be facilitated by simulation.

In this paper we present a simulation framework for WSN based on QEMU (Quick EMUlator) [2] and SystemC co-simulation that aims at validating, verifying and debugging a wireless communication protocol by emulating the execution of the protocol's binary stack on a detailed model of the node's hardware. One of the main novelties of this framework is the addition of an observer module, containing protocol properties modeled with Light Esterel [3], that can detect whether a protocol property has been violated during simulation, halting the simulation to pinpoint the source of the bug thanks to the debugging capabilities provided. This approach will be tested on a protocol named OCARI (Open Communication protocol for Ad hoc Reliable industrial Instrumentation) [4] based on the IEEE 802.15.4 standard, which is currently in its pre-industrialization phase.

In Section II, we will explain the complexity in validating a protocol stack and the need to precisely model the hardware platform upon which the stack is executed. We will then describe in Section III the new simulation environment we developed including an observer module to verify protocol properties, and in Section IV we will explain how the protocol's properties are modeled in Light Esterel and inserted into simulation. Finally, in Section V, we will provide our simulation results that demonstrate the functionality of the simulation framework we developed. We then draw conclusions and discuss further improvements to be made on this simulation framework in Section VI.

II. THE COMPLEXITY OF WSN PROTOCOL VALIDATION

Protocols are geared to serve a number of needs and constraints, some of which are contradictory, such as tolerance to RF medium temporary disturbances, deterministic behaviors, a good link budget, power saving techniques and security. The resulting compromise is complex to implement and also to validate. It is highly likely that even after a communication protocol has been industrialized, some bugs might remain. According to [5], the average of bugs in released industrial software is about 15 to 50 per 1000 lines of delivered code. This is why finding new solutions for debugging and validation of code is of great interest to both industrialists and academia.

Validation heavily relies on human driven testing of the real platform and can take a very long time in the project. Testbeds are long to set up as each node has to be handled individually for software deployment and debugging. They also suffer from scenario limitations when it comes to the number of nodes in the network and their mobility or the environmental conditions (obstacles, interference, etc.). That is why simulation is an important step in the development of wireless protocols, to better diagnose software problems before the deployment on real hardware.

Simulation can offer better flexibility on environmental conditions, as well as the possibility to test attacks on the network more easily, to validate the security aspects of the protocol. Another one of the great benefits of validating a stack on a simulator is that the scenario execution can be replayed exactly, while usual hardware test-beds cannot truly reproduce the same run, due to the asynchronous nature of the system: the CPUs of network nodes do not share the same clock and even show clock drifts. Moreover, hardware debugging is intrusive as it modifies the execution timing of the software being inspected.

Validation through simulation of a protocol at behavioral level or at C code level might be faster than validation at binary code level, but it is less reliable. Indeed, validating the source code or a behavioral model of the protocol only provides a very crude notion of time [6]. Therefore, it cannot precisely model interrupts and multitasking for instance. Yet temporary errors that are hard to reproduce in hardware validation may have their origin in wrong timer programming, missed interrupts or interrupts taken too late leading to task scheduling issues, buffer overflows and packet loss. That is why validating the binary code on a realistic platform model is a much more reliable approach.

Moreover, a simulator capable of executing the protocol's binary code has the advantage of being compatible with testing protocols for which only the binary code is provided without the source files, to test that the specifications of this protocol are met. This is why we focused on simulators capable of executing the protocols stacks binary code for our purpose of protocol validation. Only a few existing network simulators offer this advantage. To our knowledge, these simulators are TOSSIM, ATEMU, AVRORA, COOJA and Worldsens (WSim/WSNet) [7]. However, they all suffer from a few limitations, mainly in terms of the type of node platform modeled. Indeed, Atemu emulates MICA-2 motes, Cooja associated to MSPSIM emulates nodes based on the Texas Instruments MSP430 processor, and Worldsens is also limited to models of the MSP430 processor based nodes. Moreover, Avrora does not model mobility or clock drift and Tossim is not capable of capturing properties related to interruptions or the codes execution time [8]. This is the reason why we decided to develop a new simulation framework that could be more easily adapted to a larger variety of hardware platforms. To ensure the durability of this framework, we focused on open source solutions.

III. Modeling a precise node hardware model with QEMU and SystemC

Our hardware platform model was developed with QEMU and SystemC. We decided to use TLMu as the interface between both simulation environments because it is more easily adaptable to our platform model.

A. *TLMu - An Interface between QEMU and SystemC*

Based on our need to execute the binary code of protocols for a wide range of platform, we have decided to create a simulation environment based on QEMU (Quick EMUlator) [2], a popular open source environment developed in C for the rapid prototyping of virtual platforms. We have also decided to associate QEMU with SystemC, a popular C++ library to model the architecture and behavior of hardware components, to model parts of the hardware platforms absent in QEMU and the network.

TLMu [9] is a wrapper for QEMU that integrates with SystemC TLM-2.0 models, which handles the communications and time synchronization between both simulation cores. It is based on the open source hardware/software emulation framework called QEMU-SystemC [10], which was proposed in 2007 by Màrius Montón and GreenSoCs. This project aimed at attaching devices modeled in SystemC to QEMU, with QEMU as the simulation master and SystemC as the simulation slave.

An advantage of TLMu is the possibility to have multiple QEMU platforms connected to SystemC in the same simulation. It can provide either only the CPU cores or a more complete system, and the CPU emulators are built as shared libraries, one library per supported architecture (e.g., libtlmu-arm.so). Each CPU executes as a different thread in the same process as SystemC.

1) Communications between QEMU and SystemC: The wrapper loads QEMU as a shared object and accesses QEMU's main function by a loaded function pointer from the shared object. The wrapper defines callback functions. In QEMU, the SystemC environment is registered as a memory region, which when accessed uses a callback to access the TLM memory bus model using TLM transactions to read or write memory spaces in SystemC. This allows switching the control between QEMU and SystemC. A callback function also handles the communications of events to QEMU, such as interrupts from SystemC to QEMU, or reset, sleep and wake up commands.

2) Handling time and synchronization: TLMu is run by using QEMU's icount feature which means that QEMU's virtual clock (vm_clock) advances according to the number of instructions executed. In SystemC, time progresses according to the information provided by the hardware platform. TLMu may trigger a synchronization between QEMU and SystemC in various cases: when the CPU makes I/O accesses into the main emulator, when the CPU gets interrupted or after the execution of a translation block. To trigger a synchronization, QEMU calls a callback sync_time function of TLMu, and passes as a function parameter its vm_clock time. If the sync_time function estimates that enough time has passed since the last synchronization, it triggers a new synchronization. The time between synchronizations is handled by the TLM quantum keeper [11].

B. Modeling the node's hardware platform and the network

The binary stack to be tested implements the OCARI protocol on an Atmel SAM3S platform based on the ARM Cortex-M3 processor and an IEEE 802.15.4 radio module, the Atmel AT86RF233, which are connected through an SPI interface, as well as three pins for interrupt notification, reset, and sleep/wakeup command.

To develop a model of the SAM3S platform, we reused the Cortex-M3 CPU model that is available in QEMU. The memories and different peripherals of the SAM3S (timers, power management controller, SPI, etc.) were modeled in the SystemC environment according to their behavioral description, which is found in the SAM3S datasheet provided by Atmel [12]. Only the peripherals that are enabled by the Power Management Controller during the execution of OCARI's binary code, and therefore useful to the execution of OCARI's protocol, are modeled, as seen in Figure 1.

The peripherals are connected through a TLM bus and communicate through loosely timed blocking TLM transactions. These transactions are objects that are defined by TLM 2.0 containing amongst other a data pointer, a data length and an address. They are sent between different SystemC modules from TLM initiator sockets to TLM target sockets. At the reception of a transaction in a target socket, a `b_transport` function is called defining what action to take.

The interrupt mechanism was not fully implemented by TLMu, though callbacks were provided as an interface between SystemC and QEMU. In our implementation, we reused the model of the Nested Vectored Interrupt Controller (NVIC) for the ARM Cortex-M3 that was already available in QEMU to complete the interrupt mechanism.

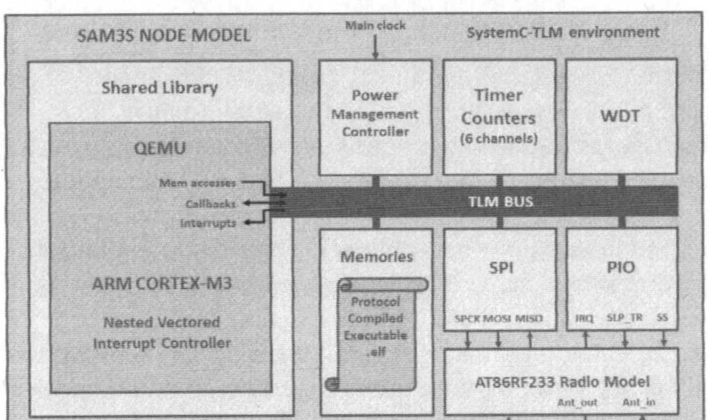

Figure 1. Simplified block diagram of the SAM3S platform modeled with SystemC and QEMU interfaced by TLMu.

The radio was also modeled in SystemC according to the AT86RF233 datasheet. The protocol controls the radio module through an SPI interface to read or write the radio registers or the frame buffer. A PIO pin is also used so that the radio can send back interrupts to the SAM3S platform. Frames that are sent out are sent as TLM transactions through the Antenna_out TLM socket. The frame is modeled as an array containing the bytes corresponding to the frame length and the Mac Protocol Data Unit (MPDU). Incoming frames are received through the Antenna_in TLM socket to later be interpreted by the protocol stack if the frame passes the radio filter.

It was verified that the model of the SAM3S and the radio were functionally correct by comparing frames output by the simulator to frames from real exchanges between nodes in a lab for similar scenarios [13]. It is possible to instantiate several models of the SAM3S platform modeled with QEMU, as well as more simple nodes that do not execute the binary code of a protocol but mimic the protocol's behavior.

In our simulation framework, all the node models are connected through a radio link module as shown in Figure 2. The radio link module relays the frames from the sender node to the other nodes according to the topology defined by the user. The user can also define times when new nodes will be added to the topology or times when a radio link between two nodes will be lost or created.

The radio link module also contains another module called the observer, which analyzes the frames exchanged as described in Section IV.

To be able to observe in an aesthetic manner the frames exchanged by the different nodes in simulation, the frames that go through the radio link module are saved in a pcap (packet capture) format file by using functions from the libpcap library to create packet headers and to encapsulate each packet. The frames in the pcap file can then be observed in a network analyzer, such as Wireshark for example. Using the same libpcap library, the radio link module is also able to extract frame packets from pcap files to generate traffic in the network, with the possibility of using frames recorded from exchanges between nodes in a lab.

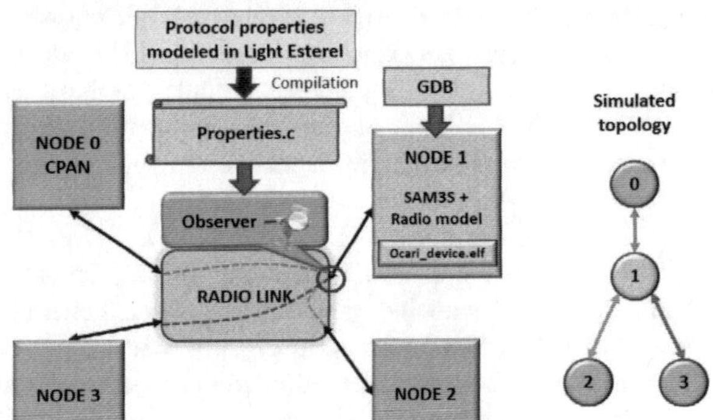

Figure 2. Connection between node models through a radio link module containing the observer focused here on node 1.

IV. Verifying Protocol Properties during Simulation

The verification of protocol properties is an important feature of the simulation framework. To implement this feature, we have developed an observer module.

A. *The observer's role*

The observer module is integrated into the simulator to analyze the frames exchanged between nodes. To have the capability of analyzing any frame that is exchanged in the network, the observer module is contained in the radio link module. Its role is to halt simulation if a protocol property is violated, so that the source of the bug causing the violation may be pinpointed thanks to the debugging capabilities provided by the simulation framework. The observer focuses on the frames sent and received from a specific node which is running the binary protocol stack under test.

B. *Modeling and integrating protocol properties into simulation*

We searched for a good solution to model protocol properties that could be easily introduced into our simulation environment. A communication protocol is considered to be a reactive system, and general purpose programming languages are not suited to design reactive systems: they are clearly inefficient to deal with the inherent complexity of such systems [14]. That is why we looked into using a language dedicated to reactive systems. Various synchronous languages have been designed such as Esterel [15]. Based on concurrency and synchronicity, they are model-based languages to allow formal verification of the system behavior. Their execution model is simple: first, the initial state is initialized and then, for each input event set, outputs are computed and then state is updated [14].

1) Light Esterel: Light Esterel (LE) [3] is a reactive synchronous programming language derived from Esterel V5 [15]. Just like Esterel, it is able to maintain a permanent interaction with its environment, such as communication protocols, man-machine interface drivers or VLSI chips.

The Light Esterel language units are named modules. Communication takes place between modules or between a module and its environment. Sub-systems communicates via events. The module interface declares the set of input events it reacts to and the set of output events it emits.

The textual or graphical Light Esterel views gives the possibility to write compact specifications for very complex systems. A system with thousands of states can generally be specified by an Esterel program of only a few hundred lines thanks to the explicit preemption and parallel operator. Moreover, this deterministic concurrent programming language can be compiled into a Finite State Machine (FSM) classically represented by an automaton. LE automata are Mealy machines and they have a set of input signals, which can be valued, to define transition triggers and a set of output signals that can be emitted when a transition is raised.

Consequently, Light Esterel programs can also be compiled into popular languages such as C, VHDL, CSharp, or other synchronous languages like Lustre. In our case we used the C program compilation of Light Esterel.

As Light Esterel has been designed to model reactive systems such as communication protocols, and because of the ease of insertion into the simulation framework, we decided to use this language to model protocol properties defined by the protocol's specifications.

2) Integration of protocol properties in the simulation framework: The objective of the observer module is to verify that the implementation of a protocol complies with its specified properties. The properties that we want to check are modeled in a LE program.

When the Light Esterel program is compiled into C to be integrated in the simulator, functions are defined where the function parameters are the inputs of the LE program and pointers to the output values.

The observer dissects the frames sent and received from a specific node that is running the binary protocol stack under test. If the information contained in those frames are relevant to the modeled protocol property, the corresponding Light Esterel C program function is called with the corresponding boolean presence predicat set to 1, followed by the signal value if the signal is valued. After the function call, the Light Esterel program outputs are checked to see whether the property has been violated, or if the conditions of the property have been met. The latter information helps in statistics on property coverage. Indeed, in certain scenarios, some properties might not be checked at all while other properties might be checked numerous times. The simulation scenarios have to be adapted in this case to make sure that all properties have been extensively put under test.

V. Experimental Results and Interpretation

To demonstrate the functionality of the simulator we developed, we tested it with the OCARI protocol, to verify that the implementation of the protocol complies with the properties from its specifications. Some simple properties that we desired to check were modeled in LE, compiled into C, and inserted into the simulator. We ran different scenarios to check that the protocol properties we modeled weren't detected as violated by the simulator. Here we describe a particular scenario where an attack on the network was simulated to see how the nodes running the OCARI protocol binary stack reacted.

In the scenario in question, 3 nodes running the OCARI protocol on full SAM3S platform models are instantiated, one is the network coordinator (CPAN) loaded with the ocari_CPAN.elf binary code, and the other two nodes are running the ocari_DEVICE.elf binary code. A fourth node is added to the simulation that will act as a node attacking

No.	Time	Source	Destination	Protocol	Info
474	24.195097	0x0001		Ocari	Ocari Beacon, Coord: 3, T1T0: 1250, Contention: 200, Colored: 100, Color Max: 3
475	24.207537	0x0002		Ocari	Ocari Beacon, Coord: 3, T1T0: 1250, Contention: 200, Colored: 100, Color Max: 3
476	24.219978	0x0003		Ocari	Ocari Beacon, Coord: 3, T1T0: 1250, Contention: 200, Colored: 100, Color Max: 3
477	24.245811	0x0001	Broadcast	Opera	Opera Hello, SeqNum: 42, Sender: 0x0001, Sym: 1, Asym: 0
478	24.259961	0x0003	Broadcast	Opera	Opera Hello, SeqNum: 40, Sender: 0x0003, Sym: 1, Asym: 0
479	24.420573	0x0003	0x0001	Connexion	Origin Address: 85:3f:4c:09:a1:cc:00:95, Random Value: 78,169, Quality: Good
480	24.420673			IEEE 802.	Ack
481	24.449789	0x0002	0x0001	Connexion	Origin Address: bb:02:26:2e:52:0b:81:37, Random Value: 17,509, Quality: Good
482	24.449889			IEEE 802.	Ack
483	24.454131	0x0003	0x0001	Connexion	Origin Address: 85:3f:4c:09:a1:cc:00:95, Random Value: 78,169, Quality: Good
484	24.454231			IEEE 802.	Ack
485	24.621632	0x0001		Ocari	Ocari Beacon, Coord: 3, T1T0: 1250, Contention: 200, Colored: 100, Color Max: 3
486	24.634073	0x0002		Ocari	Ocari Beacon, Coord: 3, T1T0: 1250, Contention: 200, Colored: 100, Color Max: 3
487	24.646514	0x0003		Ocari	Ocari Beacon, Coord: 3, T1T0: 1250, Contention: 200, Colored: 100, Color Max: 3
488	24.716770	0x0002	Broadcast	Opera	Opera Hello, SeqNum: 42, Sender: 0x0002, Sym: 2, Asym: 0
489	24.847110	0x0003	0x0001	Connexion	Origin Address: 85:3f:4c:09:a1:cc:00:95, Random Value: 76,410, Quality: Good
490	24.847210			IEEE 802.	Ack
491	24.876323	0x0002	0x0001	Connexion	Origin Address: bb:02:26:2e:52:0b:81:37, Random Value: 39,951, Quality: Good
492	24.876423			IEEE 802.	Ack
493	24.880665	0x0003	0x0001	Connexion	Origin Address: 85:3f:4c:09:a1:cc:00:95, Random Value: 76,410, Quality: Good
494	24.880765			IEEE 802.	Ack

Figure 3. Simulation output frame traces from 2 regular OCARI protocol cycles viewed with Wireshark.

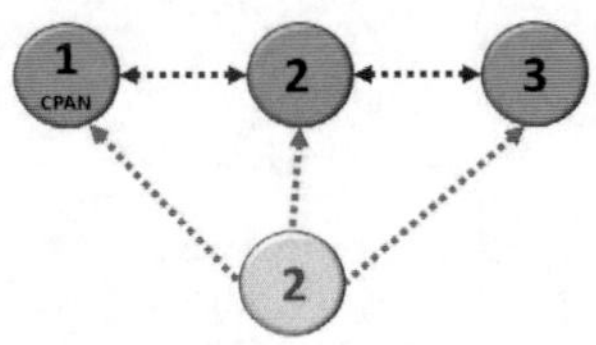

Figure 4. Network topology.

the network. The topology of the network can be seen in Figure 4.

The simulation was set up so that the attacker node is a simple node that copies a frame from the beginning of the simulation, more specifically a Beacon type frame from node 2. After 25 seconds of simulation, the attacker nodes starts sending the Beacon frame copied from node 2 at constant intervals of 50 ms. The fake beacon is received by all three other nodes in the network.

The simulation results can be observed through the terminal where the simulation was launched, but the frame exchanges can also be viewed through Wireshark, as they are saved in a pcap format. A plugin was created in Wireshark to dissect OCARI frames to correctly display frame information. Before the intervention of the attacker node, no anomaly is detected in the exchanges. In Figure 3, two cycles can be seen (a cycle beginning with a beacon frame from the CPAN) before the attacker node starts sending frames, with nodes 3 and 2 correctly relaying data to the CPAN, which are Connexion type frames with random data values for this particular application.

25 seconds into simulation, the attacker node starts sending Beacon frames pretending to be node 2. The simulation was stopped at 26.754397 seconds, as the observer in the simulator detected and indicated a "Hello" property violation from node 2. The property in question states that once nodes are associated to the CPAN, a Hello message must be sent every 2 cycles. In the frame traces observed on Wireshark, we can see that nodes 2 and 3 completely stop sending frames after 25.55445 seconds of simulation time. In Figure 5, we can observe the two last cycles before the simulation stopped where no Hello messages were sent by node 2 and 3, causing the Hello property to be violated. The violation is detected as the last Beacon frame from the CPAN is received indicating the beginning of a new cycle without a Hello frame having been received.

To know what went wrong with node 2, and why it stopped sending frames, we used GDB to know which function of the ocari_DEVICE.elf code was being executed by node 2 when the simulation stopped. We have observed that node 2 was stuck in a while loop waiting for a timer to expire, and that the while loop was initiated by the mac_wrapper_reset_MaCARI function, indicating that the node couldn't handle the frames sent by the attacker node and had to reset itself.

This experiment is an example of how this simulation environment facilitates testing protocols under more flexible scenarios and environmental conditions. Indeed, adding such an attacker node in simulation was relatively easy and would have been more complicated in a lab environment. The version of the OCARI protocol has been updated since this test with enhanced security. Not all protocol properties were inserted in simulation for these tests, only a few that we wished to check. Extra properties will be modeled and added into simulation in the future, in order to validate them under very diverse scenarios to explore the limits of the protocol.

VI. CONCLUSION AND PERSPECTIVES

In this paper, we presented a simulation framework based on QEMU/SystemC co-simulation and Light Esterel property modeling for the validation of wireless sensor network protocol implementations against their specified properties. We also showed the possibility of simulating an attack on

526	25.900000	0x0002		Ocari	Ocari Beacon, Coord: 2, T1T0: 550, Contention: 200, Colored: 100, Color Max: 0, Bitmap: 0x01
527	25.901230	0x0001		Ocari	Ocari Beacon, Coord: 3, T1T0: 1250, Contention: 200, Colored: 100, Color Max: 3, Bitmap: 0x01
528	25.943008	0x0001	Broadcast	Opera	Opera Hello, SeqNum: 44, Sender: 0x0001, Sym: 1, Asym: 0
529	25.950000	0x0002		Ocari	Ocari Beacon, Coord: 2, T1T0: 550, Contention: 200, Colored: 100, Color Max: 0, Bitmap: 0x01
530	26.000000	0x0002		Ocari	Ocari Beacon, Coord: 2, T1T0: 550, Contention: 200, Colored: 100, Color Max: 0, Bitmap: 0x01
531	26.050000	0x0002		Ocari	Ocari Beacon, Coord: 2, T1T0: 550, Contention: 200, Colored: 100, Color Max: 0, Bitmap: 0x01
532	26.100000	0x0002		Ocari	Ocari Beacon, Coord: 2, T1T0: 550, Contention: 200, Colored: 100, Color Max: 0, Bitmap: 0x01
533	26.150000	0x0002		Ocari	Ocari Beacon, Coord: 2, T1T0: 550, Contention: 200, Colored: 100, Color Max: 0, Bitmap: 0x01
534	26.200000	0x0002		Ocari	Ocari Beacon, Coord: 2, T1T0: 550, Contention: 200, Colored: 100, Color Max: 0, Bitmap: 0x01
535	26.250000	0x0002		Ocari	Ocari Beacon, Coord: 2, T1T0: 550, Contention: 200, Colored: 100, Color Max: 0, Bitmap: 0x01
536	26.300000	0x0002		Ocari	Ocari Beacon, Coord: 2, T1T0: 550, Contention: 200, Colored: 100, Color Max: 0, Bitmap: 0x01
537	26.327774	0x0001		Ocari	Ocari Beacon, Coord: 3, T1T0: 1250, Contention: 200, Colored: 100, Color Max: 3, Bitmap: 0x01
538	26.350000	0x0002		Ocari	Ocari Beacon, Coord: 2, T1T0: 550, Contention: 200, Colored: 100, Color Max: 0, Bitmap: 0x01
539	26.400000	0x0002		Ocari	Ocari Beacon, Coord: 2, T1T0: 550, Contention: 200, Colored: 100, Color Max: 0, Bitmap: 0x01
540	26.450000	0x0002		Ocari	Ocari Beacon, Coord: 2, T1T0: 550, Contention: 200, Colored: 100, Color Max: 0, Bitmap: 0x01
541	26.500000	0x0002		Ocari	Ocari Beacon, Coord: 2, T1T0: 550, Contention: 200, Colored: 100, Color Max: 0, Bitmap: 0x01
542	26.550000	0x0002		Ocari	Ocari Beacon, Coord: 2, T1T0: 550, Contention: 200, Colored: 100, Color Max: 0, Bitmap: 0x01
543	26.600000	0x0002		Ocari	Ocari Beacon, Coord: 2, T1T0: 550, Contention: 200, Colored: 100, Color Max: 0, Bitmap: 0x01
544	26.650000	0x0002		Ocari	Ocari Beacon, Coord: 2, T1T0: 550, Contention: 200, Colored: 100, Color Max: 0, Bitmap: 0x01
545	26.700000	0x0002		Ocari	Ocari Beacon, Coord: 2, T1T0: 550, Contention: 200, Colored: 100, Color Max: 0, Bitmap: 0x01
546	26.750000	0x0002		Ocari	Ocari Beacon, Coord: 2, T1T0: 550, Contention: 200, Colored: 100, Color Max: 0, Bitmap: 0x01
547	26.754397	0x0001		Ocari	Ocari Beacon, Coord: 3, T1T0: 1250, Contention: 200, Colored: 100, Color Max: 3, Bitmap: 0x01

Figure 5. Simulation traces from the two last OCARI protocol cycles before the property violation viewed with Wireshark.

the network to find weaknesses in the protocol and fix them. This simulation framework still needs some more development but shows promising results.

Future improvements on the simulation framework will include random test generation and the possibility to reproduce scenarios played out on testbeds with real nodes using the exchange traces in pcap format. There will be improvements on the radio link module to represent more diverse environmental conditions and packet loss. To obtain a better scalability, we also wish to introduce a frame generator that imitates the behavior of several nodes running the protocol under test, in order to stimulate one node that is running the protocol's binary code on a full platform model.

Verifying that the execution of the protocol respects all of its defined properties in a wide range of scenario will prove that the protocol is reliable, and will facilitate its industrialization. With this simulation framework, the great number of hardware platforms supported by the open source tools used extends the approach to a wide range of protocols for all kinds of networked embedded systems.

REFERENCES

[1] P. Suriyachai, U. Roedig, and A. Scott, "A survey of mac protocols for mission-critical applications in wireless sensor networks," *IEEE Communications Surveys & Tutorials*, vol. 14, no. 2, pp. 240–264, 2012.

[2] F. Bellard, "Qemu, a fast and portable dynamic translator." in *USENIX Annual Technical Conference, FREENIX Track*, 2005, pp. 41–46.

[3] D. Gaffé and A. Ressouche, "Algebraic framework for synchronous language semantics," in *Theoretical Aspects of Software Engineering (TASE), 2013 International Symposium on*. IEEE, 2013, pp. 51–58.

[4] K. Al Agha, M.-H. Bertin, T. Dang, A. Guitton, P. Minet, T. Val, and J.-B. Viollet, "Which wireless technology for industrial wireless sensor networks? The development of OCARI technology," *Industrial Electronics, IEEE Transactions on*, vol. 56, no. 10, pp. 4266–4278, 2009.

[5] S. McConnell, *Code complete*. Pearson Education, 2004.

[6] T. Chang, T. Watteyne, K. Pister, and Q. Wang, "Adaptive synchronization in multi-hop TSCH networks," *Computer Networks*, vol. 76, pp. 165–176, 2015.

[7] B. Musznicki and P. Zwierzykowski, "Survey of simulators for wireless sensor networks," *International Journal of Grid and Distributed Computing*, vol. 5, no. 3, pp. 23–50, 2012.

[8] A. Fraboulet, G. Chelius, and E. Fleury, "Worldsens: development and prototyping tools for application specific wireless sensors networks," in *Information Processing in Sensor Networks. 6th International Symposium on*. IEEE, 2007, pp. 176–185.

[9] "Transaction level eMulator (TLMu)," 2011, edgarigl.github.io/tlmu/. Accessed on Sep. 27, 2016.

[10] M. Montón, J. Engblom, and M. Burton, "Checkpointing for virtual platforms and SystemC-TLM," *Very Large Scale Integration (VLSI) Systems, IEEE Transactions on*, vol. 21, no. 1, pp. 133–141, 2013.

[11] "Tlm 2.0 quantum keeper," 2010, www.embecosm.com/appnotes/ean1/html/ch09s01s03.html. Accessed on Sep. 27, 2016.

[12] "Sam3s arm cortex-m3 microcontroller," 2015, www.atmel.com/products/microcontrollers/arm/sam3s.aspx. Accessed on Sep. 27, 2016.

[13] C. Barnes, J.-M. Cottin, F. Verdier, and A. Pegatoquet, "Towards the verification of industrial communication protocols through a simulation environment based on qemu and systemc," in *ACM/IEEE 19th International Conference on Models Driven Engineering Languages and Systems (MODELS 2016)*, 2016.

[14] A. Ressouche, D. Gaffé, and V. Roy, "Modular compilation of a synchronous language," in *Software Engineering Research, Management and Applications*. Springer, 2008, pp. 157–171.

[15] G. Berry, *The Esterel v5 language primer: version v5_91*. Centre de mathématiques appliquées, Ecole des mines and INRIA, 2000.

CLS : ContactLess Simulator

David Navarro, Guilherme Migliato-Marega
Université de Lyon, ECL, INSA Lyon, UCBL, CPE
INL, UMR5270
F-69134, Ecully, France
david.navarro@ec-lyon.fr

***Abstract*— A new simulator, ContactLess Simulator (CLS) has been developed in Visual C#. It is thus easy portable; several windows permit the user to configure the whole electronic system and to launch the simulation. It is specifically written to simulate contactless-powered smart systems, such as Near Field Communication (NFC) coupled to a microcontroller unit (MCU). More precisely, our study focuses on battery-less electronic systems: the MCU is supplied by the NFC circuit. To permit such a system to function, energy budget has to be explored; this is the aim of this simulator. This paper describes the considered electronic system, the models, and it details a simulation example. The simulated example is composed of a ST-Microelectronics M24LR04E NFC circuit and a Microchip PIC18LF2525 microcontroller.**

Keywords-Simulation; Modeling; NFC; Microcontroller; MCU; Energy harvesting.

I. Introduction

New trends in energy-constrained electronic systems are to harvest energy in the environment and smartly manage energy. We consider 2 kinds of harvesting: natural and artificial energy sources harvesting. Natural sources are directly given by the Nature, such as vibration, temperature, or solar rays. Many electronic systems are developed to consider these energy sources, such as for example Seebeck systems or mini-photovoltaic panels [1]. Non natural sources include for example vibration (though piezoelectric elements [2]) ambient radiofrequency waves (through RF to DC converter), or magnetic fields such as wireless powering systems.

Wireless powering systems exist since several years, and are nowadays widespread in powerful systems, such as inductive charging stations for vehicles [3], smartphones wireless chargers [4], as well as lightweight systems, such as Near Field Communication (NFC) tags and emitter. We consider such lightweight systems that are highly energy constrained. Details on NFC are given in Section II.

We focus on easy to use and graphical simulator on NFC systems, more precisely on system-level energy aspects. Many simulators in NFC field exist. We do not consider Radiofrequency Identification (RFID) or NFC so-called "simulators" that are in reality hardware-based measurements systems (that we would call debuggers or emulators), such as [5]. Many simulators focus on physical link and radiofrequency propagation aspects [6], [7]. RFIDSIM [8] is a more complete simulator that considers physical link and protocol. Others higher-level simulators focus on communication protocol and communication performance, such as NS-3 [9].

We propose in this paper a new simulator that considers energy harvesting from NFC emitter and energy balance according to the tag electrical consumption. The wireless-supplied tag is not only composed of a classical NFC circuit, but of a more complex smart system. It is described in Section II. Section III describes the models that were written in the simulator. Section IV details simulator graphical user interface, parameters, and an example result.

II. Considered NFC system

A typical NFC system is composed of an emitter and a tag. It is shown in Fig. 1.

NFC systems use Low frequency (LF) from 125 KHz to 134 KHz, high Frequency (HF) at 13.56 MHz, or ultra high frequency (UHF) at 860 – 960 MHz. We consider the 13.56 MHz frequency communication that is mostly used in NFC systems [10]. Other frequencies will be supported in further releases of CLS simulator.

The emitter outputs a powerful signal in a coil (also called "antenna") at a specific frequency. The electromagnetic field carries power and data with the help from an Amplitude Shift Keying (ASK) modulated signal. Input power at receiver (tag) depends on signal strength at emitter, antennas gains, and distance between antennas. No simple exact equation exists since communication is near field. Friis equation, used in classical long range radiofrequency communications, is not valid. Indeed, Maxwell equations have to consider E and H fields. In our case, we use electrically small antennas thus near field limit distance d depends only on wavelength λ. It t is given as [11]:

$$d = \lambda/2\pi \quad (1)$$

More precisely, the NFC system we consider (13.56 MHz, few centimeters distance between emitter and tag) is in reactive (non-radiative) near field region. Fig. 2 shows this aspect. As a result, more simple equations are used to model signal attenuation due to distance.

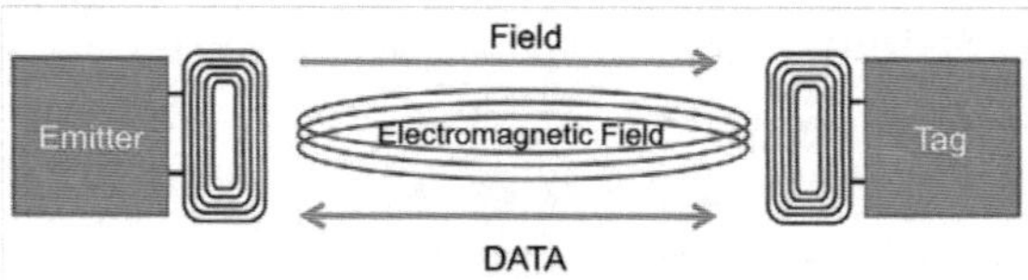

Figure 1. Typical Architecture of NFC system [12].

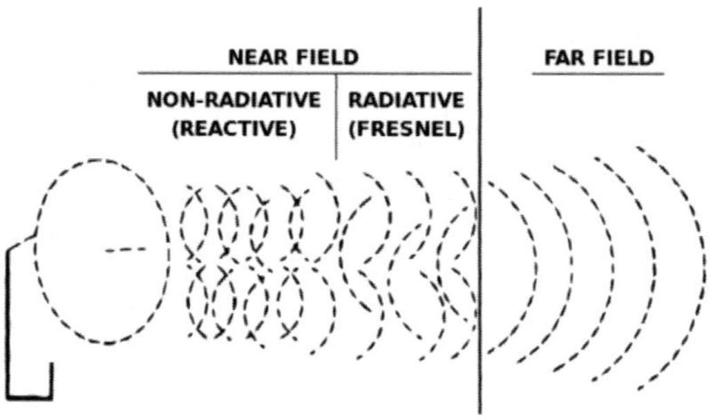

Figure 2. Radiofrequency signal propagation [14].

Received power formulas are [13]:

$$P_{RX(E)} = \left(\frac{1}{k.d^2} - \frac{1}{k.d^4} + \frac{1}{k.d^6}\right) \quad (2)$$

$$P_{RX(H)} = \left(\frac{1}{k.d^2} + \frac{1}{k.d^4}\right) \quad (3)$$

A tag is often composed of a NFC circuit that comprises 2 main blocks: energy harvesting block and data decoding block. The energy harvesting block converts the received electromagnetic field into usable energy in order to supply the circuit. The data decoding block demodulates the signal in order to recover the bit-stream. We consider in this study a smarter tag that comprises a microcontroller unit (MCU). This MCU controls the NFC circuit.

Novelty is that we focus on entire battery-less system. Neither NFC circuit nor MCU is externally supplied. The only energy source comes from electromagnetic field while NFC communications. To aim this, we choose the ST-Microelectronics M24LR04E chip. It is 13.56 MHz NFC ISO 15693 and ISO 18000-3 mode 1 compatible and it has an energy harvesting analog output that permits to supply other circuits on the board (i.e., MCU). The considered system is shown in Fig. 1, tag-side of the system is detailed in Fig. 3.

III. CLS MODELS

As it is shown in Section II, several circuits compose the system, so they have been modeled separately. Models are high-level (electronic system level), they have been written at C language level.

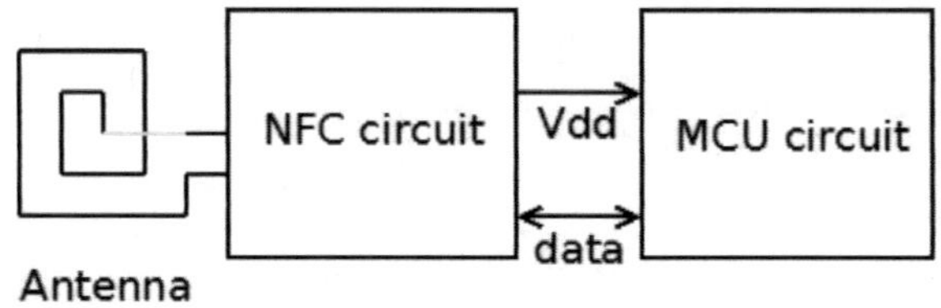

Figure 3. Considered battery-less tag.

A. *Emitter model*

The emitter is modeled according to its emitting power, frequency, distance between emitter antenna and tag antenna.

B. *Antenna model*

The emitter and tag antennas are PCB coil antennas in our prototype. Antenna gain is used to calculate propagation losses.

C. *NFC circuit model*

Several blocks in NFC circuit will be considered. RF2DC and DC2DC blocks are modeled. Performances are based on ST-Microelectronics M24LR04E circuit characteristics.

D. *MCU circuit model*

For this release, MCU is simply modeled as an electrical load. It requires a minimal voltage and consumes a nominal current. Power is calculated according to the MCU brand and model, oscillator type and operating frequency. Microchip PIC18LF2525 is modeled. Table I shows targeted MCUs.

TABLE I. TARGETTED MCUS MODELS

MCU brand	MCU model
ATMEL	ATMega-328
Microchip	PIC18LF2525
ST-Microelectronics	ST-8ML
ST-Microelectronics	STM-32
Texas Instruments	MSP-430

ATMEL, ST-Microelectronics and Texas Instruments models are under development and will be released soon.

IV. SIMULATOR & GRAPHICAL USER INTERFACE

The CLS simulator has been written in Visual C# in order to be easily portable on Microsoft 64-bit Windows operating systems. It is part of the Visual Studio Community, a free tool for academic research [15].

Graphical user interface is drawn in a horizontal way, from Emitter on the left towards Load (Electronic system) on the right. Fig. 4 shows the main window of CLS simulator. Architecture presented Section II (Fig. 1) is recognizable. Each Element has to be setup before simulation is run.

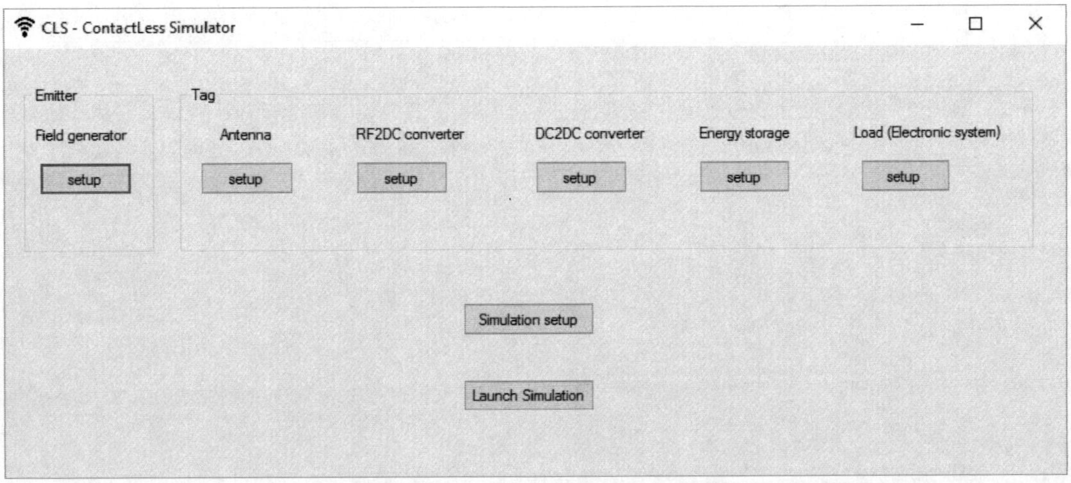

Figure 4. CLS Simulator graphical user interface

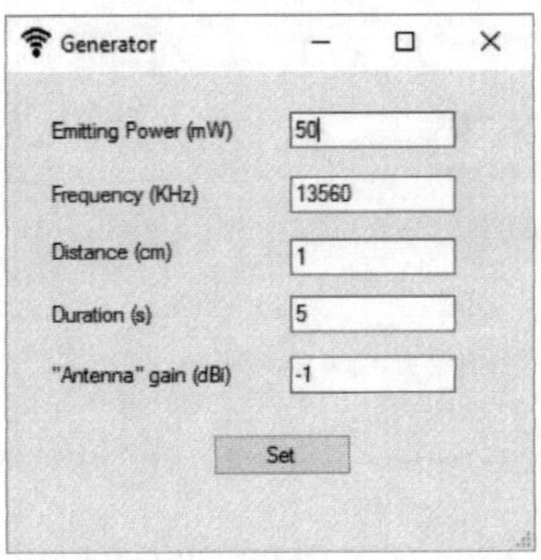

Figure 5. Electromagnetic field parameters at Emitter

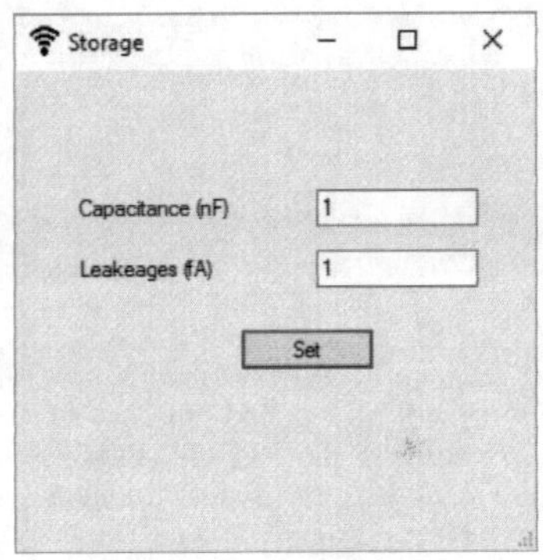

Figure 6. Energy storage parameters

A. *Tag antenna*

The tag antenna parameter is the gain (in dBi). At tag antenna output, the received electromagnetic field is known. More precisely the received power is known according to all above parameters; signal attenuation due to propagation is calculated. According to (2) and (3), as communication is near field, power of magnetic field decays as the inverse sixth power of distance [16]. Such a model is used.

B. *Tag RF2DC converter and DC2DC converter*

The RF2DC and DC2DC converters efficiencies (in %) are expressed in these windows. Efficiencies can alternatively be replaced by a transfer function to match a realistic circuit. In our example, we choose this option and we set equations from ST-Microelectronics M24LR04E datasheet.

C. *Energy storage*

The energy storage parameters are used to calculate the amount of energy that can be saved in a switched capacitor, used as a super-capacitor. Parameters are capacitance value (in nF) and total leakages (in fA) of switches and capacitor (Fig.6).

The role of this module is to further simulate energy storage versus energy usage durations. It will lead to an energy budget analysis.

D. *Load (electronic system)*

For this simulator release, the load is a MCU (microcontroller unit). When a MCU is chosen, the "Configure MCU" button opens a new window. Oscillator type is entered.

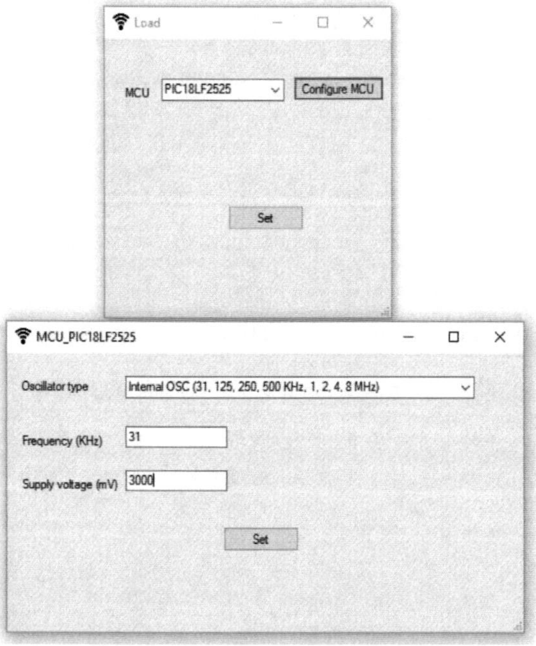

Figure 7. Load (electronic system) parameters

For this example, Microchip PIC18LF2525, it can be external RC (up to 4 MHz), external XTAL (crystal oscillator, up to 40 MHz), and internal OSC (from the internal 8MHz source or the INTRC 31KHz source, several frequencies are available according to frequency post-scaler). Frequency (in KHz) and supply voltage are then entered. All these parameters are taken from Microchip PIC18LF2525 datasheet; from current voltage versus frequency, current versus voltage and current versus frequency curves. User can enter the supply voltage he would like to obtain from the energy harvesting block. This field is dedicated to future features.

E. Simulation setup

The simulation setup permits to configure a simulation time and a simulation step for transient analysis. These parameters will be used in future release, for the moment, only static simulations are run.

F. Launch simulation & result window

In main window, *Launch simulation* button is pressed to simulate the system that user has configured. All data are calculated and written in several output files, and graphical results are displayed on a window. This window is automatically opened. Static results in Fig. 8 are obtained for parameters in table II.

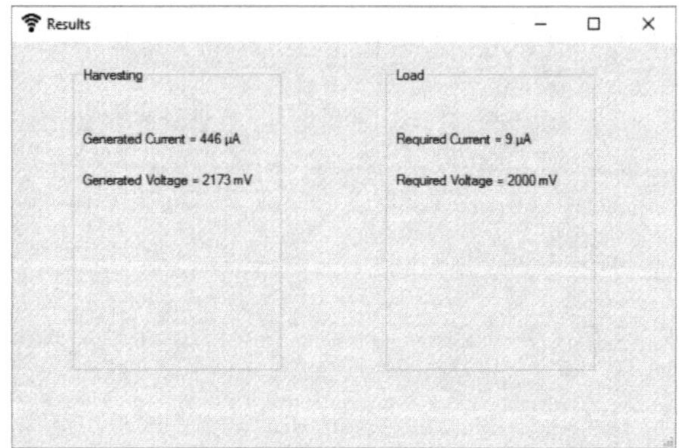

Figure 8. Result window.

TABLE II. PARAMETERS USED FOR TEST EXAMPLE

Emitting power	30 mW
Frequency	13560 MHz
Distance	1 cm
Antennas gain (Emitter & tag)	-1 dBi
RF2DC & DC2DC converters	Equations from M24LR04E
Switches leakages	100 fA
MCU brand/model	Microchip/PIC18LF2525
MCU Oscillator	Internal OSC, 31KHz
MCU Voltage	2V to 5.5V

With the help from Fig. 8, generated current from energy harvesting circuit can be compared to required current from MCU; generated voltage can be compared to minimal supply voltage of the MCU.

V. CONCLUSION

We presented first release of CLS: ContactLess Simulator. It permits to configure a NFC system: emitter and tag. Tag is battery-less (self supplied), it comprises an energy harvesting module and a microcontroller unit (MCU). CLS was developed with Microsoft Visual C#, its graphical interface is fully based on windows where parameters are set. A launch button runs the simulation and displays a result window. For this release, a static simulation is run and displays the harvested power (voltage and current) and the required power (voltage and current) for the MCU. Further releases will support transient analysis, energy calculation, and more electronic circuits in library.

REFERENCES

[1] S. Roundy, D. Steingart, L. Frechette, P. Wright, J. Rabaey, "Power Sources for Wireless Sensor Networks", Springer, Wireless Sensor Networks, Lecture Notes in Computer Science, Volume 2920, pp. 1–17, 2004.

[2] W. S. Wang, W. Magnin, N. Wang, M. Hayes, B. O'Flynn, C. O'Mathuna, "Bulk Material Based Thermoelectric Energy Harvesting for Wireless Sensor, Applications", Sensors & their Applications XVI, IOP Publishing, Journal of Physics : Conference, Series 307, pp. 1-6, 2001

[3] U. K. Madawala, D. J. Thrimawithana, " A Bidirectional Inductive Power Interface for Electric Vehicles in V2G Systems", IEEE Transactions on Industrial Electronics, Volume: 58, Issue: 10, pp 4789–4796, 2011, doi: 10.1109/TIE.2011.2114312.

[4] R. Tseng, B. von Novak, S. Shevde, and K. A. Grajski, "Introduction to the alliance for wireless power loosely-coupled wireless power transfer system specification version 1.0", Wireless Power Transfer (WPT) Conference, pp. 79-83, 2013, doi: 10.1109/WPT.2013.6556887.

[5] C. Angerer, B.Knerr, M.Holzer, A.Adalan, and M. Rupp, "Flexible simulation and prototyping for RFID designs", EURASIP Workshop on RFID Technology, pp.51-54, 2007.

[6] T. Cheng, L. Jin, "Analysis and Simulation of RFID Anti-collision Algorithms", International Conference on Advanced Communication Technology, volume 1, pp 697-701, 2007.

[7] J. Wang, D. Yang, "Design of a Multi-Protocol RFID Tag Simulation Platform Based on Supply Chain", International Conference on Management and Service Science (MASS), pp.1-4, 2009.

[8] C. Floerkemeier, S. Sarma, "RFIDSim—A Physical and Logical Layer Simulation Engine for Passive RFID", IEEE Transactions on Automation Science and Engineering, vol. 6, n. 1, pp. 33-43, 2009.

[9] G. Benigno, O. Briante, and G. Ruggeri, "A sun energy harvester model for the network simulator 3", Sensing, Communication, and Networking - Workshops (SECON), pp. 1-6, 2015, doi: 10.1109/SECONW.2015.7328143.

[10] ATMEL, "Understanding the Requirements of ISO/IEC 14443 for Type B Proximity Contactless Identification Cards", Application Note, [Online, retrieved: 15th July 2016]. Available from: http://www.atmel.com/images/doc2056.pdf.

[11] P. V. Nikitin, K. V. S. Rao, and S. Lazar, "An Overview of Near Field UHF RFID", International Conference on RFID, pp. 1-8, 2007, doi: 10.1109/RFID.2007.346165.

[12] G. Proehl, "An Introduction to Near Field Communications", ST-Microelectronics [Online, retrieved: 15th July 2016]. Available from: http://www.st.com/content/st_com/en/applications/connectivity/near-field-communication-nfc.html

[13] RF Memories and Transceivers, STMicroelectronics

[14] H. G. Schantz, "Near field propagation law & a novel fundamental limit to antenna gain versus size", Antennas and Propagation International Symposium, pp 237-240, 2005, doi: 10.1109/APS.2005.1552223.

[15] G. M. Djuknic, "Method of measuring a pattern of electromagnetic radiation", US Patent 6657596-B2, 2003.

[16] Microsoft, "Visual Studio Community", [Online, retrieved: 15th July 2016]. Available from: https://www.visualstudio.com/en-us/products/visual-studio-community-vs.aspx.

[17] J. I. Agbinya, "Investigation of Near Field Inductive Communication System Models, Channels and Experiments", Progress In Electromagnetics Research B, Vol. 49, 129-153, 2013.

CAPTURE – "Widening the Net" – Indoor Positioning using Cooperative Techniques

Gary Cullen
Department of Computing,
Letterkenny Institute of Technology,
Letterkenny, Co. Donegal, Ireland
email: gary.cullen@lyit.ie

Kevin Curran, Jose Santos
Intelligent Systems Research Centre,
Ulster University, Magee College
Derry, United Kingdom

Abstract— **Context is fast becoming a fundamental requirement in modern day application development. Key to this requirement is the accuracy of the contextualized information being processed. Incorrectly interpreted context can lead to a missed opportunity or an inappropriate user interruption. Location is arguably one of the most significant contexts that can add value to an applications perceived intelligence. Timely and accurate knowledge of a user's position can vastly improve the precision of contextualized information. Many noteworthy systems have been developed that attempt to address the notion of localization in the indoor environment. With the use of a myriad of technologies and novel implementations these systems have somewhat overcome the issues surrounding the level of accuracy in indoor positioning. In actual fact, most of the research in the area of Indoor Positioning Systems (IPSs) has been primarily focused on solving the problem of positioning accuracy. All the time, an equally important issue of yield or coverage has been somewhat overlooked. Accuracy becomes somewhat meaningless, to an extent, in areas where even coarse positioning is unobtainable. It is the focus of this research to address the issue of coverage in IPSs. The concept is to utilize mobile devices to cooperatively locate devices that cannot be *'seen'* by IPS's in indoor environments. The methodology of such an approach is to use a cooperation of devices at the extremities of IPS ranges. These devices have themselves already been positioned, but can *'see'* beyond the IPSs current range and can, in concert, locate devices that they can *'see'*.**

Keywords- Cooperative Positioning; Collaborative Positioning; Self Positioning; Indoor Positioning Systems; IPS.

I. Introduction

The problem of locating people or devices in all areas of the indoor arena, is a challenge that, as of yet, remains unsolved. Many technologies and techniques have been employed in an attempt to find a solution, but none have effectively done so. It is the focus of this particular research to describe a framework and implementation whereby mobile devices can assist in a collaborative fashion to extend the capacity of an Indoor Positioning System, thereby adding to the body of research in this area to help in the effort to find a solution.

Access to location based information in mobile devices is becoming ubiquitous. Global Navigation Satellite Systems (GNSSs), such as the Global Positioning System (GPS) have the capacity to locate a mobile device with enough precision to provide adequate context to nearly any application purpose. More importantly, it has the coverage to do so at a global level, with 24 satellites offering an almost unobstructed view, providing the necessary infrastructure to deliver such vast yields. GPS, through its success, has quietly infiltrated most of our modern day lives. If you look just beneath the surface of most modern day systems, you will invariably find layers of GPS services. GPS controls key pieces of infrastructure such as, traffic management systems in modern cities. The atomic clocks on-board GPS satellites send extremely accurate timing information, which is used to synchronize traffic lights. GPS offers positioning estimates accurate enough to now automatically land airplanes and navigate emergency services directly to their destinations. The requirements to use GPS is becoming more and more trivial with advances in accuracy and the technological advancements in hardware. Unfortunately, GPS positioning signals do not have the strength to penetrate a buildings fabric, after making the near 22,000 km journey to earth. This makes its application as a Location Based System (LBS) in the indoor arena virtually redundant. A comprehensive solution to the provision of accurate position estimations and broad coverage in the indoor environment has, proven somewhat problematic to deliver. The reasons for this are wide ranging and cover a large area of research [1-6], identifying issues with reflection, refraction, absorption and diffraction. Any of these issues can introduce challenges when attempting to position using wireless signals, especially so in the indoor environment. But a fundamental problem is that one of the most commonly implemented indoor positioning solutions use existing Wi-Fi network components to locate devices within its range. Although this technique offers obvious economic rewards, utilizing a preinstalled infrastructure. These topologies were typically designed to provide network coverage to mobile devices rather than deliver an indoor location based solution. Large areas without coverage are commonplace in these networks, because network designers were not typically concerned with providing 100% coverage for mobile data. Furthermore, where a single Wireless Access Point (WAP) can adequately provide network access to mobile devices, three or more can be required to accurately position. Hallways, toilet areas or other general purpose areas that ordinarily would not require network coverage sometimes do not get dedicated WAPs. Transient users navigating these areas of the network can be un-locatable using this infrastructure. Moreover, the indoor arena is an especially noisy atmosphere, being home to other wireless devices such as Bluetooth Headsets, Cordless Phones and Microwave Ovens, which operate on the same frequency as a Wi-Fi signal [6]. Considering users spend more time in an indoor environment [7], the need for a solution is obvious. Outdoor localization has quite a few years' research and development on its indoor equivalent, this coupled with the aforementioned difficulties provides for a fertile research area at present.

This paper is organized as follows. Section II, a description of the test environment is presented. Section III describes the CAPTURE framework. An analysis of the results found during testing are presented in Section IV and evaluated in Section V. Finally, Section VI offers a conclusion and some future implementations of CAPTURE.

II. Test Environment

The main campus building at Letterkenny Institute of Technology (LyIT) was used as a live testbed for this research. The building itself consists of 3 floor levels and covers an area of approximately 20,000 sq. meters. It contains a variety of rooms and room sizes, ranging from computer labs, classrooms, lecture theatres, staff offices and toilets. The college uses a variety (CISCO 892w, CISCO Aironet 1140 Series and CISCO Aironet 2602e Series) of 802.11 Wi-Fi APs to provide network and internetwork connectivity to its users, which is primarily made up of staff and students numbering approximately 4000 in total. During the summer of 2015, a survey of the indoor positioning capacity of the Wi-Fi infrastructure of the LyIT campus was undertaken. The Ekahau Site Survey (ESS) [8] application was used to complete the survey. ESS is the industry standard for designing, planning and maintaining Wi-Fi network systems. The survey provided analysis of network connectivity and performance, which further proved our hypothesis that large areas of a building are not locatable when using existing Wi-Fi infrastructure. The Ekahau Site Survey 8.0 (ESS 8.0) system was used to perform a Throughput Site Survey, this survey measures throughput as well as jitter and packet loss to evaluate the Wi-Fi performance of a network at given locations. It collates data, which illustrates how the network is performing in that particular area of the building. ESS is most commonly used to assist with the designing and planning of new Wi-Fi networks, as well as troubleshooting issues with existing Wi-Fi implementations. It uses different observables to measure aspects of the wireless network infrastructure. These observables can measure range as well as Data Transfer Rates, Level of Interference\Noise, Signal Strength, Signal to Noise Ratio, Strongest Access Points and Ping Round Trip Time. These can then be analyzed to measure the suitability of a given area of a building to provide a level of service with a specific technology. For example, tests can be implemented and evaluated to highlight Wi-Fi blackspots or areas with low coverage or high levels of congestion or contention rates. The system generates heat maps of the surveyed area to illustrate issues relating to network or technology yield. An interesting facet of the ESS application is its ability to configure the output to measure Wi-Fi connectivity capacity of a given area, with a given infrastructure, while at the same time measure the infrastructures capability to position devices within that same surveyed area.

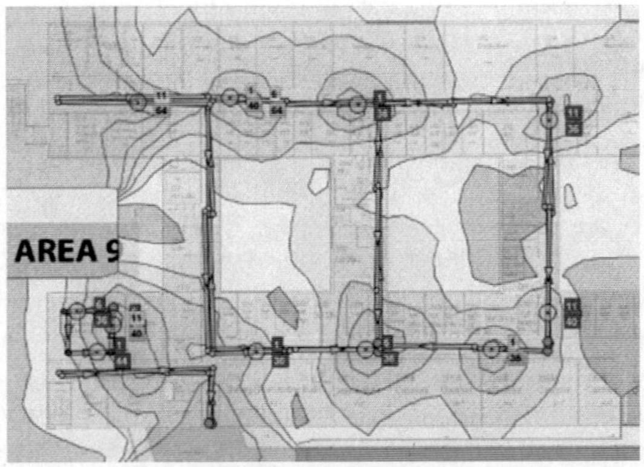

Figure 1 – Infrastructures capacity to provide Wi-Fi Connectivity

This provides the capability to clearly map the capacity of a currently installed infrastructure in any area within a building to effectively locate a mobile device. Fig. 1 Infrastructures capacity to provide Wi-Fi Connectivity, shows a sample area of the second floor of the West Wing of LyIT Letterkenny Campus, illustrating the infrastructures capacity to provide optimal connectivity to mobile devices within a Wi-Fi network.

Fig. 2 Infrastructures capacity to locate, is a heat map of the same area with precisely the same infrastructure but the representation for coverage differs dramatically. Large areas of the map cannot be used to adequately locate devices in this area of the building. These images graphically depict the challenges that designers face when attempting to implement an IPS using an endogenous infrastructure. IPS implementations can be classified as either exogenous or endogenous, endogenous is made up of infrastructure that has not been installed primarily for positioning reasons. Whilst utilizing an existing infrastructure, such as this offers many noble qualities, not least the reduced costs in procuring equipment to implement an IPS solution, the problems are obvious. Moreover, this emphasizes the hypothesis of this research and the need for a solution like CAPTURE to extend coverage into un-locatable areas of a network.

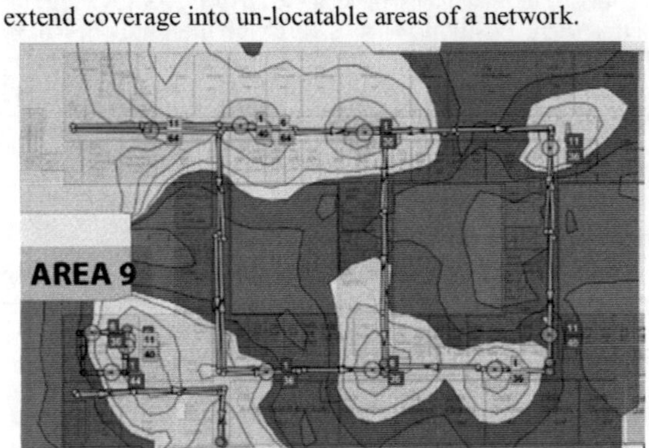

Figure 2 - Infrastructures capacity to locate

These blind spots are illustrated in the black areas in Fig. 2 Infrastructures capacity to locate, the green areas are areas where the endogenous infrastructure can adequately locate devices. Cooperative devices within the CAPTURE system that were at the edges of these green areas would already be located with the current IPS. These cooperative devices can see into these areas without coverage, in Fig. 2 Infrastructures capacity to locate, they could assist in locating devices within that area, thereby extending the reach of the IPS.

III. CAPTURE

The hypothesis of this research is that mobile devices at the boundaries of IPSs, who have themselves been located by an IPS, can assist in a cooperative approach to locate mobile devices beyond the range of the IPS but within range of the cooperating devices. CAPTURE attempts to prove this hypothesis in an augmented approach, using the Received Signal Strength (RSS) of both Bluetooth LE and Wi-Fi radio signals to ascertain range. A fundamental aspect of positioning and navigation in general, is the capacity to measure range. Range can be defined as a measurement of the distance between two points. One of the most popular ranging techniques used in indoor localization, is RSS. RSS is a measurement of the voltage that exists in a transmitted radio signal, which is an indication of the power being received by an antenna. When a signal first leaves a transmitting device, the power of the signal drops or attenuates, this is true of both wired and wireless transmissions. As a radio signal propagates through the air, some of its power is absorbed and the signal loses a specific amount of its strength, therefore, the higher the RSS value (or least negative in some devices), the stronger the signal. Knowing the amount of signal loss over a given distance provides a method to estimate the distance from a transmitting device, given a RSS.

CAPTURE then uses this RSS range observable as input for a positioning algorithm to determine the position of a lost device. The algorithm requires at least three reference devices to successfully position a *'lost'* device within a network. These devices must have *'a prior'* knowledge of their current position. That is, each of these devices have already been located by an in-house indoor positioning solution. During the tests Smartphones were used to position the lost device. RSS readings, both Bluetooth and Wi-Fi, were recorded from each device. The results of these tests are detailed in the tables in Section IV.

IV. RESULTS

The results of the experiments, which were carried out in a large campaign of measurements taken in the main campus area of Letterkenny Institute of Technology are detailed in Table 1 and Table 2. The mobile reference devices used in the tests to simulate the cooperative network were Sony Xperia Z1 C6943 Smart Phones running Google Android v5.1 (Lollipop) on a Quad-core 2.2 GHz Krait 400 CPU. Authors in [9][10] describe problems with varied RSS readings when using different phones, which most likely use different antennas. They describe the difference being up to 11.2 dBm when using disparate antenna in 25 meter tests. Lisheng et al, and Kaemarungsi and Krishnamurthy both describe these issues when testing using Wi-Fi, but because Bluetooth operates somewhat similar to Wi-Fi, it is expected that similar effects would happen with these readings when using different antenna types. Rappaport [1] also highlights issues with device orientation, which was also considered during the tests. All tests were carried out in a Line of Sight (LoS) environment offering a clear view of all phones during the tests. The average position error ranges from 0.16 meters to 65.14 meters when using Wi-Fi.

TABLE I. CAPTURE Wi-Fi RSS READINGS.

Wi-Fi RSS Readings				
Distance	**5 meters**	**10 meters**	**15 meters**	**20 meters**
Avg. RSS	-55.76	-63.16	-64.74	-64.93
Std. Dev	1.86	0.97	2.06	0.54
Avg. Position Error	0.16m	4.04m	2.62m	1.81m
Distance	**30 meters**	**40 meters**	**50 meters**	**60 meters**
Avg. RSS	-65.61	-67.67	-71.73	-70.68
Std. Dev	0.49	0.94	1.09	1.39
Avg. Position Error	10.03m	13.16m	2.72m	18.57m
Distance	**70 meters**	**80 meters**	**90 meters**	**100 meters**
Avg. RSS	-68.78	-69.14	-67.29	-69.68
Std. Dev	1.165	1.25	1.28	1.00
Avg. Position Error	39.50m	57.8m	65.59m	65.14m

The positioning errors with Bluetooth range from 0.17 to 49.81 meters.

Table II CAPTURE BLUETOOTH RSS READINGS

Bluetooth RSS Readings				
Distance	**5 Meters**	**10 Meters**	**15 Meters**	**20 Meters**
Avg. RSS	-71.54	-73.86	-75.56	-74.42
Std. Dev	3.73	3.71	3.06	3.12
Avg. Position Error	3.7 m	2.19m	0.56m	8.78m
Distance	**30 Meters**	**40 Meters**	**50 Meters**	**60 Meters**
Avg. RSS	-79.10	-82.63	-83.64	-82.70
Std. Dev	6.12	3.81	3.75	4.60
Avg. Position Error	4.08m	7.92m	0.17m	16.51m
Distance	**70 Meters**	**80 Meters**	**90 Meters**	**100 Meters**
Avg. RSS	-82.04	-81.70	-82.15	-87.91
Std. Dev	4.70	2.87	3.29	3.02
Avg. Position Error	20.40m	40.30m	49.81m	7.85m

V. CAPTURE RANGE

Another important question this research posed was just how far could CAPTURE extend an IPS? Hypothetically speaking, there is nothing to stop a device that has been located using CAPTURE, to in turn cooperatively assist in the location of devices beyond the devices that located it but within its range. With the errors rates that are currently being recorded, this would seem problematic, especially considering the error propagation that would occur with each hop. Again, hypothetically speaking, it is still plausible within the scope of the CAPTURE framework. It is accurate to say however, that any positioning system, that uses range to position, is constrained in coverage, primarily by the technology employed to measure range. The current implementation of CAPTURE uses Bluetooth and Wi-Fi to estimate range, each of which have theoretical boundaries of 200 meters. In experiments implemented in the test environment described previously, to establish the limitations of CAPTURE, RSS values were recorded for Bluetooth at a range of 173 meters and Wi-Fi at a range of 175 meters. These experiments were carried out in a LoS environment, which would reduce dramatically in a Non-LoS situation. Furthermore, the evaluated range using the recorded RSS values in these tests was 137.56 for the Bluetooth 173-meter test – a 35.44-meter average positioning error and 129.45 meters for the Wi-Fi 175-meter test – a 45.55-meter average positioning error. Although these error bounds are very high, it still nonetheless proves the fact that CAPTURE can extend into those areas by that distance. Considering the nomadic nature and resource limitations of the collaborative devices employed to implement CAPTURE, it would be nigh on impossible to equal the accuracy levels achieved by custom designed IPS's. But then, without CAPTURE these devices would not be found at all.

Although the error bounds found using this implementation are very high, the concept of CAPTURE is still nonetheless proven. That is, that a mobile device that can see another mobile device, can help in positioning it. Without CAPTURE in the test scenarios described, the lost devices would never be found. To just be able to say that these devices that cannot currently be seen by the in-house IPS can be seen when using CAPTURE, albeit with a high error bounds is still noteworthy. If the lost device was a wheelchair in a hospital, or a passenger in an airport, that a LBS used the IPS to find, it could, conceivable, be anywhere in the world. Using CAPTURE, it could be located within a certain vicinity, providing a coarse position estimate. It is not perceived that CAPTURE would be used in scenarios whereby accuracy levels were required to be within a number of feet. Nor was it ever argued that CAPTURE would be able to offer the accuracy levels that an IPS could offer with its custom designed and powerful infrastructure. But it is the authors' opinion that CAPTURE has a role and that it can fulfill that role, to allow IPS's to use mobile devices to cooperatively extend their range.

VI. CONCLUSION

The motivation behind the development of CAPTURE was to provide a technique to provide better coverage for Indoor Positioning Systems. The live tests carried out to date on CAPTURE prove that it is in fact possible and that the use of cooperating devices is key to this. The accuracy levels of CAPTURE in its current manifestation makes it unviable currently as a solution. More work is required in the area of filtering of data to remove errors and outliers as well as looking at other technologies to enhance the current implementation. Round Trip Time (RTT), could be integrated with the current version of CAPTURE to offer more accurate position estimates. Most implementation of position solutions use a hybrid of solutions to solve the positioning problem. It would be considered common practice today to use a combination of ranging techniques in a hybrid solution, in most situations to establish a more accurate ranging estimate. It is hoped that a future version of CAPTURE could incorporate such a hybrid or augmented approach.

REFERENCES

[1] T. S. Rappaport, *Wireless communications : principles and practice*, 2nd ed. ed. Upper Saddle River, N.J. ; [Great Britain]: Prentice Hall PTR, 2002.

[2] I. F. Akyildiz, W. Su, Y. Sankarasubramaniam, and E. Cayirci, "Wireless sensor networks: a survey," *Computer networks,* vol. 38, no. 4, pp. 393-422, 2002.

[3] J. D. Parsons, *The mobile radio propagation channel*, 2nd ed. ed. Chichester: Wiley, 2000.

[4] M. F. Catedra, J. Perez, F. S. d. Adana, and O. Gutierrez, "Efficient ray-tracing techniques for three-dimensional analyses of propagation in mobile communications: application to picocell and microcell scenarios," *IEEE Antennas and Propagation Magazine,* vol. 40, no. 2, pp. 15-28, 1998.

[5] Z. Yang, Z. Sun, L. Jiang, Y. Xie, and H. Kishida, "An area zoning based WLAN location system," in *Wireless Mobile and Computing (CCWMC 2009), IET International Communication Conference on*, pp. 437-440, 2009.

[6] A. Rowe, Z. Starr, and R. Rajkumar, "Using micro-climate sensing to enhance RF localization in assisted living environments," in *Systems, Man and Cybernetics, 2007. ISIC. IEEE International Conference on*, pp. 3668-3675, 2007.

[7] C. J. Matz *et al.*, "Effects of Age, Season, Gender and Urban-Rural Status on Time-Activity: Canadian Human Activity Pattern Survey 2 (CHAPS 2)," *International journal of environmental research and public health,* vol. 11, no. 2, pp. 2108-2124, 2014.

[8] Ekahau Inc. [retrieved: September, 2016] *Ekahau Wi-Fi RTLS, Active RFID Tracking Solutions, and Wi-Fi Site Survey, WLAN Planning Tools*. Available: http://www.ekahau.com/

[9] X. Lisheng *et al.*, "Variation of Received Signal Strength in Wireless Sensor Network," in *Advanced Computer Control (ICACC), 2011 3rd International Conference on*, pp. 151-154, 2011.

[10] F. D. Rosa *et al.*, "Hand-grip and body-loss impact on RSS measurements for localization of mass market devices," in *Localization and GNSS (ICL-GNSS), 2011 International Conference on*, pp. 58-63, 2011.

This page intentionally left blank.

Indoor Location Estimation based on IEEE 802.15.7 Visible Light Communication and Decision Trees

David Sánchez-Rodríguez[1,2], Itziar Alonso-González[1,2], Carlos Ley-Bosch[1,2], Javier Sánchez-Medina[3], Miguel Quintana-Suárez[1] and Carlos Ramírez-Casañas[1,2]
Department of Telematics Engineering[1]
Institute for Technological Development and Innovation in Communications[2]
Institute for Cybernetics[3]
University of Las Palmas de Gran Canaria
e-mail: david.sanchez@ulpgc.es

Abstract— **Indoor positioning estimation has become an attractive research topic due to the growing interest in location-aware services. Many research works have been proposed on solving this problem by using wireless networks. Nevertheless, there is still much work needed to achieve high accuracy levels. In the last years, the emergence of visible light communication brings a brand new approach to high accuracy indoor positioning. Among its advantages, this new technology is immune to electromagnetic interference and also allows knowing the received optical power accurately. In this paper, we propose a fingerprinting indoor location estimation methodology based on decision trees. Along with the method, we also share some experimental results using the received signal strength obtained from an IEEE 802.15.7 simulator developed by our research group. Results are encouraging. The tested model (classifier) yielded a 93% accuracy, with an average error distance for misclassified instances of 37 centimeters.**

Keywords-Indoor Location; Visible Light Communication; Decision Trees; Received Signal Strength.

I. INTRODUCTION

Indoor localization has gained considerable attention over the past decade due to the emergence of numerous location-aware services. These new services have made it possible to use applications capable of sensing their location and dynamically adjusting their settings and functions [1]. Many indoor localization approaches based on globally deployed radiofrequency systems, such as WLAN, Bluetooth and UWB, have been proposed, mainly because of their low cost and mature standardization state. Nevertheless, they usually deliver an accuracy of up to two meters because multipath propagation [2]. Visible light communication (VLC) is experiencing a growing interest due to improvements in solid state lighting and a high demand for wireless communications. VLC can offer a higher positioning accuracy [3] mainly because of two reasons: this kind of networks is not affected by electromagnetic interferences and the received optical power is more stable than radio signals and can be accurately known. For example, authors in [4] proposed a system with a positioning error about 10 centimeters using a location code and a spatial power distribution map where RSS measurements are gathered every 5 centimeters.

Indoor positioning techniques for VLC are mainly classified into two groups based on geometric properties: lateration and angulation [5]. Lateration techniques estimate the target location by measuring distances from the receiver to multiple LEDs base stations with known coordinates. The distances can be estimated involving the time of arrival (TOA), time difference of arrival (TDOA) and the received signal strength (RSS). On the other hand, with angulation techniques or angle of arrival (AOA) the target location is estimated by measuring angles to multiple base stations. Nevertheless, these techniques often require additional hardware, time synchronization between emitter and receiver, knowing every base station coordinates and extra computation. Thus, fingerprinting techniques combined with VLC can be an alternative to the aforementioned techniques because they estimate positioning by matching online measured data with pre-measured location-related data, such as RSS. Hence, only RSS information is needed and extra sensors are unnecessary. In fact, fingerprinting is one of the most commonly used techniques for RF indoor location [6]. Localization based on fingerprinting is usually carried out in two phases. The first phase (offline phase) consists on the sampling of RSS measurements for every emitter and each reference location (VLC receiver). During the second phase (online phase), the particular receiver position is estimated by feeding new measurements to the positioning model built with previously acquired samples. Most research differs in the latter phase. In this paper, we propose an indoor location estimation method based on an ensemble model of decision trees. We present some preliminary results showing the achieved high accuracy and low computational complexity.

On the other hand, in 2011, Institute of Electrical and Electronic Engineers (IEEE) published the IEEE 802.15.7 standard, which defines Physical (PHY) and Medium Access Control (MAC) layers for short-range wireless optical communications using visible light [7]. Within the last few years, many studies on VLC based positioning have been published. Nevertheless, to the best of our knowledge, to this date there is no any published indoor positioning research using this standard. This paper is the first work to use decision trees in IEEE 802.15.7 VLC networks for indoor location estimation.

With the present work, our contribution is the following: we propose an ensemble model of decision trees based indoor positioning methodology together with some promising results. Furthermore, we make use of the IEEE 802.15.7 standard on VLC to obtain RSS values, which may be a useful piece of information for other researchers and practitioners at this stage of (un)deployment of such standard.

The rest of the paper is organized as follows. In Section 2, we describe our simulator that implements the IEEE 802.15.7 standard. Next, in Section 3, we describe the ensemble model of decision trees used for VLC indoor location estimation. In Section 4, we describe the two phases of our indoor positioning method based on an ensemble model of decision trees. In Section 5, we show some experimental results that demonstrate the high accuracy of our approach. Finally, we sum up the conclusions and we present the future work.

II. SIMULATION MODEL BASED ON IEEE 802.15.7

We built our IEEE 802.15.7 simulator using OMNET++ simulation framework from the model developed by [8], designed for sensor networks based on IEEE 802.15.4 standard. We can do that due to the similarities that exist between both standards IEEE 802.15.7 and IEEE 802.15.4.

OMNeT++ provides built-in support tools for recording and analysis and visualization of simulation results. Several data can be chosen for simulation results, such as throughput, delay, packet loss and RSS.

The developed simulation model has been designed with the following premises:

- IEEE 802.15.7 star topology has been chosen, due to its importance and wide range of applications.
- For the MAC layer, we opted to use the superframe structure, since it allows the use of both contention (CAP) and no contention (CFP) access methods. In addition, the use of the superframe enables devices to enter the energy save state during the idle period.
- A VPAN identifier is assigned to each emitter in order to identify each coordinator (LED lamp).

Next subsections describe the most important features in our simulator, for a better comprehension of the presented results.

A. *Optical channel model*

The transmission medium is modeled as free space without obstacles. We chose the directed line of sight (LOS) link configuration to model the optical signal propagation, requiring a LOS between each device and the coordinator. We have considered only the direct component of the received signal to calculate the received power, despising the possible influence of reflections. According to the results presented in [9], at least 90% of total received optical power is direct light in VLC when using a receiver field of view (FOV) of 60 degrees. Therefore, to ensure the validity of our implemented model, we have configured all optical receivers using a 60 degrees FOV value.

TABLE I. PHY LAYER PARAMETERS

Parameter	Value
Transmission rate	1.25 Mbps
Optical clock rate	3.75 MHz
Coordinator optical transmission power	15 W
Half Power Angle $\theta_{1/2}$	60°
Field of Vision (FOV)	60°
Photo detector area (A)	10 mm^2
Photo detector responsivity (R)	0.54 A/W
Optical concentrator gain (G)	15
Optical filter transmission coefficient (T)	1

The adopted optical channel model facilitates reaching high transmission speeds, since the effects of multipath distortion on the optical signal are not considered. Considering only the direct component of the signal has the additional benefit of improving the efficiency of the implemented simulation model. The computational load required to run simulations of scenarios with multiple nodes including the functionality of different layers of the architecture is reduced significantly.

B. *PHY layer simulation parameters*

Table 1 shows the main configuration parameters of PHY layer used in all simulation scenarios. We selected the PHY II operating mode, intended for both indoor and outdoor environments, using MCS-ID number 16, since support for the minimum clock and data rates for a given PHY is mandatory. Because of the optical channel model used, transmitters' directivity is characterized by its half power angle, $\theta_{1/2}$ while receivers' directivity is defined by its FOV. According to [9], both parameters are assigned a value of 60 degrees, to ensure validity of the implemented channel model, since the calculation of received optical power takes in account only the direct component of the signal. In order to simplify the calculation process of the model, the values used for the concentrator gain (G) and the transmission coefficient of the optical filter (T) are set up as constant values, so they do not depend on the angle of incidence ψ.

The rest of the values selected to characterize VLC transmitters and receivers are commonly used values in literature, similar to those used in [10][11].

III. ENSEMBLE MODEL OF DECISION TREES

Indoor positioning has been a very active research area where several data mining techniques have proved useful to extract knowledge from raw data [12][13]. To solve this problem, we propose a general approach based on decision trees classifications.

Decision trees build classification models in the form of a tree structure. In general, they can handle both categorical and numerical data. A decision tree has internal nodes and leaf nodes. An internal node includes a condition or function of any feature of the dataset, which breaks down the dataset into several subsets, corresponding to two or more branches. Each leaf is assigned to one class representing the classification decision. For instance, in the location problem, the received optical power from luminaries is used in the internal node conditions, and the locations or reference points are used in the leaf nodes. Samples are classified by navigating from the root of the tree down to a leaf, according to the outcome of the condition or function along the path [14].

On the other hand, ensemble models are methods that combine the capabilities of multiple models to achieve better prediction accuracy than any of the individual model could do on its own. Ensemble methods generate multiple base models, and the final prediction is produced as the result of a combination of them, in some appropriate manner, from the prediction of each base model. For instance, the output of each base model is weighted. The success of the ensemble model is based on the ability of generating a set of base models that make errors that are as uncorrelated as possible.

In our indoor localization method, we use a weak classifier based on the C4.5 algorithm [15] to generate a decision tree as a base model. Then, the adaptive boosting (AdaBoost) algorithm [16] is used to build an ensemble model based on previous base models, that is a location estimation model formed by multiple weighted decision trees. In a previous work, we demonstrated that this combination of machine learning techniques provides excellent results for indoor localization [17].

IV. Indoor Localization Method

In this Section, we describe our positioning method based on an ensemble model of decision trees, and it is divided into two phases. The first phase is the training phase (offline phase). Coordinators send beacon frames and RSS samples are collected at reference locations (receivers) to build a dataset. From this dataset, the ensemble model is built. The second stage is the test phase (online phase) where a receiver infers its position by using the online RSS observations.

A. Training phase

In this phase, we aim at building an ensemble model of decision trees using the RSS measurements dataset as training set. Several simulations are carried out at each reference location to calculate different values of RSS. Each simulation is performed with a random orientation vector of each receiver to obtain different values. RSS data are denoted by $\varphi_{i,j}(\tau)$ and indicate the τ-th RSS value measured from i-th coordinator at the j-th receiver. The database can be represented by ψ as in (1):

$$\omega = \begin{pmatrix} \varphi_{1,1}[\tau] & \cdots & \varphi_{1,R}[\tau] \\ \vdots & \ddots & \vdots \\ \varphi_{A,1}[\tau] & \cdots & \varphi_{A,R}[\tau] \end{pmatrix} \quad (1)$$

where A is the number of coordinators, R is the number of receivers or reference locations, $\tau = 1, \ldots, N$ is the index of RSS samples and N is the number of RSS samples at each reference location.

After that, once that RSS dataset of the environment is compiled, an ensemble model of decision trees is built using boosting technique.

B. Test phase

In this phase, a dataset formed by a RSS sample from each coordinator is taken as input of ensemble model of decision trees to infer the current location. Using similar notations, the online measurements can be represented as in (2):

$$\omega_r = \begin{pmatrix} \varphi_{1,r} \\ \vdots \\ \varphi_{A,r} \end{pmatrix} \quad (2)$$

where the location r is unknown.

V. Experimental Results

Our method was tested in a simulation environment that models a 4 by 4 by 3 meters room. As shown in Fig. 1, the environment consists of 16 coordinators or LED lamps (red triangles) configured as 4 x 4 grids placed 1 meter apart from each other on the ceiling. On the lower part, we set up 100 receivers (blue circles) in a 10 x 10 grid configuration, with a 36 cm separation from each other. In order to consider different distances between receivers and coordinators, the receivers plane is set up at three different heights: 75, 100 and 125 centimeters from the floor. Receivers orientation was randomly produced for each simulation as follows: they are pointing out to the ceiling with an initial orientation vector [0,0,1] and a random (-0.2,0.2) offset is applied to each axis in each simulation. Thus, each receiver has a different orientation in each simulation.

Eleven simulations were performed on each three vertical layers. One RSS measurement was estimated at each receiver and simulation. This leads to 3.300 RSS measurements. From this dataset, training and test dataset were random split, picking the same proportion of samples at each class

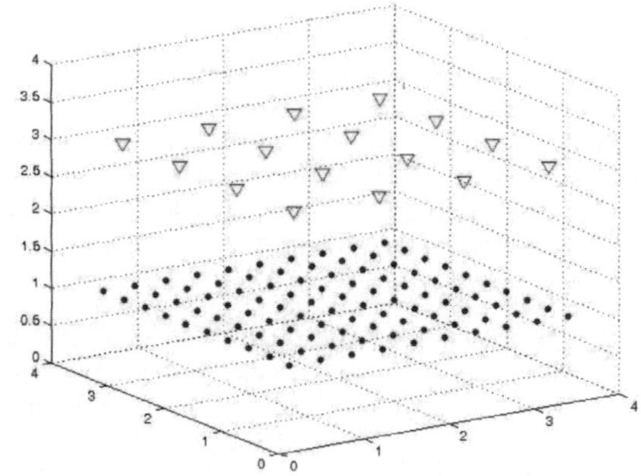

Figure 1. Network scenario with 16 coordinators and 100 receivers.

(stratified split). In order to test the robustness of the method, different training size datasets were used, from 50% to 90% of the whole dataset. The simulation parameters are provided in Table 1.

Fig. 2 shows the received optical power (lux) at 1 meter from the floor with sixteen coordinators. As it can be seen there is enough lighting to receive the beacon frame in every reference location.

For each training dataset, an ensemble model based on decision trees was generated using Weka tool in an Intel i7 2.2 GHz/8GB non-dedicated Windows machine. The classification trees were created by the C4.5 algorithm (implemented in Weka by the classifier class: *weka.classifiers.trees.J48*). The boosting method used was the metalearning AdaBoostM1 algorithm implemented by the Weka classifier class *weka.classifiers.meta.AdaBoostM1* with number of iterations equal to 10. For the validity of simulation results, all experiments were run based on 10-fold cross validation.

Experiments were focused to determine the location method accuracy. The error is the expected distance from the misclassified instance and the real location. The error is calculated by the Euclidean distance between these points, and the arithmetic mean was computed from the results of the experiments. Being a classification problem, an error simply means that a receiver was estimated to be in a wrong positioning cell, in the receivers grid.

Table II shows experimental results in terms of correctly classified instance percentage and average error distance for each training dataset size. As expected, the elapsed time to build each model increases with the training dataset size. Nevertheless, this not meaningful, because the maximum time is about thirty seconds and it must take into account that the model is generated only once, in the offline phase. On the other hand, using only five samples at each receiver for training (50% training dataset size) the model has an accuracy about 88% and an average error distance of 4.7 cm. Nevertheless, an average error distance of 39.4 cm is reached if misclassified instances are only considered. Obviously, better results are achieved by increasing training dataset size, however, the accuracy is only improved about a 5% from 50% to 90% dataset size, and the average error distance of misclassified instances improves about 2.4 cm. Fig. 3 shows the cumulative distribution function (CDF) for 90% training dataset size. As it can be seen, most of instances are correctly classified and it is about 93%. Fig. 4 shows the CDF of misclassified instances for 90% training dataset size. As it can be seen, the maximum error distance is about 50 cm. Furthermore, 86% of misclassified instances have an error distance less than 37 cm, that is, most of misclassified locations are the nearest neighbours (receivers) of exact locations.

TABLE II. EXPERIMENTAL RESULTS

Training Dataset Size (%)	Time to build Model (s)	Correctly Classified Instances (%)	Average Error Distance ± std (cm)	Average Error Distance ± std (cm) of Misclassified Instances
50	20.96	88.55	4.7 ± 0.131	39.4 ± 0.075
60	23.26	89.66	4.5 ± 0.124	37.75 ± 0.051
70	26.65	90.44	3.8 ± 0.113	37.4 ± 0.045
80	31.8	92.16	3.3 ± 0.109	37.08 ± 0.069
90	32.73	93.33	2.8 ± 0.099	37.02 ± 0.058

VI. CONCLUSIONS

In this paper, we have demonstrated that decision trees provide a high accuracy for indoor location estimation in VLC networks. This is mainly because the visible light is less susceptible to multipath effects making the propagation and

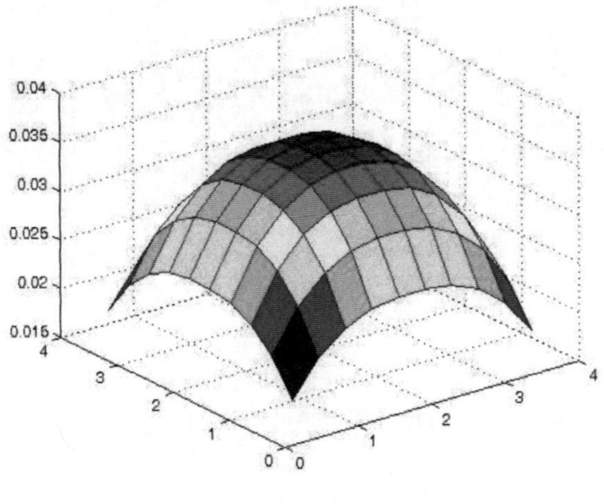

Figure 2. Distribution of the received optical power at 1 meter from the floor.

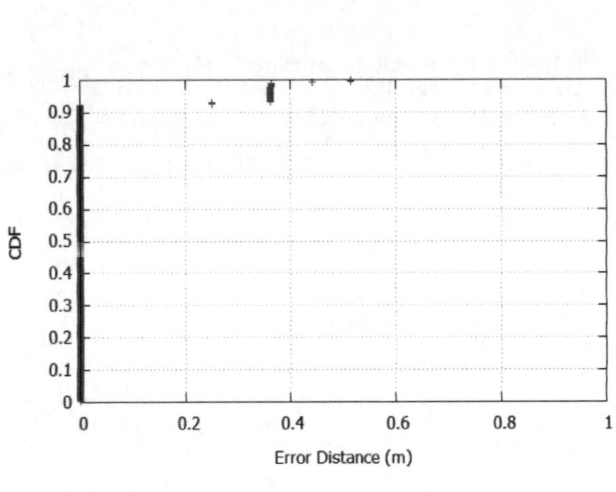

Figure 3. CDF of performance for 90% training dataset size.

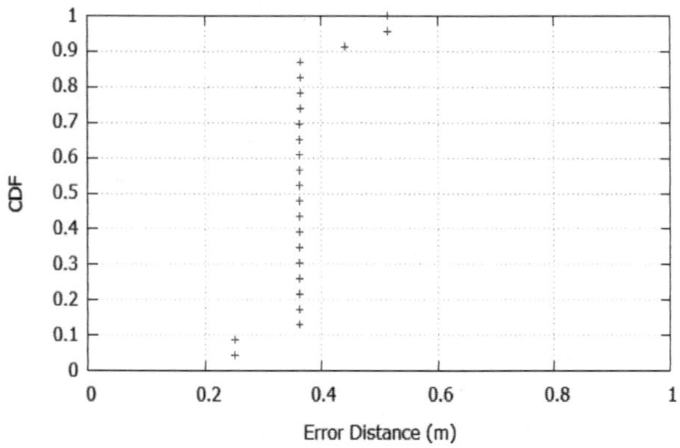

Figure 4. Misclassified instances CDF of performance for 90% training dataset size.

the received optical power more predictable. With regard to accuracy, about 93% of instances are correctly classified and average error of 2.8 cm. Furthermore, the ensemble model of decision trees achieves an average error distance of misclassified instances of 37 cm, taking account that the receivers are placed in a grid with a 36 cm separation from each other. On the other hand, the accuracy of the ensemble model improves with the training dataset size, and its effect on the elapsed time to get the model is not meaningful.

Since the average error distance of misclassified instances cannot be less than the distance among receivers when decision trees are used, in our ongoing work, we are planning to use other techniques of data mining, such as regression, to reduce the error distance.

ACKNOWLEDGMENT

This research was partially supported by the Research Program of University of Las Palmas de Gran Canaria (ULPGC2013-15).

REFERENCES

[1] R. Want and B. Schilit, "Expanding the Horizons of Location-Aware Computing", IEEE Computer, pp. 31-34, August 2001

[2] P. Bahl and V. N. Padmanabhan, "RADAR: an in-building RF-based user location and tracking system", IEEE Conference on Computer Communications (INFOCOM), pp. 775-784, 2000, doi: 10.1109/INFCOM.2000.832252.

[3] J. Armstrong, Y. A. Sekercioglu, and A. Neild, "Visible light positioning: a roadmap for international standardization", IEEE Communications Magazine, 51(12), pp. 68-73, 2013.

[4] Y. Won, S. H. Yang, D. H. Kim, and S. K. Han, "Three-dimensional optical wireless indoor positioning system using location code map based on power distribution of visible light emitting diode", IET Optoelectronics, 7(3), pp. 77-83, 2013.

[5] W. Xu, J. Wang, H. Shen, H. Zhang, and X. You, "Indoor Positioning for Multiphotodiode Device Using Visible-Light Communications", IEEE Photonics Journal, 8(1), pp. 1-11, 2016.

[6] V. Honkavirta, T. Perala, S. Ali-Loytty, and R. Piché, "A comparative survey of WLAN location fingerprinting methods", Proceedings of the 6th Workshop on Positioning, Navigation and Communication (WPNC 2009) Hannover, Germany, pp. 243–251, 2009.

[7] S. Rajagopal, R. D. Roberts, and S. K. Lim. IEEE 802.15.7 visible light communication: modulation schemes and dimming support. Communications Magazine, IEEE, 50(3), pp. 72–82, 2012.

[8] F. Chen, N. Wang, R. German, and F. Dressler, "Performance Evaluation of IEEE 802.15.4 LR-WPAN for Industrial Applications", Fifth Annual Conference on Wireless on Demand Network Systems and Services, pp. 89-96, 2008.

[9] T. Komine and M. Nakagawa, "Fundamental analysis for visible-light communication system using LED lights", IEEE Transactions on Consumer Electronics, Vol.50, Issue 1, pp. 100–107, 2004.

[10] D. Deqiang, K. Xizheng, and X. Linpeng, "An Optimal Lights Layout Scheme for Visible-Light Communication System", 8th International Conference on Electronic Measurement and Instruments, pp. 2-189 - 2-194, 2007.

[11] D. Tronghop, J. Hwang, S. Jung, and Y. Shin, "Modeling and analysis of the wireless channel formed by LED angle in visible light communication", International Conference on Information Networking, pp. 354-357, 2012.

[12] M. Youssef and A. Agrawala, "The Horus location determination system". Wireless Networks, 14, pp. 357–374, 2008.

[13] Y. Chen, Q. Yang, J. Yin, and X. Chai, "Power-efficient access-point selection for indoor location estimation", IEEE Trans. Knowl. Data Eng, 18, pp. 877–888, 2006.

[14] O. Z. Maimon and L. Rokach, "Data Mining and Knowledge" Discovery Handbook; Springer: New York, NY, USA, Volume 1 , 2005.

[15] J. R. Quinlan, "C4.5: Programs for Machine Learning", Morgan Kaufmann: San Francisco, CA, USA, Volume 1, 1993.

[16] Y. Freund, R. Schapire, and N. Abe, "A short introduction to boosting", J. Jpn. Soc. Artif. Intell, 14, pp. 771–780, 1999.

[17] D. Sánchez-Rodríguez, P. Hernández-Morera, J. M. Quinteiro, and I. Alonso-González, "A Low Complexity System Based on Multiple Weighted Decision Trees for Indoor Localization", Sensors, no. 6, pp. 14809-14829, 2015.

A New Coarse Timing Estimation Method for OFDM Signals

Soumitra Bhowmick, K.Vasudevan

Department of Electrical Engineering
Indian Institute of Technology
Kanpur, India 208016

***Abstract*—In this paper, a data aided timing synchronization scheme for Orthogonal frequency division multiplexing (OFDM) signals is proposed. The algorithm uses multiple preambles for initial (coarse) timing estimation, and it works in the time domain. We also propose a timing estimation method using one preamble which is independent of the structure of the preamble, and that works better than the other existing methods in the presence of carrier frequency offset (CFO). The performance is compared in terms of probability of erasure, probability of correct estimation and mean square error (MSE) with the existing timing synchronization methods for OFDM systems.**

Keywords*—*Timing synchronization; OFDM; Preamble; MSE; Probability of erasure; Probability of correct estimation.

I. Introduction

The main impairments in a wireless communication system are multipath fading and noise. Multipath fading introduces inter symbol interference (ISI). The major requirements of a digital communication system is to maximize the bit rate, minimize bit error rate, minimize transmit power and minimize transmission bandwidth [1]. Orthogonal frequency division multiplexing (OFDM) has emerged as a powerful technique which meets the above requirements in multipath fading channels [2]. However, OFDM is known to be very sensitive to timing and carrier frequency synchronization errors [3].

Timing estimation in OFDM systems can be achieved by either data aided (DA) or non data aided (NDA) method. In this paper, we focus on the data aided (DA) timing estimation methods. Data aided timing estimation methods proposed in the literature can be broadly classified into two categories.

1) Approaches that depend on the special structure of the preamble [3]–[7]
2) Approaches that work independent of the structure of the preamble [8]–[13].

The technique proposed in the literature by Schmidl and Cox [3] uses a preamble with two identical halves to estimate the timing synchronization. The variance of the timing estimation proposed in [3] is large due to the timing metric plateau. The performance of timing estimation is further improved by the authors in [4]–[7]. All these methods are dependent on the special structure of the preamble; hence they cannot work with other preambles and moreover the variance of the timing estimation of these methods is high in multipath fading scenario. Kang [8] proposed a technique to estimate timing offset which is independent of the preamble structure. In [8], a delayed correlation of the preamble is used for timing synchronization. The performance is further improved in [9] [10] by utilizing all correlation points without repetition. In [12] [13], a new timing estimation method using a matched filter is proposed which gives better performance than [8] [9] with less computational complexity. All these methods proposed in the literature [8]–[10] [12] [13], which are independent of the structure of the preamble utilize only one preamble for timing synchronization. Hamed [11] first proposed a timing estimation method by utilizing more than one preamble. The main drawback of these methods [8]–[12] is that the coarse timing estimation is severely degraded in the presence of carrier frequency offset (CFO). Here, we propose a new timing estimation method using multiple preambles and we also propose a modified timing estimation method which is robust to CFO.

This paper is organized as follows. The system model is presented in Section II. The proposed method is presented in Section III. The simulation results are given in Section IV and finally, the conclusions in Section V.

II. System Model

Fig. 1 shows the typical structure of a OFDM frame in the time domain. An OFDM frame contains preamble, cyclic prefix (CP) and data. The preamble is used for synchronization purpose. The mth preamble in the frequency domain can be

$\mathbf{x}_0$	$\mathbf{x}_1$	....	$\mathbf{x}_{M-1}$	*CP*	*DATA*

Figure 1: OFDM frame structure in the time domain

represented in vector form as follows.

$$\mathbf{X}_m = [X_m(0)\ X_m(1)\ ...\ X_m(N-1)] \tag{1}$$

where $0 \leq m \leq M-1$. The IFFT of the mth preamble is given by

$$x_m(n) = \frac{1}{N}\sum_{k=0}^{N-1} X_m(k)\, e^{j2\pi nk/N}. \tag{2}$$

The mth preamble in the time domain can be represented in vector form as follows

$$\mathbf{x}_m = [x_m(0)\ x_m(1)\ ...\ x_m(N-1)] \tag{3}$$

where $0 \leq k, n \leq N-1$. Let $\mathbf{x}_0$ to $\mathbf{x}_{M-1}$ be the preambles of the frame in the time domain. Let the transmitted frame be given by (Fig. 1)

$$\mathbf{x} = [\mathbf{x}_0\ ..\ \mathbf{x}_{M-1}\ \mathbf{CP}\ \mathbf{DATA}]. \tag{4}$$

Now, $\mathbf{x}$ is transmitted through the frequency selective channel. The channel is assumed to be quasi static and it is fixed for one frame and varies independently from frame to frame. Its impulse response for a given frame can be expressed as:

$$\mathbf{h} = [h(0)\, h(1)\, h(2) \ldots\ldots h(L-1)] \tag{5}$$

where L is the number of channel taps. The received signal $r(n)$ in the time domain is given by:

$$r(n) = y(n)\, e^{j2\pi n\epsilon/N} + w(n) \tag{6}$$

where

$$\begin{aligned} y(n) &= h(n) \star x(n) \\ &= \sum_{l=0}^{L-1} h(l)\, x(n-l) \,. \end{aligned} \tag{7}$$

and $w(n)$ is zero mean Gaussian noise sample and ϵ is the normalized frequency offset.

III. PROPOSED MODEL

The received signal $r(n)$ is used to estimate the start of the frame $\hat{\theta}_t$. It is assumed that the preambles $\mathbf{x}_0, \mathbf{x}_1, ..., \mathbf{x}_{M-1}$ are known to the receiver. We define the correlation function given by

$$T(d) = \sum_{n=0}^{N-1} \sum_{m=0}^{M-1} r^{\star}(d+n+mN)\, x_m(n) \tag{8}$$

$$R = \sum_{n=0}^{N-1} \sum_{m=0}^{M-1} \mid x_m(n) \mid^2 \tag{9}$$

$$G(d) = \frac{\mid T(d) \mid^2}{M.R} \tag{10}$$

The estimated start of the frame is given by

$$\hat{\theta}_t = \max_d [G(d)] \tag{11}$$

Note that in the special case of $M = 1$ in (8), $T(d)$ reduces to

$$T(d) = \sum_{n=0}^{N-1} r^{\star}(d+n)\, x_0(n) \tag{12}$$

It is equivalent to the method proposed in [12] which is a matched filtering approach using one preamble. The performance of the proposed timing metric (10) is severely degraded in the presence of CFO. Hence, we propose a modified timing metric which performs better than (10) in the presence of CFO. Let the frequency offset ϵ lie within $[-I, I]$. We divide the interval $[-I, I]$ into B sub intervals. The length of the each sub interval is 0.1. The modified correlation function $T_{CFO}(d)$ is given by

$$T_{CFO}(d) = \sum_{p=1}^{p=P} \left\{ \left| \sum_{n=0}^{N-1} \sum_{m=0}^{M-1} r^{\star}(d+n+mN) \, x_m(n)\, e^{(j2\pi(i(p))(n+mN)/N)} \right|^2 \right\} \tag{13}$$

where $i(p)$ takes equally spaced points within the interval $[-I, I]$. The spacing between two successive points is 0.1. $i(p)$ is defined as

$$i(p) = -I + (p-1)\, 0.1 \tag{14}$$

$$i(P) = I \tag{15}$$

where $1 \leq p \leq P$ and $P = B + 1$. The estimated start of the frame is given by

$$\hat{\theta}_t = \max_d [T_{CFO}(d)] \tag{16}$$

Note that in the special case of $M = 1$ in (13) $T_{CFO}(d)$ becomes

$$T_{CFO}(d) = \sum_{p=1}^{p=P} \left| \sum_{n=0}^{N-1} r^{\star}(d+n)\, x_0(n)\, e^{(j2\pi(i(p))n/N)} \right|^2 \tag{17}$$

Now (17) is the proposed timing estimation method using one preamble, which is independent of the structure of the preamble. Note that (17) gives better performance than (12) in the presence of CFO.

In the proposed method the computational complexity is high as the range of CFO increases because as the value of I increases, the value of P is also increases. If the estimated start of the frame $\hat{\theta}_t$ satisfies the condition $1 \leq \hat{\theta}_t \leq L$ then the frame is processed further, otherwise frame is discarded and considered as an erasure. Let $F1$ be the total number of frames that is considered as erasure and $F2$ be the total number of frames that is transmitted. Probability of erasure (PE) is given by

$$PE = \frac{F1}{F2}. \tag{18}$$

Let the number of detected frames is given by

$$F = F2 - F1. \tag{19}$$

The mean squared error (MSE) of the detected frames is given by

$$MSE = \frac{\sum_{f=0}^{F-1} \left(\theta_{tf} - \hat{\theta}_{tf}\right)^2}{F} \tag{20}$$

where θ_{tf} is the maximum absolute value of the channel impulse response for the fth detected frame given by

$$\theta_{tf} = \max(\text{abs}(\mathbf{h}_f)) \tag{21}$$

where $\mathbf{h}_f$ is the channel impulse response for the fth detected frame and $\hat{\theta}_{tf}$ is the estimated start of the fth detected frame.

Let $F3$ be the total number of frames for which $\hat{\theta}_t = \theta_t$, then the probability of correct estimation $P(\hat{\theta}_t = \theta_t)$ is given by

$$P(\hat{\theta}_t = \theta_t) = \frac{F3}{F2} \tag{22}$$

where θ_t is the maximum absolute value of the channel impulse response for a given frame, given by

$$\theta_t = \max(\text{abs}(\mathbf{h})) \tag{23}$$

where $\mathbf{h}$ is the channel impulse response for a given frame and $\hat{\theta}_t$ is the estimated start of that frame.

IV. SIMULATION RESULTS AND DISCUSSION

In this section, the performance of the proposed method is compared with the major existing timing synchronization methods [8]–[13] for OFDM systems, which work independent of the structure of the preamble.

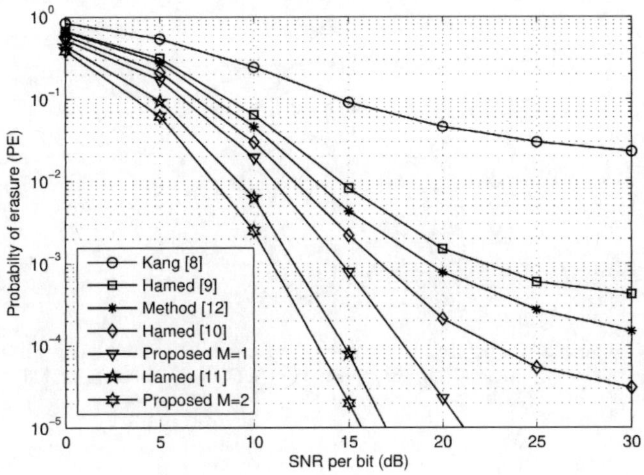

Figure 2: Probability of erasure of different estimators using randomly generated preamble in the presence of CFO [(M=1,2), I=0.5, P=11]

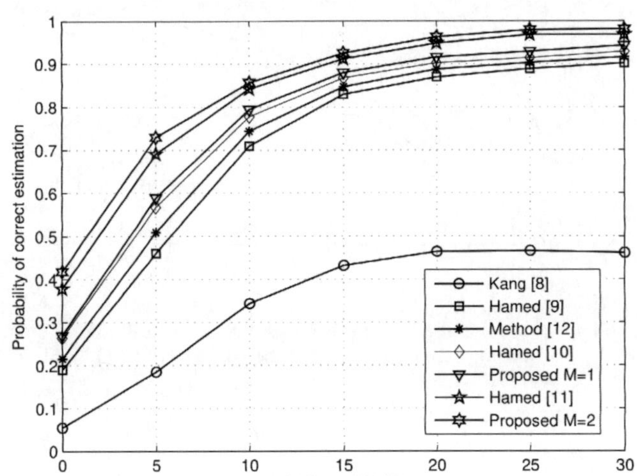

Figure 3: Probability of correct estimation of different estimators using randomly generated preamble in the presence of CFO [(M=1,2), I=0.5, P=11]

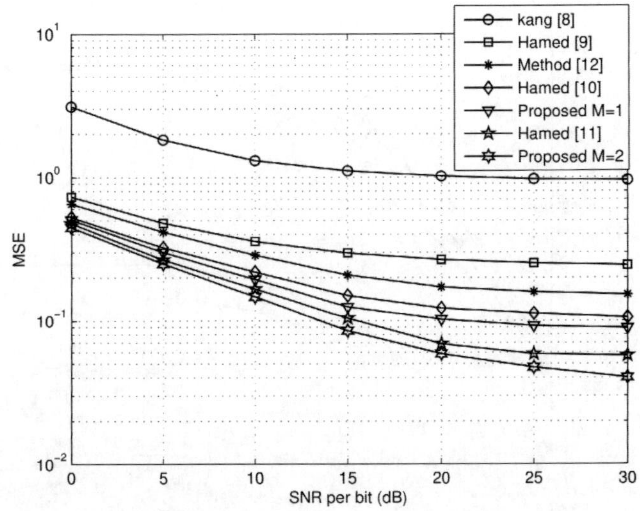

Figure 4: Timing MSE of different estimators using randomly generated preamble in the presence of CFO [(M=1,2), I=0.5, P=11]

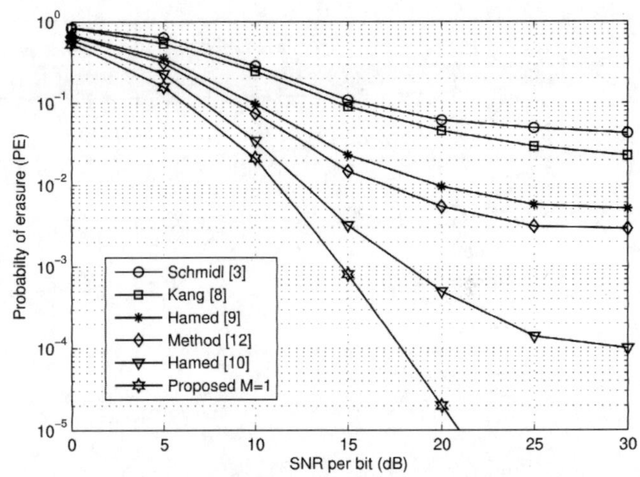

Figure 5: Probability of erasure of different estimators using Schmidl's preamble in the presence of CFO [M=1, I=0.5, P=11]

We have assumed N=64 and performed the simulations over $5*10^5$ frames. QPSK signaling is assumed. A frequency selective Rayleigh fading channel is assumed with $L = 5$ path taps and path delays $\mu_l = l$ for $l = 0, 1, ..., 4$. The channel has an exponential power delay profile (PDP) with an average power of $\exp(-\mu_l/L)$. The CFO takes random value within the range $[-I, I]$ and it varies independently from frame to frame. For the methods presented in [9] [10], we have considered all the available correlation points without repetition, i.e., $N(N-1)/2$=2016 and for the method presented in [11] we have considered all the available correlation points utilized by two preambles, i.e., N^2=4096. In order to compare with [8]–[10] [12], we consider M=1 and to compare with [11] we consider M=2. In Fig. 2, Fig. 3 and Fig. 4 probability of erasure, probability of correct estimation and timing MSE of the proposed method is compared with major existing timing synchronization methods in the presence of CFO using a randomly generated preamble. One randomly generated preamble is used for the methods presented in [8]–[10] [12] and the

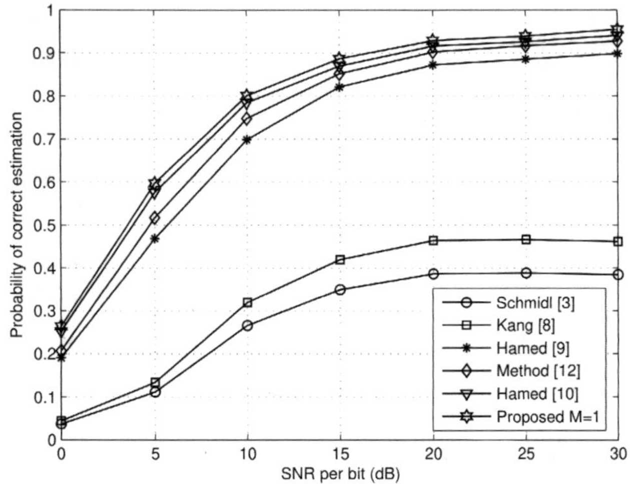

Figure 6: Probability of correct estimation of different estimators using Schmidl's preamble in the presence of CFO [M=1, I=0.5, P=11]

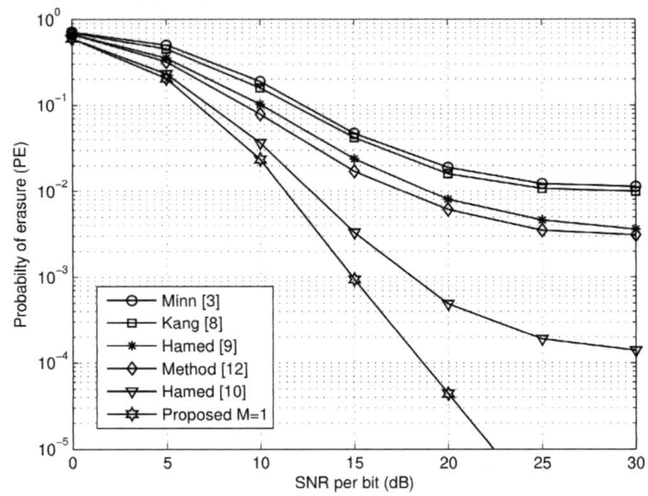

Figure 8: Probability of erasure of different estimators using Minn's preamble in the presence of CFO [M=1, I=0.5, P=11]

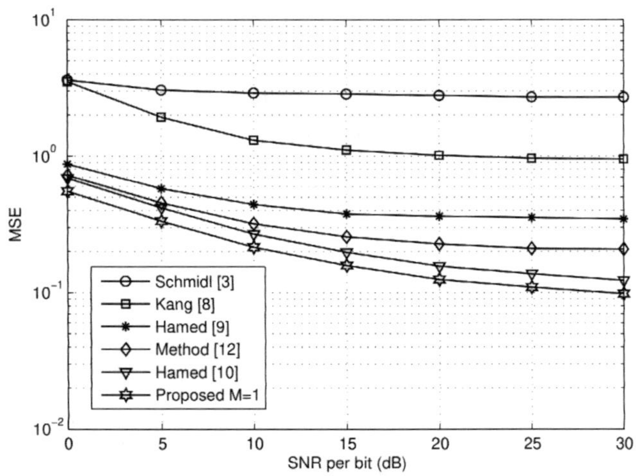

Figure 7: Timing MSE of different estimators using Schmidl's preamble in the presence of CFO [M=1, I=0.5, P=11]

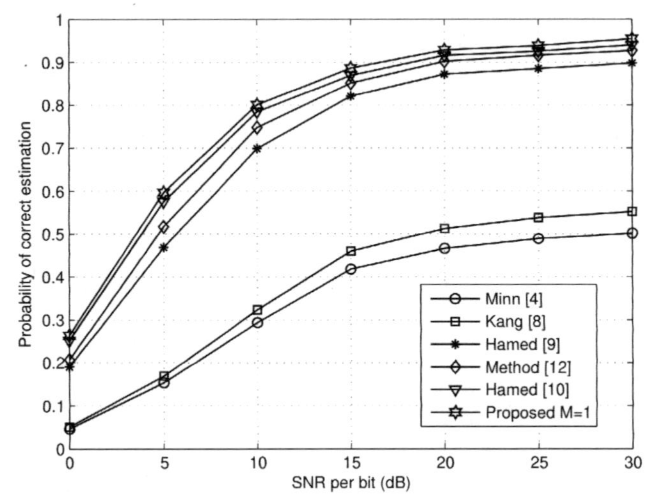

Figure 9: Probability of correct estimation of different estimators using Minn's preamble in the presence of CFO [M=1, I=0.5, P=11]

proposed method with M=1 and two randomly generated preambles are used for the method presented in [11] and the proposed method with M=2. We assume $I = 0.5$ and in the proposed method $P = 11$. From Fig. 2, Fig. 3 and Fig. 4, it is observed that proposed method performs better than the existing methods in the presence of CFO. Note that in the presence of CFO ($I \neq 0$) with $M = 1$ in the proposed method, there is a significant improvement in the performance as compared to method presented in [12]. In Fig. 5 to Fig. 13, the probability of erasure, probability of correct estimation and timing MSE of the proposed method is compared with the major existing timing synchronization methods, for different preambles. In Fig. 5 to Fig. 7, the Schmidl's preamble is used considering $M = 1$. In Fig. 8 to Fig. 10, the Minn's preamble is used considering $M = 1$ and in Fig. 11 to Fig. 13, both Schmidl's and Minn's preamble are used considering $M = 2$. We assume $I = 0.5$ and in the proposed method $P = 11$. From Fig. 5 to Fig. 13, we find that the proposed method gives the best performance. In fig. 14, probability of erasure of different estimators along with the proposed method are compared with the method proposed in [13] assuming $M = 1$. Randomly generated preamble is used. A 10 tap channel with uniform power delay profile is considered. Preamble length (N) is assumed as 128 and the number of OFDM frames simulated is $5 * 10^5$. We assume I is 3.2. For the methods presented in [9] [10], we have considered all the available correlation points without repetition, i.e., $N(N-1)/2$=8128.

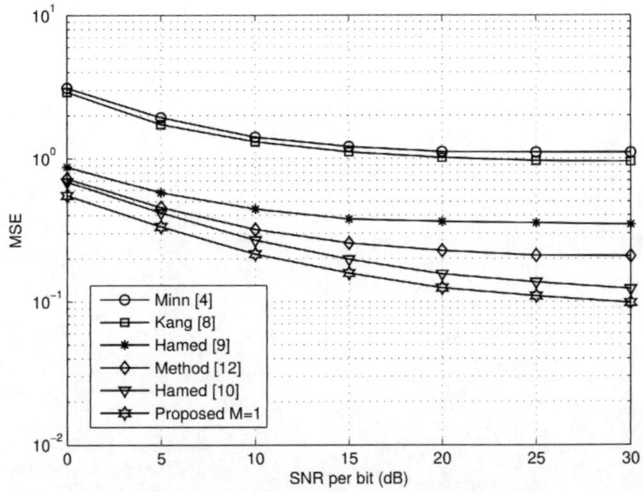

Figure 10: Timing MSE of different estimators using Minn's preamble in the presence of CFO [M=1, I=0.5, P=11]

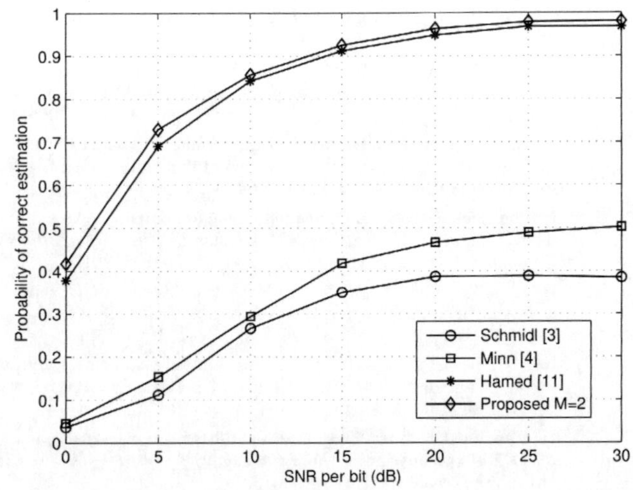

Figure 12: Probability of correct estimation of proposed estimator using Schmidl's and Minn's preamble in the presence of CFO [M=2, I=0.5, P=11]

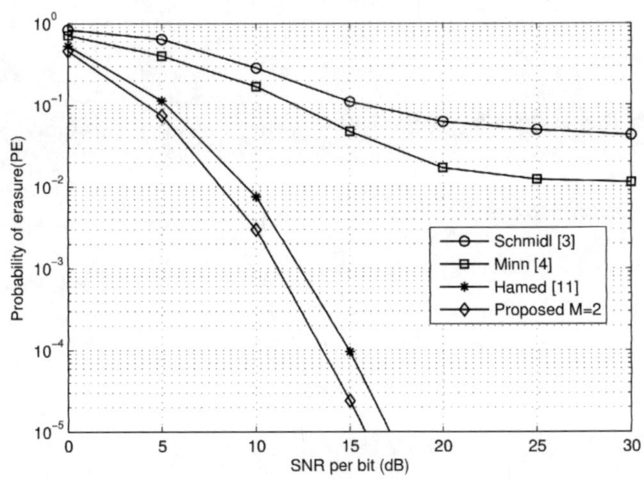

Figure 11: Probability of erasure of proposed estimator using Schmidl's and Minn's preamble in the presence of CFO [M=2, I=0.5, P=11]

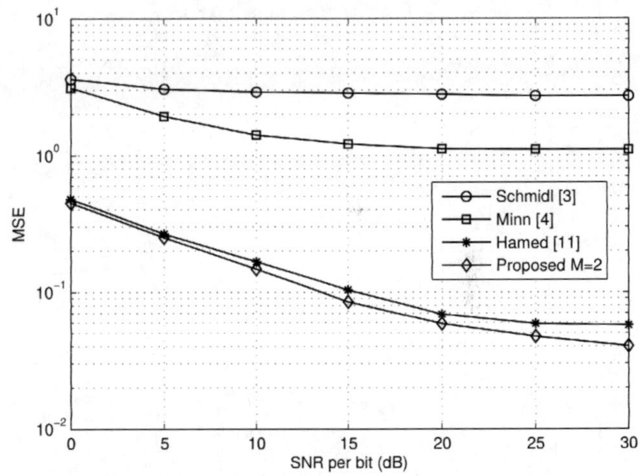

Figure 13: Timing MSE of proposed estimator using Schmidl's and Minn's preamble in the presence of CFO [M=2, I=0.5, P=11]

In the proposed method $P = 65$. It is observed that [13] gives the best performance since it is the optimum method.

V. Conclusion

In this paper, a new timing estimation method using multiple preambles has been proposed and the performance is investigated in the presence of CFO. It is observed that the proposed method performs better than most of the existing methods in the presence of CFO.

References

[1] K. Vasudevan, "Coherent detection of turbo-coded ofdm signals transmitted through frequency selective rayleigh fading channels with receiver diversity and increased throughput," *Wireless Personal Communications*, vol. 82, no. 3, pp. 1623–1642, 2015.

[2] K. Vasudevan, *Digital communications and signal processing*. Universities Press, 2007.

[3] T. M. Schmidl and D. C. Cox, "Robust frequency and timing synchronization for OFDM," *IEEE Transactions on Communications*, vol. 45, no. 12, pp. 1613–1621, 1997.

[4] H. Minn, M. Zeng, and V. K. Bhargava, "On timing offset estimation for OFDM systems," *IEEE Communications Letters*, vol. 4, no. 7, pp. 242–244, 2000.

[5] B. Park, H. Cheon, C. Kang, and D. Hong, "A novel timing estimation method for OFDM systems," *IEEE Communications Letters*, vol. 7, no. 5, pp. 239–241, 2003.

[6] J. Kim, J. Noh, and K. Chang, "Robust timing & frequency synchro-

nization techniques for OFDM-FDMA systems," in *Signal Processing Systems Design and Implementation, IEEE Workshop*, pp. 716–719, 2005.

[7] G. Ren, Y. Chang, H. Zhang, and H. Zhang, "Synchronization method based on a new constant envelop preamble for OFDM systems," *IEEE Transactions on Broadcasting*, vol. 51, no. 1, pp. 139–143, 2005.

[8] Y. Kang, S. Kim, D. Ahn, and H. Lee, "Timing estimation for OFDM systems by using a correlation sequence of preamble," *IEEE Transactions on Consumer Electronics*, vol. 54, no. 4, pp. 1600–1608, 2008.

[9] H. Abdzadeh-Ziabari, M. G. Shayesteh, and M. Manaffar, "An improved timing estimation method for OFDM systems," *IEEE Transactions on Consumer Electronics*, vol. 56, no. 4, pp. 2098–2105, 2010.

[10] H. Abdzadeh-Ziabari and M. G. Shayesteh, "Robust timing and frequency synchronization for OFDM systems," *IEEE Transactions on Vehicular Technology*, vol. 60, no. 8, pp. 3646–3656, 2011.

[11] H. Abdzadeh-Ziabari, M. G. Shayesteh, "A novel preamble-based frame timing estimator for OFDM systems," *IEEE Communications Letters*, vol. 16, no. 7, pp. 1121–1124, 2012.

[12] U. Samal and K. Vasudevan, "Preamble-based timing synchronization for OFDM systems," in *Advance Computing Conference (IACC), IEEE 3rd International*, pp. 313–318, 2013.

[13] K. Vasudevan, "Coherent detection of turbo coded ofdm signals transmitted through frequency selective rayleigh fading channels," in *Signal Processing, Computing and Control (ISPCC), IEEE International Conference*, pp. 1–6, 2013.

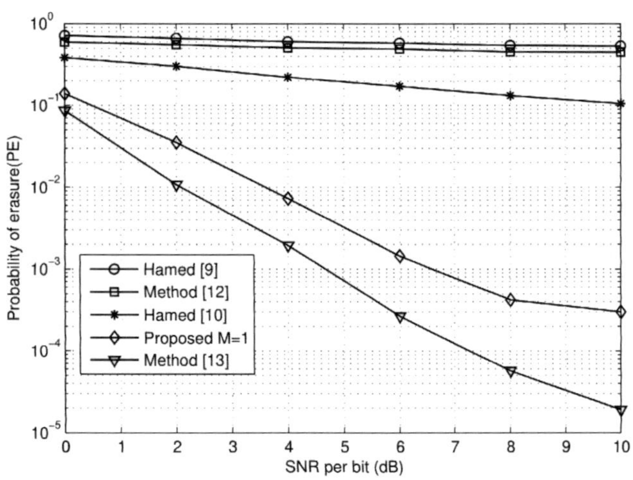

Figure 14: Probability of erasure of different estimators using randomly generated preamble in the presence of CFO [M=1, I=3.2, P=65]

A New Preamble Aided Fractional Frequency Offset Estimation in OFDM Systems

Soumitra Bhowmick, K.Vasudevan

Department of Electrical Engineering
Indian Institute of Technology
Kanpur, India 208016

***Abstract*—Carrier frequency offset (CFO) in OFDM systems can be divided in two parts, the fractional part (FFO) and the integer part (IFO). In this paper, a data aided fractional frequency offset (FFO) synchronization scheme for OFDM system is proposed. Four different algorithms to estimate the FFO are proposed. The proposed algorithms work in the time domain. An independent Rayleigh fading multipath channel in the presence of AWGN is considered. The performance is compared in terms of mean square error (MSE) of the frequency offset estimation and the computational complexity with the existing FFO estimation methods.**

***Keywords*—Carrier frequency offset (CFO); Frequency synchronization; OFDM; Preamble.**

I. INTRODUCTION

It is well known that orthogonal frequency division multiplexing (OFDM) [1] converts a frequency selective (multipath) channel into a frequency flat channel, thereby eliminating intersymbol interference (ISI). However, the presence of a carrier frequency offset (CFO) introduces inter carrier interference (ICI), which severely degrades the performance of OFDM.

There have been several methods proposed in the literature for solving the problem of CFO estimation in OFDM systems. In [2]–[5] the frequency offset is assumed to be a uniformly distributed random variable over a certain range, and is detected using maximum likelihood techniques. In the other papers CFO is usually divided into two parts: the fractional part (FFO) and the integer part (IFO). In this paper, we focus on the preamble based FFO estimation schemes. To estimate the FFO, methods proposed in the literature can be broadly classified into two categories.

1) Methods that utilize the phase shift between the repetitive parts of a preamble in the time domain [6]–[13].
2) Methods that utilize the symmetrical correlation of the preamble [14]–[18]

Schmidl and Cox [6] and Lim [8] use a preamble with two identical halves to estimate the FFO. FFO is estimated by measuring the phase shift between two identical halves of the preamble. Minn [9], Wang [11], Shi [10] use a preamble with four identical halves to estimate the FFO. FFO is estimated by measuring the phase shift between the adjacent blocks of the preamble. Tufvesson [13] proposed a different method to estimate the FFO. In [13], the received signal is multiplied by the known preamble and the FFO is estimated by measuring phase shift of the resulting signal. Morelli and Mengali [7] estimate the FFO by using a best linear unbiased estimator (BLUE), which gives better performance than [6] [8]–[11] [13]. The main drawback of the BLUE estimator [7] is its computational complexity. Zhang [14], Zhang [15], Park [16], Kim [17], Shao [18] estimate the FFO by utilizing symmetrical correlation of the preamble. Here, we propose a new method to estimate FFO using a time domain repeated preamble. The proposed method is compared with the existing methods in terms of performance in the multipath Rayleigh fading channel and the computational complexity.

This paper is organized as follows. The system model is presented in Section II. Existing FFO estimation methods are presented in Section III. The proposed method is presented in Section IV. The simulation results are given in Section V and finally, the conclusions in Section VI.

II. SYSTEM MODEL

Fig. 1 shows the typical structure of a OFDM frame in the time domain. An OFDM frame contains preamble, cyclic prefix (CP) and data. Preamble is used for synchronization purpose. Let $\mathbf{x}_p$ denotes the time domain preamble of the

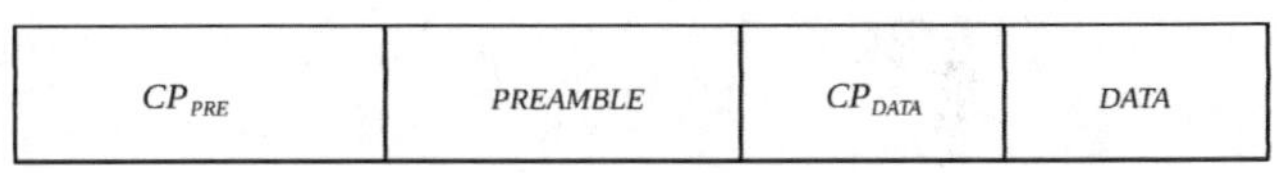

Figure 1: OFDM frame structure in the time domain

OFDM frame given by

$$\mathbf{x}_p = \left[\mathbf{A}_{N/4}\, \mathbf{A}_{N/4}\, \mathbf{A}_{N/4}\, \mathbf{A}_{N/4}\right] \tag{1}$$

where $\mathbf{A}_{N/4}$ is the sample of length $N/4$ in the time domain, which is obtained by $N/4$ point IFFT of the $N/4$ length frequency domain data. A cyclic prefix (CP) of length N_g which is denoted by $\mathbf{CP}_{\text{PRE}}$ is introduced in front of the preamble in the time domain. $\mathbf{CP}_{\text{PRE}}$ of the preamble $\mathbf{x}_p$ is given by

$$\mathbf{CP}_{\text{PRE}} = \left[x_p\left(N - N_g\right) \,...\, x_p\left(N-1\right)\right] \tag{2}$$

Let

$$\mathbf{x} = \left[\mathbf{CP}_{\text{PRE}}\, \mathbf{x}_p\right]. \tag{3}$$

Now, $\mathbf{x}$ is transmitted through the frequency selective channel. The channel is assumed to be quasi static and it is fixed for one frame and varies independently from frame to frame. Its impulse response for a given frame can be expressed as:

$$\mathbf{h} = \left[h(0)\, h(1)\, h(2) \,.....\, h(L-1)\right] \tag{4}$$

where L is the number of channel taps. The received signal $\mathbf{r}$ in the time domain is given by:

$$r(n) = y(n)\,\mathrm{e}^{j2\pi n\epsilon/N} + w(n) \tag{5}$$

where

$$\begin{aligned} y(n) &= h(n) \star x(n) \\ &= \sum_{l=0}^{L-1} h(l)\,x(n-l). \end{aligned} \tag{6}$$

where $w(n)$ is zero mean Gaussian noise sample and ϵ is the normalized frequency offset. ϵ can be divided into two parts the integer part denoted by ϵ_I (IFO) and the fractional part denoted by ϵ_F (FFO), where $-1/2 \leqslant \epsilon_F < 1/2$ [19] and $-N/2 \leqslant \epsilon_I < N/2$ or $0 \leq \epsilon_I < N$ [20]. Here, we consider the presence of FFO only. Let $z(n)$ denote the signal after discarding the CP of the received preamble $r(n)$. After discarding CP $z(n)$ is re indexed from 0 to $N-1$. We define the sub vectors $\mathbf{Z}_i$ given by

$$\mathbf{Z}_i = \left[z\left((i-1)\,N/4\right) \,.....\, z\left(iN/4-1\right)\right]^T \tag{7}$$

where $1 \leq i \leq 4$. We define the correlation functions given by

$$\mathbf{Z}_1^H\mathbf{Z}_2 = \sum_{n=0}^{N/4-1} z^\star(n).z(n+N/4) \tag{8}$$

$$\mathbf{Z}_2^H\mathbf{Z}_3 = \sum_{n=N/4}^{N/2-1} z^\star(n).z(n+N/4) \tag{9}$$

$$\mathbf{Z}_3^H\mathbf{Z}_4 = \sum_{n=N/2}^{3N/4-1} z^\star(n).z(n+N/4) \tag{10}$$

$$\mathbf{Z}_1^H\mathbf{Z}_3 = \sum_{n=0}^{N/4-1} z^\star(n).z(n+N/2) \tag{11}$$

$$\mathbf{Z}_2^H\mathbf{Z}_4 = \sum_{n=N/4}^{N/2-1} z^\star(n).z(n+N/2) \tag{12}$$

$$\mathbf{Z}_1^H\mathbf{Z}_4 = \sum_{n=0}^{N/4-1} z^\star(n).z(n+3N/4). \tag{13}$$

III. EXISTING FFO ESTIMATION METHODS

In this section, we give a brief overview of fractional frequency offset estimation methods.

1) Schmidl and Cox method: Schmidl and Cox [6] use a preamble with two identical halves to estimate the FFO, which is given by

$$\mathbf{x}_{p(sch)} = \left[\mathbf{A}_{N/2}\,\mathbf{A}_{N/2}\right] \tag{14}$$

where $\mathbf{A}_{N/2}$ is the sample of length $N/2$. In this case the $\mathbf{Z}_i$ becomes

$$\mathbf{Z}_i = \left[z\left((i-1)\,N/2\right) \,.....\, z\left(iN/2-1\right)\right]^T \tag{15}$$

where $1 \leq i \leq 2$. FFO estimation proposed by Schmidl and Cox [6] is given by

$$\hat{\epsilon}_F = \frac{2}{\pi}\arg\left(\mathbf{Z}_1^H\mathbf{Z}_2\right) = \frac{2}{\pi}\arg\left(\sum_{n=0}^{N/2-1} z^\star(n).z(n+N/2)\right). \tag{16}$$

2) Minn and Bhargava method: Minn and Bhargava [9] use a preamble with four identical halves (as given in the system model) to estimate the FFO. FFO estimation proposed by Minn and Bhargava [9] is given by

$$\hat{\epsilon}_F = \frac{2}{\pi}\arg(\psi_1) \tag{17}$$

where ψ_1 is given by

$$\psi_1 = \mathbf{Z}_1^H\mathbf{Z}_2 + \mathbf{Z}_3^H\mathbf{Z}_4 \tag{18}$$

3) Wang and Faulkner method: Wang and Faulkner [11] use a preamble with four identical halves (as given in the system model) to estimate the FFO. FFO estimation proposed by Wang and Faulkner [11] is given by

$$\hat{\epsilon}_F = \frac{2}{\pi}\arg(\psi_2) \tag{19}$$

where ψ_2 is given by

$$\psi_2 = \mathbf{Z}_2^H\mathbf{Z}_3 + \mathbf{Z}_3^H\mathbf{Z}_4 \tag{20}$$

4) Shi and Serpedin method: Shi and Serpedin [10] use a preamble with four identical halves (as given in the system model) to estimate the FFO. FFO estimation proposed by Shi and Serpedin [10] is given by

$$\hat{\epsilon}_F = \frac{2}{\pi}\arg(\psi_3) \tag{21}$$

where ψ_3 is given by

$$\psi_3 = \mathbf{Z}_1^H\mathbf{Z}_2 + \mathbf{Z}_2^H\mathbf{Z}_3 + \mathbf{Z}_3^H\mathbf{Z}_4 \tag{22}$$

5) Morelli and Mengali method: Morelli and Mengali [7] use a preamble with T identical halves to estimate the FFO, given by

$$\mathbf{x}_{p(morelli)} = \left[\mathbf{A}_{N/T}\,\mathbf{A}_{N/T}\,.....\,\mathbf{A}_{N/T}\right] \tag{23}$$

where T is given by

$$T = 2^j \tag{24}$$

where j is a positive integer and $\mathbf{A}_{N/T}$ is the sample of length N/T. FFO estimation proposed by Morelli and Mengali [7] is given by

$$\hat{\epsilon}_F = \frac{T}{2\pi}\sum_{m=1}^{H} w(m)\,\phi(m) \tag{25}$$

where $w(m)$ is given by

$$w(m) = 3\frac{(T-m)(T-m+1) - H(T-H)}{H\left(4H^2 - 6TH + 3T^2 - 1\right)} \tag{26}$$

$\phi(m)$ is given by

$$\phi(m) = \left[\arg\{R(m)\} - \arg\{R(m-1)\}\right] \tag{27}$$

and $1 \leq m \leq H$. where

$$R(k) = \sum_{n=kM}^{N-1} z^\star(n-kM)\,z(n) \tag{28}$$

and $0 \leq k \leq H$ and $H = T/2$ and $M = N/T$.

6) Park and Cheon method: Park and Cheon [16] use symmetrical correlation to estimate the FFO. Preamble used in [16] is given by

$$\mathbf{x}_{p(park)} = \left[\mathbf{A}_{N/4}\, \mathbf{B}_{N/4}\, \mathbf{A}^{\star}_{N/4}\, \mathbf{B}^{\star}_{N/4}\right] \tag{29}$$

where $\mathbf{A}_{N/4}$ is the sample of length $N/4$. $\mathbf{A}^{\star}_{N/4}$ is the conjugate of $\mathbf{A}_{N/4}$. $\mathbf{B}_{N/4}$ is designed to be the time reversed version (symmetric) of $\mathbf{A}_{N/4}$. $\mathbf{B}^{\star}_{N/4}$ is the conjugate of $\mathbf{B}_{N/4}$. The proposed FFO estimation in [16] is given by

$$\hat{\epsilon}_F = \frac{1}{\pi}\arg\left(\sum_{n=0}^{N/4-1} z^{\star}(n) . z(n+N/2)\right). \tag{30}$$

7) Shao method: Shao [18] uses symmetrical correlation to estimate the FFO. Preamble used in [18] is given by

$$\mathbf{x}_{p(shao)} = \left[\mathbf{A}_{N/4}\, \mathbf{B}^{\star}_{N/4}\, \mathbf{A}^{\star}_{N/4}\, \mathbf{B}_{N/4}\right] \tag{31}$$

where $\mathbf{A}_{N/4}$ is the sample of length $N/4$. $\mathbf{A}^{\star}_{N/4}$ is the conjugate of $\mathbf{A}_{N/4}$. $\mathbf{B}_{N/4}$ is designed to be the time reversed version (symmetric) of $\mathbf{A}_{N/4}$. $\mathbf{B}^{\star}_{N/4}$ is the conjugate of $\mathbf{B}_{N/4}$. The proposed FFO estimation in [18] is given by

$$\hat{\epsilon}_F = \frac{1}{\pi}\arg\left(\sum_{n=0}^{N/2-1} z^{\star}(n)\, z(N-n)\right). \tag{32}$$

IV. PROPOSED MODEL

The proposed method uses a preamble with four identical halves as mentioned in the system model. Correlation functions between the adjacent blocks are given by $\mathbf{Z}_1^H\mathbf{Z}_2$, $\mathbf{Z}_2^H\mathbf{Z}_3$, $\mathbf{Z}_3^H\mathbf{Z}_4$ and the correlation functions between the nonadjacent blocks are given by $\mathbf{Z}_1^H\mathbf{Z}_3$, $\mathbf{Z}_2^H\mathbf{Z}_4$, $\mathbf{Z}_1^H\mathbf{Z}_4$. In [9]–[11], the FFO is estimated by utilizing the correlation between the adjacent blocks of the preamble. In proposed method, we utilize only the non adjacent blocks of the preamble.

A. Proposed algorithm 1

The FFO estimate is

$$\hat{\epsilon}_F = \frac{1}{\pi}\arg(\psi_4) \tag{33}$$

where ψ_4 is either given by

$$\psi_4 = \mathbf{Z}_1^H\mathbf{Z}_3 \tag{34}$$

or

$$\psi_4 = \mathbf{Z}_2^H\mathbf{Z}_4 \tag{35}$$

B. Proposed algorithm 2

The FFO estimate is

$$\hat{\epsilon}_F = \frac{1}{\pi}\arg(\psi_5) \tag{36}$$

where ψ_5 is given by

$$\psi_5 = \mathbf{Z}_1^H\mathbf{Z}_3 + \mathbf{Z}_2^H\mathbf{Z}_4 \tag{37}$$

C. Proposed algorithm 3

The FFO estimate is

$$\hat{\epsilon}_F = \frac{2}{3\pi}\arg(\psi_6) \tag{38}$$

where ψ_6 is given by

$$\psi_6 = \mathbf{Z}_1^H\mathbf{Z}_4 \tag{39}$$

D. Proposed algorithm 4

The FFO estimate is

$$\hat{\epsilon}_F = \frac{1}{2\pi}\arg(\psi_5) + \frac{1}{3\pi}\arg(\psi_6) \tag{40}$$

V. SIMULATION RESULTS AND DISCUSSION

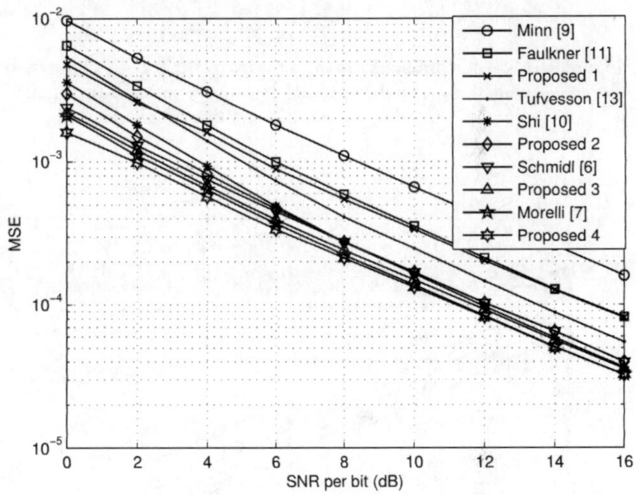

Figure 2: Mse performance of the proposed method in comparison with the previous methods that use time domain repeated preamble to estimate FFO in AWGN channel

In this section, the performance of the proposed method is compared with the major existing fractional frequency offset synchronization methods We have assumed N=128 and performed the simulations over 10^4 frames. Length N_g of the cyclic prefix (CP) is 16. QPSK signaling is assumed. Frequency selective Rayleigh fading channel is assumed with path taps $L = 5$ and path delays $\mu_l = l$ for $l = 0, 1, ..., 4$. The channel has an exponential power delay profile (PDP) with an average power of $\exp(-\mu_l/L)$. The CFO takes random value within the range $[-0.5, 0.5]$ and it varies from frame to frame. In order to compare with the methods in [9]–[11] along with the proposed method the value of j and T for the method proposed in [7] are set to 2 and 4 respectively.

Fig. 2 and Fig. 3 show the comparison of the proposed method with the existing methods that use time domain repeated preamble to estimate FFO in AWGN channel and multipath channel respectively. As indicated in Fig. 2 and Fig. 3 the proposed algorithm 1 performs better than the methods in [9] and [11] with less computational complexity. The proposed algorithm 2 performs better than the methods in

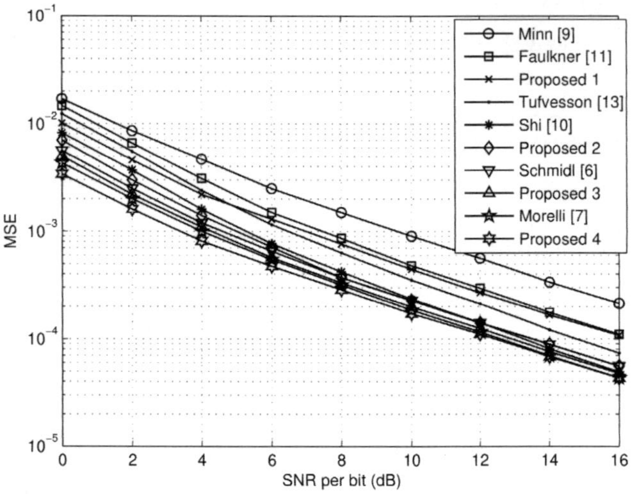

Figure 3: Mse performance of the proposed method in comparison with the previous methods that use time domain repeated preamble to estimate FFO in multipath channel

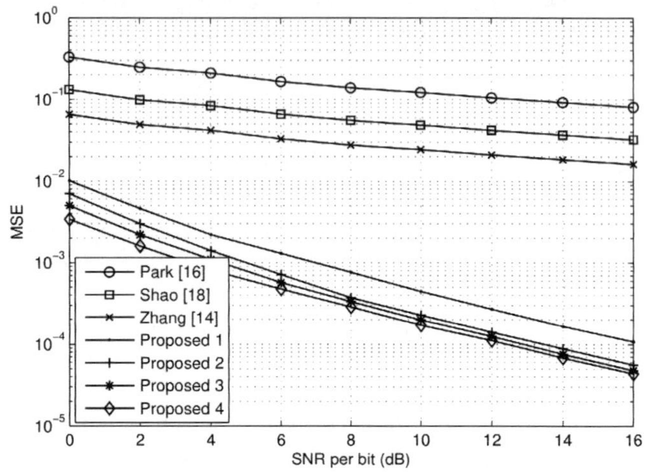

Figure 5: Mse performance of the proposed method in comparison with the previous methods that use symmetrical correlation of the preamble to estimate FFO in multipath channel

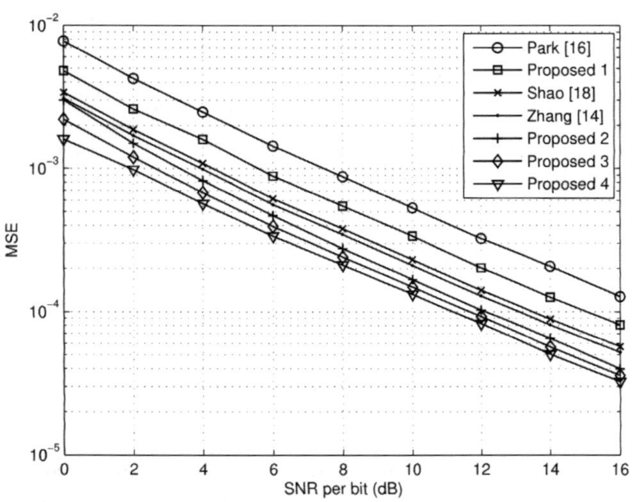

Figure 4: Mse performance of the proposed method in comparison with the previous methods that use symmetrical correlation of the preamble to estimate FFO in AWGN channel

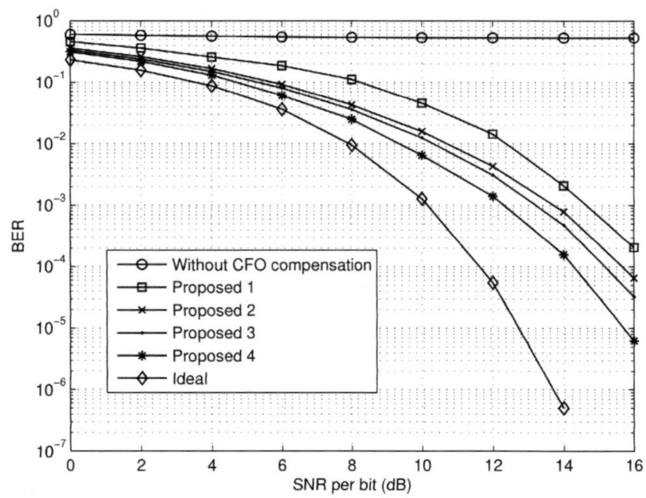

Figure 6: Ber performance of the proposed methods in AWGN channel

[9]–[11] and [13]. Computational complexity of the proposed algorithm 2 is the same as for the methods in [9] and [11] but less as compared to methods proposed in [13] and [10]. Proposed algorithm 3 performs better than the methods given in [6] [9]–[11] and [13] with less computational complexity. Proposed algorithm 4 gives the best performance because it gives the better result as compared to method in [7] with less computational complexity as indicated in Fig. 2 and Fig. 3.

Fig. 4 and Fig. 5 shows the comparison of the proposed method with the existing methods that use symmetrical correlation of the preamble to estimate FFO in AWGN channel and multipath channel respectively. It is observed that the performance of the symmetrical correlation methods [16] [14] and [18] are degraded in the presence of multipath as compared to AWGN channel. It is also observed that the proposed methods perform better than the existing symmetrical correlation methods in the presence of multipath. In table 1, the computational complexity of different estimators along with the proposed methods is given. Fig. 6 shows the ber performance of the proposed methods in AWGN channel. It is observed that proposed algorithm 4 performs better than the other methods.

VI. CONCLUSION

In this paper, the performance of different existing data aided fractional frequency offset estimator schemes are com-

TABLE I: COMPUTATIONAL COMPLEXITY

Method	Multiplications	Addition	Division
Schmidl	$(N/2)+1$	$(N/2-1)$	0
Minn	$(N/2)+1$	$(N/2)-1$	0
Faulkner	$(N/2)+1$	$(N/2)-1$	0
Shi	$(3N/4)+1$	$(3N/4)-1$	0
Morelli	$9N/4+23, T=4, H=2$	$9N/4-2, T=4, H=2$	$2, T=4, H=2$
Park	$N/4+1$	$N/4-1$	0
Shao	$N/2+1$	$N/2-1$	0
Proposed 1	$(N/4)+1$	$(N/4)-1$	0
Proposed 2	$(N/2)+1$	$(N/2-1)$	0
Proposed 3	$(N/4)+1$	$(N/4-1)$	0
Proposed 4	$(3N/4)+2$	$(3N/4-1)$	0

pared with the proposed methods. The proposed methods give better result as compared to existing techniques.

REFERENCES

[1] K. Vasudevan, *Digital communications and signal processing*. Universities Press, 2007.

[2] K. Vasudevan, "Coherent detection of turbo-coded ofdm signals transmitted through frequency selective rayleigh fading channels with receiver diversity and increased throughput," *Wireless Personal Communications*, vol. 82, no. 3, pp. 1623–1642, 2015.

[3] K. Vasudevan, "Synchronization of bursty offset qpsk signals in the presence of frequency offset and noise," in *TENCON 2008-2008 IEEE Region 10 Conference*, pp. 1–6, 2008.

[4] K. Vasudevan, "Coherent detection of turbo coded ofdm signals transmitted through frequency selective rayleigh fading channels," in *Signal Processing, Computing and Control (ISPCC), 2013 IEEE International Conference*, pp. 1–6, 2013,

[5] K. Vasudevan, "Iterative detection of turbo-coded offset qpsk in the presence of frequency and clock offsets and awgn," *Signal, Image and Video Processing*, vol. 6, no. 4, pp. 557–567, 2012.

[6] T. M. Schmidl and D. C. Cox, "Robust frequency and timing synchronization for OFDM," *IEEE Transactions on Communications*, vol. 45, no. 12, pp. 1613–1621, 1997.

[7] M. Morelli and U. Mengali, "An improved frequency offset estimator for OFDM applications," in *Communication Theory Mini-Conference, 1999.* IEEE, pp. 106–109, 1999.

[8] Y. S. Lim and J. H. Lee, "An efficient carrier frequency offset estimation scheme for an OFDM system," in *Vehicular Technology Conference, 2000. IEEE-VTS Fall VTC 2000. 52nd*, vol. 5, pp. 2453–2458, 2000.

[9] H. Minn, V. K. Bhargava, and K. B. Letaief, "A robust timing and frequency synchronization for ofdm systems," *IEEE Transactions on Wireless Communications*, vol. 2, no. 4, pp. 822–839, 2003.

[10] K. Shi and E. Serpedin, "Coarse frame and carrier synchronization of OFDM systems: a new metric and comparison," *IEEE Transactions on Wireless Communications*, vol. 3, no. 4, pp. 1271–1284, 2004.

[11] K. Wang, M. Faulkner, J. Singh and I.Tolochko, "Timing synchronization for 802.11a WLANs under multipath channels," ATNAC'03, pp. 1-5, 2003.

[12] H.-T. Hsieh and W.-R. Wu, "Maximum likelihood timing and carrier frequency offset estimation for OFDM systems with periodic preambles," *IEEE Transactions on Vehicular Technology*, vol. 58, no. 8, pp. 4224–4237, 2009.

[13] F. Tufvesson, O. Edfors, and M. Faulkner, "Time and frequency synchronization for ofdm using pn-sequence preambles," in *Vehicular Technology Conference, 1999. VTC 1999-Fall. IEEE VTS 50th*, vol. 4, pp. 2203–2207, 1999.

[14] Z. Zhang, M. Zhao, H. Zhou, Y. Liu, and J. Gao, "Frequency offset estimation with fast acquisition in ofdm system," *IEEE Communications Letters*, vol. 8, no. 3, pp. 171–173, 2004.

[15] Z. Zhang, J. Liu, C. Wang, K. Sohraby, and Y. Liu, "Joint frame synchronization and carrier frequency offset estimation in ofdm systems," in *Electro Information Technology, 2005 IEEE International Conference* , pp. 1–5, 2005.

[16] B. Park, H. Cheon, C. Kang, and D. Hong, "A novel timing estimation method for ofdm systems," *IEEE Communications Letters*, vol. 7, no. 5, pp. 239–241, 2003.

[17] J. Kim, J. Noh, and K. Chang, "Robust timing & frequency synchronization techniques for ofdm-fdma systems," in *Signal Processing Systems Design and Implementation, 2005 IEEE Workshop*, pp. 716–719, 2005.

[18] H. Shao, Y. Li, J. Tan, Y. Xu, and G. Liu, "Robust timing and frequency synchronization based on constant amplitude zero autocorrelation sequence for ofdm systems," in *Communication Problem-Solving (ICCP), 2014 IEEE International Conference*, pp. 14–17, 2014.

[19] M. Morelli, A. D'andrea, and U. Mengali, "Frequency ambiguity resolution in OFDM systems," *IEEE Communications Letters*, vol. 4, no. 4, pp. 134–136, 2000.

[20] H. Abdzadeh-Ziabari and M. G. Shayesteh, "Sufficient statistics, classification, and a novel approach for frame detection in ofdm systems," *IEEE Transactions on Vehicular Technology*, vol. 62, no. 6, pp. 2481–2495, 2013.

Coherent Turbo Coded MIMO OFDM

K. Vasudevan

Dept. of EE
IIT Kanpur
India
Email: vasu@iitk.ac.in

***Abstract*—The minimum average signal-to-noise ratio (SNR) per bit required for error-free transmission over a fading channel is derived, and is shown to be equal to that of the additive white Gaussian noise (AWGN) channel, which is -1.6 dB. Discrete-time algorithms are presented for timing and carrier synchronization, as well as channel estimation, for multiple input multiple output (MIMO) orthogonal frequency division multiplexed (OFDM) systems. The algorithms can be implemented on programmable hardware and there is a large scope for parallel processing.**

***Index Terms*—MIMO; OFDM; coherent detection; matched filtering; turbo codes; frequency selective Rayleigh fading; channel capacity.**

I. Introduction

As the world prepares for 5G [1]–[3] with its capabilities like gigabits per second peak data rate for each user, smart antennas, massive multiple input multiple output (MIMO) transmitters and receivers [4]–[6] and millimeter wave frequencies [7]–[10], the question remains [11]: What is the operating signal-to-noise ratio (SNR) per bit of the present day mobile phones? The mobile phones indicate a typical received signal strength of -100 dBm (10^{-10} mW), however this is not the SNR per bit. It appears that the research in telecommunications engineering is primarily driven by two groups namely the RF (radio frequency) and microelectronics. It also appears that advancement of technology implies asking for more: more data rate, more bandwidth, more antennas and finally more transistors on a single chip. However, there is yet another group in telecommunications, which asks for less. This is the algorithms group (perhaps this group has been too busy writing too many complicated equations) for the physical layer of telecommunication systems. The task of this group is to develop discrete-time algorithms that would minimize the bite-error-rate, by consuming the minimum possible transmit power. This aspect of telecommunications is expected to assume significance in future.

The main contribution of this paper is to develop discrete-time algorithms for coherently detecting multiple input, multiple output (MIMO), orthogonal frequency division multiplexed (OFDM) signals, transmitted over frequency selective Rayleigh fading channels. Carrier frequency offset and additive white Gaussian noise (AWGN) are the other impairments considered in this work. The minimum SNR per bit required for error-free transmission over MIMO channels is derived. The capacity of single-user MIMO systems under different assumptions about the channel impulse response (also called the channel state information or CSI) and the statistics of the channel impulse response (also called channel distribution information or CDI) is discussed in [12]. The capacity of MIMO Rayleigh fading channels in the presence of interference and receive correlation is discussed in [13]. The low SNR capacity of MIMO fading channels with imperfect channel state information is presented in [14]. To the best of our knowledge, other than the work in [15], which deals with turbo coded single input single output (SISO) OFDM, and [11] [16], which deal with turbo coded single input multiple output (SIMO) OFDM, discrete-time algorithms for the coherent detection of turbo coded MIMO OFDM systems have not been discussed earlier in the literature. Simulations results for a 2×2 turbo coded MIMO OFDM system indicate that a BER of 10^{-5}, is obtained at an SNR per bit of just 5.5 dB, which is a 2.5 dB improvement over the performance given in [11].

This paper is organized as follows. Section II presents the system model. The discrete-time algorithms for the coherent receiver are given in Section III. The simulation results are presented in Section IV. Finally, Section V concludes the paper.

II. System Model

We assume a MIMO-OFDM system with N_t transmit and N_r receive antennas, with QPSK modulation. The data from each transmit antenna is organized into frames, as shown in Fig. 1(a), similar to [11] [15] [16]. Note the presence of the cyclic suffix, whose purpose will be explained later. In Fig. 1(b), we observe that only the data and postamble QPSK symbols are interleaved. The buffer QPSK symbols (B) are sent to the IFFT without interleaving. In Fig. 1, the subscript k refers to the kth frame, n denotes the time index in a frame and $1 \leq n_t \leq N_t$ is the index to the transmit antenna. The total length of the frame is

$$L = L_p + L_{cs} + L_{cp} + L_d. \tag{1}$$

Let us assume a channel span equal to L_h. The channel span assumed by the receiver is [15] [16]

$$L_{hr} = 2L_h - 1 \tag{2}$$

Note that L_h depends on the delay spread of the channel, and is measured in terms of the number of symbols. Recall that, the delay spread is a measure of the time difference between

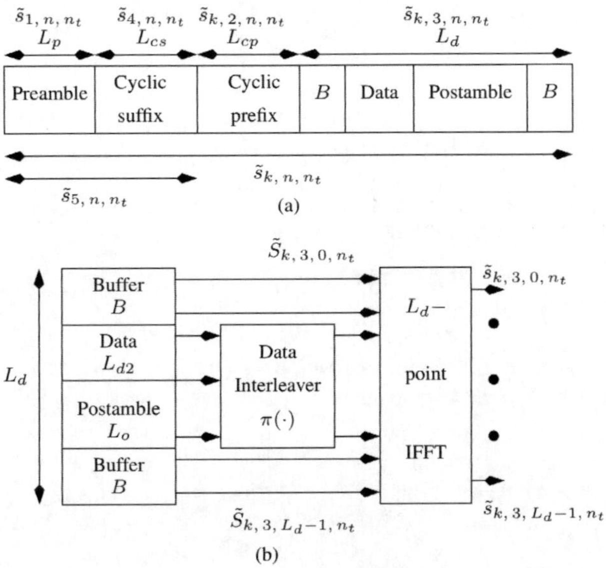

Fig. 1. The frame structure in the time domain.

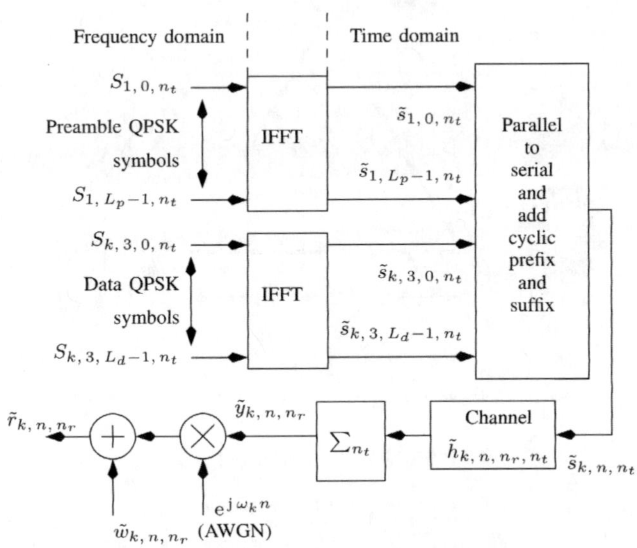

Fig. 2. Block diagram of the transmitter.

the arrival of the first and the last multipath signal, as seen by the receiver. Typically

$$L_h = d_0/(cT_s) \tag{3}$$

where d_0 is the distance between the longest and shortest multipath, c is the velocity of light and T_s is the symbol duration. We have assumed a situation where the mobile is close to the base station and the longest path is reflected from the cell edge, which is approximately equal to the cell diameter d_0, as shown in Fig. 3. For $L_h = 10$, $1/T_s = 10^7$ bauds and $c = 3\times 10^8$ meters per sec, we get $d_0 = 300$ meters. Similarly with $L_h = 10$ and $1/T_s = 10^8$ bauds we obtain $d_0 = 30$ meters. In other words, as the baud rate increases, the cell size needs to decrease, and consequently the transmit power decreases, for the same channel span L_h. The length of the cyclic prefix and suffix is [17]:

$$L_{cp} = L_{cs} = L_{hr} - 1. \tag{4}$$

Throughout the manuscript, we use tilde to denote complex quantities. However, complex QPSK symbols will be denoted without a tilde e.g., $S_{1,\,n,\,n_t}$. Boldface letters denote vectors or matrices. The channel coefficients $\tilde{h}_{k,\,n,\,n_r,\,n_t}$ associated with the receive antenna n_r ($1 \le n_r \le N_r$) and transmit antenna n_t ($1 \le n_t \le N_t$) for the kth frame are $\mathscr{CN}(0,\,2\sigma_f^2)$ and independent over time n, that is:

$$\frac{1}{2}E\left[\tilde{h}_{k,\,n,\,n_r,\,n_t}\tilde{h}^*_{k,\,n-m,\,n_r,\,n_t}\right] = \sigma_f^2\delta_K(m) \tag{5}$$

where "*" denotes complex conjugate and $\delta_K(\cdot)$ is the Kronecker delta function. This implies a uniform power delay profile. Note that a uniform power delay profile is the worst case channel model, since all the multipath components have the same power. The channel is assumed to be quasi-static, that is $\tilde{h}_{k,\,n,\,n_r,\,n_t}$ is time-invariant over one frame and varies independently from frame-to-frame. The AWGN noise samples $\tilde{w}_{k,\,n,\,n_r}$ for the kth frame at time n and receive antenna n_r are $\mathscr{CN}(0,\,2\sigma_w^2)$. The frequency offset ω_k for the kth frame is uniformly distributed over $[-0.04,\,0.04]$ radian [18]. We assume that ω_k is fixed for a frame and varies randomly from frame-to-frame. The block diagram of the transmitter is given in Fig. 2.

With reference to Fig. 1(a) and 2, note that:

$$\begin{aligned}
\tilde{s}_{1,\,n,\,n_t} &= \frac{1}{L_p}\sum_{i=0}^{L_p-1} S_{1,\,i,\,n_t}\mathrm{e}^{\,\mathrm{j}\,2\pi ni/L_p} \\
&\quad \text{for } 0 \le n \le L_p - 1 \\
\tilde{s}_{k,\,3,\,n,\,n_t} &= \frac{1}{L_d}\sum_{i=0}^{L_d-1} S_{k,\,3,\,i,\,n_t}\mathrm{e}^{\,\mathrm{j}\,2\pi ni/L_d} \\
&\quad \text{for } 0 \le n \le L_d - 1 \\
\tilde{s}_{k,\,2,\,n,\,n_t} &= \tilde{s}_{k,\,3,\,L_d-L_{cp}+n,\,n_t} \\
&\quad \text{for } 0 \le n \le L_{cp} - 1 \\
\tilde{s}_{4,\,n,\,n_t} &= \tilde{s}_{1,\,n,\,n_t} \\
&\quad \text{for } 0 \le n \le L_{cs} - 1 \\
\tilde{s}_{5,\,n,\,n_t} &= \tilde{s}_{1,\,n,\,n_t} + \tilde{s}_{4,\,n-L_p,\,n_t}.
\end{aligned} \tag{6}$$

From (6), it is clear that the preamble is independent of the frame k. However, each transmit antenna has its own preamble, for the purpose of synchronization and channel estimation at the receiver.

The preamble in the frequency domain, for each transmit antenna is generated as follows. Let $\pi_p(i)$, for $0 \le i \le L_p - 1$, denote the interleaver map for the preamble. Let

$$\mathbf{S}_r = \left[\; S_{r,\,0} \quad \ldots \quad S_{r,\,L_p-1} \;\right]^T_{L_p\times 1} \tag{7}$$

denote a random vector of QPSK symbols. The preamble vector for the transmit antenna n_t is first initialized by

$$\begin{aligned}\mathbf{S}_{1,\,n_t} &= \begin{bmatrix} S_{1,\,0,\,n_t} & \ldots & S_{1,\,L_p-1,\,n_t} \end{bmatrix}^T_{L_p\times 1} \\ &= \mathbf{0}_{L_p\times 1}.\end{aligned} \tag{8}$$

Next, we substitute

$$\mathbf{S}_{1,\,\pi_p(i_4:i_5),\,n_t} = \mathbf{S}_r(i_4 : i_5). \tag{9}$$

where $i_4 : i_5$ denotes the range of indices from i_4 to i_5, both inclusive, and

$$\begin{aligned} i_4 &= (n_t-1)L_p/N_t \\ i_5 &= i_4 + L_p/N_t - 1. \end{aligned} \tag{10}$$

Note that the preamble in the frequency domain for each transmit antenna has only L_p/N_t non-zero elements, the rest of the elements are zero. Moreover, due to $\pi_p(\cdot)$, the L_p/N_t non-zero elements are randomly interspersed over the L_p subcarriers in the frequency domain, for each transmit antenna.

By virtue of the preamble construction in (8), (9) and (10), the preambles in the frequency and time domains corresponding to transmit antennas n_t and m_t satisfy the relation (using Parseval's energy theorem):

$$\begin{aligned} S_{1,\,i,\,n_t} S^*_{1,\,i,\,m_t} &= (2N_tL_p/L_d)\delta_K(n_t-m_t) \\ &\quad \text{for } 0 \le i \le L_p-1 \\ \Rightarrow \tilde{s}_{1,\,n,\,n_t} \odot_{L_p} \tilde{s}^*_{1,\,-n,\,m_t} &= \begin{cases} 0 & \text{for } n_t \ne m_t, \\ & 0 \le n \le L_p-1 \\ (2L_p/L_d)\delta_K(n) & \\ & \text{for } n_t = m_t \end{cases} \end{aligned} \tag{11}$$

where "$\odot_{L_p}$" denotes the L_p-point circular convolution. In other words, the preambles corresponding to distinct transmit antennas are orthogonal over L_p samples. Moreover, the autocorrelation of the preambles in frequency and time domain, can be approximated by a weighted Kronecker delta function (this condition is usually satisfied by random sequences having zero-mean; the approximation gets better as L_p increases).

We assume $S_{k,\,3,\,i,\,n_t} \in \{\pm 1 \pm \mathrm{j}\}$. Since we require:

$$E\left[|\tilde{s}_{1,\,n,\,n_t}|^2\right] = E\left[|\tilde{s}_{k,\,3,\,n,\,n_t}|^2\right] = 2/L_d \stackrel{\Delta}{=} \sigma_s^2 \tag{12}$$

we must have $S_{1,\,i,\,n_t} \in \sqrt{L_pN_t/L_d}\,(\pm 1 \pm \mathrm{j})$. In other words, the average power of the preamble part must be equal to the average power of the data part, in the time domain.

Due to the presence of the cyclic suffix in Fig. 1 and (6), and due to (11), we have

$$\begin{aligned} &\tilde{s}_{5,\,n,\,n_t} \star \tilde{s}^*_{1,\,L_p-1-n,\,m_t} \\ &= \begin{cases} 0 & \text{for } L_p-1 \le n \le L_p+L_{hr}-2, \\ & n_t \ne m_t \\ (2L_p/L_d)\delta_K(n-L_p+1) & \\ & \text{for } n_t = m_t \end{cases} \end{aligned} \tag{13}$$

where "$\star$" denotes linear convolution.

The signal for the kth frame and receive antenna n_r can be written as (for $0 \le n \le L + L_h - 2$):

$$\begin{aligned} \tilde{r}_{k,\,n,\,n_r} &= \sum_{n_t=1}^{N_t} \left(\tilde{s}_{k,\,n,\,n_t} \star \tilde{h}_{k,\,n,\,n_r,\,n_t}\right) \mathrm{e}^{\,\mathrm{j}\,\omega_k n} + \tilde{w}_{k,\,n,\,n_r} \\ &= \tilde{y}_{k,\,n,\,n_r}\mathrm{e}^{\,\mathrm{j}\,\omega_k n} + \tilde{w}_{k,\,n,\,n_r} \end{aligned} \tag{14}$$

where $\tilde{s}_{k,\,n,\,n_t}$ is depicted in Fig. 1(a) and

$$\tilde{y}_{k,\,n,\,n_r} = \sum_{n_t=1}^{N_t} \tilde{s}_{k,\,n,\,n_t} \star \tilde{h}_{k,\,n,\,n_r,\,n_t}. \tag{15}$$

Note that any random carrier phase can be absorbed in the channel impulse response.

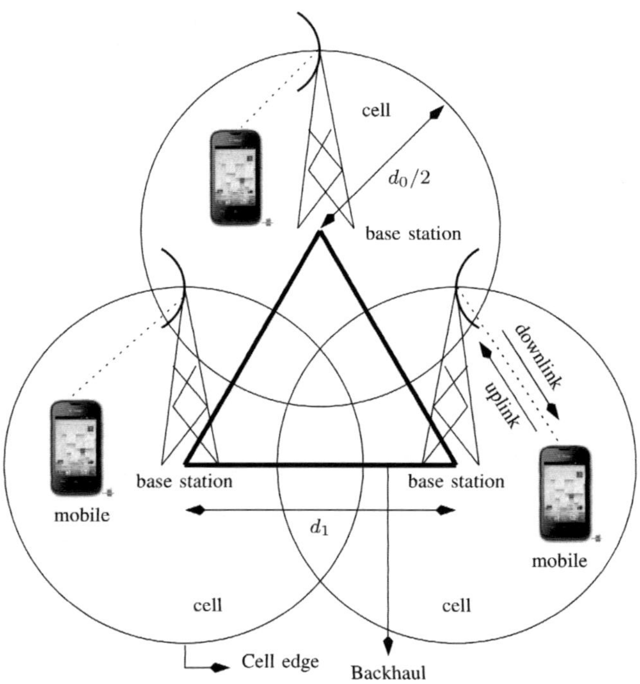

Fig. 3. System block diagram.

The system block diagram is depicted in Fig. 3. The base stations are interconnected by a high data-rate backhaul. Note that $d_1 < d_0$. In order to obtain symmetry, the backhaul forms an equilateral triangle of length d_1. The base station is at the center of each cell, whose diameter is d_0. The uplink and downlink transmissions between the mobiles and base station could be carried out using time division duplex (TDD) or frequency division duplex (FDD). Time division (TDMA), frequency division (FDMA), code division (CDMA), orthogonal frequency division (OFDMA), for downlink transmissions and filterbank multicarrier (FBMC), for uplink transmissions [19], are the possible choices for multiple access (MA) techniques.

III. RECEIVER

In this section, we discuss the discrete-time receiver algorithms.

A. Start of Frame (SoF) and Coarse Frequency Offset Estimate

The start of frame (SoF) detection and coarse frequency offset estimation is performed for each receive antenna $1 \leq n_r \leq N_r$ and transmit antenna $1 \leq n_t \leq N_t$, as given by the following rule (similar to (22) in [15] and (24) in [16]): choose that value of m and ν_k which maximizes

$$\left| \left(\tilde{r}_{k,\,m,\,n_r} \, \mathrm{e}^{-\mathrm{j}\,\nu_k m} \right) \star \tilde{s}^*_{1,\,L_p-1-m,\,n_t} \right| . \tag{16}$$

Let $\hat{m}_k(\cdot)$ denote the time instant and $\hat{\nu}_k(\cdot)$ denote the coarse estimate of the frequency offset (both of which are functions of n_r and n_t), at which the maximum in (16) is obtained. Note that (16) is a two-dimensional search over m and ν_k, which can be efficiently implemented in hardware, and there is a large scope for parallel processing. In particular, the search over ν_k involves dividing the range of ω_k ($[-0.04,\, 0.04]]$ radians) into B_1 frequency bins, and deciding in favour of that bin which maximizes (16). In our simulations, $B_1 = 64$ [15] [16].

Note that in the absence of noise and due to the properties given in (13)

$$\hat{m}_k(n_r,\, n_t) = L_p - 1 + \mathrm{argmax}_m \left| \tilde{h}_{k,\,m,\,n_r,\,n_t} \right| \tag{17}$$

where argmax_m corresponds to the value of m for which $\left| \tilde{h}_{k,\,m,\,n_r,\,n_t} \right|$ is maximum. We also have

$$L_p - 1 \leq \hat{m}_k(n_r,\, n_t) \leq L_p + L_h - 2. \tag{18}$$

If $\hat{m}_k(\cdot)$ lies outside the range in (18), the frame is declared as erased (not detected). This implies that the peak in (16) is due to noise, and not due to the channel. The average value of the coarse frequency offset estimate is given by

$$\hat{\omega}_k = \frac{\sum_{n_r=1}^{N_r} \sum_{n_t=1}^{N_t} \hat{\nu}_k(n_r,\, n_t)}{N_r N_t}. \tag{19}$$

B. Channel Estimation

We assume that the SoF has been estimated using (16) with outcome $m_{0,\,k}$ given by (assuming the condition in (18) is satisfied for all n_r and n_t):

$$m_{0,\,k} = \hat{m}_k(1,\,1) - L_p + 1 \quad 0 \leq m_{0,\,k} \leq L_h - 1 \tag{20}$$

and the frequency offset has been perfectly canceled [15] [16]. Observe that any value of n_r and n_t can be used in the computation of (20). We have taken $n_r = n_t = 1$. Define

$$m_{1,\,k} = m_{0,\,k} + L_h - 1. \tag{21}$$

For the sake of notational simplicity, we drop the subscript k in $m_{1,\,k}$, and refer to it as m_1. The steady-state, preamble part of the received signal for the kth frame and receive antenna n_r can be written as:

$$\tilde{\mathbf{r}}_{k,\,m_1,\,n_r} = \sum_{n_t=1}^{N_t} \tilde{\mathbf{s}}_{5,\,n_t} \tilde{\mathbf{h}}_{k,\,n_r,\,n_t} + \tilde{\mathbf{w}}_{k,\,m_1,\,n_r} \tag{22}$$

where

$$\begin{aligned}
\tilde{\mathbf{r}}_{k,\,m_1,\,n_r} &= \left[\, \tilde{r}_{k,\,m_1,\,n_r} \;\; \ldots \;\; \tilde{r}_{k,\,m_1+L_p-1,\,n_r} \,\right]^T \\
&\quad [L_p \times 1] \;\; \text{vector} \\
\tilde{\mathbf{w}}_{k,\,m_1,\,n_r} &= \left[\, \tilde{w}_{k,\,m_1,\,n_r} \;\; \ldots \;\; \tilde{w}_{k,\,m_1+L_p-1,\,n_r} \,\right]^T \\
&\quad [L_p \times 1] \;\; \text{vector} \\
\tilde{\mathbf{h}}_{k,\,n_r,\,n_t} &= \left[\, \tilde{h}_{k,\,0,\,n_r,\,n_t} \;\; \ldots \;\; \tilde{h}_{k,\,L_{hr}-1,\,n_r,\,n_t} \,\right]^T \\
&\quad [L_{hr} \times 1] \;\; \text{vector} \\
\tilde{\mathbf{s}}_{5,\,n_t} &= \begin{bmatrix} \tilde{s}_{5,\,L_{hr}-1,\,n_t} & \ldots & \tilde{s}_{5,\,0,\,n_t} \\ \vdots & \ldots & \vdots \\ \tilde{s}_{5,\,L_p+L_{hr}-2,\,n_t} & \ldots & \tilde{s}_{5,\,L_p-1,\,n_t} \end{bmatrix} \\
&\quad [L_p \times L_{hr}] \;\; \text{matrix}
\end{aligned} \tag{23}$$

where L_{hr} is the channel length assumed by the receiver (see (2)), $\tilde{\mathbf{s}}_{5,\,n_t}$ is the channel estimation matrix and $\tilde{\mathbf{r}}_{k,\,m_1,\,n_r}$ is the received signal vector *after* cancellation of the frequency offset. Observe that $\tilde{\mathbf{s}}_{5,\,n_t}$ is independent of m_1 and due to the relations in (11) and (13), we have

$$\tilde{\mathbf{s}}^H_{5,\,m_t} \tilde{\mathbf{s}}_{5,\,n_t} = \begin{cases} \mathbf{0}_{L_{hr} \times L_{hr}} & \text{for } n_t \neq m_t \\ (2L_p/L_d)\mathbf{I}_{L_{hr}} & \text{for } n_t = m_t \end{cases} \tag{24}$$

where $\mathbf{I}_{L_{hr}}$ is an $L_{hr} \times L_{hr}$ identity matrix and $\mathbf{0}_{L_{hr} \times L_{hr}}$ is an $L_{hr} \times L_{hr}$ null matrix. The statement of the ML channel estimation is as follows. Find $\hat{\mathbf{h}}_{k,\,n_r,\,m_t}$ (the estimate of $\tilde{\mathbf{h}}_{k,\,n_r,\,m_t}$) such that:

$$\left(\tilde{\mathbf{r}}_{k,\,m_1,\,n_r} - \sum_{m_t=1}^{N_t} \tilde{\mathbf{s}}_{5,\,m_t} \hat{\mathbf{h}}_{k,\,n_r,\,m_t} \right)^H \left(\tilde{\mathbf{r}}_{k,\,m_1,\,n_r} - \sum_{m_t=1}^{N_t} \tilde{\mathbf{s}}_{5,\,m_t} \hat{\mathbf{h}}_{k,\,n_r,\,m_t} \right) \tag{25}$$

is minimized. Differentiating with respect to $\hat{\mathbf{h}}^*_{k,\,n_r,\,m_t}$ and setting the result to zero yields [17] [20]:

$$\hat{\mathbf{h}}_{k,\,n_r,\,m_t} = \left(\tilde{\mathbf{s}}^H_{5,\,m_t} \tilde{\mathbf{s}}_{5,\,m_t} \right)^{-1} \tilde{\mathbf{s}}^H_{5,\,m_t} \tilde{\mathbf{r}}_{k,\,m_1,\,n_r}. \tag{26}$$

Observe that when $m_{0,\,k} = L_h - 1$ in (20), and noise is absent (see (29) in [15] and (35) in [16]), we obtain:

$$\hat{\mathbf{h}}_{k,\,n_r,\,m_t} = \left[\, \tilde{h}_{k,\,0,\,n_r,\,m_t} \;\; \ldots \;\; \tilde{h}_{k,\,L_h-1,\,n_r,\,m_t} \;\; 0 \;\; \ldots \;\; 0 \,\right]^T. \tag{27}$$

Similarly, when $m_{0,\,k} = 0$ and in the absence of noise:

$$\hat{\mathbf{h}}_{k,\,n_r,\,m_t} = \left[\, 0 \;\; \ldots \;\; 0 \;\; \tilde{h}_{k,\,0,\,n_r,\,m_t} \;\; \ldots \;\; \tilde{h}_{k,\,L_h-1,\,n_r,\,m_t} \,\right]^T. \tag{28}$$

To see the effect of noise on the channel estimate in (26), consider

$$\tilde{\mathbf{u}} = \left(\tilde{\mathbf{s}}^H_{5,\,m_t} \tilde{\mathbf{s}}_{5,\,m_t} \right)^{-1} \tilde{\mathbf{s}}^H_{5,\,m_t} \tilde{\mathbf{w}}_{k,\,m_1,\,n_r}. \tag{29}$$

It can be shown that

$$E\left[\tilde{\mathbf{u}} \tilde{\mathbf{u}}^H \right] = \frac{\sigma^2_w L_d}{L_p} \mathbf{I}_{L_{hr}} \stackrel{\Delta}{=} 2\sigma^2_u \mathbf{I}_{L_{hr}}. \tag{30}$$

Therefore, the variance of the ML channel estimate (σ_u^2) tends to zero as $L_p \to \infty$ and L_d is kept fixed. Conversely, when L_d is increased keeping L_p fixed, there is noise enhancement [11] [16].

C. Fine Frequency Offset Estimation

The fine frequency offset estimate is obtained using the following rule: choose that value of time instant m and frequency offset $\nu_{k,\,f}$ which maximizes:

$$\left|\left(\tilde{r}_{k,\,m,\,n_r}\,\mathrm{e}^{-\mathrm{j}\,(\hat{\omega}_k+\nu_{k,\,f})m}\right)\star \tilde{y}^*_{1,\,k,\,L_2-1-m,\,n_r,\,n_t}\right| \tag{31}$$

where

$$\begin{aligned} L_2 &= L_{hr}+L_p-1 \\ \hat{y}_{1,\,k,\,m,\,n_r,\,n_t} &= \tilde{s}_{1,\,m,\,n_t}\star \hat{h}_{k,\,m,\,n_r,\,n_t} \end{aligned} \tag{32}$$

where $\hat{h}_{k,\,m,\,n_r,\,n_t}$ is obtained from (26). The fine frequency offset estimate ($\hat{\nu}_{k,\,f}(n_r,\,n_t)$) is obtained by dividing the interval $[\hat{\omega}_k - 0.005,\ \hat{\omega}_k + 0.005]$ radian ($\hat{\omega}_k$ is given in (19)) into $B_2 = 64$ frequency bins [21]. The reason for choosing 0.005 radian can be traced to Fig. 5 of [16]. We find that the maximum error in the coarse estimate of the frequency offset is approximately 0.004 radian over 10^4 frames. Thus the probability that the maximum error exceeds 0.005 radian is less than 10^{-4}. However, from Table V in this paper, we note that the maximum error in the frequency offset is 2.4×10^{-2} radians for $L_p = 512$, and 1.1×10^{-2} for $L_p = 1024$, both of which are larger than 0.005 radian. By observing this trend, we expect that for larger values of L_p, say $L_p = 4096$, the maximum error in the coarse frequency offset estimate would be less than 0.005 radians. Increasing L_p would also imply an increase in L_d, for the same throughput (see (51)). The average value of the fine frequency offset estimate is given by:

$$\hat{\omega}_{k,\,f} = \frac{\sum_{n_r=1}^{N_r}\sum_{n_t=1}^{N_t}\hat{\nu}_{k,\,f}(n_r,\,n_t)}{N_r N_t}. \tag{33}$$

D. Super Fine Frequency Offset Estimation

The fine frequency offset estimate in (33) is still inadequate for turbo decoding and data detection when $L_d \gg L_p$ [15]. Note that the residual frequency offset is equal to:

$$\omega_k - \hat{\omega}_k - \hat{\omega}_{k,\,f}. \tag{34}$$

This residual frequency offset is estimated by interpolating the FFT output and performing postamble matched filtering at the receiver [11] [16]. If the interpolation factor is I, then the FFT size is IL_d (interpolation in the frequency domain is achieved by zero-padding the FFT input in the time domain, and then taking the IL_d-point FFT). Let

$$m_{2,\,k} = m_{1,\,k} + L_p + L_{cs} \tag{35}$$

where $m_{1,\,k}$ is defined in (21). Once again, we drop the subscript k from $m_{2,\,k}$ and refer to it as m_2. Define the FFT input in the time domain as:

$$\tilde{\mathbf{r}}_{k,\,m_2,\,n_r} = \left[\ \tilde{r}_{k,\,m_2,\,n_r}\ \ \ldots\ \ \tilde{r}_{k,\,m_2+L_d-1,\,n_r}\ \right]^T \tag{36}$$

which is the data part of the received signal in (14) for the kth frame and receive antenna n_r, assumed to have the residual frequency offset given by (34). The output of the IL_d-point FFT of $\tilde{\mathbf{r}}_{k,\,m_2,\,n_r}$ in (36) is denoted by

$$\tilde{R}_{k,\,i,\,n_r} = \sum_{n=0}^{L_d-1}\tilde{r}_{k,\,m_2+n,\,n_r}\mathrm{e}^{-\mathrm{j}\,2\pi i n/(IL_d)} \tag{37}$$

for $0 \le i \le IL_d - 1$.

The coefficients of the postamble matched filter is obtained as follows [11] [16]. Define

$$\tilde{G}''_{k,\,i,\,n_r} = \sum_{n_t=1}^{N_t}\hat{H}_{k,\,i_3,\,n_r,\,n_t}S_{k,\,3,\,i,\,n_t}\quad \text{for } i_0 \le i \le i_1 \tag{38}$$

where $\hat{H}_{k,\,i,\,n_r,\,n_t}$ is the L_d-point FFT of the channel estimate in (26), and

$$\begin{aligned} i_0 &= B + L_{d2} \\ i_1 &= i_0 + L_o - 1 \\ i_3 &= B + \pi(i - B) \end{aligned} \tag{39}$$

where $\pi(\cdot)$ is the data interleaver map, B, L_{d2} and L_o are the lengths of the buffer, data and postamble respectively, as shown in Fig. 1(b). Let

$$\tilde{G}'_{k,\,i_3,\,n_r} = \begin{cases} \tilde{G}''_{k,\,i,\,n_r} & \text{for } i_0 \le i \le i_1 \\ 0 & \text{otherwise} \end{cases} \tag{40}$$

where $0 \le i_3 \le L_d - 1$, the relation between i_3 and i is given in (39). Next, we perform interpolation:

$$\tilde{G}_{k,\,i_4,\,n_r} = \begin{cases} \tilde{G}'_{k,\,i,\,n_r} & \text{for } 0 \le i \le L_d - 1 \\ 0 & \text{otherwise} \end{cases} \tag{41}$$

where $0 \le i_4 \le IL_d - 1$ and $i_4 = iI$. Finally, the postamble matched filter is $\tilde{G}^*_{k,\,IL_d-1-i,\,n_r}$, which is convolved with $\tilde{R}_{k,\,i,\,n_r}$ in (37). Note that due to the presence of the cyclic prefix, any residual frequency offset in the time domain, manifests as a circular shift in the frequency domain. The purpose of the postamble matched filter is to capture this shift. The role of the buffer symbols is explained in [11] [16]. Assume that the peak of the postamble matched filter output occurs at $m_{3,\,k}(n_r)$. Ideally, in the absence of noise and frequency offset

$$m_{3,\,k}(n_r) = IL_d - 1. \tag{42}$$

In the presence of the frequency offset, the peak occurs to the left or right of $IL_d - 1$. The average superfine estimate of the residual frequency offset is given by:

$$\hat{\omega}_{k,\,sf} = 2\pi/(IL_d N_r)\sum_{n_r=1}^{N_r}\left[m_{3,\,k}(n_r) - IL_d + 1\right]. \tag{43}$$

E. Noise Variance Estimation

The noise variance is estimated as follows, for the purpose of turbo decoding:

$$\hat{\sigma}_w^2 = \frac{1}{2L_pN_r}\sum_{n_r=1}^{N_r}\left(\tilde{\mathbf{r}}_{k,\,m_1,\,n_r} - \sum_{n_t=1}^{N_t}\tilde{\mathbf{s}}_{5,\,n_t}\hat{\mathbf{h}}_{k,\,n_r,\,n_t}\right)^H \left(\tilde{\mathbf{r}}_{k,\,m_1,\,n_r} - \sum_{n_t=1}^{N_t}\tilde{\mathbf{s}}_{5,\,n_t}\hat{\mathbf{h}}_{k,\,n_r,\,n_t}\right). \quad (44)$$

F. Turbo Decoding

In this section, we assume that the frequency offset has been perfectly canceled, that is, $\tilde{\mathbf{r}}_{k,\,m_2,\,n_r}$ in (36) contains no frequency offset. The output of the L_d-point FFT of $\tilde{\mathbf{r}}_{k,\,m_2,\,n_r}$ for the kth frame is given by:

$$\tilde{R}_{k,\,i,\,n_r} = \sum_{n_t=1}^{N_t}\tilde{H}_{k,\,i,\,n_r,\,n_t}S_{k,\,3,\,i,\,n_t} + \tilde{W}_{k,\,i,\,n_r} \quad (45)$$

for $0 \le i \le L_d - 1$, where $\tilde{H}_{k,\,i,\,n_r,\,n_t}$ is the L_d-point FFT of $\tilde{h}_{k,\,n,\,n_r,\,n_t}$ and $\tilde{W}_{k,\,i,\,n_r}$ is the L_d-point FFT of $\tilde{w}_{k,\,n,\,n_r}$. It can be shown that [15] [16]

$$\begin{aligned}\frac{1}{2}E\left[\left|\tilde{W}_{k,\,i,\,n_r}\right|^2\right] &= L_d\sigma_w^2\\ \frac{1}{2}E\left[\left|\tilde{H}_{k,\,i,\,n_r,\,n_t}\right|^2\right] &= L_h\sigma_f^2.\end{aligned} \quad (46)$$

The generating matrix of each of the constituent encoders is given by (41) in [16]. For the purpose of turbo decoding, we consider the case where $N_r = N_t = 2$. The details of turbo decoding can be found in [16], and will not be discussed here. Suffices to say that corresponding to the transition from state m to state n, at decoder 1, for the kth frame, at time i, we define (for $0 \le i \le L_{d2} - 1$):

$$\gamma_{1,\,k,\,i,\,m,\,n} = \exp\left(-Z_{1,\,k,\,i,\,m,\,n}/\left(2L_d\hat{\sigma}_w^2\right)\right) \quad (47)$$

where $Z_{1,\,k,\,i,\,m,\,n}$ is given by

$$\min_{\text{all } S_{m,\,n,\,2}}\sum_{n_r=1}^{2}\left|\tilde{R}_{k,\,i,\,n_r} - \sum_{n_t=1}^{2}\hat{H}_{k,\,i,\,n_r,\,n_t}S_{m,\,n,\,n_t}\right|^2 \quad (48)$$

where $S_{m,\,n,\,n_t}$ denotes the QPSK symbol corresponding to the transition from state m to state n in the trellis, at transmit antenna n_t. Observe that $\hat{\sigma}_w^2$ is the estimate of σ_w^2 obtained from (44). Observe that the minimization in (48) is over all possible QPSK symbols, at $n_t = 2$ and index i. Similarly, for the transition from state m to state n, at decoder 2, for the kth frame, at time i, we define (for $0 \le i \le L_{d2} - 1$):

$$\gamma_{2,\,k,\,i,\,m,\,n} = \exp\left(-Z_{2,\,k,\,i,\,m,\,n}/\left(2L_d\hat{\sigma}_w^2\right)\right) \quad (49)$$

where $Z_{2,\,k,\,i,\,m,\,n}$ is given by

$$\min_{\text{all } S_{m,\,n,\,1}}\sum_{n_r=1}^{2}\left|\tilde{R}_{k,\,i,\,n_r} - \sum_{n_t=1}^{2}\hat{H}_{k,\,i,\,n_r,\,n_t}S_{m,\,n,\,n_t}\right|^2. \quad (50)$$

Now, (47) and (49) are used in the forward and backward recursions of the BCJR algorithm [16].

G. Summary of the Receiver Algorithms

The receiver algorithms are summarized as follows:

1) Estimate the start-of-frame and the frequency offset (coarse) using (16), for each receive antenna. Obtain the average value of the frequency offset ($\hat{\omega}_k$) using (19).
2) Cancel the frequency offset by multiplying $\tilde{r}_{k,\,n,\,n_r}$ in (14) by $\mathrm{e}^{-\mathrm{j}\hat{\omega}_k n}$, and estimate the channel using (26), for each n_r and n_t.
3) Obtain $\tilde{y}_{1,\,k,\,m,\,n_r,\,n_t}$ from (32) and the fine frequency offset using (33).
4) Cancel the frequency offset by multiplying $\tilde{r}_{k,\,n,\,n_r}$ in (14) by $\mathrm{e}^{-\mathrm{j}(\hat{\omega}_k+\hat{\omega}_{k,\,f})n}$, and estimate the channel again using (26), for each n_r and n_t.
5) Obtain the average superfine frequency offset estimate using (43). Cancel the offset by multiplying $\tilde{r}_{k,\,n,\,n_r}$ in (14) by $\mathrm{e}^{-\mathrm{j}(\hat{\omega}_k+\hat{\omega}_{k,\,f}+\hat{\omega}_{k,\,sf})n}$.
6) Obtain the noise variance estimate from (44).
7) Take the L_d-point FFT of $\tilde{\mathbf{r}}_{k,\,m2,\,n_r}$ and perform turbo decoding.

IV. Simulation Results

In this section, we present the simulation results for the proposed turbo coded MIMO OFDM system with $N_t = N_r = 2$. The SNR per bit is defined in (61). Note that one data bit (two coded QPSK symbols) is sent simultaneously from two transmit antennas. Hence, the number of data bits sent from each transmit antenna is $\kappa = 0.5$, as given in (61). We have also assumed that $\sigma_f^2 = 0.5$. The frame parameters are summarized in Table I. The throughput is defined as [11] [16]:

TABLE I
FRAME PARAMETERS.

Parameter	Value (QPSK symbols)
L_p	512, 1024
L_d	4096
B	4
L_o	256, 512
L_{d2}	3832, 3576
L_h	10
$L_{cp} = L_{cs}$	18

$$\mathscr{T} = \frac{L_{d2}}{L_d + L_p + L_{cp} + L_{cs}}. \quad (51)$$

The throughput of various frame configurations is given in Table II. The BER simulation results for the turbo coded MIMO OFDM system with $N_t = N_r = 2$ is shown in Fig. 4. Here "Id" denotes the ideal receiver. For the practical receivers ("Pr"), the interpolation factor for superfine frequency offset estimation is $I = 16$. The practical receiver with $L_p = 1024$, $L_o = 512$ attains a BER of 10^{-5} at an SNR per bit of 5.5 dB, which is 1 dB better than the receiver

TABLE II
THROUGHPUT.

L_p	L_o	L_{d2}	$\mathscr{T}$
512	256	3832	82.515%
1024	512	3576	69.356%

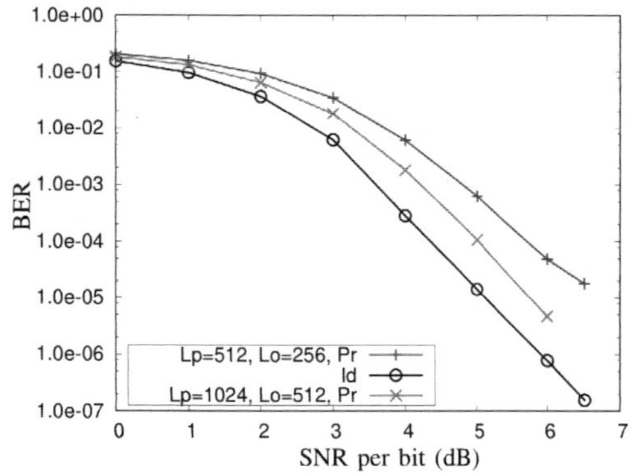

Fig. 4. BER simulation results.

with $L_p = 512$, $L_o = 256$. This is due to the fact that the variance of the channel estimation error with $L_p = 512$ is twice that of $L_p = 1024$ (see (30)). This difference in the variance of the channel estimation error affects the turbo decoding process. Moreover, the practical receiver in Fig. 4 with $L_p = 1024$, $L_o = 512$ is 2.5 dB better than the practical receiver with one transmit and two receive antennas in Fig. 10 of [11]. The probability of frame erasure (this happens when

TABLE III
PROBABILITY OF FRAME ERASURE.

Frame configuration	Probability of erasure
$L_p = 512$, $L_o = 256$	2.98×10^{-2}
$L_p = 1024$, $L_o = 512$	7×10^{-4}

(18) is not satisfied) at 0 dB SNR per bit is shown in Table III. Clearly, as L_p increases, the probability of erasure decreases.

TABLE IV
RMS FREQUENCY OFFSET ESTIMATION ERROR.

Frame configuration	Coarse	Fine	Superfine
$L_p = 512$ $L_o = 256$	1.71×10^{-3}	3.38×10^{-4}	5.85×10^{-5}
$L_p = 1024$ $L_o = 512$	3.3×10^{-4}	9.2×10^{-5}	4.3×10^{-5}

Finally, the root mean square (RMS) and maximum frequency

TABLE V
MAXIMUM FREQUENCY OFFSET ESTIMATION ERROR.

Frame configuration	Coarse	Fine	Superfine
$L_p = 512$ $L_o = 256$	2.4×10^{-2}	1.6×10^{-2}	2.6×10^{-4}
$L_p = 1024$ $L_o = 512$	1.2×10^{-2}	3.9×10^{-4}	1.82×10^{-4}

offset estimation errors in radians, at 0 dB SNR per bit, are given in Tables IV and V.

V. CONCLUSIONS

Discrete-time algorithms for the coherent detection of turbo coded MIMO OFDM system are presented. Simulations results for a 2×2 turbo coded MIMO OFDM system indicate that a BER of 10^{-5}, is obtained at an SNR per bit of just 5.5 dB, which is a 2.5 dB improvement over the performance given in the literature. The minimum average SNR per bit for error-free transmission over fading channels is derived and shown to be equal to -1.6 dB, which is the same as that for the AWGN channel.

Future work could address the issues of peak-to-average power ratio (PAPR) and extension of the proposed concepts to massive MIMO systems.

APPENDIX

A. The Minimum Average SNR per bit for Error-free Transmission over Fading Channels

In this appendix, we derive the minimum average SNR per bit for error-free transmission over MIMO fading channels. Consider the signal

$$\tilde{r}_n = \tilde{x}_n + \tilde{w}_n \qquad \text{for } 0 \le n < N \tag{52}$$

where $\tilde{x}_n$ is the transmitted signal (message) and $\tilde{w}_n$ denotes samples of zero-mean noise, not necessarily Gaussian. All the terms in (52) are complex-valued or two-dimensional and are transmitted over one complex dimension. Here the term dimension refers to a communication link between the transmitter and the receiver carrying only real-valued signals. We also assume that $\tilde{x}_n$ and $\tilde{w}_n$ are ergodic random processes, that is, the time average statistics is equal to the ensemble average. The time-averaged signal power over two-dimensions is given by, for large values of N:

$$\frac{1}{N}\sum_{n=0}^{N-1} |\tilde{x}_n|^2 = P'_{\text{av}}. \tag{53}$$

The time-averaged noise power per dimension is

$$\frac{1}{2N}\sum_{n=0}^{N-1} |\tilde{w}_n|^2 = \sigma'^2_w = \frac{1}{2N}\sum_{n=0}^{N-1} |\tilde{r}_n - \tilde{x}_n|^2. \tag{54}$$

The received signal power over two-dimensions is

$$\begin{aligned}\frac{1}{N}\sum_{n=0}^{N-1}|\tilde{r}_n|^2 &= \frac{1}{N}\sum_{n=0}^{N-1}|\tilde{x}_n+\tilde{w}_n|^2 \\ &= \frac{1}{N}\sum_{n=0}^{N-1}|\tilde{x}_n|^2+|\tilde{w}_n|^2 \\ &= P'_{\text{av}}+2\sigma'^2_w \\ &= E\left[|\tilde{x}_n+\tilde{w}_n|^2\right] \end{aligned} \tag{55}$$

where we have assumed independence between $\tilde{x}_n$ and $\tilde{w}_n$ and the fact that $\tilde{w}_n$ has zero-mean. Note that in (55) it is necessary that either $\tilde{x}_n$ or $\tilde{w}_n$ or both, have zero-mean.

Next, we observe that (54) is the expression for a $2N$-dimensional noise hypersphere with radius $\sigma'_w\sqrt{2N}$. Similarly, (55) is the expression for a $2N$-dimensional received signal hypersphere with radius $\sqrt{N(P'_{\text{av}}+2\sigma'^2_w)}$.

Now, the problem statement is: how many noise hyperspheres (messages) can fit into the received signal hypersphere, such that the noise hyperspheres do not overlap (reliable decoding), for a given N, P'_{av} and σ'^2_w? The solution lies in the volume of the two hyperspheres. Note that a $2N$-dimensional hypersphere of radius R has a volume proportional to R^{2N}. Therefore, the number of possible messages is

$$M=\frac{\left(N\left(P'_{\text{av}}+2\sigma'^2_w\right)\right)^N}{\left(2N\sigma'^2_w\right)^N}=\left(\frac{P'_{\text{av}}+2\sigma'^2_w}{2\sigma'^2_w}\right)^N \tag{56}$$

over N samples (transmissions). The number of bits required to represent each message is $\log_2(M)$, over N transmissions. Therefore, the number of bits per transmission, defined as the channel capacity, is given by [22]

$$\begin{aligned} C &= \frac{1}{N}\log_2(M) \\ &= \log_2\left(1+\frac{P'_{\text{av}}}{2\sigma'^2_w}\right) \quad \text{bits per transmission} \end{aligned} \tag{57}$$

over two dimensions or one complex dimension (here again the term "dimension" implies a communication link between the transmitter and receiver, carrying only real-valued signals. This is not to be confused with the $2N$-dimensional hypersphere mentioned earlier or the M-dimensional orthogonal constellations in [23]).

Proposition A.1: Clearly, the channel capacity is additive over the number of dimensions. In other words, channel capacity over D dimensions, is equal to the sum of the capacities over each dimension, provided the information is independent across dimensions [11]. Independence of information also implies that, the bits transmitted over one dimension is not the interleaved version of the bits transmitted over any other dimension.

Proposition A.2: Conversely, if C bits per transmission are sent over $2N_r$ dimensions, (N_r complex dimensions), it seems reasonable to assume that each complex dimension receives C/N_r bits per transmission [11].

Note that, when

$$\begin{aligned}\tilde{x}_n &= \sum_{n_t=1}^{N_t}\tilde{H}_{k,\,n,\,n_r,\,n_t}S_{k,\,3,\,n,\,n_t} \\ \tilde{w}_n &= \tilde{W}_{k,\,n,\,n_r}\end{aligned} \tag{58}$$

as given in (45), the channel capacity remains the same as in (57). We now define the average SNR per bit for MIMO systems having N_t transmit and N_r receive antennas. We assume that κ information bits are transmitted simultaneously from each transmit antenna. The amount of information received by each receive antenna is $\kappa N_t/N_r$ bits per transmission, over two dimensions (due to Proposition A.2). Assuming independent channel frequency response and symbols across different transmit antennas, the average SNR of $\tilde{R}_{k,\,i,\,n_r}$ in (45) can be computed from (46) as:

$$\text{SNR}_{\text{av}}=\frac{2L_h\sigma_f^2P_{\text{av}}N_t}{2L_d\sigma_w^2}=\frac{P'_{\text{av}}}{2\sigma'^2_w} \tag{59}$$

for $\kappa N_t/N_r$ bits, where

$$P_{\text{av}}=E\left[|S_{k,\,3,\,i,\,n_t}|^2\right]. \tag{60}$$

The average SNR per bit is

$$\begin{aligned}\text{SNR}_{\text{av},\,b} &= \frac{2L_h\sigma_f^2P_{\text{av}}N_t}{2L_d\sigma_w^2}\cdot\frac{N_r}{\kappa N_t} \\ &= \frac{L_h\sigma_f^2P_{\text{av}}N_r}{L_d\sigma_w^2\kappa} \\ &= \frac{P'_{\text{av}}}{2\sigma'^2_w}\cdot\frac{N_r}{\kappa N_t}.\end{aligned} \tag{61}$$

Moreover, for each receive antenna we have

$$C=\kappa N_t/N_r \quad \text{bits per transmission} \tag{62}$$

over two dimensions. Substituting (61) and (62) in (57) we get

$$\begin{aligned} C &= \log_2\left(1+C\cdot\text{SNR}_{\text{av},\,b}\right) \\ \Rightarrow \text{SNR}_{\text{av},\,b} &= \frac{2^C-1}{C}.\end{aligned} \tag{63}$$

Clearly as $C\to 0$, $\text{SNR}_{\text{av},\,b}\to\ln(2)$, which is the minimum SNR required for error-free transmission over MIMO fading channels.

REFERENCES

[1] J. G. Andrews *et al.*, "What will 5g be?" *IEEE Journal on Selected Areas in Communications*, vol. 32, no. 6, pp. 1065–1082, June 2014.

[2] C. L. I *et al.*, "New paradigm of 5g wireless internet," *IEEE Journal on Selected Areas in Communications*, vol. 34, no. 3, pp. 474–482, March 2016.

[3] O. Galinina, A. Pyattaev, S. Andreev, M. Dohler, and Y. Koucheryavy, "5g multi-rat lte-wifi ultra-dense small cells: Performance dynamics, architecture, and trends," *IEEE Journal on Selected Areas in Communications*, vol. 33, no. 6, pp. 1224–1240, June 2015.

[4] J. Hoydis, S. ten Brink, and M. Debbah, "Massive mimo in the ul/dl of cellular networks: How many antennas do we need?" *IEEE Journal on Selected Areas in Communications*, vol. 31, no. 2, pp. 160–171, February 2013.

[5] F. Rusek *et al.*, "Scaling up mimo: Opportunities and challenges with very large arrays," *IEEE Signal Processing Magazine*, vol. 30, no. 1, pp. 40–60, Jan 2013.

[6] E. Bjrnson, E. G. Larsson, and M. Debbah, "Massive mimo for maximal spectral efficiency: How many users and pilots should be allocated?" *IEEE Transactions on Wireless Communications*, vol. 15, no. 2, pp. 1293–1308, Feb 2016.

[7] T. S. Rappaport, W. Roh, and K. Cheun, "Mobile's millimeter-wave makeover," *IEEE Spectrum*, vol. 51, no. 9, pp. 34–58, Sept 2014.

[8] Z. Pi and F. Khan, "An introduction to millimeter-wave mobile broadband systems," *IEEE Communications Magazine*, vol. 49, no. 6, pp. 101–107, June 2011.

[9] T. S. Rappaport *et al.*, "Millimeter wave mobile communications for 5g cellular: It will work!" *IEEE Access*, vol. 1, pp. 335–349, 2013.

[10] ——, "Broadband millimeter-wave propagation measurements and models using adaptive-beam antennas for outdoor urban cellular communications," *IEEE Transactions on Antennas and Propagation*, vol. 61, no. 4, pp. 1850–1859, April 2013.

[11] K. Vasudevan, "Coherent detection of turbo-coded ofdm signals transmitted through frequency selective rayleigh fading channels with receiver diversity and increased throughput," *Wireless Personal Communications*, vol. 82, no. 3, pp. 1623–1642, 2015. [Online]. Available: http://dx.doi.org/10.1007/s11277-015-2303-8

[12] A. Goldsmith, S. A. Jafar, N. Jindal, and S. Vishwanath, "Capacity limits of mimo channels," *IEEE Journal on Selected Areas in Communications*, vol. 21, no. 5, pp. 684–702, June 2003.

[13] Y. Wang and D. W. Yue, "Capacity of mimo rayleigh fading channels in the presence of interference and receive correlation," *IEEE Transactions on Vehicular Technology*, vol. 58, no. 8, pp. 4398–4405, Oct 2009.

[14] F. Benkhelifa, A. Tall, Z. Rezki, and M. S. Alouini, "On the low snr capacity of mimo fading channels with imperfect channel state information," *IEEE Transactions on Communications*, vol. 62, no. 6, pp. 1921–1930, June 2014.

[15] K. Vasudevan, "Coherent detection of turbo coded ofdm signals transmitted through frequency selective rayleigh fading channels," in *Signal Processing, Computing and Control (ISPCC), 2013 IEEE International Conference on*, Sept 2013, pp. 1–6.

[16] ——, "Coherent detection of turbo-coded OFDM signals transmitted through frequency selective rayleigh fading channels with receiver diversity and increased throughput," *CoRR*, vol. abs/1511.00776, 2015. [Online]. Available: http://arxiv.org/abs/1511.00776

[17] ——, *Digital Communications and Signal Processing, Second edition (CDROM included)*. Universities Press (India), Hyderabad, www.universitiespress.com, 2010.

[18] H. Minn, V. K. Bhargava, and K. B. Letaief, "A Robust Timing and Frequency Synchronization for OFDM Systems," *IEEE Trans. on Wireless Commun.*, vol. 2, no. 4, pp. 822–839, July 2003.

[19] B. Farhang-Boroujeny, "Ofdm versus filter bank multicarrier," *IEEE Signal Processing Magazine*, vol. 28, no. 3, pp. 92–112, May 2011.

[20] S. Haykin, *Adaptive Filter Theory*, 3rd ed. Prentice Hall, 1996.

[21] K. Vasudevan, "Iterative Detection of Turbo Coded Offset QPSK in the Presence of Frequency and Clock Offsets and AWGN," *Signal, Image and Video Processing, Springer*, vol. 6, no. 4, pp. 557–567, Nov. 2012.

[22] J. G. Proakis and M. Salehi, *Fundamentals of Communication Systems*. Pearson Education Inc., 2005.

[23] K. Vasudevan, "Digital Communications and Signal Processing, Third edition," 2016, URL: http://home.iitk.ac.in/ vasu/book0.pdf [accessed: 2016-09-26].

Experiments with OpenFlow and IEEE802.11 Point-to-Point Links in a WMN

Michael Rademacher*, Florian Siebertz†, Moritz Schlebusch‡ and Karl Jonas§
Department of Computer Science, Bonn-Rhein-Sieg University of Applied Sciences
Grantham-Allee 20, 53757 Sankt Augustin
Email: *michael.rademacher@h-brs.de, †florian.siebertz@inf.h-brs.de, ‡moritz.schlebusch@inf.h-brs.de, §karl.jonas@h-brs.de

***Abstract*—Software Defined Networking (SDN) and Wireless Mesh Networks (WMNs) evolved to be sophisticated technologies used in a variety of applications. However, a combined approach called Wireless Mesh Software Defined Network (wmSDN) has not been widely addressed in the research community. Our idea in this field consists of WiFi-based point-to-point links managed by the OpenFlow protocol. We investigate two different issues regarding this idea. First, which WiFi operational mode is suitable in an OpenFlow managed broadcast domain? Second, does the performance decrease compared with other routing or switching principles? Therefore, we set up a real-world testbed and a suitable simulation environment. Unlike previous work, we show that it is possible to use WiFi links without conducting Media Access Control (MAC) address rewriting at each hop by utilizing the 4-address-mode.**

***Keywords*–SDN; OpenFlow; WDS; wmSDN; SDWN; WiFi**

I. Introduction

SDN and OpenFlow started as an academic experiment but emerged to a paradigm that challenges the limitations of current static network infrastructures [1]. SDN related research and applications mainly focus on wired infrastructures. However, recent work discusses the advantages also in the context of wireless networks, especially in the backhaul segments [2]. WMNs have been a research topic for several years and they are used successfully for last-mile connectivity [2]. In this case, a WMN is used with multiple radios and Commercial Off-the-Shelf (COTS) WiFi transmitters over long-distance to form what is called a WiFi-based Long Distance (WiLD) network [3].

Our motivation is a combination of SDN and WiLD as already introduced in Hadzic et al. [2]. The following are - by no means exhaustive - examples for benefits of such a combination:

- If SDN based infrastructure is already utilized in the core part of a network it feels natural to extend it further into the last-mile.
- SDN maintains a centralized network state. This provides the flexibility to configure, manage, secure and optimize the network resources using SDN applications.
- In WMNs, traffic pattern can change on a relatively small time-scale. With a centralized SDN based structure, the network can react to these changes based on global knowledge.
- With an increased number of mesh nodes in the network, multiple gateways providing interconnection to public networks become mandatory. SDN applications can handle these multiple gateways and configure the flows accordingly.

In this work, we share first experiences running commodity IEEE 802.11 hard- and software in combination with a recent OpenFlow implementation. We found that a major challenge for the usage of, e.g., the Open vSwitch (OVS) in combination with WiFi (IEEE 802.11) is the handling of MAC addresses. In fact, the usage of wireless links is currently marked as not supported by the OVS. The documentation summarizes this issue as follows: "Wireless base stations generally only allow packets with the source MAC address of NICs that completed the initial handshake. Therefore, without MAC rewriting, only a single device can communicate over a single wireless link." [4].

The remainder of this paper is structured as follows. In Section II, we summarize related work in the context of wmSDN. In Section III, the principles of combining OpenFlow and OVS, as well as the different possible addressing modes in IEEE 802.11 are described. Section IV is twofold, presenting our methodology: First, we describe a small testbed based on COTS hardware. Afterwards, we introduce a wmSDN simulation environment running the same OpenFlow software components used in the testbed. In Section V, we describe our experiments and the results. This paper closes with a summary and an outlook on future work items.

II. Software Defined Wireless Networks

SDN is an architecture where network control is decoupled from the task of forwarding packets. This is achieved by removing the decision making process regarding the handling of packets from every single device. A centralized controller entity is deployed instead, conducting decisions for all devices in the network [1].

Software Defined Wireless Networks (SDWNs) or wmSDNs are beginning to form themselves on top of the experiences gathered in wired networks. What differs is the need for handling the new layer of complexity that is added through wireless interfaces. The terms wmSDN or SDWN are used in two different ways in the research community. SDWN describes a SDN controlled network in which the backbone is typically wired but interconnects several wireless access networks. The term wmSDN is often used to describe a wireless SDN backbone network. In the following, we summarize important contributions in both research fields.

Different generic architectures with the goal of implementing SDN into existing wireless technologies and networks have been proposed [5][6][7]. In Hadzic et al. [2], a concept for integrating SDN into a wireless backhaul infrastructure is presented. A more detailed thought is given to how control- and data-plane must be adapted in order to provide the setup and configuration of diverse wireless interfaces. The authors propose additional modules in the control plane that gather information regarding the spectrum management and link capacity in the entire network via an extended southbound interface.

In Dely et al. [8], the authors present an IEEE 802.11 architecture where packets are forwarded between virtual Access Points (APs) and stations based on MAC layer processing via OpenFlow. This enables applications like dynamic spectrum use, on-demand scaling, and improved roaming. Only the access part of the network utilizes wireless SDN technology in this case.

One possibility of using OpenFlow alongside link configuration mechanisms is the extension of the existing OpenFlow protocol with new functionality. Guimaraes et al. [9] propose additional control messages to be included into the protocol for querying the link state and setting interface parameters. The controller has to be extended in order to handle the additional configuration aspects. Nascimento et al. [10] take a similar approach by deploying a wmSDN that extends the OpenFlow protocol capabilities with new control messages. Additionally, it is proposed to include the IEEE 802.11 MAC header into the list of headers that can be examined by OpenFlow to handle forwarding on each hop. The authors identify that it is necessary to manipulate the source and destination addresses of each packet as it traverses through the network. The proposed solution is to exchange the addresses at each hop. This is taken into account by adding new actions to the flow table.

Another approach is presented in Dely et al. [11]. The OpenFlow protocol and controller remain unchanged, while the wireless configuration and monitoring is done via a separate monitoring and control server that communicates with agents on each device. This server handles the topology, associations between stations, and monitors changes in order to adapt the network accordingly. All control data, including the OpenFlow protocol, is managed through a separate Service Set Identifier (SSID) and the Optimized Link State Routing (OLSR) protocol. The packet forwarding problem mentioned above is addressed in the same way through manipulating the MAC addresses on each hop.

Hurtado-Borràs et al. [12] examine a wireless backhaul with Multi-Radio (MR) wireless switches. The controller is attached in-band, with a preconfigured path through the use of one parent interface on each node, indicating the next hop towards the controller. The issue of wireless status and configuration is addressed by extending the interface between controller and node accordingly.

The OVS can be used to bring OpenFlow capabilities onto a large number of devices. Although it is not meant for wireless networks explicitly, a number of projects have succeeded in adapting it for this scenario. Lee et al. [13] propose an open-source platform for wireless research on the basis of OVS. Mihailescu et al. [14] utilize the OVS in their wireless nodes combined with a local controller that handles the local status and configuration. Detti et al. [15] use the OVS to build OpenFlow capable, wireless devices. The controller is connected in-band via the same SSID and in combination with OLSR to route OpenFlow control messages. Similar to the other works, MAC-rewriting is used in order to enable packet forwarding. In Lima et al. [16], the authors deploy the

Table 1. Address field combinations of IEEE 802.11.

Control Bits		Address Field				
To DS	From DS	1	2	3	4	Usage
0	0	RA=DA	TA=SA	BSSID	N/A	ad-hoc
0	1	RA=DA	TA=BSSID	SA	N/A	AP
1	0	RA=BSSID	TA=SA	DA	N/A	Station
1	1	RA	TA	DA	SA	WDS

OVS on OpenWRT driven commodity hardware similar to our approach, comparing operation with and without OpenFlow and between different controllers.

III. OpenFlow Based Switching and IEEE 802.11

One of the main concepts of SDN is that the network appears to the applications and policy engines located at the centralized controller as a single, logical switch [17]. Since IEEE 802.11 implies a different addressing principle, a seamless integration is proving challenging, as described in Section II. MAC rewriting for every packet is proposed by other research to tackle this issue and enabling packet forwarding via IEEE 802.11 links on OpenFlow capable switches [15][11]. In this section, we investigate the basics for an operation of different IEEE 802.11 modes on OpenFlow enabled switches.

When running a layer 2 OpenFlow switching application, an OpenFlow network can operate similar to a common switched network. The manipulation of flows is based on the ingress port and the destination MAC address. However, in SDN, the initial decision for a manipulation is made at the centralized controller and not on the switches themselves.

The following steps summarize the process of a packet arriving at an OpenFlow enabled switch, i.e., the OVS. If no existing flow matches the packet, it is sent to the controller. Different actions are applied based on the source and destination address. If the source MAC address is unknown to the controller, the controller learns it by binding the address to the ingress port on the switch. If the destination MAC address is unknown to the controller, the controller initiates a flood on all remaining ports of the switch. If the destination MAC address is known to the controller after learning it from the source MAC address of a different packet, the controller installs a flow rule on the switch. When a flow has been installed on the switch successfully, future packets are processed on the switch itself. More details about this example and additional applications can be found in the work [18].

The MAC addressing in IEEE 802.11 differs from IEEE 802.3. The current IEEE 802.11 standard [19] distinguishes between five different address types:

- Transmitter Address (TA): The individual MAC address that identifies the station that has transmitted onto the wireless medium.
- Receiver Address (RA): The individual or group MAC address that identifies the intended immediate recipient on the wireless medium.
- Source Address (SA): The individual MAC address from which the transfer was originally initiated.
- Destination Address (DA): The individual or group MAC address that identifies the final recipients.

- Basic Service Set Identifier (BSSID): The address of a set of stations that are associated successfully.

Up to four different address fields can be used at the same time and four different combinations are specified in the current standard as listed in Tab. 1. The number of address fields used and their contents are controlled by two bits in the MAC header - To DS and From DS. In the last case, To DS and From DS are set to "1", resulting in all four address fields being used. The first two address fields are set to RA and TA respectively, while the last two are set to the DA and SA. This mode of operation is commonly known as 4-address-mode or Wireless Distribution System (WDS).

IV. Methodology

We utilize two different evaluation environments for our use-case of a wmSDN: A real world testbed using COTS hardware and a simulation environment. Despite the different nature and scope of both approaches, we ensure that they share the same configuration and software as far as possible. All wireless links use the IEEE 802.11n standard, either in the 2.4 GHz or 5 GHz band. The channel width is limited to 20 MHz and the Modulation and Coding Scheme (MCS) is fixed to index number 7. This MCS results in no Multiple-Input and Multiple-Output (MIMO) usage and a maximum physical-layer bitrate of 65 Mbps. The main reasons for the fixed MCS is to avoid undesired effects of a rate-controller. At the moment of writing, MIMO is not supported in the used simulation software ns-3 3.24. Therefore, we also limit our experiments to Single-Input and Single-Output (SISO) in the real-world testbed.

Two main software components are necessary for our network evaluation: An OpenFlow capable switch and a controller. Ryu [20] in version 3.26 is used as the OpenFlow controller, running the preinstalled OpenFlow 1.3 layer two switching module operating on a i686 fanless mini-pc system running Ubuntu 14.04. For the switching part, we choose the latest version 2.3.90 of the OVS [4].

Both components are used on the actual devices and in the simulation environment. All devices are connected out-of-band to the controller via a dedicated wired control network. Individual configurations for the testbed and the simulation are summarized in the following subsections. Additional documentation, configurations and materials are available to the research community on our website [21].

A. Testbed

The testbed consists of TP-Link WDR4300 routers version 1.7, running OpenWRT 15.05 "Chaos Calmer" (rev. 47499, Kernel 3.18.23). The OVS enables OpenFlow on the routers which we therefore call wireless switches. The wireless configuration is conducted in the respective OpenWRT configuration files. To enable the 4-address-mode, we set the option "wds" on the wireless interfaces as enabled.

B. Simulation

For our simulation, we use ns-3 in combination with the Mininet framework [22]. The main reason for this choice is ns-3's limited ability to enable OpenFlow and our desire to use the same OpenFlow components in the testbed and in the simulation. We build upon the work done in [23]. The author implements Mininet and ns-3 enhancements, enabling the ns-3 modeling of links between container-virtualized Mininet nodes. The connection is done by combining Linux virtual network devices, called TAP-devices, and a ns-3 module called TAP-bridge. In our case, the TAP-device connects to the ns-3 process by using a file descriptor. When packets generated at a Mininet host arrive at the ns-3 process, they are forwarded by the TAP-bridge to the ns-3 net device and transmitted across the emulated ns-3 WiFi channel using the Friis propagation loss model. Two additional modifications are necessary to build the desired simulation environment: First, the adaption of a ns-3 patch, enabling wireless links in 4-address-mode [23]. Second, preparation of wmSDN devices based on Mininet nodes.

V. Experiments

In the first part of this section, we evaluate the forwarding issue for IEEE 802.11 links in an OpenFlow managed broadcast domain. Afterwards, we evaluate the performance of a wmSDN in a simple multi-hop chain topology.

A. IEEE 802.11 and OpenFlow

In this section, we present the results obtained when integrating WiFi links operating in different modes, as shown in Tab. 1, into a broadcast domain managed with OpenFlow. For simplicity, we reduce this experiment to a minimal topology. We use two of our OpenFlow enabled wireless switches (S1,S2) described in Subsection IV-A and two hosts (H1,H2) connected to the OpenFlow managed Ethernet ports. To evaluate the packet exchange, we use a dedicated sniffing system running a WiFi card in monitor mode.

The packet exchange for the experiments is shown in Fig. 1. Exemplary, we choose the Address Resolution Protocol (ARP) to display the behavior. ARP-request are sent between two hosts (H1,H2) over one IEEE 802.11 hop (S1,S2). Three different modes for the IEEE 802.11 interfaces are used independently. The labels on the arrows show the MAC addresses:

- Destination (dst) and source (src) for IEEE 802.3
- 1–4 for IEEE 802.11 according to Tab. 1

All interfaces are managed by the OVS and the OpenFlow protocol, while the wireless switches are controlled out-of-band by the OpenFlow controller. In all experiments, H1 asks for the hardware address of H2. The ARP-request arrives at the OVS on S1 and is forwarded to the wireless interface. Depending on the WiFi mode, the previous dst and src addresses are matched differently to the 802.11 header.

The first experiment is conducted using what is commonly known as ad-hoc mode on S1 and S2. In this mode, dst and src addresses are matched to the first two addresses in the 802.11 packet header. The Independent Basic Service Set (IBSS) is added in address field 3. Due to the fact that the dst address is a broadcast address, the receiving wireless station accepts the packet. The OVS running on S2 floods the packet to H2 where the ARP-reply is generated, which is again sent back to S2. The ARP-reply is sent on the wireless interface with the first address field set to H1. This results in the receiving wireless interface on S1 not processing the frame, as it is not the target. The communication is unsuccessful.

The second experiment is conducted using the AP mode on S1 and the station mode on S2. Again, due to the broadcast

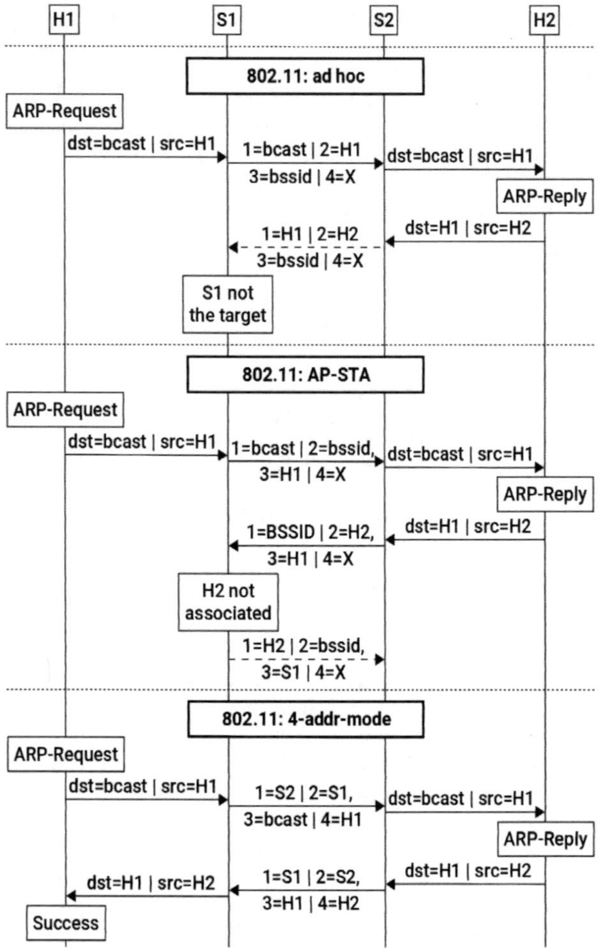

Figure 1. ARP-requests between two hosts are transmitted over one OpenFlow controlled wireless link in different modes.

address, the frame arrives at H2, which generates the ARP-reply. The ARP-reply is forwarded by S2. The transmission is unsuccessful because address field 2 in the 802.11 header is set to H2. The OVS forwards the packet on the wireless port, but the wireless AP does not accept the packet, since H2 is not associated with the AP. In fact, the AP sends a deauthentication frame with the destination set to H2. This deauthentication is ignored by S2.

The last experiment shows the results using the 4-address-mode on S1 and S2. Due to the usage of four addresses, the communication is successful. In fact, the first two addresses in the IEEE 802.11 header can be described as link scope while the last two addresses retain the original communication between the two hosts. This behavior is transparent to the OVS.

B. Performance Measurements

In this subsection, we present different performance measurements conducted in our testbed and in the simulation environment. All configuration and parameters from the testbed are adapted to the simulation as far as possible. We compare the following cases:

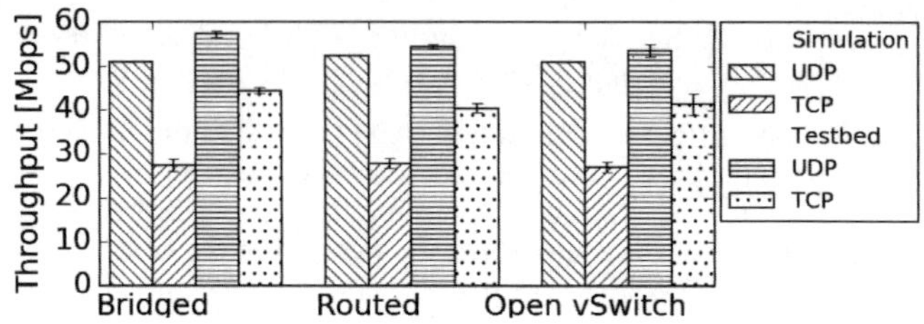

Figure 2. Results of the performance test using four OpenFlow enabled wireless routers and the simulation environment.

- Linux kernel *bridging*, as used by the IEEE 802.11s mesh protocol [24] with WiFi interfaces in 4-address-mode.
- IP based Linux kernel *routing*, as used by different routing protocols in Multi-Radio Multi-Channel (MR-MC) WMNs [25] with WiFi interfaces in AP and station mode.
- An OpenFlow managed network, as shown in the previous section using WiFi interfaces in 4-address-mode.

In this experiment, conducted indoors and under laboratory conditions, four dual-band wireless switches are arranged in the corners of a square plane spanning 3x3 meters in a clear line of sight environment. The four devices are configured to form a chain topology, utilizing two 5 GHz and one 2.4 GHz links on independent channels. One server and one client are connected to the first and the last router via Ethernet. The performance measurements are conducted with artificial User Datagram Protocol (UDP) and Transmission Control Protocol (TCP) traffic using the well-known tool iPerf. Each test is executed five times, lasting 5 minutes in total. The same topology is implemented in the developed simulation environment. For real-world tests, e.g., Rademacher et al. [26] demonstrate the effects that are accompanied by using IEEE 802.11 over longer distances and their influence on parameters like throughput and jitter.

The results of our tests are shown in Fig. 2. Due to the fixed MCS, the maximum physical data rate is bounded by 65 Mbps. First, we describe the results from the testbed and afterwards from the simulation environment.

In our testbed scenario, we measure a maximum unidirectional UDP rate of 57.2 ± 0.7 Mbps for the bridged mode test. This throughput is close to a saturation of all wireless links considering the 802.11n MAC overhead. A slight performance decrease for the routed (54.3 ± 0.4 Mbps) and OVS (53.4 ± 1.3 Mbps) case has been obtained. For the Linux bridged mode, packet headers are not evaluated or changed. In the case of IP based routing, an IP table lookup and address rewrite is necessary. In the case of OVS, for every packet, the flow tables are evaluated.

Similar observations can be made for TCP, although the throughput is consistently lower due to the incurring overhead (bridged: 44.3 ± 0.7 Mbps, routed: 40.4 ± 1.1 Mbps, OVS: 41.3 ± 2.3 Mbps). Performance differences between bridging, routing and OVS have also been reported by other research in the case of wired networks [27]. However, the measurements show that the performance of OVS managed wireless links using the 4-address-mode is comparable to already established approaches.

The measured simulated throughput differs in some aspects from the results obtained in the testbed environment. Noticably, all three cases show the same results for UDP ($\approx 51Mbps$) and TCP ($\approx 27Mbps$). Compared to the testbed, UDP throughput is slightly, and TCP traffic is considerably lower. This behavior could indicate a performance bottleneck within the simulation environment. Due to it's complex architecture, further research is needed in order to identify the source of the bottleneck.

VI. Summary

In this work, we present the difficulty of using wireless links and OpenFlow enabled switches. Because of the way packet forwarding is realized in OpenFlow, just adding the respective interface to the OVS is not sufficient. To evaluate the solution of a wmSDN multi-channel network, we developed a testbed and simulation environment. The same OpenFlow software components were used in both environments.

The results show that with ad-hoc and AP Station mode and the fact that packet headers are not modified at each hop, using OpenFlow does not work with the 802.11 encapsulation. We successfully show that using the 4-address-mode on the wireless links resolves this issue. Thus, it is possible to preserve source and destination addresses from the IEEE 802.3 frames and to insert the respective WiFi address information per link automatically. Unlike previous work, we demonstrate the general applicability of using OpenFlow in an IEEE 802.11 based wmSDN without the need for manually overwriting MAC addresses at each hop.

To show the feasibility of this solution, we compare the throughput of OpenFlow controlled wireless bridging with 4-address-mode enabled to traditional bridging and classic routing in a simulation environment and a testbed. In the testbed enviroment, using COTS hardware, the performance difference between all three solutions are negligible. In our opinion this technology combination provides interesting capabilities in different use-cases - for example in a WiLD network used for internet provisioning in rural areas.

A. Future Work

Several important issues remain unaddressed and need further investigation. Especially for a complete wmSDN solution suitable to function as a WiLD. While we have limited the presented research in this work to an evaluation in a laboratory testbed, the suitability for WiLD networks still needs to be evaluated. This includes in-band connections of the controller, a discovery algorithm for the wireless SDN switches, monitoring of wireless link states, and multiple internet gateways. Instead of using the simple OpenFlow switching application, a more sophisticated routing approach based on this data is desired.

Acknowledgment

This work has been funded by the Federal Ministry of Education and Research of the Federal Republic of Germany (Foerderkennzeichen 16KIS0332, Virtualisierung von Netzfunktionen in Funknetzen auf der Basis von Software Defined Networks). The authors alone are responsible for the content of this paper.

References

[1] D. Kreutz, F. M. V. Ramos, P. E. Verissimo, C. E. Rothenberg, S. Azodolmolky, and S. Uhlig, "Software-Defined Networking: A Comprehensive Survey," in Proceedings of the IEEE, vol. 103, no. 1, Jan. 2015, pp. 14–76.

[2] S. Hadzic, C. Niephaus, O. G. Aliu, G. Ghinea, and M. Kretschmer, "Wireless Back-haul: a software defined network enabled wireless Back-haul network architecture for future 5G networks," IET Networks, vol. 4, no. 6, Nov. 2015, pp. 287–295.

[3] M. Rademacher, "Performance estimation and optimization of the IEEE802.11 MAC layer for long distance point-to-point links," Hochschule Bonn-Rhein-Sieg, Tech. Rep., 2015, [Retrieved: Sep. 2016]. [Online]. Available: http://opus.bib.hochschule-bonn-rhein-sieg.de/opus-3.3/volltexte/2015/30

[4] The Linux Foundation, "Open vSwitch – Frequently Asked Questions," [Retrieved: Sep. 2016]. [Online]. Available: https://github.com/openvswitch/ovs/blob/master/FAQ.md

[5] C. Bernardos, A. De La Oliva, P. Serrano, A. Banchs, L. Contreras, H. Jin, and J. Zuniga, "An Architecture for Software Defined Wireless Networking ," Wireless Communications, IEEE, vol. 21, no. 3, June 2014, pp. 52–61.

[6] S. Tomovic, K. Yoshigoe, I. Maljevic, M. Pejanovic-Djurisic, and I. Radusinovic, "SDN-based concept of QoS aware heterogeneous wireless network operation," in Telecommunications Forum Telfor (TELFOR), 2014 22nd, Nov. 2014, pp. 27–30.

[7] H. Ali-Ahmad, C. Cicconetti, A. De la Oliva, V. Mancuso, M. R. Sama, P. Seite, and S. Shanmugalingam, "An sdn-based network architecture for extremely dense wireless networks," in Future Networks and Services (SDN4FNS), 2013 IEEE SDN for. IEEE, 2013, pp. 1–7.

[8] P. Dely, J. Vestin, A. Kassler, N. Bayer, H. Einsiedler, and C. Peylo, "CloudMAC - An OpenFlow based Architecture for 802.11 MAC Layer Processing in the Cloud," in Globecom Workshops (GC Wkshps), 2012 IEEE, Dec. 2012, pp. 186–191.

[9] C. Guimaraes, D. Corujo, and R. Aguiar, "Enhancing OpenFlow with Media Independent Management Capabilities," in Communications (ICC), 2014 IEEE International Conference on, June 2014, pp. 2995–3000.

[10] V. Nascimento, M. Moraes, R. Gomes, B. Pinheiro, A. Abelem, V. Borges, K. Cardoso, and E. Cerqueira, "Filling the Gap Between Software Defined Networking and Wireless Mesh Networks," in Network and Service Management (CNSM), 2014 10th International Conference on, Nov. 2014, pp. 451–454.

[11] P. Dely, A. Kassler, and N. Bayer, "Openflow for wireless mesh networks," in Computer Communications and Networks (ICCCN), 2011 Proceedings of 20th International Conference on. IEEE, 2011, pp. 1–6.

[12] A. Hurtado-Borràs, J. Pala-Solé, D. Camps-Mur, and S. Sallent-Ribes, "SDN wireless backhauling for Small Cells," in 2015 IEEE International Conference on Communications (ICC). IEEE, 2015, pp. 3897–3902.

[13] S. Lee, Y.-H. Kim, and S. Yang, "Open-source Wireless Switch for Experimental Research Vitalization for B4G/5G Networks," in Ubiquitous and Future Networks (ICUFN), 2014 Sixth International Conf on, July 2014, pp. 125–126.

[14] M. Mihailescu, H. Nguyen, and M. Webb, "Enhancing Wireless Communications with Software Defined Networking," in Military Communications and Information Systems Conference (MilCIS), 2015, Nov. 2015, pp. 1–6.

[15] A. Detti, C. Pisa, S. Salsano, and N. Blefari-Melazzi, "Wireless Mesh Software Defined Networks (wmSDN)," in Wireless and Mobile Computing, Networking and Communications (WiMob), 2013 IEEE 9th International Conference on, Oct. 2013, pp. 89–95.

[16] L. Lima, D. Azevedo, and S. Fernandes, "Performance evaluation of openflow in commodity wireless routers," in Network Operations and Management Symposium (LANOMS), 2015 Latin American. IEEE, 2015, pp. 17–22.

[17] O. N. Foundation, "Software-defined networking: The new norm for networks," ONF White Paper, 2012.

[18] N. McKeown, T. Anderson, H. Balakrishnan, G. Parulkar, L. Peterson, J. Rexford, S. Shenker, and J. Turner, "OpenFlow: enabling innovation in campus networks," ACM SIGCOMM Computer Communication Review, vol. 38, no. 2, 2008, pp. 69–74.

[19] IEEE Standards Association and others, "Wireless LAN Medium Access Control (MAC) and Physical Layer (PHY) Specifications," IEEE Std 802.11-2012 (Revision of IEEE Std 802.11-2007), Feb. 2012, pp. 1–2793.

[20] NN, "Ryu - a component-based software defined networking framework," [Retrieved: Sep. 2016]. [Online]. Available: https://osrg.github.io/ryu/

[21] ——, "MC-Lab Homepage," [Retrieved: Sep. 2016]. [Online]. Available: http://mc-lab.de

[22] ——, "Mininet - An Instant Virtual Network on your Laptop," [Retrieved: Sep. 2016]. [Online]. Available: http://mininet.org/

[23] P. Jurkiewicz, "Link modeling using ns 3," https://github.com/mininet/mininet/wiki/Link-modeling-using-ns-3, [Retrieved: Sep. 2016].

[24] G. R. Hiertz, D. Denteneer, S. Max, R. Taori, J. Cardona, L. Berlemann, and B. Walke, "IEEE 802.11s: The WLAN Mesh Standard," IEEE Wireless Communications, vol. 17, no. 1, Feb. 2010, pp. 104–111.

[25] A. Raniwala and T.-c. Chiueh, "Architecture and algorithms for an ieee 802.11-based multi-channel wireless mesh network," in Proceedings IEEE 24th Annual Joint Conference of the IEEE Computer and Communications Societies., vol. 3. IEEE, 2005, pp. 2223–2234.

[26] M. Rademacher, M. Chauchet, and K. Jonas, "A Token-Based MAC For Long-Distance IEEE802. 11 Point-To-Point Links," ITG-Fachbericht-Mobilkommunikation–Technologien und Anwendungen, 2016.

[27] A. Bianco, R. Birke, L. Giraudo, and M. Palacin, "OpenFlow Switching: Data Plane Performance," Communications (ICC), 2010 IEEE International Conference on, 2010, pp. 1–5.

RSS-Based Indoor Positioning with Weighted Iterative Nonlinear Least Square Algorithm

Veli İlçi
Map and Cadastre Program
Hitit University
Çorum, Turkey
E-mail: veliilci@hitit.edu.tr

V. Engin Gülal
Geomatic Engineering
Yildiz Technical University
İstanbul, Turkey
E-mail: egulal@yildiz.edu.tr

Hüseyin Çizmeci
Computer Programming Program
Hitit University
Çorum, Turkey
E-mail: hcizmeci@hitit.edu.tr

Mustafa Coşar
Computer Engineering
Hitit University
Çorum, Turkey
E-mail: mustafacosar@hitit.edu.tr

Reha Metin Alkan
Geomatic Engineering
İstanbul Technical University
İstanbul, Turkey
E-mail: alkanr@itu.edu.tr

***Abstract*— In recent years, researches on indoor positioning have become one of the most studied subject. This paper presents a real-time Wi-Fi-based indoor localization system using 2.4 GHz Wi-Fi signals. This experiment consists of two main phases. In the first phase, establishing a relationship between the received signal strength and the distance via signal propagation model, the distances between the mobile devices and the access points were determined using the log-distance path loss model. In the second stage, to test the usability and the performance of weighted iterative nonlinear least square algorithm for Wi-Fi based indoor positioning application, coordinates of the mobile device were estimated using this algorithm. This system runs on mobile devices in real time at line-of-sight indoor environments.**

Keywords - Indoor positioning; RSS; signal propagation model; weighted least square; Wi-Fi; 2.4 GHz.

I. INTRODUCTION

In recent years, academic and commercial studies on indoor positioning that have focused on producing real-time, and accurate location information has become one of the important investigation issues [1]. In the outdoor environments, sufficient 3D positioning accuracies can be obtained using Global Navigation Satellite Systems (GNSS) [2]. However, GNSS signals are losing its influence due to various reasons, such as multipath and reflection in indoor environments. Therefore, the accuracy obtained in outdoors environments can't be achieved in indoor environments using GNSS. In recent years, in order to obtain the desired positioning accuracy in indoor areas, many studies have been conducted using different technologies such as GNSS [3], Ultra-Wide Band (UWB) [4], Radio Frequency Identification (RFID) [5], Infrared (IR), Bluetooth [6] and Wireless Local Area Network (WLAN) [7]. Among these technologies, WLAN stands out because of using the pre-existing Wi-Fi infrastructure within buildings, and also Wi-Fi signals can be received by smartphones and tablets. So, WLAN-based indoor localization does not require any additional cost or hardware. Therefore, WLAN-based indoor localization has been frequently investigated in recent years.

Various classifications in many studies have been made for indoor positioning system. One of these classifications has been made depending on the distances named as rangeless and the range-based classification [8]. Rangeless algorithms are working regardless of the distance. Range-based location algorithms determine the location of the mobile device using the distances from the reference devices. Range-based algorithms are classified as Received Signal Strength (RSS), Angle of Arrival (AOA), Time of Arrival (TOA), and Time Difference of Arrival (TDOA) [9]. TOA, TDOA and AOA algorithms require dedicated equipment to perform the distance and angle measurements, so they require additional costs [10]. However, RSS-based algorithms require no additional hardware or cost.

In the literature, RSS-based indoor positioning is divided into two different approaches named as fingerprinting and propagation model-based [11]. The Fingerprinting approach consists of two phases named as offline and online phases. In the offline phase, a radio-map is created in the workspace using the signal strength values received from all Access

Points (APs). In the online phase, the position of the device is established by matching the RSS values that of the offline phase. The major drawback of this approach is requires more labor during the offline phase measurements. The Propagation model-based approach consists of two phases. In the first phase, distances between the mobile device and APs are determined using signal propagation models and in the second phase, the mobile device's position is determined using three or more distances with positioning algorithms [12], such as Trilateration, Least Squares, Extended Kalman Filter, etc. Such distances can be determined by performing special applications in the workspace or obtained using predetermined signal propagation models without requiring any additional applications such as the ITU Path loss model [ITU] proposed by the International Communication Union and Log-distance path loss model and etc. RSS signals are affected by external factors in indoor environments such as fading, diffraction and multipath, so the distance estimation stage is one of the most critical phases for RSS-based indoor positioning applications [13].

In this study, a RSS-based indoor positioning study has been conducted at a direct line-of-sight indoor environment. The Log-distance path loss model used to determine the distances between the mobile device and APs and the position of the mobile device was established using the weighted iterative nonlinear least square method (WINLSQ). Positioning accuracy of the used method was tested experimentally at 27 different points.

The outline of the paper is arranged as follows. Section 2 formulates the distance estimation stage using signal propagation model, and positon estimation of the mobile device using WINLSQ is described in Section 3. Section 4 describes the study area and evaluates experimental results, and finally, the conclusion of the paper is presented in Section 5.

II. Signal Propagation Model

The ranges between the mobile devices and APs are usually estimated through RSS signals due to ease of implementation and not requiring any additional costs [14]. Signal propagation models are used to obtain RSS-based ranges. RSS are affected by environmental conditions depending on obstacles, multipath, scattering, reflection, shadowing and diffraction in indoor areas [15]. So, ranges obtained using the RSS can include large range errors, and this directly affects the accuracy of the position estimation.

Signal strength decreases logarithmically depending on the distance [16]. To model the relationship between the distance and RSS in the indoor or outdoor environments, many signal propagation models have been proposed. Due to its ease of use, log-distance path loss model is mostly used in the literature [17].

Log-distance path loss model is represented in the following equations [15-16]:

$$PL(dB) = PL(d_0) + 10n\log_{10}(\frac{d}{d_0}) + X_\sigma \quad (1)$$

$$PL(d_0) = -20\log_{10}\lambda + 20\log_{10}(4\pi) + 20\log_{10}(d_0) \quad (2)$$

where, $PL(d_0)$ is the path loss at the reference distance, n is the path loss exponent depends heavily on the studied indoor environment and building type, d is the distance between the receiver and the transmitter in meters, d_0 is the reference distance in meters usually chosen as 1 meter, X_σ is the Gaussian random variable with zero mean and standard deviation of σ dB, and λ is the wavelength of the signal in meters.

III. Weighted Iterative Nonlinear Least Square Algorithm

Minimizing the square error, linear and non-linear parameters can be estimated using least square algorithms [8]. In the absence of variance information, non-linear parameter estimation can be accepted [18]. The solution of non-linear least square needs linearization using a few algorithms, such as the Taylor series.

In the literature, many least square algorithms are used to solve the positioning problem for indoor localization problem. In this study, we use the WINLSQ algorithm that is proposed in [19]. In this algorithm, the observation model is given as;

$$z = h(x) + v \quad (3)$$

where, z is the measurement vector, and the function of the state vector X is represented by $h(x)$. The equation (4) can be obtained with the linearization of the nonlinear measurement vector around the current state estimation $\hat{X}$ [20].

$$z = h(\hat{x}) + H\delta x + v \quad (4)$$

where, the innovation of the state vector is presented as:

$$\delta x = x - \hat{x} \quad (5)$$

and, design matrix is represented as:

$$H = \frac{dh(x)}{dx} \quad (6)$$

The measurement misclosure vector δz can be obtained by rearranging the equation (4):

$$\delta z = H\delta x + v \quad (7)$$

The solution (8), covariance matrix of the solution (9) and new state vector (10) are given respectively as:

$$\delta\hat{x} = (H^T R^{-1} H)^{-1} H^T R^{-1} \delta z \quad (8)$$

$$C_{\delta\hat{x}} = (H^T R^{-1} H)^{-1} \quad (9)$$

$$\hat{x}_{updated} = \hat{x} + \delta\hat{x} \quad (10)$$

where, R is the observation covariance matrix. The iteration of this process continues until $|\delta\hat{x}| < \text{threshold}$. The residual vector (11) and its covariance matrix (12) are given as follows:

$$r = z - h(\hat{x}) \quad (11)$$

$$C_r = R - H(H^T R^{-1} H)^{-1} H^T \quad (12)$$

IV. Experimental Results

This experiment consists of two main phases, distance estimation using the Log-distance path loss model and position estimation using WINLSQ. To assess the performance of this system, a static test is conducted at 27 different points (named as observed points) in the application area. Four similar ASUS DSL-AC68U APs are placed in the corners of the application area that is 10 m x 9.6 m at line-of-sight indoor environment. In Fig. 1, red and green points indicate the locations of APs and the observed points, respectively, in the experimental area. Two dimensional geodetic coordinates of APs and the observation points were determined accurately using the total station, and that is accepted as the reference coordinates. Simultaneously transmitted 2.4 GHz Wi-Fi signals (IEEE 802.11ac) from the APs were collected by a Samsung Note 5 mobile device that has an Android operating system. These signals were converted into distances using the Log-distance path loss model, and the position of the 27 observed points were estimated using the WINLSQ algorithm. JAVA programming language was used with the JAMA basic linear algebra package to make all the calculations. The data was collected 150 times at all of the observation points, and the coordinates of these points was obtained using the mentioned algorithms in real time by mobile device. The differences between the obtained coordinates and the known coordinates, and the mean value of the differences are depicted in Fig. 2.

According to the values in Fig. 2, the positioning error values are varying between 0.81-13.16 m. Mean values of these errors is 3.73m, and standard deviation of the errors are 2.37 m. While errors of 26 observed points are up to 7.13 m, exceptionally only the 22th point's positioning error is more than 8 m. This is the reason that huge RSS fluctuations received from AP-2 and AP-3 during the measurement of 27th point. These values were tested with the χ^2 test, and they passed the test successfully at a 95% confidence level.

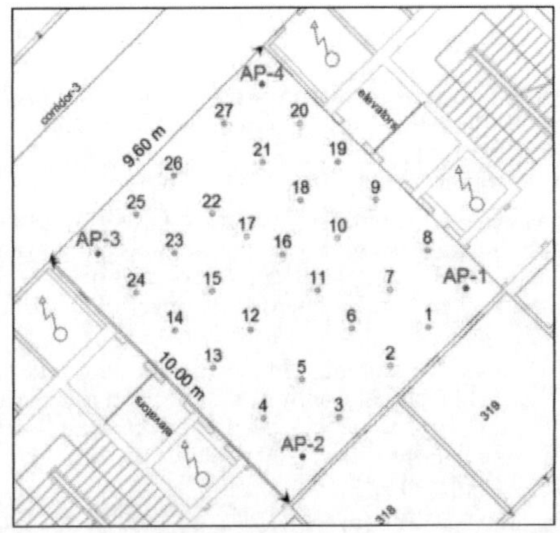

Figure 1.Experimental area

V. CONCLUSIONS

In this paper, we examined the usability of the weighted iterative nonlinear least square algorithm in a 2.4 GHz Wi-Fi based indoor environment to find the position of the mobile device. The relationship between the distance and RSS was determined using log-distance path loss model via received signals strength. Weighted iterative nonlinear least square algorithm was adopted for estimation of the position.

Obtained results indicated that 92 percent of the error values were smaller 5 meter. Although, these results are enough for many indoor positioning applications, some error values are still very huge. It is clear that this situation emerges from the fluctuations of the RSS values. In order to eliminate this fluctuation, raw signal values have been filtered using other algorithms before finding the distances.

ACKNOWLEDGENT

The authors would like to thanks the Hitit University Scientific Research Projects Units for supporting this research (MUH19002.15.004).

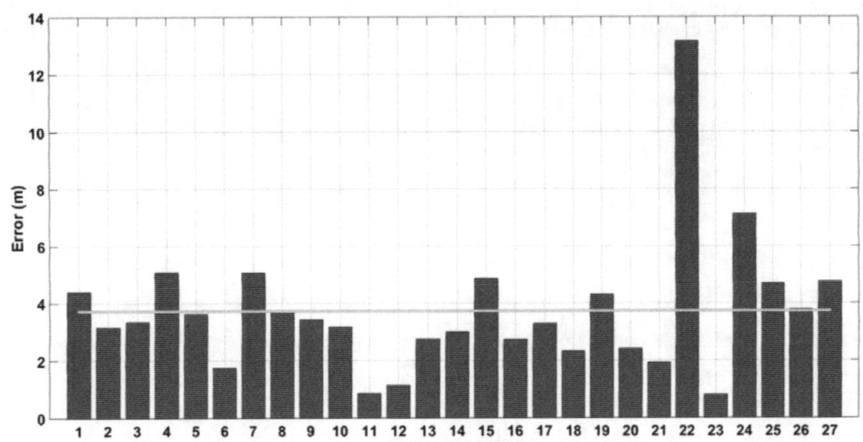

Figure 2. The differences between reference and estimated coordinates are shown as the blue bars and mean value of differences are shown as the green line.

References

[1] J. Yim, S. Jeong, K. Gwon, and J. Joo, "Improvement of Kalman Filters for WLAN based Indoor Tracking," Expert Systems with Applications, vol.37, pp.426-433, 2010, doi:10.1016/j.eswa.2009.05.047.

[2] J. Wang, R. V. Prasad, X. An, and I. G. M. M. Niemegeers, "A study on wireless sensor network based indoor positioning systems for context-aware applications," Wireless Communications and Mobile Computing, vol. 12, issue. 1, pp. 53-70, 2012.

[3] I. Selmi, and N. Samama, "Indoor positioning with GPS and GLONASS-like signal use of new codes and a repealite-based infrastructure in a typical museum building," annals of telecommunications, vol. 69, pp. 641-655, 2014, doi: 10.1007/s12243-014-0422-y.

[4] C. Basaran, J. Yoon, S. H. Son, and T. Park, "Self-Configuring Indoor Localization Based on Low-Cost Ultrasonic Range Sensors," Sensors, vol.14, pp.18728-18747, 2014, doi:10.3390/s141018728.

[5] L. Geng, M. F. Bugallo, A. Athalye, and P. M. Djurić, "Indoor Tracking With RFID Systems," IEEE Journal of Selected Topics in Signal Processing, vol. 8, no. 1, pp. 96-105, February 2014, doi: 10.1109/JSTSP.2013.

[6] C. Liang, et al., "Bayesian Fusion for Indoor Positioning Using Bluetooth Fingerprints," Wireless Personal Communications, vol. 70, pp. 1735-1745, 2013, doi:10.1007/s11277-012-0777-1.

[7] J. Yim, "Development of Web Services for WLAN-based Indoor Positioning and Floor Map Repositories," International Journal of Control and Automation, vol.7, no.3, pp.63-74, 2014, doi:10.14257/ijca.2014.7.3.07.

[8] H. Li, "Low-Cost 3D Bluetooth Indoor Positioning with Least Square," Wireless Personal Communications, vol.78, no.2, pp.1331-1344, 2014, doi: 10.1007/s11277-014-1820-1.

[9] R. Khan, S. U. Khan, S. Khan, and M. U. A. Khan, "Localization Performance Evaluation of Extended Kalman Filter in Wireless Sensor Networks," Procedia Computer Science, vol. 32, pp. 117-124, 2014.

[10] P. Tarrio, A. M. Bernardos, J. A. Besada and J. R. Casar, "A new positioning technique for RSS-Based localization based on a weighted least squares estimator," 2008 IEEE International Symposium on Wireless Communication Systems, Reykjavik, pp. 633-637, 2008, doi: 10.1109/ISWCS.2008.4726133.

[11] M. A. Al-Ammar, et al., "Comparative Survey of Indoor Positioning Technologies, Techniques, and Algorithms," Cyberworlds (CW), 2014 International Conference on, Santander, pp. 245-252, 2014.

[12] J. Cota-Ruiz, J. G. Rosiles, E. Sifuentes, and P. Rivas-Perea, "A Low-Complexity Geometric Bilateration Method for Localization in Wireless Sensor Networks and Its Comparison with Least-Squares Methods," Sensors, vol. 12, pp. 839-862, 2012.

[13] R. Khan, F. Sottile, and M. A. Spirito, "Hybrid Positioning through Extended Kalman Filter with Inertial Data Fusion," International Journal of Information and Electronics Engineering, vol. 3, no. 1, pp. 127-131, January 2013.

[14] J. Koo and H. Cha, "Localizing WiFi Access Points Using Signal Strength," IEEE Communications Letters, vol. 15, no. 2, pp. 187-189, February 2011, doi: 10.1109/LCOMM.2011.121410.101379

[15] J. S. Seybold, "Introduction to RF Propagation," 1th ed., vol. 1, John Wiley&Sons:USA, 2005, pp. 210-217.

[16] T. S. Rappaport, "Wireless Communications: Principles and Practice," Prentice Hall PTR, Upper Saddle River, NJ, 2001.

[17] F. Xiao, M. Wu, H. Huang, R. Wang, and S. Wang, "Novel Node Localization Algorithm Based on Nonlinear Weighting Least Square for Wireless Sensor Networks," International Journal of Distributed Sensor Networks, vol. 2012, Article ID 803840, 6 pages, 2012, doi:10.1155/2012/803840.

[18] W. Wang, H. Ma, Y. Wang, and M. Fu, "Performance analysis based on least squares and extended Kalman filter for localization of static target in wireless sensor networks," Ad Hoc Networks, vol. 25, part A, pp. 1- 15, February 2015.

[19] Y. Zhuang, Z. Syed, J. Georgy, and N. El-Sheimy, "Autonomous smartphone-based WiFi positioning system by using access points localization and crowdsourcing," Pervasive and Mobile Computing, vol. 18, pp. 118-136, April 2015, doi: http://dx.doi.org/10.1016/j.pmcj.2015.02.001.

[20] Y. Zhuang, B. Wright, Z. Syed, Z. Shen, and N. El-Sheimy, "Fast WiFi access point localization and autonomous crowdsourcing," Ubiquitous Positioning Indoor Navigation and Location Based Service (UPINLBS), 2014, Corpus Christ, TX, pp. 272-280, 2014, doi: 10.1109/UPINLBS.2014.

Wireless Relay System with Two Sections in κ-μ Short-Term Fading Channel

Dragana Krstic, Mihajlo Stefanovic, Radmila Gerov
Faculty of Electronic Engineering,
University of Niš,
Niš, Serbia
Email: dragana.krstic@elfak.ni.ac.rs

Zoran Popovic
Technical College of vocational studies
Zvecan, Serbia
Email: zpopovic@vts-zvecan.edu.rs

Abstract—**The wireless relay communication mobile radio system will be considered in this article. This system has two sections. The desired signal in both sections is subjected to κ-μ short- term fading. The outage probability is calculated for two cases. For the first case, the outage probability is defined as probability that the signal envelope in any sections falls below the specified threshold. For the second case, the outage probability is defined as probability that output signal envelope falls below the determined threshold. The influence of the Rician κ factor and multipath fading severity parameter on the outage probability is analyzed for both cases.**

Keywords-κ-μ distribution; cumulative distribution function; probability density function; outage probability

I. INTRODUCTION

In this article, the wireless communication relay system operating over κ-μ multipath fading environment is considered. The relay system has two sections. The κ-μ distribution describes signal envelopes in channels with dominant components [1] [2].

The κ-μ distribution is characterized by two parameters [3]. The parameter κ is Rician factor, which is defined as the ratio of dominant component power and scattering components power. The parameter μ is related to the number of clusters in propagation channel. The κ-μ small scale fading is more severe for less values of parameter μ. Also, the κ-μ multipath fading is more severe for lesser value of dominant component power and higher values of scattered components power. The κ-μ distribution is general distribution from which Rayleigh, Rician and Nakagami-m distribution can be derived [4]. The κ-μ distribution reduces to Nakagami-m distribution for $\kappa=0$, to Rician distribution for $\mu=1$, and to Rayleigh distribution for $\kappa=0$ and $\mu=1$. When Rician factor goes to infinity, κ-μ multipath fading channel becomes no fading channel. Also, when parameter μ goes to infinity, there is no fading in the channel [5].

There are two ways to define the outage probability in wireless relay systems. One way to define the outage probability is as a probability that signal level at any section falls below of the determined threshold. In this case, the outage probability can be calculated from cumulative distribution function of the minimum of the signal envelope at sections of wireless communication system. In the second definition, the outage probability can be calculated as probability that signal envelope at output of wireless relay communication system falls below the determined threshold. For this case, the outage probability can be calculated as cumulative distribution function of product of two κ-μ distributions [6].

There are some works in technical literature dealing with performance analysis of wireless relay communication systems in the presence of multipath fading [7]-[14]. Beside, several papers treated minimum, product and ratio of random variables and how they could be applied in performance analysis of relay communication systems [13] [14]. Since the distribution of random variables is of interest in wireless communications, the probability density functions of minimum of ratios of Rayleigh, Rician, Nakagami-m, Weibull and α-μ random variables are derived in [13]. These formulas are used for studying the outage probability in multi-hop systems working over fading channels in the presence of cochannel interference. The general, closed-form expressions for the probability density function (PDF) and cumulative distribution function (CDF) of the ratio of the products of two independent α-μ variables are presented in [14]. The obtained solutions are applicable in analysis of multihop wireless communication systems in the presence of different fading.

According to the authors' knowledge, relay radio system in the presence of κ-μ short-term fading in the first and the second sections is not processed in publicly available literature. Consequently, such system is analyzed in this work. The Rician factor and fading severity parameter are the same for both sections. In this paper, probability density function and cumulative distribution function of minimum of two κ-μ random variables are determined. The cumulative distribution function is the outage probability of the proposed wireless relay system. Furthermore, PDF and CDF of product of two κ-μ random variables are evaluated and also the outage probability of proposed system can be calculated from cumulative distribution function. The signal envelope at output of considered relay system can be evaluated as product of two κ-μ random variables. The results obtained here can be applied in performance analysis and design of relay radio systems working over κ-μ multipath fading channels.

This article consists of five sections. After an introduction to the topic and description of the works in the field, in the second section, the probability density function and cumulative distribution function of minimum of two κ-μ random variables are performed. Then, in third section, PDF and CDF of product of two κ-μ random variables are carried out. Numerical results are given and discussed in the forth section, and some conclusions, with described possibilities for further work, are given in the last section.

II. Probability Density Function and Cumulative Distribution Function of Minimum of Two κ-μ Random Variables

The probability density function of κ-μ random variable x_1 is:

$$p_{x_1}(x_1)=\frac{2\mu(k+1)^{\frac{\mu+1}{2}}}{k^{\frac{\mu-1}{2}}e^{k\mu}\Omega_1^{\frac{\mu+1}{2}}}\cdot$$

$$\cdot\sum_{i_1=0}^{\infty}\left(\mu\sqrt{\frac{k(k+1)}{\Omega_1}}\right)^{2i_1+\mu-1}\frac{1}{i_1!\Gamma(i_1+\mu)}\cdot x_1^{2i_1+2\mu-1}e^{-\frac{\mu(k+1)}{\Omega_1}x_1^2},\ x_1\geq 0, \quad (1)$$

where κ is Rician factor, μ is severity parameter and Ω_1 is signal envelope average power.

The random variable x_2 follows also κ-μ distribution:

$$p_{x_2}(x_2)=\frac{2\mu(k+1)^{\frac{\mu+1}{2}}}{k^{\frac{\mu-1}{2}}e^{k\mu}\Omega_2^{\frac{\mu+1}{2}}}\cdot$$

$$\cdot\sum_{i_2=0}^{\infty}\left(\mu\sqrt{\frac{k(k+1)}{\Omega_2}}\right)^{2i_2+\mu-1}\cdot\frac{1}{i_2!\Gamma(i_2+\mu)}\cdot$$

$$x_2^{2i_2+2\mu-1}e^{-\frac{\mu(k+1)}{\Omega_2}x_2^2},\ x_2\geq 0 \quad (2)$$

Cumulative distribution function of x_1 is [5, eq. 2]:

$$F_{x_1}(x_1)=\frac{2\mu(k+1)^{\frac{\mu+1}{2}}}{k^{\frac{\mu-1}{2}}e^{k\mu}\Omega_1^{\frac{\mu+1}{2}}}\cdot\sum_{i_1=0}^{\infty}\left(\mu\sqrt{\frac{k(k+1)}{\Omega_1}}\right)^{2i_1+\mu-1}\frac{1}{i_1!\Gamma(i_1+\mu)}\cdot$$

$$\cdot\frac{1}{2}\left(\frac{\Omega_1}{\mu(k+1)}\right)^{i_1+\mu}\cdot\gamma\left(i_1+\mu,\frac{\mu(k+1)}{\Omega_1}x_1^2\right),\ x_1\geq 0, \quad (3)$$

where $\gamma(n, x)$ is incomplete Gamma function of argument x and order n [15].

Cumulative distribution function of x_2 is:

$$F_{x_2}(x_2)=\frac{2\mu(k+1)^{\frac{\mu+1}{2}}}{k^{\frac{\mu-1}{2}}e^{k\mu}\Omega_2^{\frac{\mu+1}{2}}}\cdot\sum_{i_2=0}^{\infty}\left(\mu\sqrt{\frac{k(k+1)}{\Omega_2}}\right)^{2i_2+\mu-1}\frac{1}{i_2!\Gamma(i_2+\mu)}\cdot$$

$$\cdot\frac{1}{2}\left(\frac{\Omega_2}{\mu(k+1)}\right)^{i_2+\mu}\gamma\left(i_2+\mu,\frac{\mu(k+1)}{\Omega_2}x_2^2\right),\ x_2\geq 0 \quad (4)$$

In wireless relay system, the outage probability can be defined in two different ways, as it is described above. When the signal level at any section falls under the defined threshold, the outage probability can be calculated from cumulative distribution function of the minimum of the signal envelopes at sections of wireless communication system.

Let analyze the minimum x of two random variables x_1 and x_2. It is define as:

$$x=\min(x_1,x_2) \quad (5)$$

PDF of x is [8]:

$$p_x(x)=p_{x_1}(x)F_{x_2}(x)+p_{x_2}(x)F_{x_1}(x) \quad (6)$$

Cumulative distribution function of minimum x of two κ-μ random variables is [13, eq. (26)]:

$$F_x(x)=1-(1-F_{x_1}(x))(1-F_{x2}(x))=$$

$$=1-(1-\frac{2\mu(k+1)^{\frac{\mu+1}{2}}}{k^{\frac{\mu-1}{2}}e^{k\mu}\Omega_1^{\frac{\mu+1}{2}}}\cdot\sum_{i_1=0}^{\infty}\left(\mu\sqrt{\frac{k(k+1)}{\Omega_1}}\right)^{2i_1+\mu-1}\frac{1}{i_1!\Gamma(i_1+\mu)}\cdot$$

$$\cdot\frac{1}{2}\left(\frac{\Omega_1}{\mu(k+1)}\right)^{i_1+\mu}\gamma\left(i_1+\mu,\frac{\mu(k+1)}{\Omega_1}x^2\right)\Bigg)\cdot$$

$$\Bigg(1-\frac{2\mu(k+1)^{\frac{\mu+1}{2}}}{k^{\frac{\mu-1}{2}}e^{k\mu}\Omega_2^{\frac{\mu+1}{2}}}\cdot\sum_{i_2=0}^{\infty}\left(\mu\sqrt{\frac{k(k+1)}{\Omega_2}}\right)^{2i_2+\mu-1}\cdot\frac{1}{i_2!\Gamma(i_2+\mu)}\cdot$$

$$\cdot\frac{1}{2}\left(\frac{\Omega_2}{\mu(k+1)}\right)^{i_2+\mu}\gamma\left(i_2+\mu,\frac{\mu(k+1)}{\Omega_2}x^2\right)\Bigg) \quad (7)$$

Cumulative distribution function of minimum of two κ-μ random variables is the outage probability of wireless relay communication system with two sections over κ-μ multipath fading channel.

III. Probability Density Function and Cumulative Distribution Function of Product of Two κ-μ Random Variables

By the second definition, the outage probability of wireless relay system can be calculated as probability that signal envelope at the output of wireless relay communication system lessens below the predetermined threshold. For this case, the outage probability can be calculated as cumulative distribution function of product of two κ-μ distributed signals.

Product of two κ-μ random variables x_1 and x_2 is:

$$x=x_1\cdot x_2,\ x_1=\frac{x}{x_2} \quad (8)$$

Conditional PDF of x is [10]:

$$p_x(x/x_2)=\left|\frac{dx_1}{dx}\right|p_{x_1}\left(\frac{x}{x_2}\right)=\frac{1}{x_2}p_{x_1}\left(\frac{x}{x_2}\right) \quad (9)$$

After integration, the expression for $p_x(x)$ becomes:

$$p_x(x)=\int_0^\infty dx_2 \frac{1}{x_2} p_{x_1}\left(\frac{x}{x_2}\right) p_{x_2}(x_2)=$$

$$=\frac{2\mu(k+1)^{\frac{\mu+1}{2}}}{k^{\frac{\mu-1}{2}} e^{k\mu}\Omega_1^{\frac{\mu+1}{2}}}\cdot\sum_{i_2=0}^{\infty}\left(\mu\sqrt{\frac{k(k+1)}{\Omega_1}}\right)^{2i_1+\mu-1}\cdot\frac{1}{i_1!\Gamma(i+\mu)}\cdot$$

$$\cdot\frac{2\mu(k+1)^{\frac{\mu+1}{2}}}{k^{\frac{\mu-1}{2}} e^{k\mu}\Omega_2^{\frac{\mu+1}{2}}}\cdot\sum_{i_2=0}^{\infty}\left(\mu\sqrt{\frac{k(k+1)}{\Omega_2}}\right)^{2i_2+\mu-1}\cdot\frac{1}{i_2!\Gamma(i_2+\mu)}$$

$$x^{2i_1+2\mu-1}\int_0^\infty dx_2\, x_2^{-1-2i_1-2\mu+1+2i_2+2\mu-1} e^{-\frac{\mu(k+1)}{\Omega_1}\frac{x^2}{x_2^2}-\frac{\mu(k+1)}{\Omega_2}x_2^2}=$$

$$=\frac{2\mu(k+1)^{\frac{\mu+1}{2}}}{k^{\frac{\mu-1}{2}} e^{k\mu}\Omega_1^{\frac{\mu+1}{2}}}\cdot\sum_{i_2=0}^{\infty}\left(\mu\sqrt{\frac{k(k+1)}{\Omega_1}}\right)^{2i_1+\mu-1}\cdot\frac{1}{i_1!\Gamma(i+\mu)}\cdot$$

$$\cdot\frac{2\mu(k+1)^{\frac{\mu+1}{2}}}{k^{\frac{\mu-1}{2}} e^{k\mu}\Omega_2^{\frac{\mu+1}{2}}}\cdot\sum_{i_2=0}^{\infty}\left(\mu\sqrt{\frac{k(k+1)}{\Omega_2}}\right)^{2i_2+\mu-1}\cdot\frac{1}{i_2!\Gamma(i_2+\mu)}$$

$$x^{2i_1+2\mu-1}\left(\frac{\Omega_2 x^2}{\Omega_1}\right)^{i_2-i_1} K_{2i_2-2i_1}\left(2\sqrt{\frac{\mu^2(k+1)^2x^2}{\Omega_1\Omega_2}}\right) \tag{10}$$

Cumulative probability density of x is:

$$F_x(x)=\int_0^x dt\, p_x(t)=$$

$$=\frac{2\mu(k+1)^{\frac{\mu+1}{2}}}{k^{\frac{\mu-1}{2}} e^{k\mu}\Omega_1^{\frac{\mu+1}{2}}}\cdot\sum_{i_2=0}^{\infty}\left(\mu\sqrt{\frac{k(k+1)}{\Omega_1}}\right)^{2i_1+\mu-1}\cdot\frac{1}{i_1!\Gamma(i+\mu)}\cdot$$

$$\cdot\frac{2\mu(k+1)^{\frac{\mu+1}{2}}}{k^{\frac{\mu-1}{2}} e^{k\mu}\Omega_2^{\frac{\mu+1}{2}}}\cdot\sum_{i_2=0}^{\infty}\left(\mu\sqrt{\frac{k(k+1)}{\Omega_2}}\right)^{2i_2+\mu-1}\cdot\frac{1}{i_2!\Gamma(i_2+\mu)}\cdot$$

$$\cdot\int_0^\infty dx_2\, x_2^{2i_2-2i_1-1} e^{-\frac{\mu(k+1)}{\Omega_2}x_2^2}\cdot\int_0^x dt\, t^{2i_1+2\mu-1} e^{-\frac{\mu(k+1)}{\Omega_1}\frac{x^2}{x_2^2}}=$$

$$=\frac{2\mu(k+1)^{\frac{\mu+1}{2}}}{k^{\frac{\mu-1}{2}} e^{k\mu}\Omega_1^{\frac{\mu+1}{2}}}\cdot\sum_{i_2=0}^{\infty}\left(\mu\sqrt{\frac{k(k+1)}{\Omega_1}}\right)^{2i_1+\mu-1}\cdot\frac{1}{i_1!\Gamma(i+\mu)}\cdot$$

$$\cdot\frac{2\mu(k+1)^{\frac{\mu+1}{2}}}{k^{\frac{\mu-1}{2}} e^{k\mu}\Omega_2^{\frac{\mu+1}{2}}}\cdot\sum_{i_2=0}^{\infty}\left(\mu\sqrt{\frac{k(k+1)}{\Omega_2}}\right)^{2i_2+\mu-1}\cdot\frac{1}{i_2!\Gamma(i_2+\mu)}\cdot$$

$$\cdot\int_0^\infty dx_2\, x_2^{2i_2-2i_1-1} e^{-\frac{\mu(k+1)}{\Omega_2}x_2^2}$$

$$\cdot\frac{1}{2}\left(\frac{\Omega_1}{\mu(k+1)x_2^2}\right)^{i_1+\mu}\gamma\left(i_1+\mu,\frac{\mu(k+1)}{\Omega_1}\frac{x^2}{x_2^2}\right)\Bigg), \tag{11}$$

where $\gamma(n, x)$ is incomplete Gamma function.

After substituting (10) into (11), the previous expression for CDF becomes:

$$F_x(x)=\frac{2\mu(k+1)^{\frac{\mu+1}{2}}}{k^{\frac{\mu-1}{2}} e^{k\mu}\Omega_1^{\frac{\mu+1}{2}}}\cdot$$

$$\cdot\sum_{i_2=0}^{\infty}\left(\mu\sqrt{\frac{k(k+1)}{\Omega_1}}\right)^{2i_1+\mu-1}\cdot\frac{1}{i_1!\Gamma(i_1+\mu)}\cdot$$

$$\cdot\frac{2\mu(k+1)^{\frac{\mu+1}{2}}}{k^{\frac{\mu-1}{2}} e^{k\mu}\Omega_2^{\frac{\mu+1}{2}}}\cdot\sum_{i_2=0}^{\infty}\left(\mu\sqrt{\frac{k(k+1)}{\Omega_2}}\right)^{2i_2+\mu-1}\cdot\frac{1}{i_2!\Gamma(i_2+\mu)}\cdot$$

$$\cdot\frac{1}{2}\left(\frac{\Omega_1}{\mu(k+1)}\right)^{i_1+\mu}\frac{1}{i_1+\mu}\left(\frac{\mu(k+1)}{\Omega_1}x^2\right)^{i_1+\mu}\cdot$$

$$\cdot\sum_{j_1=0}^{\infty}\frac{1}{(i_1+\mu+1)(j_1)}\cdot\left(\frac{\mu(k+1)x^2}{\Omega_1}\right)^{j_1}\cdot$$

$$\cdot\int_0^\infty dx_2\, x_2^{2i_2-2i_1-1+2i_1+2\mu-2i_1-2\mu-2j_1} e^{-\frac{\mu(k+1)}{\Omega_1}\frac{x^2}{x_2^2}-\frac{\mu(k+1)}{\Omega_2}x_2^2}=$$

$$=\frac{2\mu(k+1)^{\frac{\mu+1}{2}}}{k^{\frac{\mu-1}{2}} e^{k\mu}\Omega_1^{\frac{\mu+1}{2}}}\cdot\sum_{i_2=0}^{\infty}\left(\mu\sqrt{\frac{k(k+1)}{\Omega_1}}\right)^{2i_1+\mu-1}\cdot\frac{1}{i_1!\Gamma(i+\mu)}\cdot$$

$$\cdot\frac{2\mu(k+1)^{\frac{\mu+1}{2}}}{k^{\frac{\mu-1}{2}} e^{k\mu}\Omega_2^{\frac{\mu+1}{2}}}\cdot\sum_{i_2=0}^{\infty}\left(\mu\sqrt{\frac{k(k+1)}{\Omega_2}}\right)^{2i_2+\mu-1}\cdot\frac{1}{i_2!\Gamma(i_2+\mu)}\cdot$$

$$\cdot\frac{1}{2}\frac{1}{i_1+\mu}x^{2i_1+2\mu}\cdot\sum_{j_1=0}^{\infty}\frac{1}{(i_1+\mu+1)(j_1)}\cdot\left(\frac{\mu(k+1)x^2}{\Omega_1}\right)^{j_1}\cdot$$

$$\left(\frac{\Omega_2x^2}{\Omega_1}\right)^{\frac{i_2}{2}-\frac{i_1}{2}-\frac{j_1}{2}} K_{i_2-i_1-j_1}\left(2\sqrt{\frac{\mu^2(k+1)^2x^2}{\Omega_1\Omega_2}}\right) \tag{12}$$

Here, $K_n(x)$ is the modified Bessel function of the second kind [16, eq. (3.471.9)].

IV. NUMERICAL RESULTS

The cumulative distribution function of minimum of two κ-μ random variables versus signal envelope is presented in Fig. 1. The CDF is plotted for $\mu_1=\mu_2=2$ and variable parameters κ_1 and κ_2. It is visible that CDF increases with increasing of the signal envelope. The cumulative distribution function decreases for larger values of Rician factor κ_1. Also, one can see from Fig. 1 that CDF is bigger for higher values of Rician factor κ_2.

The cumulative distribution function of product of two κ-μ random variables depending on the signal envelope is presented in Fig. 2. The parameters μ_1 and μ_2 are equal to each other and have a value of 2. It is possible to see from Fig. 2 that CDF becomes bigger with increasing of the signal envelope. Fig. 2 shows that CDF is less for higher values of Rician factors κ_1 and κ_2.

The system performance is better for smaller values of the outage probability, i.e., cumulative distribution function. This can be achieved by increasing the Ricean factors κ_1 and κ_2.

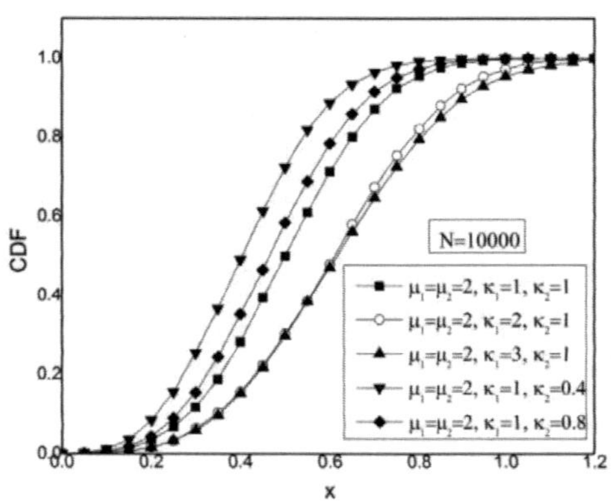

Figure 1. The cumulative distribution function of minimum of two κ-μ random variables.

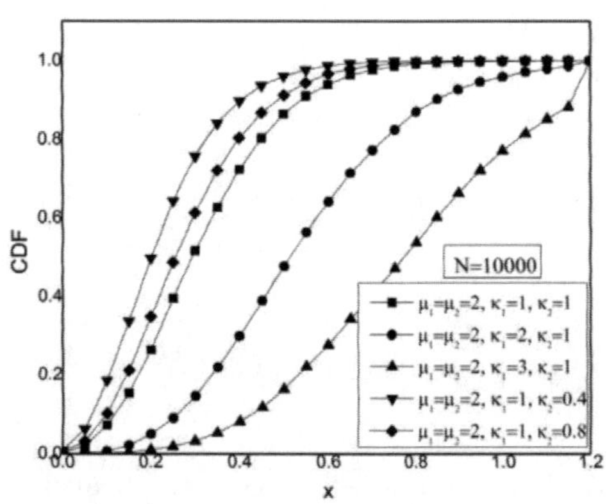

Figure 2. The cumulative distribution function of the product of two κ-μ random variables.

Since Rician factor is the ratio of dominant component power and scattering components power, it is evident that bigger dominant component powers and smaller scattering components give better system performance.

V. CONCLUSION

In this article, the communication relay radio system with two sections is analyzed. Both sections are exposed to κ-μ multipath fading.

The outage probability is defined in two ways. For the first, the outage probability is probability that signal envelope at one of sections becomes less than the specified threshold. The outage probability for this case can be calculated as a CDF of minimum of signal envelopes from both sections. The outage probability is calculated in the closed form. The influence of Rician κ factors on the outage probability is then analyzed.

For the second way, the outage probability is presented as probability that communication relay system output signal envelope drops below the defined threshold. The outage probability for this case is equal to the CDF of product of signal envelopes at sections. The fading parameters influence on the outage probability is described also.

The obtained formulas for the outage probability for relay (κ-μ)-(κ-μ) channels could be used for calculation the outage probability of other relay channels. For $\kappa_1=0$ and $\kappa_2=0$, (κ-μ)-(κ-μ) relay channel reduces to Nakagami-Nakagami relay channel; for $\mu_1=1$ and $\mu_2=1$, (κ-μ), (κ-μ) distribution becomes Rician-Rician channel [18]. Because of that, this article has general importance.

Results of this analysis can be used by designers of relay systems in terms of the presence of fading with the κ-μ distribution. The designers of these systems can choose optimal parameters for given value of the outage probability. Because of the generality of the results, the presence of other types of fading can also be covered with this investigation.

In our further work, the other system characteristics can be determined. Further, the outage probability for relay radio system with three sections can be derived. Besides, the performance for similar relay systems in the presence of other small-scale general fading distributions, such as α-μ, α-η-μ, or α-λ-μ, can be calculated too.

ACKNOWLEDGMENT

This paper has been partially supported by the Ministry of Education, Science and Technological Development of Republic of Serbia under the projects TR-33035 and III-44006.

REFERENCES

[1] M. K. Simon and M. S. Alouini, Digital Communication over Fading Channels, USA: John Wiley & Sons. 2000.

[2] W. C. Y. Lee, Mobile communications engineering, Mc-Graw-Hill, NewYork, USA, 2003.

[3] M. D. Yacoub, The k-μ distribution, http://www.eletrica.ufpr.br/anais/sbrt/SBrT19/001000000008700059.pdf, retrieved 31 Aug. 2016.

[4] S. L. Cotton and W. G. Scanlon, "High-order statistics for k-μ distribution", IEE Electron. Lett., vol. 43, issue 22, 25 Oct.

2007, pp. 1215 – 1217, Print ISSN 0013-5194, Online ISSN 1350-911X, DOI: 10.1049/el:20072372.

[5] D. Krstić, Z. Jovanović, R. Gerov, D. Radenković, and V. Milenković, "Statistics of k-μ Random Variable", Proc. of the 18th International Conference on Mathematical Methods, Computational Techniques and Intelligent Systems, MAMECTIS'16, Venice, Italy, January 29-31, 2016, pp. 163-171.

[6] D. Krstic, M. Stefanovic, V. Milenkovic, M. Masadeh Bani Yassein, S. Aljawarneh, and Z. Popovic, "Wireless Relay System with Two Sections in the Presence of κ-μ and η-μ Multipath Fading", IEEE International Conference on Internet of Things and Pervasive Systems IoT-SP-2016, in conjunction with The International Conference on Engineering & MIS 2016, Agadir, Morocco, 22- 24 Sept. 2016.

[7] N. Mpisias, doctoral disertation, http://dione.lib.unipi.gr/xmlui/bitstream/handle/unipi/5818/Mpisias.pdf?sequence=2.

[8] A. Papoulis and S. U. Pillai, Probability, random variables and stochastic processes, McGraw Hill, 4th edition, 2002.

[9] J. Galambos and I. Simonelli, Products of Random Variables: Applications to Problems of Physics and to Arithmetical Functions, July 20, 2004 by CRC Press, 344 Pages, ISBN 9780824754020 - CAT# DK2935.

[10] A. G. Glen, L. M. Leemis, and J. H. Drew, "Computing the distribution of the product of two continuous random variables", Computational Statistics & Data Analysis, Vol. 44, Issue 3, 1 January 2004, pp. 451–464.

[11] S. H. Stein, "Sums and Products of Jointly Distributed Random Variables: A Simplified Approach", Journal of Statistics Education, Cleveland State University, Vol. 13, Number 3, 2005, http://www.amstat.org/publications/jse/v13n3/stein.html.

[12] E. Mekić, M. Stefanović, P. Spalević, N. Sekulović, and A. Stanković, "Statistical analysis of ratio of random variables and its application in performance analysis of multi-hop wireless transmissions", Mathematical Problems in Engineering, vol. 2012, Article ID 841092, 10 pages, http://dx.doi.org/10.1155/2012/841092.

[13] A. Stanković, Č. Stefanović, N. Sekulović, Z. Popović, and M. Stefanović, "The Distribution of Minimum of Ratios of Two Random Variables and Its Application in Analysis of Multi-hop Systems", Radioengineering, Vol. 21, No. 4, Dec. 2012, pp. 1156-1162.

[14] A. Matović, E. Mekić, N. Sekulović, M. Stefanović, M. Matović, and C. Stefanović, "The Distribution of the Ratio of the Products of Two Independent α-μ Variates and Its Application in the Performance Analysis of Relaying Communication Systems", Mathematical Problems in Engineering, vol. 2013, Article ID 147106, 6 pages, http://dx.doi.org/10.1155/2013/147106.

[15] Incomplete Gamma Function, http://mathworld.wolfram.com/IncompleteGammaFunction.html, retrieved 31 Aug. 2016.

[16] Modified Bessel Function of the Second Kind, http://mathworld.wolfram.com/ModifiedBesselFunctionoftheSecondKind.html, retrieved 31 Aug. 2016.

[17] I. S. Gradshteyn and I. M. Ryzhik, Table of Integrals, Series, and Products, 7 th ed. New York: Academic, 2007.

[18] P. M. Shankar, Fading and Shadowing in Wireless Systems, Springer, Dec 7, 2011. DOI 10.1007/978-1-4614-0367-8.

Experimental Analysis on How Access Point Scanning Impacts on TCP Throughput over IEEE 802.11n Wireless LAN

Kento Kobayashi, Yoshiki Hashimoto, Masataka Nomoto, Ryo Yamamoto, Satoshi Ohzahata, and Toshihiko Kato
University of Electro-Communications
Tokyo, Japan
e-mail: k1552010@edu.cc.uec.ac.jp, hys3224@net.is.uec.ac.jp, noch@net.is.uec.ac.jp, ryo_yamamoto@is.uec.ac.jp, ohzahata@is.uec.ac.jp, kato@is.uec.ac.jp

Abstract— **In IEEE 802.11 wireless LAN, there is a problem that the access point scanning at stations which uses the power management function gives impacts on the performance of TCP communication. In paper, we show the result of experiments on this problem for uploading and downloading TCP data transfer over 802.11n wireless LAN. For the uploading transfer, we analyze the influence to TCP throughput focusing on the TCP small queues that limit the amount of data in wireless LAN's sending queue. As for the downloading transfer, we discuss the influence by the TCP congestion control algorithm at TCP senders and A-MPDU transmission rate at the access point.**

Keywords- WLAN; IEEE802.11n; Access Point Scanning; Power Management; TCP Small Queues; TCP Congestion Window Validation.

I. Introduction

Nowadays, 802.11n [1] is one of most widely adopted IEEE wireless LAN (WLAN) standards. It establishes high speed data transfer using the higher data rate support (e.g., 300 Mbps), the frame aggregation in Aggregated MAC Protocol Data Unit (A-MPDU) and the Block Acknowledgment mechanism. On the other hand, TCP introduces some new functions to establish high performance over high speed WLANs. CoDel [2] and TCP small queues [3], which aim to resolve the Bufferbloat problem [4] are examples.

We reported some performance evaluation results on TCP behaviors over 802.11n [5][6]. In those evaluations, we have encountered the situation that the TCP throughput decreases periodically. By analyzing the captured WLAN frame logs during the performance degradation, its reason is detected to be periodically transmitted data frames without data (*Null data frames*) with the power management field set to 1 in the WLAN header. These frames are used by WLAN stations to inform access points that they are going to sleep and to ask the associated access point not to send data frames. It is pointed out that WLAN stations use Null data frames to scan another available access point periodically [7].

Through more detailed performance analysis, we found that the impacts of Null data frames on TCP data transfer vary by the functions of TCP used in the communication. Specifically, the TCP sender behaviors and the throughput degradation depend on the direction of TCP data transfer (uploading from station to access point or downloading in the reverse direction), whether the TCP small queues are used or not, and what kind of congestion control algorithm is used. This paper shows the results of experimental analysis about the impacts on TCP throughput given by Null data frames used for the access point scanning. The rest of this paper consists the following sections. Section 2 shows the technologies relevant to this paper. Section 3 explains the experimental settings. Sections 4 and 5 give the results of the experiments for uploading TCP data transfer and downloading TCP data transfer, respectively. In the end, Section 6 gives the conclusions of this paper.

II. Relevant Technologies

A. Power management function and Null data frames

As described above, IEEE 802.11 standards introduce the power management function. In the WLAN frame format depicted in Fig. 1 (a), bit 12 of the Frame Control field is the *Power Management field* (shown in Fig. 1 (b)). By setting this bit to 1, a station informs the associated access point that it is going to the *power save mode*, in which the station goes to sleep and wakes up only when the access point sends beacon frames. By setting the bit to 0, it informs the access point that it goes back to the *active mode*.

This function is used for several purposes. One example is the case that a station is actually going to sleep to save its power consumption for some time period. In this case, a station wakes up only at the timing of receiving beacon frames from the access point. If the access point has data frames to deliver to the sleeping station, it indicates, in the Traffic Indication Map element in a beacon frame, that there are some frames to the station. In response to this information, the station requests the delivery of data frames by use of a PS-Poll frame.

Another is the access point scanning. For example, a Lunix terminal executing the NetworkManager application searches periodically for an access point which provides

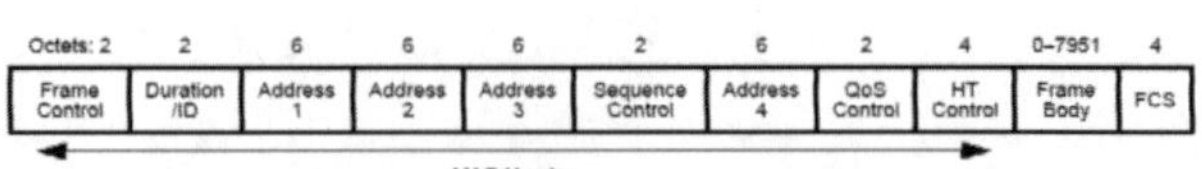

(a) Structure of WLAN frame.

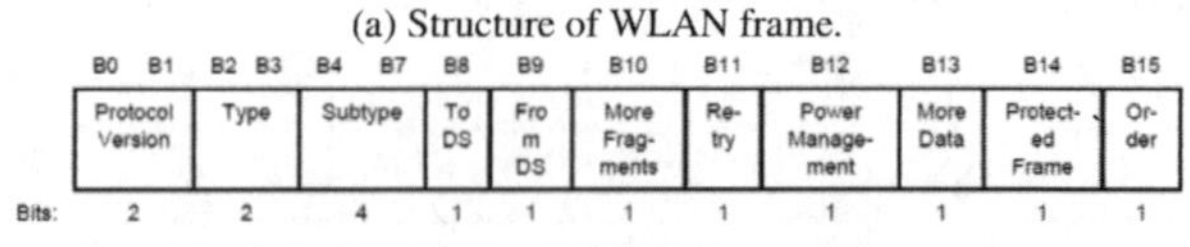

(b) Structure of Frame Control field.
Fig. 1. IEEE 802.11 WLAN frame format [1].

stronger radio signal than the access point with which the terminal is associated [8]. There are two schemes for the access point scanning; the passive scanning in which a station waits for a beacon frame from another access point, and the active scanning in which a station sends a probe request frame and waits for a probe response frame for the request. In either scheme, a station needs to ask the current access point to stop sending data frames to it. For this purpose, the station sends a frame with the Power Management field set to 1.

Null data frames are used by WLAN stations to inform access points of the transfer to the power save mode or to the active mode [9]. This is a frame which contains no data (Frame Body in Fig. 1 (a)). An ordinary data frame has the type of '01' and the subtype of '0000' in the Frame Control field. That is, B3 and B2 in Fig. 1 (b) are 0 and 1, and B7 through B4 are all 0. On the other hand, Null data frame has the type of '01' and the subtype of '0100'. While an ordinary data frame has three Address fields, a Null data frame has only two Address fields; the transmitter is a station MAC address and the receiver is an access point MAC address. By using Null data frames with the Power Management field set to 0 or 1, stations can request the power management function for access points.

B. TCP small queues

In the Linux operating system with version 3.6 and later, a mechanism called TCP small queues [3] is installed in order to cope with the Bufferbloat problem. It keeps watch on the queues in Linux schedulers and device drivers in a sending terminal, and if the amount of data stored in the queues is larger than the predefined queue limit, it suspends the TCP module until the amount of stored data becomes smaller than the limit. During this TCP suspension, the data which applications transmitted is stored in the TCP send socket buffer, which may cause the application to be suspended if the TCP send socket buffer becomes full. After the TCP module is resumed, it processes the application data stored in the send socket buffer.

The default value of the predefined queue limit is 128 Kbyte, and it is adjustable by changing the following parameter;

/proc/sys/net/ipv4/tcp_limit_output_bytes.

This mechanism is different from the other mechanisms against the Bufferbloat problem, such as CoDel, in the point that no TCP segments are discarded intentionally to protect the increase of buffered data in sending queues, which may cause a large communication delay.

C. Congestion window validation

The TCP congestion control uses the congestion window size (*cwnd*) maintained in TCP senders. TCP senders transmits TCP data segments under the limitation of cwnd and the window size advertised by TCP receivers. In general, cwnd is increased when TCP senders receive TCP acknowledgment (ACK) segments and decreased when any data segments are retransmitted.

This mechanism is considered to work well under the assumption that the throughput of data transfer is limited by cwnd. When the throughput is controlled by an application in a TCP sender, however, the data amount floating over network without acknowledged (it is called *flight size*) might be smaller than cwnd. In this case, cwnd also increases when an ACK segment is delivered to the sender and the value of cwnd becomes much larger than the current flight size. This means that the value of cwnd is invalid in this stage. If the TCP sender changes its status from application limited to cwnd limited suddenly, TCP segments corresponding to an invalid, i.e., too large cwnd value will rush into network.

In order to resolve such a problems, the congestion window validation (CWV) mechanism is proposed. RTC 2861 [10] proposes the following two rules. (1) A TCP sender halves the value of cwnd if no dat segments are transmitted during a retransmission timeout period. (2) When a TCP sender does not send data segment more than cwnd during a round-trip time (RTT), then it decreases cwnd to

$$(cwnd + sent\ data\ size)/_2$$

in the next RTT time frame.

RFC 7661 [11] revises the above rules and defines a new rule that, if the data size acknowledged during one RTT is smaller than half of cwnd, a TCP sender does not increase cwnd in the next RTT time frame. It defines the procedure in the case of congestion separately.

III. EXPERIMENTAL SETTINGS

Fig. 2 shows the configuration of the performance evaluation experiment we conducted. Two stations conforming to 802.11n with 5GHz band are associated with one access point, which is connected to a server through 1Gbps Ethernet. One station called STA1 is located at a near position to the access point, and communicates with the server through the access point. The other station called STA2 is used to monitor WLAN frames exchanged between STA1 and the access point.

We use commercially available notebooks for the stations and the server. The access point used is also off-the-shell product. The detailed specification of the notebook and the access point is shown in Table 1. The access point is able to use the 40 MHz channel bandwidth and provides the MAC level data rate from 6.5 Mbps to 300 Mbps.

In the experiment, the data is generated by iperf [12] in the upload direction from STA1 to the server and the download direction from the server to STA1. The conditions for the experiment are the followings.

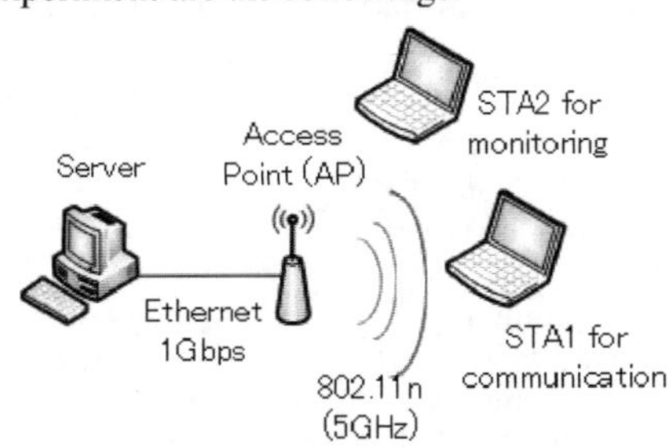

Fig. 2. Network configuration in experiment.

TABLE I. SPECIFICATION OF NOTEBOOK AND ACCESS POINT.

NOTE	Manufacturer/Model	DELL Insilon 14
	Operating system	Ubuntu 14.04LTS (kernel 3.13) or Ubuntu 12.04LTS (kernel 3.2)
	WLAN driver	ath9k
AP	Manufacturer/Model	BUFFALO AirStation WZR-HP-AG300H
	WLAN chip	Atheros AR7161
	WLAN driver	ath9k

- Use or non-use of the TCP small queues, and
- use of CUBIC TCP [13] or TCP NewReno [14] as a congestion control mechanism.

When we use the TCP small queues, we installed Ubuntu 14.04LTS in the notebook, and in the case not to use it, we installed Ubuntu 12.04 LTS.

During the data transmissions, the following detailed performance metrics are collected for the detailed analysis of the communication;

- the packet trace at the server, STA1 and STA2 , by use of *tcpdump*,
- the TCP throughput for every second, calculated from packet trace at TCP sender,
- the WLAN related metrics, such as the MAC level data rate, the number of A-MPDUs sent for a second and the number of MPDUs aggregated in an A-MPDU, from the device driver ath9k [15] at the access point and STA1, and
- the TCP congestion window size at the server, by use of *tcpprobe* [16].

IV. ANALYSIS OF UPLOADING TCP DATA TRANSFER

In the experiments for uploading TCP data transfer, the results were different depending on whether the TCP small queues are used or not. On the other hand, the TCP congestion control algorithms did not affect the results so much. This section shows the results for uploading TCP data transfer focusing on the use or non-use of TCP small queues using CUBIC TCP.

A. *Results when TCP small queues are used*

Fig. 3 shows the time variation of TCP throughput and cwnd in the case that the TCP small queues are used in STA1. From this result, we can say that the throughput degradations occur periodically. Specifically, each *throughput degraded period* is around 10 sec. and such a period happens approximately once in 120 sec. In a *normal period*, the average TCP throughput is 136 Mbps, but it decreases to as much as 57 % in a throughput degraded period.

On the other hand, cwnd does not decrease even in a throughput degraded period, which means that there are no packet losses. Besides that, the increase of cwnd is depressed throughout the TCP communication. In this result, the value of cwnd is limited to around 200 packets.

Fig. 4 shows the packet trace, captured by STA2, of WLAN frames without data in the throughput degraded period starting at time 25 sec. This is the result of analysis

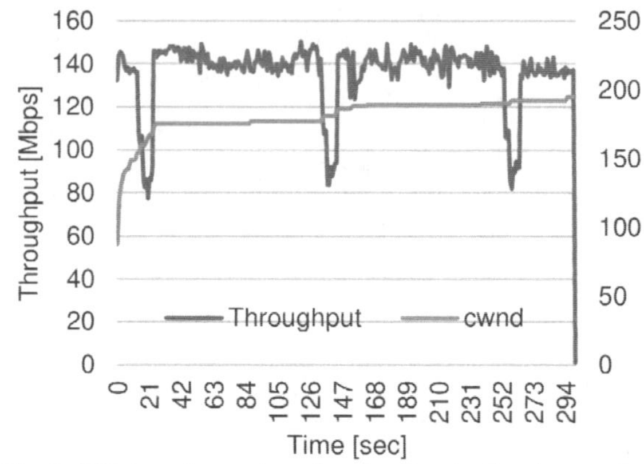

Fig. 3. TCP throughput and cwnd vs. time in uploading data transfer with TCP small queues.

by Wireshark and contains the number of frame, the time of packet capture measeured from the TCP SYN segment, the source and destination MAC address, the protocol type (802.11), the frame length, and the information including name and parameters.

The frame whose number is 105,932, shown inverted to blue in the figure, is a Null data frame. For this frame, the Info column says that "Flags=. . .P. . .TC." This means that the Power Management field is set to 1 in this frame. The transmitter of this frame is STA1, whose MAC address is "LiteonTe_0b:ce:0c," and its receiver is the access point whose MAC address is "BuffaloI_27:2a:39." The sequence control ("SN" in the figure) is 1750 in this frame. In this packet trace, this Null data frame is not acknowledged by the access point. Instead, the same Null data frames are retransmitted eight times by the frames with numbers 105,933 through 105,953. They have the same sequence control (1750), and the Retry field in the Frame Control field is set to 1, as indicated "Flags=. . .PR. .TC" in the figure. From the fourth retransmission, a RTS frame is used before sending a Null data frame and the access point responds it by returning a CTS frame, which allows STA1 to send a Null data frame. But, from the fourth to the seventh retransmissions, the access point does not send any ACK frames. In the end, the access point sends an ACK frame at the eighth retransmission (see the frame with number 105,954). During these frame exchanges, it takes 1.8 msec.

Then, the frame with number 105,955 is a beacon frame broadcasted by the access point. The duration between the ACK frame (No. 105,954) and this beacon frame is 90 msec in the figure.

24 msec after the beacon frame is transmitted, STA1 sends a Null data frame with the Power Management field set to 0, whose number and sequence control is 105,956 and 1751, respectively. Again, this Null data frame is retransmitted four times. In this case, although STA2 captures the corresponding ACK frames from the access point, STA1 retransmits it, repeatedly. After this frame is acknowledged by the ACK frame with number 105,966, STA1 transmit the next Null data frame whose sequence control 1752, and it is immediately acknowledged. These frame exchanges take 1.3 msec.

No.	Time	Source	Destination	Protocol	Length	Info
105931	25.814733	LiteonTe_0b:ce:0c	BuffaloI_27:2a:39	802.11	58	802.11 Block Ack, Flags=........C
105932	25.815296	LiteonTe_0b:ce:0c	BuffaloI_27:2a:39	802.11	57	Null function (No data), SN=1750, FN=0, Flags=...P...TC
105933	25.815318	LiteonTe_0b:ce:0c	BuffaloI_27:2a:39	802.11	57	Null function (No data), SN=1750, FN=0, Flags=...PR..TC
105934	25.815323	LiteonTe_0b:ce:0c	BuffaloI_27:2a:39	802.11	57	Null function (No data), SN=1750, FN=0, Flags=...PR..TC
105935	25.815326	LiteonTe_0b:ce:0c	BuffaloI_27:2a:39	802.11	57	Null function (No data), SN=1750, FN=0, Flags=...PR..TC
105938	25.815343	LiteonTe_0b:ce:0c	BuffaloI_27:2a:39	802.11	58	802.11 Block Ack, Flags=........C
105939	25.817033	LiteonTe_0b:ce:0c	BuffaloI_27:2a:39	802.11	46	Request-to-send, Flags=...P....C
105940	25.817054		LiteonTe_0b:ce:0c	802.11	40	Clear-to-send, Flags=........C
105941	25.817066	LiteonTe_0b:ce:0c	BuffaloI_27:2a:39	802.11	57	Null function (No data), SN=1750, FN=0, Flags=...PR..TC
105942	25.817070	LiteonTe_0b:ce:0c	BuffaloI_27:2a:39	802.11	46	Request-to-send, Flags=...P....C
105943	25.817073		LiteonTe_0b:ce:0c	802.11	40	Clear-to-send, Flags=........C
105944	25.817077	LiteonTe_0b:ce:0c	BuffaloI_27:2a:39	802.11	57	Null function (No data), SN=1750, FN=0, Flags=...PR..TC
105945	25.817080	LiteonTe_0b:ce:0c	BuffaloI_27:2a:39	802.11	46	Request-to-send, Flags=...P....C
105946	25.817083		LiteonTe_0b:ce:0c	802.11	40	Clear-to-send, Flags=........C
105947	25.817088	LiteonTe_0b:ce:0c	BuffaloI_27:2a:39	802.11	57	Null function (No data), SN=1750, FN=0, Flags=...PR..TC
105948	25.817091	LiteonTe_0b:ce:0c	BuffaloI_27:2a:39	802.11	46	Request-to-send, Flags=...P....C
105949	25.817095		LiteonTe_0b:ce:0c	802.11	40	Clear-to-send, Flags=........C
105950	25.817099	LiteonTe_0b:ce:0c	BuffaloI_27:2a:39	802.11	57	Null function (No data), SN=1750, FN=0, Flags=...PR..TC
105951	25.817102	LiteonTe_0b:ce:0c	BuffaloI_27:2a:39	802.11	46	Request-to-send, Flags=...P....C
105952	25.817105		LiteonTe_0b:ce:0c	802.11	40	Clear-to-send, Flags=........C
105953	25.817111	LiteonTe_0b:ce:0c	BuffaloI_27:2a:39	802.11	57	Null function (No data), SN=1750, FN=0, Flags=...PR..TC
105954	25.817116		LiteonTe_0b:ce:0c	802.11	40	Acknowledgement, Flags=........C
105955	25.907580	BuffaloI_27:2a:39	Broadcast	802.11	379	Beacon frame, SN=3924, FN=0, Flags=........C, BI=100, SSID=klab-n/a
105956	25.931649	LiteonTe_0b:ce:0c	BuffaloI_27:2a:39	802.11	57	Null function (No data), SN=1751, FN=0, Flags=.......TC
105958	25.931677		LiteonTe_0b:ce:0c	802.11	40	Acknowledgement, Flags=........C
105959	25.931682	LiteonTe_0b:ce:0c	BuffaloI_27:2a:39	802.11	57	Null function (No data), SN=1751, FN=0, Flags=....R..TC
105960	25.931686		LiteonTe_0b:ce:0c	802.11	40	Acknowledgement, Flags=........C
105961	25.931691	LiteonTe_0b:ce:0c	BuffaloI_27:2a:39	802.11	57	Null function (No data), SN=1751, FN=0, Flags=....R..TC
105962	25.932891	LiteonTe_0b:ce:0c	BuffaloI_27:2a:39	802.11	57	Null function (No data), SN=1751, FN=0, Flags=....R..TC
105963	25.932914	LiteonTe_0b:ce:0c	BuffaloI_27:2a:39	802.11	46	Request-to-send, Flags=........C
105964	25.932918		LiteonTe_0b:ce:0c	802.11	40	Clear-to-send, Flags=........C
105965	25.932922	LiteonTe_0b:ce:0c	BuffaloI_27:2a:39	802.11	57	Null function (No data), SN=1751, FN=0, Flags=....R..TC
105966	25.932927		LiteonTe_0b:ce:0c	802.11	40	Acknowledgement, Flags=........C
105967	25.932937	LiteonTe_0b:ce:0c	BuffaloI_27:2a:39	802.11	54	Null function (No data), SN=1752, FN=0, Flags=.......TC
105968	25.932940		LiteonTe_0b:ce:0c	802.11	40	Acknowledgement, Flags=........C

Fig. 4. An example of packet trace during throughput degraded period focusing on WLAN frames without data

During this sequence, STA1 and the access point do not send any data frames. This paper refers to the time period as a *sleeping period*. After the last Null data frame with the Power Management field set to 0 is acknowledged, the data transfer from STA1 is restarted. But, several hundred milliseconds later, the similar communication sequence including the Null data frames and beacon frame occurs, and it goes to another sleeping period. This paper refers to the period when data frames are transmitted between sleeping periods as an *awoken period*. During a performance degraded period, there are around 26 pairs of sleeping period and awoken period.

The relationship among those periods are shown in Fig. 5. In the evaluation result, the throughput degraded periods and the normal periods are repeated as shown at the top of this figure. The average duration for them is around 10 sec. and 110 sec., respectively. A throughput degraded period consists of sleeping periods and awoken periods. The average duration for them is 110 msec and 320 msec, respectively. As described in Fig. 4 before, a sleeping period consists of a period sending Null data frames with the Power Management field set to 1, a period waiting for a beacon frame, and a period sending Null data frames with the Power Management field set to 0. The average durations for the individual periods are shown in Fig. 5.

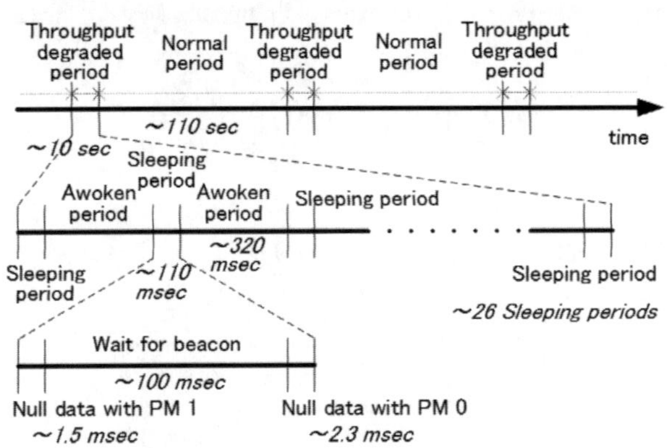

Fig. 5. Detailed analysis of time periods.

On the other hand, Fig. 3 shows that the increase of cwnd is suppressed even if there are no packet losses. The reason is considered to be the collaboration of the TCP small queues and CWV. As described before, CWV intends to be used when a TCP communication is application limited. In the case the TCP small queues are used, however, it is possible that the data transfer stops when the buffered data in the sending queue for WLAN device exceeds the predefined queue limit, even if the flight size is smaller than cwnd. In this case, the MAC level data rate dominates the throughput instead of cwnd in the TCP level, and therefore, the control by CWV becomes effective. Actually, the source program of the TCP small queues implements a procedure such that, when the unacknowledged data amount is smaller than the current value of cwnd in the slow start phase, cwnd is not incremented even if a new ACK segment arrives. Note that this procedure itself is not conforming to RFC 2861 strictly but similar to RFC 7661, which was not standardized when the TCP small queues were introduced.

B. Results when TCP small queues are not used

Fig. 6 shows the time variation of TCP throughput and cwnd in the case that the TCP small queues are not used in STA1. In this case, the throughput degradations also occur periodically. In the normal periods, the average throughput is 174 Mbps, which is 38 Mbps higher than the case using the TCP small queues. This result seems to come from the fact that the cwnd value goes up to 970 packets. On the other hand, in the throughput degraded periods, the

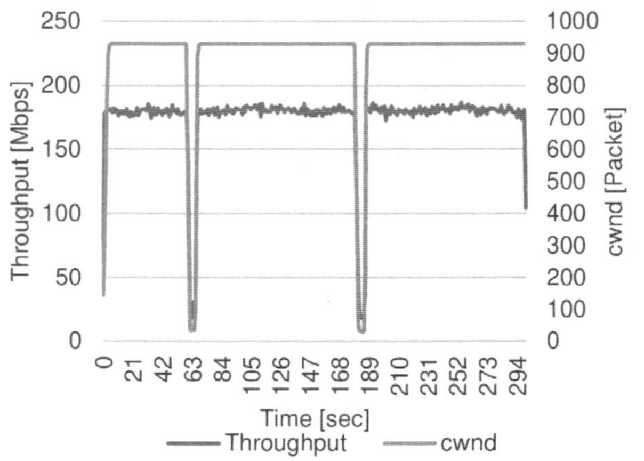

Fig. 6. TCP throughput and cwnd vs. time in uploading data transfer without TCP small queues.

throughput decreases as low as 10 % of that in the normal period. The value of cwnd decreases largely in the throughput degraded periods.

The reason for the periodic throughput degradation is also the periodic access point scanning using Null data frames with the power management function. In this case, however, there are some differences compared with the case of the TCP small queues. At first, the value of cwnd in a normal period is large. The reason is that there are no packet losses in this period and ACK segments increase cwnd because the TCP communication is cwnd limited. It should be noted that the large cwnd results in a lot of packets being stored in the sending queue at STA1. It is considered that these queued packets invoke packet losses and, as a result, cwnd decreases largely in a throughput degraded period. This is the second difference. In turn, the decrease of cwnd reduces the throughput in this period largely.

V. Analysis of Downloading TCP Data Transfer

In the experiments for downloading TCP data transfer, the results were not different depending on the use or non-use of TCP small queues. This is because neither the TCP small queues nor CWV are implemented at the access point. Instead, the results slightly depended on the TCP congestion control algorithms in the server. This section shows these results.

A. Results when CUBIC TCP is used

Fig. 7 shows the time variation of TCP throughput and cwnd in the case that CUBIC TCP is used at the server. From this figure, we can say that the periodic throughput degradation also occurs at the downloading TCP data transfer. By analyzing the monitoring results of WLAN frames captured by STA2, we confirmed that there are periodic exchanges of Null data frames and beacon frames between STA1 and the access point, which is similar with the sequence in the uploading TCP data transfer. So, in the case of downloading TCP data transfer, the access point scanning by WLAN stations reduces the throughput.

As shown in the figure, cwnd at the server takes the value between 350 and 500 packets. The drops of cwnd indicate that packet losses occur frequently. The increase of cwnd takes a cubic curve of time, which is characteristic for CUBIC TCP.

In contrary to the upload results, the throughput in a throughput degraded period drops sharply, although the cwnd value does not decrease largely during this period. In addition, the throughput just after a throughput degraded period is rather low. In order to investigate those results, we checked the number of A-MPDUs sent in one second by the access point, and the number of MPDUs contained in one A-MPDU. The results are given in Fig. 8. This figure shows that both A-MPDUs and MPDUs per A-MPDU decrease largely in throughput degraded periods. This result accounts for the throughput reduction. Besides that, the number of MPDUs aggregated in an A-MPDU is low just after a throughput degraded period. This is considered the reason for low throughput in this time frame.

B. Results when TCP NewReno is used

Fig. 9 shows the time variation of TCP throughput and cwnd in the case that TCP NewReno is used at the server. Fig. 10 shows the time variation of the number of A-MPDUs sent in one second by the access point, and the number of MPDUs contained in one A-MPDU. From Fig. 9, it is

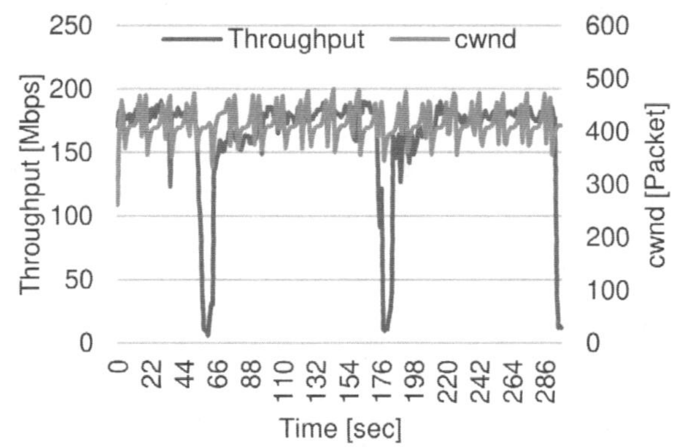

Fig. 7. TCP throughput and cwnd vs. time in downloading data transfer using CUBIC TCP at server.

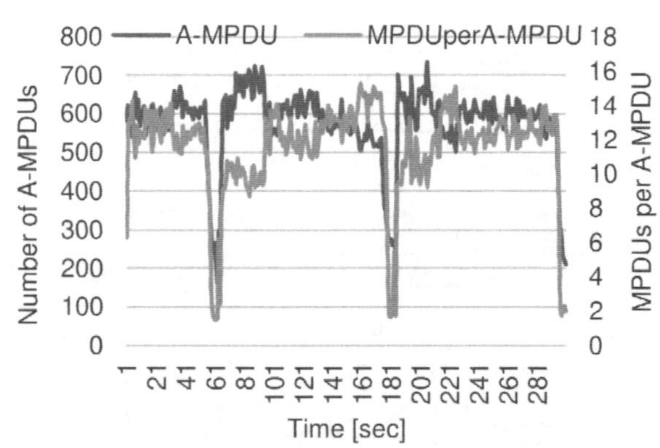

Fig. 8. Number of A-MPTU and number of MPTUs in A-MPDU vs. time in downloading data transfer using CUBIC TCP at server.

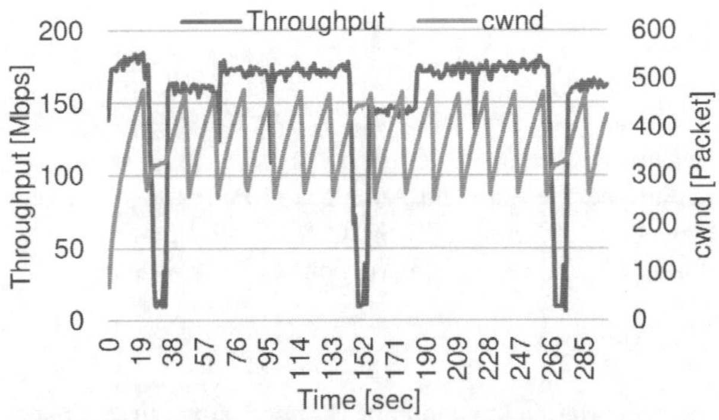

Fig. 9. TCP throughput and cwnd vs. time in downloading data transfer using TCP NewReno at server.

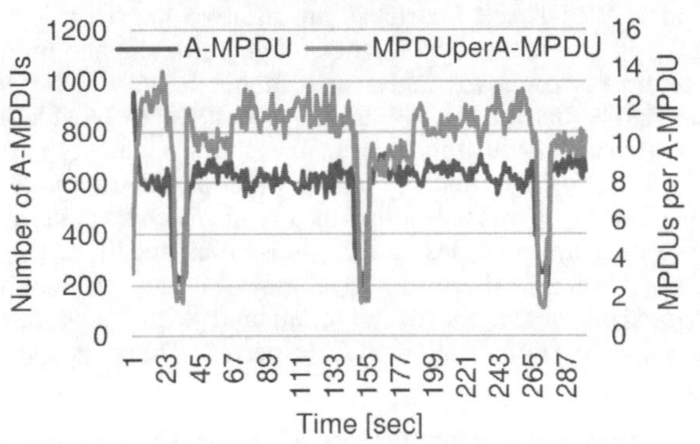

Fig. 10. Number of A-MPTU and number of MPTUs in A-MPDU vs. time in downloading data transfer using TCP NewReno at server.

confirmed that the throughput is degraded sharply in every 120 sec. From the monitoring results of WLAN frames captured by STA2, we also confirmed the periodic exchanges of Null data frames and beacon frames between STA1 and the access point. This is an access point scanning by STA1 and the reason for the throughput reduction.

This figure also shows that cwnd at the server takes the value between 300 and 500 packets, and that cwnd drops frequently, similarly with the case of CUBIC TCP. The increase of cwnd takes a linear curve along with time, which is characteristic for TCP NewReno.

While the throughput in a throughput degraded period drops sharply, the cwnd value does not decrease largely. The throughput just after a throughput degraded period is rather low. These are similar with the case of CUBIC TCP. As Fig. 10 shows, the numbers of transmitted A-MPDUs and MPDUs per A-MPDU decrease largely in throughput degraded periods. Besides that, the number of MPDUs aggregated in an A-MPDU is low just after a throughput degraded period. This will be the reason for low throughput in this time frame. These results are similar with the case of CUBIC TCP.

VI. CONCLUSIONS

This paper discussed the results on performance evaluation on the periodic TCP throughput degradation in IEEE 802.11n WLAN. The degradation is invoked by the periodic access point scanning using Null data frames with the Power Management field set to on and off. We showed that the throughput degradation is different depending on whether the TCP small queues are used or not in an uploading TCP data transfer, and what type of TCP congestion control algorithms are used in a downloading TCP data transfer. In the uploading data transfer, the TCP small queues and the congestion window validation suppress both of the increase of congestion window size in a normal period and its decrease in a throughput degradation period. So, the throughput degradation invoked by the access point scanning is smaller than the case when the TCP small queues are not used. In the downloading data transfer, the congestion control algorithms give some impacts on the time variation of congestion window size. However, the actual reason for the throughput degradation is the decrease in the transmission rate of A-MPDUs and the number of MPDUs in one A-MPDU, which are observed at an access point.

REFERENCES

[1] IEEE Standard for Information technology: Local and metropolitan area networks Part 11: Wireless Medium Access Control (MAC) and Physical Layer (PHY) Specifications, 2012.

[2] K. Nichols and V. Jacobson, "Controlling Queue Delay," ACM Queue, Networks, vol.10, no.5, pp. 1-15, May 2012.

[3] Eric Dumazet, "[PATCHv2 net-next] tcp: TCP Small Queues",http://article.gmane.org/gmane.network.routing.codel/68, 2012, retrieved Sept. 2016. .

[4] J. Gettys and K. Nichols, "Bufferbloat: Dark Buffers in the Internet," ACM Queue, Virtualization, vol. 9, no.11, pp. 1-15, Nov. 2011.

[5] M. Nomoto, T. Kato, C. Wu, and S. Ohzahata, "Resolving Bufferbloat Problem in 802.11n WLAN by Weakening MAC Loss Recovery for TCP Stream," Proc. PDCN 2014, pp.293-300, Feb. 2014.

[6] Y. Hashimoto, M. Nomoto, C. Wu, S. Ohzahata, and T. Kato, "Experimental Analysis on Performance Anomaly for Download Data Transfer at IEEE 802.11n Wireless LAN," Proc. ICN 2016, pp.22-27, Feb. 2016.

[7] My80211.com, "802.11: Null Data Frames," http://www.my80211.com/home/2009/12/5/80211-null-data-frames.html, Dec. 2009, retrieved Jun. 2016. .

[8] ath9k-devel@lists.ath9k.org, "disable dynamic power save in AR9280," http://comments.gmane.org/gmane.linux.drivers.ath9k.devel/5199, Jan. 2011, retrieved Jun. 2016. .

[9] W. Gu, Z. Yang, D. Xuan, and W. Jia, "Null Data Frame: A Double-Edged Sword in IEEE 802.11 WLANs," IEEE Trans. Parallel & Distributed Systems, vol. 21, no. 7, pp.897-910, Jul. 2010.

[10] N, Handley, J. Padhye, and S. Floyd, "TCP Congestion Window Validation," IETF RFC 2861, Jun. 2000.

[11] G. Fairhurst, A. Sathiaseelan, and R. Secchi, "Updating TCP to Support Rate-Limited Traffic," IETF RFC 7661, Oct. 2015.

[12] iperf, http://iperf.sourceforge.net/, retrieved Jun. 2016.

[13] S. Ha, I. Rhee, and L. Xu, "CUBIC: A New TCP-Friendly High-Speed TCP Variant," ACM SIGOPS Operating Systems Review, vol. 42, no. 5, pp. 64-74, July 2008.

[14] S. Floyd, T. Henderson, and A. Gurtov, "The NewReno Modification to TCP's Fast Recovery Algorithm," IETF RFC 3728, April 2004.

[15] ath9k Linux Wireless, http://sireless.kernel.org/enusers/Drivers/ath9k, retrieved Jun. 2016.

[16] Linux foundation: tcpprobe, http://www.linuxfoundation.org /collaborate/workgroups/networking/ tcpprobe, retrieved Jun. 2016.

Using Number of Retransmissions to Improve Routing in Ad-hoc NETworks

Tiguiane Yélémou
Polytechnic University of Bobo Dioulasso,
School of Computer Science, Burkina Faso
Email: tyelemou@gmail.com

Philippe Meseure and Anne-Marie Poussard
University of Poitiers, XLIM CNRS Lab, France
Email: (Philippe.Meseure, anne.marie.poussard)@univ-poitiers.fr

***Abstract*—In this paper, we analyze the effectiveness of usual metrics and Quality of Service (QoS) methods used to improve routing in wireless networks, when considering the erroneous nature of radio links. We first analyze an additive metric based on Bit Error Rate (BER) and we propose a new metric similar to hop-count metric where retransmissions are accurately taken into account. With this number of retransmissions-based metric, the distance between two adjacent nodes will not be 1, but 1 plus the cost of retransmissions required on the link. Our approach is a light and immediate way to evaluate link quality. It does not imply additional network overhead and costly computation. To test the efficiency of this new metric, we have implemented it into the well-known Optimized Link State Routing protocol. Realistic simulation results show that this metric outperforms traditional metrics like the ones based on delay, BER or Expected Transmission Count.**

Keywords*—*Wireless networks; QoS metrics; Routing protocols; OLSR protocol; cross layer approach.

I. INTRODUCTION AND MOTIVATIONS

Routing in wireless networks is still an issue. It remains hazardous to guarantee any quality of service (QoS) for such networks. Most algorithms compute paths by relying on a selected metric. This allows them to compare computed paths and find the best. However, most of the used metrics do not take into account all specific characteristics of ad hoc wireless networks such as erroneous links, interference, etc. In this context, a node may need several attempts to transmit data successfully. Unfortunately, retransmissions imply additional delays, decrease throughput and increase communication overhead in the network. In critical cases, communications fail after several attempts.

In order to guarantee a certain level of QoS, routing protocols should be smart enough to pick a stable and good quality communication route in order to avoid retransmission and packets loss. In recent years, many QoS approaches have been proposed that take into account link quality in the choice of routes. Nevertheless, these methods arise many issues. Indeed, some approaches rely on link estimation that are hard to measure in practice (for instance, the bit error rate). Others require costly analysis of the network and imply a substantial communication overhead. Finally, some approaches choose routes that maximize packet delivery ratio, but at the cost of a high number of intermediate nodes and/or delay.

To make protocols more reliable, an effective and simple estimation of link quality must be proposed, as well as a link quality-aware computation of shortest paths . In this paper, we focus on metrics related to the packet loss rate criterion. First, the Bit Error Rate (BER) as QoS link criterion is analyzed and a BER-based metric as an additive metric is designed. Second, to evaluate link quality, a light, efficient and immediate solution is proposed and a new metric based on the number of retransmissions at Medium Access Control (MAC) level is proposed. With this metric, the shortest path is expressed not exactly in terms of number of hops but rather in terms of number of transmissions. In a realistic environment taking into account obstacles in the propagation medium, these two metrics (the BER-based and number of transmissions count-based ones) are tested and compared with those based on number of hops, delay and Expected Transmission Count (ETX).

The remainder of this paper is organized as follows. In Section II, related work is presented and shortcomings of commonly used metrics are highlighted. In Section III, a thorough study of BER-based metric is drawn. In Section IV, our new metric is described. In Section V, performance results of the well known Optimized Link State Routing (OLSR) protocol enhanced with this new metric is presented and compared with delay, ETX and BER based ones. We conclude and present some perspectives in Section VI.

II. RELATED WORK

Wireless networks offer a lower QoS than wired ones. To address the QoS requirements of multimedia applications, several metrics have been proposed and incorporated into routing protocols for a judicious choice of data transmission routes. The provided performances have been mixed. In this section, critical overview of the most commonly encountered metrics is made. The costs (in terms of routing load and additional time) generated by measure and use of these metrics in routing protocols are analyzed. Here, the speech focuses on Packet Delivery Ratio (PDR)-based metrics. BER-based metric is analyzed in Section III.

Packet loss in Mobile Ad hoc NETwork (MANET) is due to many factors. Among them, buffer overflows, transmission loss and link breakages are the most dominant [1]. In addition, a received packet whose delay is over the tolerable delay threshold is also considered as a lost packet. Loss caused by over-threshold delay can only be monitored at the receiver, requiring a feedback message be sent to the source for QoS purpose. Packet loss caused by buffer overflow and maximum retransmissions exceeding, are the only information that can be obtained from intermediate nodes. Successful design of a metric that takes into account all of these components is very delicate.

Many approaches measure the packet loss rate by injecting probing packets into the network. A large number of sample packets are required to accurately estimate a highly variable link. Shi et al. [2] evaluate the number of probing packets needed to get an accurate result as follows: $N = \frac{1-p}{m^2 p}$ where p is the packet loss probability and m the coefficient of variation. According to this formula, we see that this active measurement scheme is not suitable for MANETs. For example, for a link with 10% mean packet loss rate ($p = 0.1$), 900 samples must be sent on that link to get a measurement result where standard deviation is within 10% of the loss probability (i.e., $m = 0.1$). When each node should send probe packets, these can cause a large overhead in MANETs, thus skewing the obtained results. Furthermore, it takes some time for measurements. For example, if one sample packet is sent every 1 second, 15 minutes are needed to send 900 samples. This shows that the active measurement scheme is obviously not suitable for a wireless network particularly in mobility context. In order to overcome this dilemma (amount overhead), Link Quality Ranking (LQR) [3] uses the following trade-off. Instead of estimating a link-layer metric for each link, LQR performs a pairwise comparison of the physical-layer metrics and selects the best link. One problem faced when broadcasting probe-based estimators, is that they decouple link estimation from data traffic. If a link goes bad and packets are lost, the link estimate will not reflect this change until the next routing beacon is dropped [4].

The average rates of the link packet loss are commonly used. Link quality of a route is evaluated by summing the metric values of every link on the route [5][6]. This way of using this metric is questionable. The average or the sum of link quality measurements along one route may hide the worst link. Indeed, if the quality of a link among one route is rather bad, the packets can not be delivered successfully although the average or sum value is rather good.

The PDR metric is often used as a multiplicative metric [7]. A blind multiplication applied to this metric strongly favors long paths. In such a case, inter-hop interference may be significant. Indeed, the intermediate node can not simultaneously receive a packet from a neighbor upstream and send another to a downstream neighbor. Additional delay due to intra-communication interference is often not taken into account. It has an impact on throughput but not necessarily on packet delivery ratio.

ETX routing metric [6] is one of the most popular among this class of metrics. It is developed to improve the performance of routing in static wireless mesh networks where hop count is not suitable. The ETX of a link is calculated using the forward and reverse delivery ratios of the link. These delivery ratios are measured using probe packets. For two adjacent nodes X and Y, X measures probe delivering rate by determining the ratio between the number of probes received from Y and the number of expected ones. When X sends a probe, it includes the calculated ratio in the message. Y does the same. Hence, each node knows the ratio in both directions of a link (one is calculated, the other is provided by the neighbor). The metric is then obtained by:

$$ETX = \frac{1}{PDR_{X \to Y} \times PDR_{Y \to X}} \tag{1}$$

It can be noted that, although ETX distinguishes two PDR values for respectively upstream and downstream direction, the obtained link metric is the same for both directions. ETX is therefore symmetric. We consider this point as a drawback of the approach. Indeed, if a link is asymmetric, we think that this link should be used but only for traffic in the reliable direction. Only ACK messages should be sent in the unreliable direction, since these messages are small and then are more likely to be transmitted correctly. Besides, this metric is independent on network load. A detailed analysis of OLSR [8] with the original hysteresis [9] and ETX routing metric revealed that the original hysteresis performs better than ETX-based protocols in a large dense mesh network. An analysis was then carried out on the ETX protocols. It revealed that in realistic networks, using the ETX algorithm, the predicted losses are twice the actual losses that are experienced even in ideal lab conditions for 802.11 [8]. Shi et al. [10] present the design and selection of appropriate routing metrics as the principal issue to guarantee efficient routing in self-organizing networks. They attempt to analyze, compare and summarize traffic-based routing metrics in the Expected Number of Transmissions (ETX) family. Several studies [11][12][13] have been proposed to improve the metric, but its fundamental limits remain.

Delay based-metrics are also questionable. Delay at each node is composed of input queuing delay, processing delay, output queuing delay, transmission delay, propagation delay, and retransmission delay. Most of QoS-based delay metric focus only on transmission delay at MAC layer [14][15], while the other components of delay take a significant portion of the total hop-to-hop delay. Li et al. [16] consider queuing delay at network layer, but their estimation method is complex. In practice, it is not easy to obtain the number of packets waiting in network-layer buffer.

Delay is closely related to packet loss rate. A packet loss that induces retransmissions grows delay and also network congestion significantly. These network performance measures depend on the quality of used links and ambient flow. Delay and link loss ratios are often subject to high variation. End-to-end delay changes with network load as interface queue lengths vary. This can cause routes to oscillate away from a good path once the path is used. Delay must be calculated easily to avoid additional delay due to complex process.

In addition to the sensitivity of the link quality criterion measurement, many authors have questioned the use of these QoS values. In [2][17][18][19][20], the authors highlight the complexity and exorbitant cost (overhead and computing time) of route-discovery approach with admission control processes.

III. BER-BASED METRIC

The BER criterion characterizes the network at the lowest level of the transmission chain (physical layer). Measuring the error rate at this level provides a more refined estimation of quality of radio links. It allows the study of physical

TABLE I. EXPECTED NUMBER OF TRANSMISSIONS DEPENDING ON BER.

ber	$nb_{transmissions}$
10^{-5}	1.05
10^{-4}	1.51
2.10^{-4}	2.27
3.10^{-4}	3.42
4.10^{-4}	5.15
5.10^{-4}	7.76

phenomena that influence the quality of communication. This link quality criterion has a direct impact on packet delivery rate and average communications delay.

Delahaye [21][22] uses a ray-tracer propagation model called CRT for a better estimate of the radio channel in Network Simulator (NS). The BER used in [23][24] is the result of simulation of this realistic channel model. The use of this metric in the MANET routing protocols (OLSR, Ad hoc On-demand Distance Vector, Zone Routing Protocols) has significantly improved PDR and delay. However, this metric has many drawbacks in actual implementation. The BER metric is quite hard to measure in practice. A first method consists in injecting probe packets in the network. Knowing every binary elements that a packet should contain, the receiver is able to evaluate the bit error rate by counting how many bits are erroneous. Nevertheless, the packet should be large enough to allow a precise measure of BER but its size is in practice limited to the maximal transfer unit of the network. Note that control packets are too small and cannot be used to evaluate BER. So, this method generates an additional load for the network [25]. Another approach consists in sending impulses and measuring the impulse response associated with a transmission. The main drawback is that this method requires an adapted physical layer. These disadvantages are presented in [2].

Moreover, using BER as an additive metric induces long end-to-end transmission path [24]. These long paths with an overall good BER value would potentially permit a better packet delivery ratio, but they generate a long delay and induce a poor throughput. First, long paths increase intra-communication interference. Second, they also increase the vulnerability of established routes, particularly in mobility or dense networks and multi-communication contexts. For all these reasons, the BER-based metrics remain theoretical.

Against these BER metric limits, we invested a new metric based on the number of retransmissions required to make a data transmission over a link successful. We can note that the number of packet retransmissions is highly related to the bit error rate ber. If we suppose a multimedia stream with constant packet size of n bits, the packet error rate is $per = 1 - (1 - ber)^n$. Furthermore, the expected number of transmissions to get a successful packet can be computed as the mathematical expectation of the stochastic variable per. It equals $1/(1-per)$. Therefore, the expected number of transmissions is equal:

$$nb_{transmissions} = \frac{1}{(1 - ber)^n} \quad (2)$$

Table I shows how the expected number of transmissions depends on BER, for 512-byte-long packets ($n = 4096$).

We see that when BER equals $4e^{-4}$ or more, the expected number of transmissions is beyond the number of attempts that a default MAC layer allows to successfully deliver a packet. If possible, these links should not be used.

We therefore propose a new metric based on the number of transmissions and more precisely the number of retransmissions (that appear when the first attempt is not successful). As shown in Table I, this metric is highly related to BER, but, it does not require to be measured. It appears as a low-level but effective measure of the quality of links. This metric only requires that each MAC layer computes a mean value of the number of transmissions required to send packets to each neighbor, including the large ones. It is therefore not a costly measure. The next section is devoted to this metric.

IV. RETRANSMISSION-BASED METRIC

In this section, first, the choice of route when intra communication interference (different transmissions for the same communication) is taken into account is discussed. In a second step, the design of our number of retransmissions-based metric is presented. In a third step, this metric is compared with the ETX metric.

In this new metric, the estimated cost of retransmission, compared to the cost of the first attempt, must be evaluated, and delay seems a convenient way to evaluate it.

Let us evaluate the transmission time between a source S and its neighbor D. Let's consider a given constant time $t1$ corresponding to a successful first transmission. If transmission fails, the additional time for each retransmission is $t2$. For more details on different timing at MAC level see [26][17]. To simplify, $t1$ is supposed to include processing time to pass from routing level to MAC level, Request To Send / Clear To sent (RTS/CTS) mechanism [27] time and propagation time, and $t2$ includes additional ACKnowledge (ACK) packet waiting timeout, RTS/CTS mechanism time and propagation time (hence t2>t1).

Thereby, the delay is:

$$t = t1 + (n - 1) \times t2$$

where n is the total number of transmissions. We normalize this equation to get our new metric (called PR for Packet Retransmission) as follows:

$$PR = \frac{t}{t1} = 1 + (n - 1) \times a. \quad (3)$$

with $a = \frac{t2}{t1}$

Note that this metric appears as the number of hops penalized by a weighted number of retransmissions $a \times (n-1)$. It equals 1 if no retransmission is needed, but it can have a greater value if retransmissions occur. This value can be seen as an equivalent (but not integer) number of intermediate hops. PR is therefore an additive metric, since equivalent number of hops can be cumulated. In a sense, it is an alternative to the simple number of hops metric: this new metric is based on the number of intermediate nodes to access a recipient, but unlike the standard number of hops, it takes into account the quality of links.

To evaluate this metric, the number of packet transmissions must be determined. This information is available at the MAC level (it is a part of the communication statistics at the MAC layer) and, by a cross layer approach, is operated at routing level. There is no need to use special probes contrary to what is required in most metrics. When the used packet size is small (such as hello packet), the number of transmissions is almost always 1 (no retransmission) when the used link exists. On the contrary, large packets allow a better estimate of the quality of a link with this metric. In our protocols, all packets are taken into account.

Note that a is a mean value that represents retransmission cost. To calibrate the value of a, we use a statistical approach. A realistic propagation model taking into account the obstacles, with data packets in a multi-communication context, allowed us to find the value 1.65 for a with 0.1 as standard deviation. In-depth study could better refine the value of a. This parameter may vary depending on the nature (dense or less dense) and congestion level of the studied network.

To test the effectiveness of this new metric, it has been incorporated in OLSR as the metric used for path selection. At each node, the metric is calculated from the number of retransmissions required to make data transmissions successful over a given link. The obtained information is recorded as a new field in the record of neighbors and is disseminated through the network thanks to Topology Control (TC) messages. As it is an additive metric, a path length is computed as the sum of the metric of each of its links.

V. Performance Evaluation

In this section, we briefly present the five different protocols implementing the metrics we analyze. Then, we present our experimental setup and simulation conditions. We conclude the section with an analysis of simulation results.

A. Routing protocols

We compare the performance of five routing protocols, the standard one OLSR-3626 and four modified ones, OLSR-delay, OLSR-ETX, OLSR-BER and OLSR-PR.

OLSR-3626 refers to the standard OLSR described in RFC-3626 [9]. Route selection criterion used in this protocol is the minimum number of hops needed to reach destination.

The four other protocols are based on standard OLSR. Basically, they consider another metric than the number of hops. These metrics are additive: the distances of a route is the sum of the distance of all elementary links on the route. A node computes the shortest path, in term of the considered metric, toward each destination and records it in its routing table.

OLSR-delay chooses delay as metric. Link delay measures are based on Hello messages. Considering OLSR-ETX, ETX metric is implemented like in [28]. The delivery ratio is based on Hello messages. OLSR with BER consideration (OLSR-BER) consists in selecting the path with the lowest global BER described in Section III. OLSR-PR is based on PR metric as described in Section IV.

TABLE II. Simulation parameters.

Parameters	Values
Network simulator	NS 2
Simulation time	100s
Simulation area	1000m*1000m
Maximum number of transmissions	4
Transmission power	0.1W
Data types	CBR
Data packet size	512 bytes
MAC layer	IEEE 802.11a

B. Experimental setup

To show the effectiveness of new QoS approaches for protocol enhancements, t work, evaluations often rely on simulation. Most of the time, experiments do not take into account any environment parameters when modeling the propagation channel. They often consider only the direct ray between transmitter and receiver assuming that no obstacle disturbs transmissions. Furthermore, other effects such as multiple paths induced by the environment are not taken into account although they highly influence the quality of the received signal [29][30][31]. If the environment is not considered, the obtained results are biased and rather optimistic. The influence of bad links is thus highly underestimated. To compute more convincing simulations, we must use a realistic model of wave propagation taking into account the environment characteristics. Therefore, we enhanced NS2 [32] with a communication ray-tracer (CRT) simulator that has been developed at the XLIM-SIC laboratory [21]. Our BER-based protocol directly relies on BER values computed by this CRT software. The global parameters for the simulations are given in Table 2.

C. Simulation results

We simulate OLSR protocol based on our new metric and compare results with standard and the most common enhanced ones. Communication concerns simultaneous transmissions between ten source-destination couples during 100s. The number of hops between transmitters and receivers varies from 2 to 6. To compare the obtained results, we consider two criteria: packet delivery ratio (PDR) and average end-to-end delay. Our metric considers both quality of links in terms of transmission error and some kind of delay estimation to select shortest paths. It is important to note that, for these results, BER estimation time for all links is not taken into account. The BER measurement is supposed completed before the packet transmission begins. Different protocols are analyzed in fixed-nodes context.

In this set of simulation scenarios, the number of nodes increases from 10 to 50. We study the protocols'performance under the influence of path breakages in low densities, routing overhead and new paths in high densities (high network connectivity).

Fig. 1 shows that all these enhanced OLSR outperform the standard one (OLSR-3626) in delay. This means that the shortest path based on the number of hops metric is not suitable for communications in realistic environment (Couto et. al have produced the same result [28]). These results show that our approach (OLSR-PR) always finds best paths in term of end-to-end delay than other protocols. Considering the PDR criterion, OLSR-BER and OLSR-PR outperform the others (Fig. 2). Very often, OLSR-BER is slightly better than OLSR-PR. The difference does not exceed 10 points. An analysis of simulation trace files (statistical results) shows that the paths found by OLSR-3626 is shorter (in terms of number of hops), followed by OLSR-PR. The average length of the paths used by OLSR-BER and OLSR-ETX are the longest.

The best performance of OLSR-PR against OLSR-BER and OLSR-ETX is due to the intra-communication interference effect and additionnal processing time at the intermediate nodes that are larger for the latter. Our new approach allows to better optimize the number of hops. But the poorer performance of OLSR-3626 is due to the fact that some of the used links have a very poor quality, resulting in too many retransmissions.

Regarding PDR parameter as shown in Fig. 2, although OLSR-PR often seems less efficient than OLSR-BER, a thorough analysis shows that it has delivered more packets (it provides the best throughput). This has an impact on the end-to-end delay since additionnal packets delivered by OLSR-PR and not by OLSR-BER require longer delays, so the average delay is degrated.

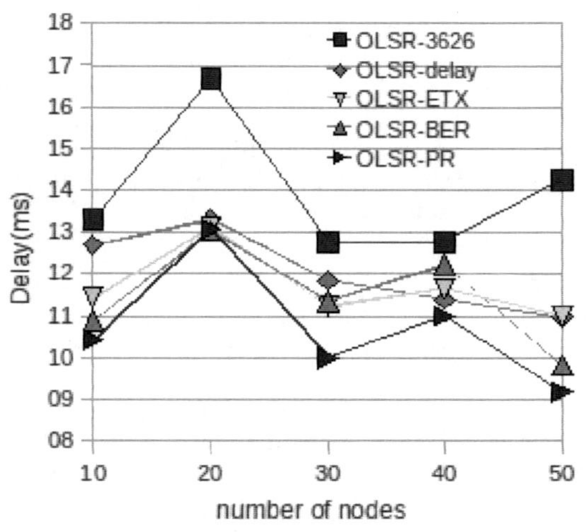

Fig. 1. Delay evolution with number of nodes.

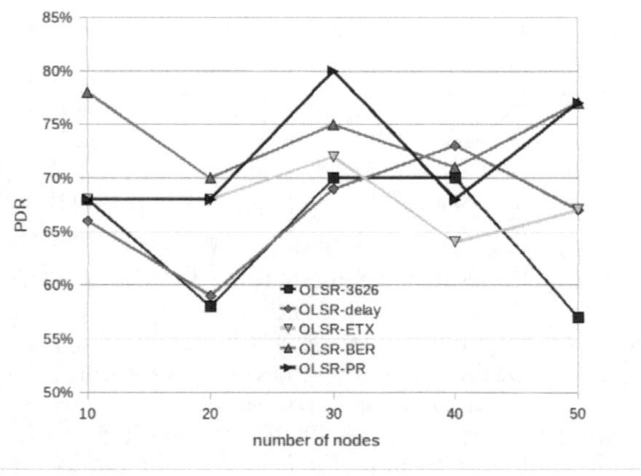

Fig. 2. PDR evolution with number of nodes.

VI. Conclusion and Prospects

We conducted a critical analysis of existing metrics used in QoS routing, then we proposed a metric based on the number of retransmissions required to manage data transmission over a link. With our QoS approach, the distance between a node and its neighbor will not be 1 but $1 + a * (n - 1)$ where n represents the average number of transmissions required to make transmissions successful and a is a parameter to weight retransmission cost. We chosed to base a on expected transmission delay, that is, the ratio between the average delay required for a retransmission over the delay necessary for an initial successful transmission. This metric indirectly relates to BER since the latter affects the number of retransmissions. In addition, it takes into account the real time network load. Its estimation does not induce additional routing load or a large computation time. Without considering the complexity of the BER measurement, this number of retransmision-based metric is a compromise between the number of hops metric that does not take into account the quality of links and metrics based on packet delivery ratio that induce too long paths.

We integrated this new metric in OLSR. Paths that require less retransmission are preferred in routing table calculation process. Simulation results in fixed-nodes context show that this approach improves the average transmission delay and is better than traditional metrics. For delay-sensitive applications, it is better to use a retransmission-based metric to quantify links.

For better PDR and delay performance, neighbor links and MPR node selection should be reconsidered. In future work, we intend to evaluate performances of our new metric in mobility nodes context.

References

[1] I. Chlamtac, M. Conti, and J. J. N. Liu, "Mobile ad hoc networking: imperatives and challenges," *Ad Hoc Networks*, vol. 1, no. 1, pp. 13 – 64, 2003.

[2] L. Shi, A. Fapojuwo, N. Viberg, W. Hoople, and N. Chan, "Methods for calculating bandwidth, delay, and packet loss metrics in Multi-Hop IEEE802.11 ad hoc networks," in *IEEE Vehicular Technology Conference (VTC)*, pp. 103–107, May 2008.

[3] M. Zuniga, I. Irzynska, J. Hauer, T. Voigt, C. A. Boano, and K. Roemer, "Link quality ranking: Getting the best out of unreliable links," in *IEEE International Conference on Distributed Computing in Sensor Systems and Workshops (DCOSS)*, pp. 1–8, June 2011.

[4] R. Fonseca, O. Gnawali, K. Jamieson, and P. Levis, *Four-Bit Wireless Link Estimation*. 2007.

[5] G. Karbaschi and A. Fladenmuller, "A link-quality and congestion-aware cross layer metric for multi-hop wireless routing," in *IEEE International Conference on Mobile Adhoc and Sensor Systems Conference*, IEEE, Nov. 2005.

[6] D. S. J. D. Couto, D. Aguayo, J. Bicket, and R. Morris, "a high-throughput path metric for multi-hop wireless routing," *Wireless Networks*, vol. 11, pp. 419–434, July 2005.

[7] F. Ingelrest and D. Simplot-Ryl, "Maximizing the delivery of mpr broadcasting under realistic physical layer assumptions," *Journal of Computer Science and Technology*, vol. 23, no. 3, pp. 451–460, 2008.

[8] D. Johnson and G. Hancke, "Comparison of two routing metrics in olsr on a grid based mesh network," *Ad Hoc Netw.*, vol. 7, pp. 374–387, Mar. 2009.

[9] T. Clausen and P. Jacquet, "Optimized link state routing protocol (OLSR)," Oct. 2003. IETF RFC 3626.

[10] F. Shi, D. Jin, and J. Song, "A survey of traffic-based routing metrics in family of expected transmission count for self-organizing networks," *Computers and Electrical Engineering*, vol. 40, no. 6, pp. 1801 – 1812, 2014.

[11] P. Esposito, M. Campista, I. Moraes, L. Costa, O. Duarte, and M. Rubinstein, "Implementing the expected transmission time metric for OLSR wireless mesh networks," in *Wireless Days (WD)*, pp. 1–5, Nov. 2008.

[12] R. Draves, J. Padhye, and B. Zill, "Routing in multi-radio, multi-hop wireless mesh networks," in *Proceedings of the 10th annual international conference on Mobile computing and networking (MOBICOM)*, pp. 114–128, 2004.

[13] A. Cerpa, J. L. Wong, M. Potkonjak, and D. Estrin, "Temporal properties of low power wireless links: Modeling and implications on multi-hop routing," in *In ACM MobiHoc*, pp. 414 – 425, ACM Press, 2005.

[14] R. Draves, J. Padhye, and B. Zill, "Routing in multi-radio, multi-hop wireless mesh networks," in *Proceedings of the 10th annual international conference on Mobile computing and networking*, MobiCom '04, (New York, NY, USA), pp. 114–128, ACM, 2004.

[15] Y. Yang, "Designing routing metrics for mesh networks," in *In WiMesh*, 2005.

[16] H. Li, Y. Cheng, C. Zhou, and W. Zhuang, "Minimizing end-to-end delay: A novel routing metric for multi-radio wireless mesh networks," in *IEEE INFOCOM*, pp. 46–54, Apr. 2009.

[17] S. Su, Y. Su, and J. Jung, "A novel QoS admission control for ad hoc networks," in *IEEE Wireless Communications and Networking Conference (WCNC)*, pp. 4193–4197, Mar. 2007.

[18] B. Bakhshi and S. Khorsandi, "Complexity and design of qos routing algorithms in wireless mesh networks," *Computer Communications*, vol. 34, no. 14, pp. 1722 – 1737, 2011.

[19] Z. Wang and J. Crowcroft, "Quality-of-service routing for supporting multimedia applications," *IEEE Journal on Selected Areas in Communications*, vol. 14, pp. 1228–1234, Sept. 1996.

[20] K. A. Al-Soufy and A. M. Abbas, "A path robustness-based quality of service routing for mobile ad hoc networks," in *2010 IEEE 4th International Conference on Internet Multimedia Services Architecture and Application (IMSAA)*, pp. 1–6, IEEE, Dec. 2010.

[21] R. Delahaye, Y. Pousset, A.-M. Poussard, C. Chatellier, and R. Vauzelle, "A realistic physic layer modeling of 802.11g ad hoc networks in outdoor environments with a computation time optimization," in *Proceedings of the Eleventh World Multi-Conference on Systemics, Cybernetics and Informatics (WMSCI)*, (Orlando, Florida, USA), 2007.

[22] R. Delahaye, A.-M. Poussard, Y. Pousset, and R. Vauzelle, "Propagation models and physical layer quality criteria influence on ad hoc networks routing," in *Telecommunications, 2007. ITST '07. 7th International Conference on ITS*, pp. 1–5, June 2007.

[23] T. Yélémou, P. Meseure, and A. M. Poussard, "A new ber-based approach to improve olsr protocol," in *2011 Eighth International Conference on Wireless and Optical Communications Networks*, pp. 1–5, May 2011.

[24] T. Yélémou, P. Meseure, and A. M. Poussard, "Improving zrp performance by taking into account quality of links," in *2012 IEEE Wireless Communications and Networking Conference (WCNC)*, pp. 2956–2960, April 2012.

[25] J. Ledy, H. Boeglen, A. Poussard, B. Hilt, and R. Vauzelle, "A Semi-Deterministic channel model for VANETs simulations," *International Journal of Vehicular Technology*, vol. 2012, pp. 1–8, 2012.

[26] IEEE, "Wireless lan medium access control (MAC) and physical layer (PHY) specifications (IEEE standard 802.11, part 11)," June 1999.

[27] J. Weinmiller, H. Woesner, J. pierre Ebert, and A. Wolisz, "Analyzing the rts/cts mechanism in the dfwmac media access protocol for wireless lans," 1995.

[28] D. S. J. De Couto, D. Aguayo, J. Bicket, and R. Morris, "A high-throughput path metric for multi-hop wireless routing," in *Proceedings of the 9th Annual International Conference on Mobile Computing and Networking*, MobiCom '03, (New York, NY, USA), pp. 134–146, ACM, 2003.

[29] J. Gozalvez, M. Sepulcre, and R. Bauza, "Impact of the radio channel modelling on the performance of vanet communication protocols," *Telecommunication Systems*, pp. 1–19, 2010.

[30] W. Hamidouche, R. Vauzelle, C. Olivier, Y. Pousset, and C. Perrine, "Impact of realistic mimo physical layer on video transmission over mobile ad hoc network," in *Personal, Indoor and Mobile Radio Communications, 2009 IEEE 20th International Symposium on*, pp. 187–191, 2009.

[31] M. Günes, M. Wenig, and A. Zimmermann, "Realistic mobility and propagation framework for manet simulations," in *Proceedings of the 6th International IFIP-TC6 Conference on Ad Hoc and Sensor Networks, Wireless Networks, Next Generation Internet*, NETWORKING'07, (Berlin, Heidelberg), pp. 97–107, Springer-Verlag, 2007.

[32] L. Breslau, D. Estrin, K. Fall, S. Floyd, J. Heidemann, A. Helmy, P. Huang, S. McCanne, K. Varadhan, Y. Xu, and H. Yu, "Advances in network simulation," *COMPUTER*, vol. 33, May 2000.

Energy Efficient Communications with Device-to-Device Links in Cellular Networks

Radwa Ahmed Osman[*#], Xiao-Hong Peng[*] and Zuoyin Tang[*]
[*]School of Engineering & Applied Science, Aston University
Birmingham, UK.
[#]College of Engineering & Technology Arab Academy for Science, Technology & Maritime Transport
Alexandria, Egypt.
Email:{osmanmra, x-h.peng, z.tang1}@aston.ac.uk

Abstract—**Device-to-Device (D2D) communications in cellular networks allow devices to communicate directly without going through the base station. The D2D underlaying cellular networks method is aimed to increase network energy efficiency, as specified for Long-Term Evolution Advanced (LTE-A) and 5G systems. In this paper, we examine the performance of both cooperative and non-cooperative communications modes based on the energy models we establish, within a mobile network where both user equipment (UE) to base station and D2D transmission links co-exist. We show that the source-destination distance is an important factor to decide whether to use the cooperative or non-cooperative transmission scheme in order to achieve better energy efficiency. We have also investigated the effects of choosing different numbers of relaying branches and relays in each branch on the performance of the network. This investigation leads to identifying optimal transmission schemes for maximizing energy efficiency under varying environmental conditions.**

Keywords-Energy efficiency; cooperative communications; D2D communications.

I. INTRODUCTION

Device-to-Device (D2D) communications, which enable direct data transmission between devices such as user equipment (UE) without help from existing infrastructures such as base stations (BSs) or access points (APs), has been investigated as a promising technique for future cellular networks [1]. It can reduce signaling overhead and save the limited resources of local cells and the network as a whole. The existing research in this area has been mainly focused on how D2D communications can run efficiently as an underlay to cellular networks to save energy consumption of UEs and BS and improve network performance such as spectral efficiency and throughput [2] [3].

D2D communications normally take place through a direct and reliable link between D2D devices to satisfy the quality-of-service (QoS) requirement for both D2D links and the cellular system simultaneously. However, meeting these requirements faces challenges from physical and resource limitations, including high loss rates due to changes in terrain, multipath fading, Doppler spread, interference and noise. This will not only reduce network performance but also waste the limited power of the devices involved.

Cooperative communications through applying relaying techniques including decode-and-forward (DF) and amplify-and-forward (AF) are commonly used to overcome these problems, to enhance the transmission reliability by creating diversity [4][5]. These techniques can enable cellular user equipment (UE) to help each other through relaying other device's data and sharing their limited resources. However, involving more relay nodes will consume more energy, although this can be mitigated to some degree through proper power allocation schemes [6].

In this work, we examine the energy efficiency performance of a mobile cellular network that accommodates both D2D and UE assisted relaying communications. We also investigate the strengths and limitations of cooperative transmission schemes in this scenario, in comparison with non-cooperative schemes, under different conditions, such as transmission distance, relaying method, channel condition (path loss exponent) and interference. Through this investigation we can identify proper transmission schemes for optimizing the energy performance of the network in varied conditions. In addition, we derive the closed form outage probability that contributes to establishing the models of energy efficiency.

The remainder of this paper is organized as follows. Section II discusses the relevance of this research with other work. Energy efficiency models for both cooperative and non-cooperative transmission schemes in a cellular network are presented in Section III. Simulation results and discussions are provided in Section IV. Finally, the paper is concluded in Section V.

II. RELATED WORK

Most literature has been focused on the interference coordination issue between D2D and cellular communication links. The problem of maximizing cellular offloading with D2D communication was studied in [7], which is mainly focused on the communication aspects, including interference avoidance and energy efficiency. Multi-user multiple-input and multiple-output (MIMO) systems are also considered to obtain the maximal possible energy efficiency for cellular networks [8]. Currently, the cooperative D2D idea was exploited for enhancing social ties in human social networks [9] to promote efficient cooperation among devices.

In the energy efficiency aspect, work in [10] showed that the best position of devices can be found to minimize the total power used for the network, while in [11], multihop D2D communications where one UE may help other two UEs to exchange information has been investigated in order to enhance energy efficiency. Most of the works reported have investigated energy efficiency and spectral efficiency over non-cooperative or cooperative communication links using only one relay branch. There is a lack of information regarding how to choose a specific transmission scheme and determine the number of relaying branches and the number of relays in each branch under different conditions such as the changing transmission distance between source and destination nodes, in order to find a solution for ensuring the best QoS within a network.

In this paper, based on the initial work for wireless sensor networks [12], our investigation will identify the conditions for establishing appropriate transmission strategies among different commonly used transmission schemes in the context of a cellular network that includes both D2D and UE-to-BS links with cooperative as well as non-cooperative communications. This investigation is based on the development of analytical energy efficiency models for these transmission schemes, and involves performance analysis on, in particular, the trade-offs between cooperative and non-cooperative transmission schemes.

III. ENERGY EFFICIENCY MODEL

In this section, the analytical models of the required transmitting power, outage probability and energy efficiency in the context of a cellular network and D2D communication links are established for both cooperative and non-cooperative transmission schemes. Based on these models, an adaptive transmission strategy can be developed to optimize the energy performance.

Given a cellular network with a number of D2D pairs and cellular user equipment (CUE) and BS, the optimization of the system performance is achieved by maximizing the overall energy efficiency with an outage probability target:

$$Max \sum EE_{bi} \quad s.t. \{p_{outS\text{-}D}\} \tag{1}$$

where EE_{bi} is the energy efficiency of the i-th transmission link either between CUE and BS or between D2D devices, and $p_{outS\text{-}D}$ is the fixed outage probability target.

Different transmission schemes involving D2D and CUE-to-BS links are shown in Fig. 1, including both non-cooperative and cooperative communications in CUE-BS links. In the cooperative communications scenario (Fig. 1 (b)), relaying with a varied numbers of branches and relays in each branch are illustrated and will be considered in analytical modeling in connection with D2D transmission in Subsections III.*A* & III.*B*.

We consider a cellular cell in which the transmission links are subject to narrowband Rayleigh fading with Additive White Gaussian Noise (AWGN) and propagation path-loss. The channel fades for different links are assumed to be statistically mutually independent.

A. Non-Cooperative Transmission Scheme

Consider the scenario shown in Fig. 1(a) where in addition to communication between cellular users through the base station, which forms CUE-BS links, cellular users can also communicate with each other directly in the D2D mode. It is assumed that the distance between any D2D pair is shorter than that of the CUE-BS link in a cellular cell. When a D2D pair communicate by reusing the uplink (UL) resource of an active CUE that is transmitting data to the BS, the active CUE will interfere with to the D2D receiver (DRx) and at the same time the D2D transmitter (DTx) causes interference to the BS.

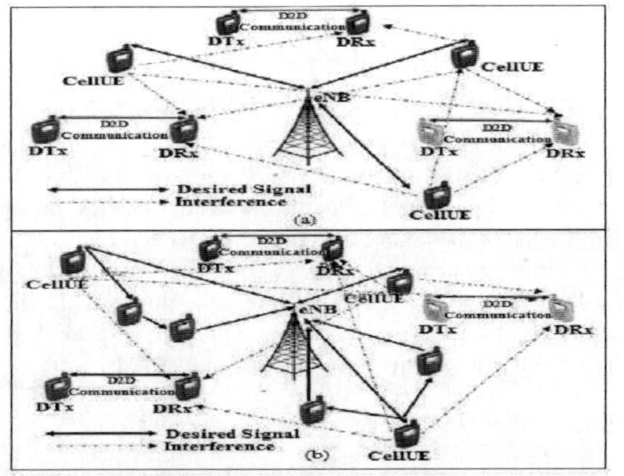

Figure 1. Transmission schemes in a cellular network: (a) CUE-BS using non-cooperative communications and direct D2D, and (b) CUE-BS using cooperative communications and direct D2D.

The energy efficiency (EE) in this scheme is given by:

$$EE_1 = EE_{CB} + EE_{D2D} = \frac{R_{CB}}{P_{CB}} + \frac{R_{D2D}}{P_{D2D}} \tag{2}$$

where EE_{CB}, R_{CB} and P_{CB} are the energy efficiency, achievable rate and power consumption of the CUE-BS link, respectively. EE_{D2D}, R_{D2D} and P_{D2D} are the energy efficiency, data rate and power consumption of the D2D link, respectively. Let B be the system bandwidth. The achievable rates R_{CB} and R_{D2D} in bits/s are expressed as:

$$R_{CB} = B \log_2 (1 + SINR_{CB}) \tag{3}$$

$$R_{D2D} = B \log_2 (1 + SINR_{D2D}) \tag{4}$$

and the signal-to-interference-and-noise ratios of the CUE-BS link, $SINR_{CB}$, and the D2D links, $SINR_{D2D}$ are given by:

$$SINR_{CB} = \frac{P_C |h_{CB}|^2 \gamma_{CB}}{P_D |h_{DB}|^2 \gamma_{DB} + N} \tag{5}$$

$$SINR_{D2D} = \frac{P_D |h_{DD}|^2 \gamma_{DD}}{P_C |h_{CD}|^2 \gamma_{CD} + N} \tag{6}$$

where P_C and P_D are the transmitting power of the CUE transmitter and D2D transmitter, respectively, N is the thermal noise power at any receiver, $|h_{ij}|^2$ is the channel fading coefficient between transmitter i (i= {C (CUE),D (DTx)}) and receiver j (j = {B (BS),D (DRx) }) where h_{ij} follows a complex normal distribution $CN(0, 1)$, and γ_{ij} is path loss between transmitter i and receiver j with the same index sets used for $|h_{ij}|^2$, which is given by [13]:

$$\gamma_{ij} = \frac{G\lambda^2}{(4\pi)^2 d_{ij}^{\alpha} M_l N_f} \quad (7)$$

where d_{ij} is the distance between transmitter i and receiver j with the same index sets for i and j as described above, G is the total gain of the transmit and receive antennas, α is the path loss exponent, λ is the wavelength, M_l is the link margin and N_f is the noise figure at the receiver.

An outage occurs when *SINR* at the receiver falls below a threshold β in the CUE-BS link or η in the D2D link, which allows error free decoding. The outage probability of the single-hop transmission is given by [14]:

$$p_{outCB} = p(SINR_{CB} \le \beta) = 1 - \frac{P_C |h_{CB}|^2 \gamma_{CB}}{\beta P_D |h_{DB}|^2 \gamma_{DB} + P_C |h_{CB}|^2 \gamma_{CB}} \exp\left(\frac{\beta N}{P_C |h_{CB}|^2 \gamma_{CB}}\right) \quad (8)$$

$$p_{outD2D} = p(SINR_{D2D} \le \eta) = 1 - \frac{P_D |h_{DD}|^2 \gamma_{DD}}{\eta P_C |h_{CD}|^2 \gamma_{CD} + P_D |h_{DD}|^2 \gamma_{DD}} \exp\left(\frac{\eta N}{P_D |h_{DD}|^2 \gamma_{DD}}\right) \quad (9)$$

Due to the short distance between any D2D pairs, which means that the power of DTx is so low that the interference caused by DTx can be neglected. In addition, assume $\eta N << P_D |h_{DD}|^2 \gamma_{DD}$, so (8) and (9) can be rewritten as:

$$p_{outCB} = 1 - \exp\left(\frac{\beta N}{P_C |h_{CB}|^2 \gamma_{CB}}\right) \quad (10)$$

$$p_{outD2D} = 1 - \frac{P_D |h_{DD}|^2 \gamma_{DD}}{\eta P_C |h_{CD}|^2 \gamma_{CD} + P_D |h_{DD}|^2 \gamma_{DD}} \quad (11)$$

Energy consumption is largely proportional to the requirement of maintaining a certain level of transmission reliability or the successful transmission rate. In order to maintain a required level of the reliability of a transmission link, denoted by $U(0 \le U \le 1)$, the maximum outage probability is bounded by:

$$p_{out} \le 1 - U \quad (12)$$

Replacing p_{out} by p_{outCB} in (10) and p_{outD2D} in (11), respectively, and taking the nature logarithm on the both sides of the expression in (12) when replacing p_{out} by p_{outCB}, we then have:

$$\frac{\beta N}{P_C |h_{CB}|^2 \gamma_{CB}} \le \ln(U^{-1}) \quad (13)$$

$$\frac{P_D |h_{DD}|^2 \gamma_{DD}}{\eta P_C |h_{CD}|^2 \gamma_{CD} + P_D |h_{DD}|^2 \gamma_{DD}} \ge U \quad (14)$$

The main objective for performance optimization is to maximize the overall energy efficiency under different environmental conditions. Thus, the transmit power required to satisfy the reliability requirement or be constrained by the outage probability for the direct transmission must be:

$$P_C \ge \frac{\beta N}{|h_{CB}|^2 \gamma_{CB}} (\ln(U^{-1}))^{-1} \quad (15)$$

$$P_D \ge \frac{U \eta P_C |h_{CD}|^2 \gamma_{CD}}{(1-U)|h_{DD}|^2 \gamma_{DD}} \quad (16)$$

Therefore, the overall energy efficiency in *bits/J* of both CUE-BS and D2D links using direct transmission are expressed as:

$$EE_1 = \frac{R_{CB}}{P_C + P_0} + \frac{R_{D2D}}{P_D + P_0} \quad (17)$$

where P_0(J/s) is the internal circuitry power consumption of user devices.

B. Cooperative Transmission Scheme

In cooperative transmission, CUEs communicate with the BS through relay devices in addition to the direct CUE-BS link. D2D communications involve direct transmission between any two UE devices including CUE-Relay and Relay-Relay links, as shown in Fig.1(b). Relays receive the noisy version of the transmitted symbol and transmit the received symbol after some processing to the next relay or the BS. In this case, the active CUE and the transmitting relays will interfere with the D2D receiver (DRx) and at the same time the D2D transmitter (DTx) causes interference to the receiving relays and BS.

The energy efficiency in this scenario is given by:

$$EE_2 = EE_{Coop} + EE_{D2D} = \frac{R_{Coop}}{P_{coop}} + \frac{R_{D2D}}{P_{D2D}} \quad (18)$$

where EE_{Coop}, R_{Coop} and P_{Coop} are the energy efficiency, achievable rate and overall power consumption of the cooperative CUE-BS link, respectively. The achievable rate R_{Coop} in bits/s is expressed as:

$$R_{Coop} = \mathrm{B} \, log_2\left(1 + SINR_{CB} + \textstyle\sum_{j=1}^{K} SINR_{rjB}\right) \quad (19)$$

where K is the number of relaying branches. The signal-to-interference-and-noise ratios of the j-th Relay-BS (R-BS) link, $SINR_{rjB}$ is given by:

$$SINR_{rjB} = \frac{P_{CC} |h_{rjB}|^2 \gamma_{rjB}}{P_D |h_{DB}|^2 \gamma_{DB} + N} \quad (20)$$

where P_{CC} is the transmitting power of cooperative relays, h_{rjB} is the channel coefficient of the cooperative R-BS link. In this paper, we present two types of cooperative transmission schemes: 1) using multiple (K) relaying branches with one relay in each branch, and 2) using multiple relaying branches and with multiple (n) relays in each branch. The selective decode and forward (SDF) relaying protocol is used in these two schemes and relays perform cooperation when the information from the CUE is correctly received by them. We assume that the selection combining technique is used at the destination on the received packets. For the transmission scheme shown in

Fig. 1(b), the outage probability is given by jointly considering the outages in CUE-BS, CUE-R and R-BS links, i.e.

$$p_{outcoop} = p(SNR_{CB} \leq \beta) \cap p(SNR_{Cr} \leq \beta)$$
$$+ p(SNR_{CB} \leq \beta) \cap p(SNR_{Cr} > \beta) \cap p(SNR_{rB} \leq \beta) \quad (21)$$

When we have multiple (K) branches and multiple relay (n) in each branch:

$$p_{outcoop} \approx (\beta)^{(K+1)} N^{(K+1)} \Big(\Big(1/P_C \gamma_{CB} |h_{CB}|^2 \Big(1/P_C \gamma_{Cr_1} |h_{Cr_1}|^2 +$$
$$\textstyle\sum_{i=2}^{n} \Big(d^{\alpha}_{r_1 r_i} / P_{CC_i} \gamma_{r_1 r_i} |h_{r_1 r_i}|^2 \Big) + d_{r_n B} / P_{CCn} \gamma_{r_n B} |h_{r_n B}|^2 \Big)^K \Big) \quad (22)$$

where P_C and P_{CC} are the transmit power at the CUE and relays, respectively. We set the transmit power to be proportional to the distance between two communicating nodes. For broadcast transmission, e.g., when the CUE transmits, the longest distance, i.e., the distance between the CUE and the BS, d_{CB}, is considered. So, the power between the two communicating nodes is given by:

$$P_{ij} = \Lambda_{ij}{}^{\alpha} P_C \quad (23)$$

where Λ_{ij} denotes the power coefficient between node i and node j. In our model, we assume that the value of Λ_{ij} depends on the distance of the CUE-BS, relay-relay or relay-destination link. For example, the transmit power for the relay-destination link is:

$$P_{rB} = \Lambda_{rB}{}^{\alpha} P_C = \left(\frac{d_{rB}}{d_{CB}}\right)^{\alpha} P_C \quad (24)$$

As Equation (22) can be rewritten as:

$$p_{outcoop} \approx (\beta)^{(K+1)} N^{(K+1)} / P_C{}^{(K+1)} \Big(1/\gamma_{CB} |h_{CB}|^2 \Big(1/\gamma_{Cr_1} |h_{Cr_1}|^2 +$$
$$\textstyle\sum_{i=2}^{n} \Big(1/\gamma_{r_1 r_i} \Lambda^{\alpha}_{r_1 r_i} |h_{r_1 r_i}|^2 \Big) + 1/\gamma_{r_n B} \Lambda^{\alpha}_{r_n B} |h_{r_n B}|^2 \Big)^K \Big) \quad (25)$$

We can formulate the power minimization problem by specifying a required reliability level, in a similar way to the method used in Subsection III. *A*. The optimization problem can be stated as follows: Optimize P_C or P_{CC} so that

$$Max \textstyle\sum EE_2 s.t. \{p_{outcoop} \leq 1 - U\} \quad (26)$$

Both P_C and P_{CC}(contained in $p_{outcoop}$) are involved in the optimization process for the cooperative transmission mode. And the transmitted power used in the selective decode–and-forward scheme with multiple relays, P_T, is bounded by:

$$P_T \geq \beta N_0 \Big(1/\gamma_{CB} |h_{CB}|^2 \Big(1/\gamma_{Cr_1} |h_{Cr_1}|^2 + \textstyle\sum_{i=2}^{n} \Big(1/\gamma_{r_1 r_i} \Lambda^{\alpha}_{r_1 r_i} |h_{r_1 r_i}|^2 \Big)$$
$$+ 1/\gamma_{r_n B} \Lambda^{\alpha}_{r_n B} |h_{r_n B}|^2 \Big)^K \Big)^{(1/(K+1))} \Big(\ln(Q_s^{-1}) \Big)^{-(1/(K+1))} \quad (27)$$

Therefore, the overall consumed power can be expressed as:

$$P_{coop} = (p_{outCr})(P_C + P_0) + (1 - p_{outCr}) \Big(\big((K * n) * \Lambda_{rB}{}^{\alpha} + 1 \big) P_C + (K * n + 1) P_0 \Big) \quad (28)$$

The first term on the right-hand side corresponds to the consumed energy when the relay is not able to correctly decode the message from the CUE, which means that this link is in outage. In this case, only the CUE consumes transmit power and the destination node and K relays consume receive power. The second term counts for the event that the CUE-Relay link is not in outage, hence transmit and processing power at relays and receive power at the destination are consumed.

The optimization problem with one constraint variable and its Lagrangian is given by:

$$\frac{\partial P_{coop}}{\partial P_T} + \zeta \frac{\partial p_{outcoop}}{\partial P_T} = 0 \quad (29)$$

Where ζ denotes the Lagrangian factor. The derivatives of the overall power consumption P_{coop} and the outage probability $p_{outcoop}$ with respect to the transmit power P_T lead to:

$$\left(K \left(\sum_{i=1}^{n} X_i \right) + 1 \right) \xi / \mu + b_{Cr} / P_{coop}^2 \big(nKP_{Tx} + (K(n-1)+1) P_{Rx} \big) -$$
$$\zeta \Big[b_{CB} (K+1) \big(b_{Cr1} + \textstyle\sum_{i=2}^{n} b_{r1ri} + b_{rnB} \big)^K \Big] / P_{coop}^{K+2} = 0 \quad (30)$$

Based on P_{coop} resulting from the above optimization process, the energy efficiency can then be obtained through (18).

IV. NUMERICAL RESULTS AND DISCUSSION

In this section, we examine the energy efficiency of different transmission schemes under various channel and transmission conditions in a cellular network shown in Fig. 1 using computer simulation. We then show how the transmission scheme can be chosen in an adaptive way to optimize the energy performance. The network settings used for simulation are listed in TABLE 1. Given a certain network topology, we randomly choose a CUE-BS pair and apply different transmission schemes for comparison purposes. Assume the achievable rate R in this scenario to be 1 Mbit/s, and the required system reliability level (U) to be 0.999.

Fig. 2 shows the energy efficiency performance of both cooperative and non-cooperative schemes. As we can observe, cooperative transmission outperforms the non-cooperative transmission when the transmission range is beyond 17 meters for the CUE-BS link (Fig. 2(a)) and 2 meters for the D2D link (Fig. 2(b)), respectively. We can see from Fig. 2(a) that the non-cooperative direct transmission has considerably higher energy efficiency than cooperative schemes for short-range transmission, i.e., d_{CB}<17m in the case of cooperative transmission using K=2 branches with n=1 relay per branch, and d_{CB}<44m in the

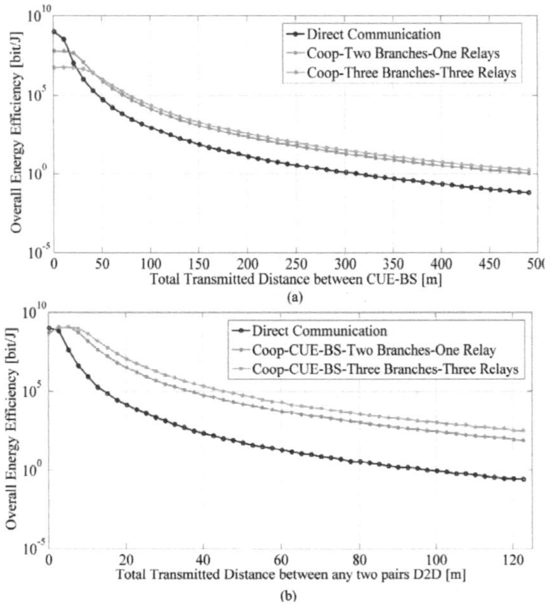

Figure 2. Energy efficiency vs Total transmitted distance (β = η =0 dB).

TABLE 1. SIMULATION PARAMETERS

Parameters	Value
N	-100dBm
B	10 MHz
U	0.999
Max P_C or P_D	250 mW
P_0	100 mW
fc	2 GHz
Ml	4 dB
Nf	1 dB
G	5 dBi
α	4

case of cooperative transmission using K=3 branches with n=3 relays per branch.

When the distance of the CUE-BS link is short the transmit power of CUE is proportionally low according to (23), so the interference of CUE to the D2D receiver DRx is low as well. This reduces the overall required transmit power from DTx and then increases energy efficiency for short distance transmission, as shown in Fig. 2(b).

Fig. 3depicts energy efficiency against the numbers of CUEs and D2D pairs which uniformly distributed in a cellular cell. Substantial performance gaps in energy efficiency can be observed from Fig.3(a) and Fig. 3(b) between the direct transmission scheme in CUE-BS or D2D links and the optimal transmission schemes using cooperative relaying.

Results in Fig. 4 show how energy efficiency varies with the threshold of SINR (β) for both cooperative and non-cooperative schemes with different distances in CUE-BS links (d_{CB}). When distance is 10m (Fig. 4(a)) using direct transmission is most energy efficient and significantly better than cooperative transmission for β<9dB. This is because within a short distance direct

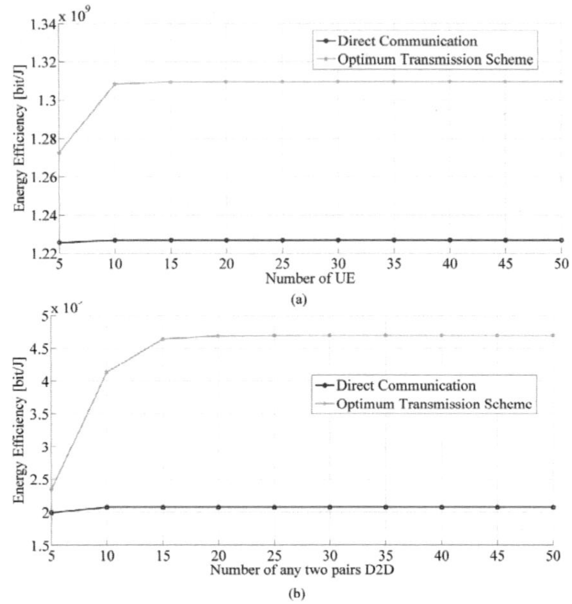

Figure 3. Energy efficiency vs numbers of CUEs and D2D (β = η =0 dB).

transmission is good enough to meet the reliability requirement while having a less number of transmitters than the cooperative transmission scheme. When the SINR threshold becomes higher, the scheme with one relay and one branch (n=1, K=1) performs better than others, but schemes with more branches and relays for this short distance leads to the increase of the transmit power and then the decrease of energy efficiency.

When the transmission range increases (d_{CB}=35m), the energy efficiency of direct transmission decreases as shown in Fig. 4(b). It can be seen that transmission with two relaying branches(with one relay each) in addition to the direct link is most energy efficient for the relatively good channel conditions (β<5dB). When the SINR threshold becomes higher, other schemes with more relays and branches (n>1, K>1) perform better than others. For β>5dB, transmission with three branches and three relays per branch are the best in terms of energy efficiency, with a trend that more relays are needed to maintain the highest possible efficiency when the channel condition gets worse. This is because using more than one relay in each branch will lead to the transmit power of relays being significantly reduced due to shortened distance between devices.

In Fig.4(c), the energy performance of the same set of transmission schemes is displayed but the distance is 100m. In this scenario, transmission with multiple branches (K= 3) and three relays (n=3) per branch is more efficient than direct transmission, and schemes with two branches (K=2) with one relay (n=1) each in all channel conditions. This indicates that the diversity created through cooperation has an impact on the increment of energy efficiency. In addition, it reveals that when channel conditions get worse, having additional relays in a branch is a simple and effective way to prevent transmission failure events while keeping energy consumption as low as possible.

There are a number of factors that can affect energy consumption in a cellular networks. Cooperative transmission involves additional paths and devices (relays) compared to direct transmission, which costs more energy.

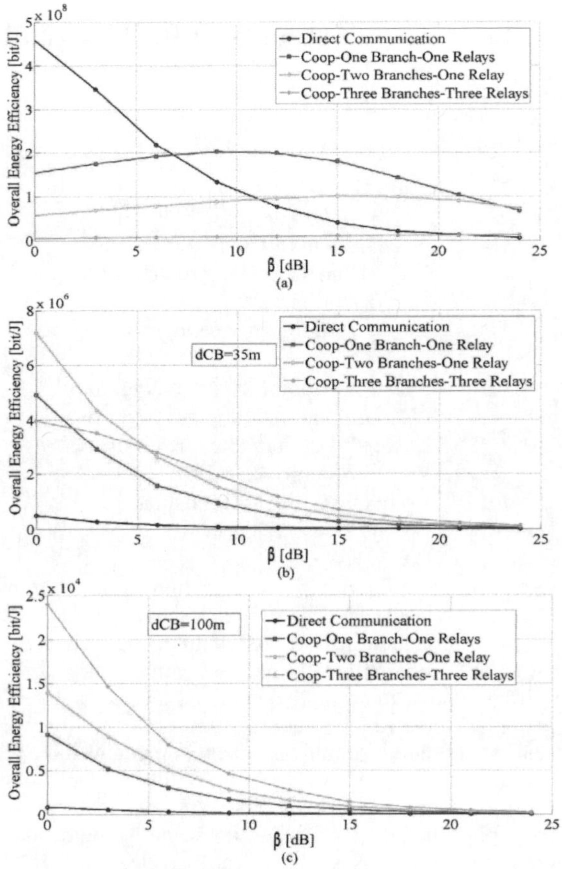

Figure 4. Energy efficiency vs β.

But the diversity it creates can save energy by reducing the number of retransmissions due to the reduced packet loss rate. In addition, increasing the number of relays in each branch reduces the distance of each transmission hop, resulting in lower transmit power needed for relays. But when the number of relays increases, the total circuitry power will accumulate as it depends on the number of transmitting devices and is independent from the transmission distance. As a result, the total energy consumption will increase if too many branches and relays are used.

Therefore, to achieve the best energy performance proper transmission schemes including in both CUE-BS and D2D links should be selected given the transmission conditions, such as the source-destination distance and channel quality. The results of this work provide an effective guidance for deciding when and how the cooperative or direct transmission scheme should be employed. Based on our investigation, an energy-efficient transmission strategy can be formed in cellular networks by adaptively choosing cooperative or non-cooperative transmission schemes for varied network and transmission conditions.

V. Conclusion

We have investigated the energy performance of a cellular network supporting both D2Dcommunications and CUE-BS links in either cooperative or non-cooperative transmission modes. Based on the outage probability and energy efficiency models derived, we have shown that cooperative and non-cooperative transmission schemes can be used collectively alongside D2D communications to achieve the highest possible energy efficiency depending on environmental conditions such as the channel quality and transmission range. Adaptive transmission strategies based on the results presented in this paper can therefore be derived to optimize the energy performance in such a network.

References

[1] A.Asadi, Q. Wang, and V. Mancuso, "A Survey on device-to-device communication in cellular networks,"IEEE Commun. Surveys Tuts., vol. 16, pp. 1801–1819, April 2014.

[2] K. Dopller, M. Rinne, C. Wijting, C. Ribeiro, and K. Hugl, "Device-to-device communication as an underlay to LTE-Advanced networks," IEEE Commun. Mag., vol. 47, pp. 42-49, Dec. 2009.

[3] P. Janis, et al., "Device-to-device communication underlaying cellular communications systems," Int. Journal of Communications, Network and System Sciences, vol. 2, no. 3, pp. 169–178, 2009.

[4] B. Li, H. Li, W. Wang, Q. Yin, and H. Liu,"Performance analysis and optimization for energy-efficient cooperative transmission inrandom wireless sensor network," IEEE Trans. on Wireless Commun., vol. 12, pp. 4647-4657, August 2013.

[5] A. Nasri, R. Schober, and I. F. Blake,"Performance and optimization of amplify-and-forward cooperative diversity systems ingeneric noise and interference," IEEE Trans. on Wireless Commun.,vol. 10, pp.1132-1143, January 2011.

[6] G. Chen, O. Alnatouh, and J. Chambers,"Outage probability analysis for a cognitive amplify-and-forward relay network with single and multi-relay selection," IET Commun., vol. 7, pp.1974-1981, November 2013.

[7] J. Jiang,Z. Zhang, B. Li, and B. Li,"Maximized cellular traffic offloading via device-to-device content sharing,"IEEE Journal on Selected Area in Commun.,vol. 34, pp. 82-91, January 2016.

[8] E. Björnson, L. Sanguinetti, J. Hoydis, and M.Debbah, "Optimal design of energy-efficient multi-userMIMO systems: Is massive MIMO the answer?,"IEEE Trans. on Wireless Commun., vol. 14, pp. 3059-3075, June 2015.

[9] X. Chen, B. Proulx, X. Gong, and J. Zhang,"Exploiting social ties for cooperative D2D communications: A mobile social networking case," IEEE Trans. on Networking, vol. 23, pp.1471-1484, October 2015.

[10] A. S. Ibrahim, Z. Han, and K.J.R. Liu,"Distributed energy-efficient routing in wireless networks," IEEE Trans. on Wireless Commun., vol. 7, pp. 3930 - 3941, October 2008.

[11] L. Wei, R. Q. Hu, Y. Qian, and G. Wu, "Energy efficiency and spectrum efficiency of multihop device-to-device communications underlaying cellular networks," IEEE Trans. on Vehichual Technology, vol. 6, pp. 367-380, January 2016.

[12] O. R. Ahmed, X.-H. Peng, and Z. Tang, "Energy efficient adaptive cooperative communications in wireless sensor networks," Proc. 15th IEEE Int. Conf. on Computer and Information Technology, October 2015.

[13] A. Goldsmith,*Wireless Communications*, 1st edition. Cambridge University Press, 2005.

[14] H. Min, W. Seo, J. Lee, S. Park and D. Hong, "Reliability improvement using receive mode selection in device-to-device uplink period underlaying cellular networks," IEEE Trans. on Wireless Commun., vol. 10, pp. 413-951, Februaury 2011.

Network Traffic Prediction for Load Balancing in Cloud Access Point Controller

Zhifei Zhang, Shilei Cheng
School of Computer and Information Technology
Beijing Jiaotong University
Beijing, China
zhfzhang@bjtu.edu.cn

Jingpeng Tang, Abraham Teng
Department of Computer Science
Utah Valley University
Orem, Utah, USA
jtang@uvu.edu

Damian Lampl, Kendall Nygard
Department of Computer Science
North Dakota State University
Fargo, ND, USA
kendall.nygard@ndsu.edu

Abstract— **In cluster cloud access controller (AC) solutions, load balancing algorithms typically consider the number of access points (APs), the number of users, the network traffic at the ACs, as well as central processing unit (CPU) and memory usage. However, because the network traffic has bursts and the user traffic on APs is unbalanced, it is not enough to consider only these factors. We report on the development of new traffic prediction models and their use in load balancing algorithms. The methods are evaluated with simulation experiments using MATLAB and CLOUDSIM. The methods utilize phase space reconstruction sequencing of the user network traffic. The result is improved load balancing efficiency when compared with alternative existing approaches.**

Keywords- cloud controller; wireless access point; load balancing; network traffic prediction.

I. INTRODUCTION

Traditional load balancing algorithms are usually divided into static load balancing algorithms [1] and dynamic load balancing algorithms [2] according to their strategy. Static load balancing algorithms do not consider the runtime operating state of each node in the cluster, but allocates the load of each node with a predetermined load balancing strategy based on its processing capacity. Dynamic load balancing algorithms monitor and collect information on the load of each node, such as CPU utilization, storage, memory and bandwidth utilization, in order to calculate the load balancing weight of each node in real time, and then distribute the traffic to corresponding nodes. Popular static load balancing algorithms include random balancing, polling, hash target address, and source address hash [3]. Dynamic load balancing algorithms include least connection, weighted least connection scheduling, weighted polling and minimum response time [4]. In addition to the classical algorithms, heuristic optimization algorithms, such as genetic algorithms [5], ant colony optimization [6][7], simulated annealing [8] and particle swarm optimization algorithms [9], are also used for scheduling problems.

In the conventional AC-AP architecture, AC is the most important equipment since it manages the AP's configuration, controls the station's access authentication and even forwards the station's packets centrally. With the progress of cloud technology, many companies have released Control and Provisioning of Wireless Access Points (CAPWAP) protocol-based cloud AC management systems. Examples include Ruckus, Relay2 and Google, and some domestic enterprises have also released cloud AC management systems. With the dramatic increase of AP, clustered cloud ACs (called AC pools) have become necessary to obtain performance requirements and unified resource management. Therefore, delivering an incoming AP to its proper cloud AC has become increasingly important in clustered cloud AC systems.

Our proposed load balancing strategy works as follows. First, the user traffic prediction model is set up and the user traffic is predicted based on its partially similar characteristics. Then, the incoming AP's load is predicted based on the user's traffic predictions. Finally, the incoming AP is distributed to a target cloud AC based on the AP's load predictions by the load balancer.

The rest of paper is organized as follows. Section II presents the wireless user traffic characteristics. Section III specifies the user traffic prediction model and its features. Section IV proposes the load balancing algorithm. Section V simulates and evaluates the performance of our proposed algorithm. The paper concludes with section VI.

II. RELATED WORK

Research on wireless user traffic typically involves obtaining its regular pattern through analysis of the user traffic data. It is known that the user traffic has self-similarity, periodicity [10] and burst characteristics [11]. Most studies on the characteristics of wireless user traffic take the statistical data for analyzing during a certain period of time. In [12][13], based on the statistical result of the user number and user network traffic, it is proved that the user number and user network traffic of an AP has partial similarity with a period measured in days.

According to the CAPWAP protocol used in centralized forwarding mode, AP control packets and data packets are forwarded to the AC through a CAPWAP tunnel. In [14], it is proved that the CPU utilization and memory usage increases rapidly in centralized forwarding mode, while remaining almost constant in local forwarding mode when the number of AP and the number of users remains unchanged, and the user network traffic is increasing. Therefore, it indicates that the user traffic has no impact on network control messages between APs and ACs. Furthermore, the CPU utilization and memory usage increases in both the local forwarding mode and the centralized forwarding mode when the number of AP and user network traffic remains unchanged and the number of users is increased. As we know, there are many more data packets than management packets in centralized forwarding mode; load on cloud AC mainly depends on the user network traffic in centralized forwarding mode.

As shown in Figure (1), the traffic of 140 APs during 7 days while sampling 1440 time points per day illustrates that the traffic varies rapidly during a day but implies a period of day similarity.

Because network traffic has been shown to include attributes of self-similarity, periodicity and burst, a Poisson model is not suitable to describe the characteristics of the network traffic. Moving average models predict a result based on the historical average and require smaller storage space as well as less calculation compared to other models. Weighted moving average methods give different weights to history data, so the predicted value obtained may go awry since the user traffic is partial-similar data. An exponential smoothing model is a time-series forecasting method based on the moving average method and includes the single exponential smoothing, second-order exponential smoothing, and cubic exponential smoothing models. Exponential smoothing models are simple and practical with the potential to reach a high predictive accuracy in some cases.

Artificial neural networks are suitable for large-scale data because of their memorizing, calculating, learning and other

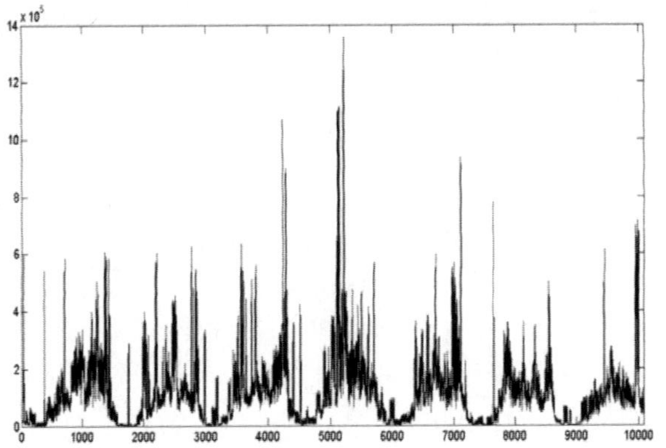

Figure 1. Traffic of 140 Aps for 7 days

intelligent features. Therefore, the neural network prediction method can be used to describe the non-linear characteristics of network traffic and exhibits better performance than autoregressive (AR), autoregressive moving average (ARMA) [15] and other linear network prediction methods. Specifically, since the neural network can remember the variation of network traffic during the training process, which results in less effect on the forecast value of the number of prediction steps, it is suitable for long-term prediction. The autoregressive integrated moving average (ARIMA) model for network traffic prediction gives a bigger error prediction deviation because of its multiple difference on non-stationary time series, which makes the characteristics of network traffic disappear. Furthermore, due to the long time required for its prediction algorithm, the ARIMA model cannot guarantee the required performance necessary for real-time network traffic forecasting. In this paper, we focus on wireless user network traffic prediction by the moving average model, exponential smoothing model [16] and back propagation (BP) neural network model [17], and select the suitable AC network traffic prediction model by comparing the prediction results of these three models.

In the centralized forwarding mode, the traffic will be forwarded to the AC after the AP successfully accesses the AC, which requires a load balancing strategy to not only consider the current load of the AC, but also take into account the long period load prediction. In consequence, we take the prediction as the AC's load after a long time prediction for user network traffic.

III. USER TRAFFIC PREDICTION MODEL

In this paper, due to the user network traffic periodic partial similar characteristics, the user network traffic time series phase space is reconstructed according to Takens' embedding theorem [18], and the reconstructed series are used to predict the user network traffic of the next day.

Given the user network traffic time series as:

$$X(i) = \{X(1), X(2), X(3) \cdots X(N*T)\}, T = 1440, \quad (1)$$

with the total sequence length being $N*T$, The reconstructed sequences of the same time each day:

$$Y_n(k) = \{X(n), X(n+T) \cdots X(n+k*T)\}, \\ k = 1,2 \cdots N-1, N > 1, \quad (2)$$

forms T reconstruction sequences set:

$$Y_n(k), n = 1,2, \cdots T. \quad (3)$$

In consequence, modeling the network traffic by secondary exponential smoothing as following:

$$S_n^{(1)}(N+1) = \alpha Y_n(N) + (1-\alpha) S_n^{(1)}(N), \quad (4)$$

$$S_n^{(2)}(N+1) = \alpha S_n^{(1)}(N+1) + (1-\alpha) S_n^{(2)}(N), \quad (5)$$

TABLE I. SQUARED ERROR OF DIFFERENT MODEL

Average AP Number per Day	Moving Average Model SSE(10^{15})	Second Exponential Model SSE(10^{15})	BP neural network model SSE(10^{15})
1	0.027	0.028	0.278
2	0.114	0.118	0.492
3	0.145	0.123	0.614
4	0.252	0.234	0.797
5	0.348	0.370	1.080
6	2.215	1.637	2.623
7	2.226	1.657	3.754
8	2.418	1.728	8.305
9	2.454	1.722	12.32
10	2.492	1.795	14.19

where n is the time index of a day and N is the day index, $S_n^{(1)}(N)$ is the single exponential smoothing value of Nth day n^{th} time slot, $S_n^{(2)}(N)$ is the second exponential smoothing value of Nth day n^{th} time, α is the Smoothness index where $0<\alpha<1$.

$$a_n(N+1) = 2S_n^{(1)}(N+1) - S_n^{(2)}(N+1), \quad (6)$$

$$b_n(N+1) = \frac{\alpha}{1-\alpha}\left[S_n^{(1)}(N+1) - S_n^{(2)}(N+1)\right], \quad (7)$$

where $a_n(N+1)$, $b_n(N+1)$ are intermediate variables. And the network traffic prediction of AC for the next day is:

$$F_n(N+1) = a_n(N+1) + b_n(N+1). \quad (8)$$

The user network traffic sequence $Y_n(k)$ based on the moving average, second exponential smoothing, and BP neural network models are modeled and predicted respectively. We take $n_{max} = 1440$ sample data per day and calculate the squared error for different models. Given the prediction value to be $F_n(k)$ and the real value to be $Y_n(k)$, the sum of squared error on the kth day is [19]

$$SSE = \sum_{n=1}^{n_{max}} [F_n(k) - Y_n(k)]^2 . \quad (9)$$

The prediction results in Table (1) show that the moving average and second exponential smoothing models have similar sum of squared errors when the AP number is small.

TABLE II. SECOND EXPONENTIAL SMOOTHING MODEL WITH CONSTANT AND DYNAMIC EXPONENT

	Fixed Exponent	Dynamic Exponent
SSE(10^{13})	2.5674	1.0156

The second exponential smoothing model has the smallest sum of squared error among the three models and is therefore more suitable for wireless user network traffic prediction, although all of their sum of squared errors increase when the AP number increases. On the other hand, the exponential smoothing model takes less execution time than the BP neural network model, and the moving average model has the shortest execution time. After taking into account the practical application, the exponential smoothing models and moving average models both meet the time requirements for our AC-AP architecture. In conclusion, the second exponential smoothing model is used to predict the user network traffic when correcting the load balancing algorithm.

For the second exponential smoothing models, the smoothness index α is an important factor in algorithm prediction precision. In addition, the greater value of α results in a faster model prediction process. Usually, the smoothness index α is a constant determined by experience when the network traffic is predicted by second exponential smoothing models. However, it is very hard to set α by experience on the case of AC-AP architecture because the connection time and order is unknown, and the network traffic for each user on the AP is different. Therefore, in this paper, a dynamic exponential smoothing [20] model is used to dynamically adjust the smoothness index α in order to decrease prediction deviation.

The user network traffic in time nth of one day may vary sharply compared to its historical data because of the traffic's periodical and burst characteristics. In addition, the value of the exponent α is constantly adjusted based on the smallest network traffic deviation. Experiments for fixed index and dynamic index exponential smoothing models are shown in Table (2).

IV. THE PROPOSED ALGORITHM

As shown in Figure (2), there are m cloud ACs $AC_1, AC_2 \cdots AC_m$ and k APs $AP_1, AP_2 \cdots AP_k$. The AC load balancer relays an AP's packet to a cloud AC and vice versa. To simplify the algorithm, it is assumed that the each AP-AC tunnel has the same quality and the same configuration for every AP.

For cluster cloud ACs set:

$$AC = \{AC_1, AC_2 \cdots AC_m\}, \; m > 1. \quad (10)$$

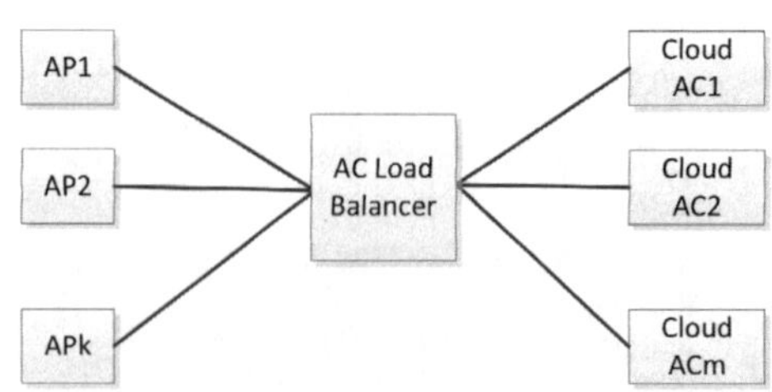

Figure 2. AC Load Balancing Model

Let AC nodes have the same configuration, $L(AC_i)$ represents the mean user network traffic of cloud AC_i. The sum of all cloud AC's mean user network traffic gives as:

$$L_{SUM} = \sum_{i=1}^{m} L(AC_i) \quad , \tag{11}$$

and $C_N(AC_i)$ represents the current AP number managed by cloud AC_i , therefore, the sum of AP managed by all cloud AC's gives as:

$$C_{NSUM} = \sum_{i=1}^{m} C_N(AC_i) \quad . \tag{12}$$

Let the weight coefficient be β, where 0<β<1. Given β=0.5 defines the weighted traffic load $T(AC_i)$ of AC_i as:

$$T(AC_i) = \beta \frac{C_N(AC_i)}{C_{NSUM}} + (1-\beta) \frac{L(AC_i)}{L_{SUM}} \, . \tag{13}$$

Finally, the minimum traffic load $T_{min}(AC)$ among cluster cloud AC set is:

$$T_{min}(AC) = \min\{T(AC_i), i = 1,2 \cdots m\} \tag{14}$$

V. SIMULATION AND EVALUATIONS

This section presents the simulation setup and evaluations using MATLAB and CLOUDSIM simulation tools. The wireless user network traffic prediction and the process for APs accessing ACs is simulated by MATLAB, while the process time of cloud AC is simulated by CLOUDSIM after APs access ACs successfully.

Euclidean distance is widely used in the sequence similarity research [21]. The Euclidean distance between sequence $X(k) = \{X_1, X_2 \cdots X_n\}$ and sequence $Y(k) = \{Y_1, Y_2 \cdots Y_n\}$ is given as:

$$D(X, Y) = \sqrt{\sum_{i=1}^{n} (X_i - Y_i)^2} \quad . \tag{15}$$

A. *MATLAB Simulation*

Based on 140 APs 14 days of experimental data, the process for AP accessing 3 ACs is simulated through the traffic prediction & AP number algorithm, AP number only algorithm, current traffic load algorithm, and current traffic & AP number algorithm respectively.

After all the AP access the 3 cloud ACs system successfully, the traffic sequence is taken from each AC for 1440 sample data points per day. The similarity of traffic sequence is indicated by their Euclidean distance $D(X, Y)$ which reflects the load balancing among cluster cloud ACs.

TABLE III. LOAD EUCLIDEAN DISTANCE FOR ALTERNATIVE ALGORITHMS

Euclidean Distance	Traffic Prediction & AP Number Algorithm	AP Number Algorithm	Current Traffic Load Algorithm	Current Traffic & AP Number Algorithm
$D(L_1, L_2)$ (10^6)	2.7477	2.8207	2.8409	2.8083
$D(L_2, L_3)$ (10^6)	2.8292	2.7969	2.7960	2.8272
$D(L_1, L_3)$ (10^6)	2.8603	2.8997	2.8251	2.8269
Summary (10^6)	8.4372	8.5173	8.4620	8.4625

Let L1, L2 and L3 be the load sequence of AC1, AC2 and AC3 respectively, the average Euclidean distance for a 100 times simulations is shown in Table (3).

A smaller Euclidean distance indicates a higher similarity. The sum Euclidean distance of the traffic prediction & AP number algorithm is 0.94%, 0.30% and 0.30% smaller compared to the AP number algorithm, current traffic load algorithm, and current traffic & AP number algorithm respectively. Therefore, the traffic prediction & AP number algorithm is more efficient for cluster cloud ACs load balancing algorithm.

B. *CLOUDSIM Simulation*

After all the AP access the 3 cloud ACs system successfully with the load balancing algorithm through the traffic prediction & AP number algorithm, AP number only algorithm, current traffic load algorithm, and current traffic & AP number algorithm respectively, the traffic sequence is taken from each AC for 1440 sample data points per day. The process time is simulated through CLOUDSIM and the Euclidean distance for the process time sequence is calculated to evaluate the different load balancing algorithms' efficiencies.

In this simulation, one broker and three virtual hosts with node id 1, 2 and 3 are created with simulation parameters as MIPS = 250, RAM = 512MB, bandwidth = 1000Mbps and the image space size =10000MB. The broker takes the load of AC obtained from the MATLAB simulation and delivers the traffic to different virtual host which represents the cloud AC.

Let T1, T2 and T3 be the process time sequence of AC1, AC2 and AC3 respectively. The average Euclidean distance for a 5 times simulations is illustrated in Table (4).

As before, a smaller Euclidean distance means higher similarity. The sum Euclidean distance of the traffic prediction & AP number algorithm is 1.8%、0.32%、0.17% smaller compared to the AP number algorithm, current traffic load algorithm, and current traffic & AP number algorithm respectively. Therefore, the process time simulation by CLOUDSIM gives a result similar to the load simulation of MATLAB, and the traffic prediction & AP

TABLE IV. PROCESS TIME EUCLIDEAN DISTANCE FOR DIFFERENT ALGORITHMS

Process Time Euclidean Distance	Traffic Prediction & AP Number Algorithm	AP Number Algorithm	Current Traffic Load Algorithm	Current Traffic & AP Number Algorithm
$D(T_1, T_2)$ (10^6)	2.0236	2.0856	2.0741	2.0473
$D(T_2, T_3)$ (10^6)	2.0547	2.0652	2.0434	2.0591
$D(T_1, T_3)$ (10^6)	2.0774	2.1206	2.0582	2.0597
Total (106)	6.1557	6.2714	6.1757	6.1661

number algorithm is more efficient for cluster cloud ACs load balancing.

To sum up, in the centralized forwarding mode, since the user network traffic in AC has similarity with a period of a day, it is feasible to predict the user traffic and take the prediction into account for cluster cloud ACs load balancing. The resultant traffic prediction & AP number algorithm gives a better result among cluster cloud ACs load balancing algorithms.

VI. CONCLUSIONS

In this work, the load balancing strategy is studied for APs accessing cluster cloud ACs. The similarity of wireless user network traffic is researched and a prediction algorithm is proposed to forecast the network traffic. The algorithm efficiency is compared with their load and process time Euclidean distance using simulation with MATLAB and CLOUDSIM. The simulations show that the second exponential smoothing model is more suitable for wireless user traffic prediction and the traffic prediction & AP number algorithm is more efficient among cluster cloud ACs load balancing algorithms.

REFERENCES

[1] Chonggun Kim, Kameda H. An algorithm for optimal static load balancing in distributed computer systems [J].Computers, IEEE Transactions on, 1995(41):381-384.

[2] Whang K Y, Kim SW, Wiederhold G. Dynamic Maintenance of Data Distribution for Selectivity Estimation [J].VLDB Journal, 1994, 3(1):29-51.

[3] Ben-Asher Y, Cohen A, Schuster A. The impact of task-length parameters on the performance of the random load-balancing algorithm[C]. Parallel Processing Symposium, 1992 Proceedings, Sixth International, 1992:82-85.

[4] Haddad E. Optimal dynamic redistribution of divisible load in distributed real-time systems[C]. Real-Time Applications, 1994 Proceedings of the IEEE Workshop on, 1994.21-26.

[5] J Gu, J Hu, T Zhao, and G Sun. A new resource scheduling strategy based on genetic algorithm in cloud computing environment [J] Journal of Computers, 2012, 7(1):42-52.

[6] Gupta E, Deshpande V. A Technique Based on Ant Colony Optimization for Load Balancing in Cloud Data Center[C]. Information Technology (ICIT), 2014 International Conference on, 2014:12-17.

[7] Xu Zhihong, Hou Xiangdan, Sun Jizhou. Ant algorithm-based task scheduling in gridcomputing[C]. Proceedings of the IEEE Canadian conference on electrical and computer engineering, 2003:1107-1110.

[8] Paletta M, Herrero P. An Awareness-Based Simulated Annealing Method to Cover Dynamic Load-Balancing in Collaborative Distributed Environments[C]. Web Intelligence and Intelligent Agent Technologies, 2009 WI-IAT 09 IEEE/WIC/ACM International Joint Conferences on, 2009:371-374.

[9] Zhao Yongyi, Xia Shengxian. Research on Load Balancing for Multidimensional Network Services Based on Particle Swarm Optimization Algorithm[C]. Intelligent Networks and Intelligent Systems (ICINIS), 2010 3rd International Conference on, 2010:411-414.

[10] Groschwitz N K, Polyzos G C. A time series model of long-term NSFNET backbone traffic[C], Communications, 1994. ICC'94, SUPERCOMM/ICC'94, Conference Record, 'Serving Humanity Through Communications.' IEEE International Conference on. IEEE, 1994: 1400-1404.

[11] Erramilli A, Singh R P, Pruthi P. Chaotic maps as models of packet traffic[C], Proc. 14th Int. Teletraffic Cong. 1994, 1: 329-338.

[12] McNett M, Voelker G M. Access and mobility of wireless PDA users [J]. ACM SIGMOBILE Mobile Computing and Communications Review, 2005, 9(2): 40-55.

[13] Balachandran A, Voelker G M, Bahl P. Characterizing user behavior and network performance in a public wireless LAN[C], ACM SIGMETRICS Performance Evaluation Review. ACM, 2002, 30(1): 195-205.

[14] Songqun Huo, Research on the networking and forwarding technologies in WLAN [D], Beijing University of Posts and Telecommunications, 2010:45-48.

[15] Xue Ke, Li Zengzhi, Liu Liu and Song Chengquan, Network traffic prediction based on ARIMA model [J]. Microelectronics and Computer, 2004, 21(7):84-87.

[16] LIU Y, JIN X. Research on Network Traffic Prediction-based Dynamic Exponential Smoothing Model [J]. Fire Control and Command Control, 2008, 3: 029.

[17] Li Z, Qin L, Xue K, et al. A Novel BP Neural Network Model for Traffic Prediction of Next Generation Network[C], Natural Computation, 2009. ICNC '09. Fifth International Conference on. IEEE, 2009:32-38.

[18] Lu Jinjun, Wang Zhiquan, Internet traffic data follow forecast by RBF neural network based on phase space reconstruction, Transactions of Nanjing University of Aeronautics & Astronautics [J], 2006, 23(4):316-322.

[19] Hecht-Nielson R. Theory of the back propagation neural networks [M]. Washington D. C. Proceedings of IEEE international Joint conference on Neural Networks. 1989.

[20] Bonsdorff H. A comparison of the ordinary and a varying parameter exponential smoothing [J]. Journal of Applied Probability, 1989.784-792.

[21] Keogh E. Fast similarity search in the presence of longitudinal scaling in time series databases[C], Tools with Artificial Intelligence, 1997. Proceedings, Ninth IEEE International Conference on. IEEE, 1997: 578-58.

Energy Efficiency in MC-DS/CDMA Cooperative Networks: Centralized and Distributed Solutions

Lucas D. Hiera Sampaio and Taufik Abrão
State University of Londrina, Brazil
Email: dr.lucas.sampaio@ieee.org; taufik@uel.br

Álvaro R. C. Souza and Paul J. E. Jeszensky
Polytechnic School of the University of São Paulo
Brazil. Email: alvarorcsouza@usp.br; pjej@usp.br

***Abstract*—The energy efficiency (EE) maximization on the uplink of multi-carrier direct sequence code division multiple access (MC-DS/CDMA) cooperative wireless networks is an NP-hard optimization problem of great interest for future networks systems. This paper presents three centralized solutions and two distributed ones: the centralized solutions include an iterative solution based on the Dinkelbach method and two heuristic approaches, *i.e.*, the Firefly algorithm (FA) and the Particle Swarm Optimization (PSO) algorithm. The distributed solutions are based on a game theory framework and employ two different algorithms for resource allocation: the classical waterfilling algorithm adapted to the discussed problem and the Verhulst distributed power control algorithm (V-DPCA). Simulations were conducted in order to establish which technique has the best EE, spectral efficiency (SE) and complexity tradeoff.**

Keywords–Cooperative Networks; MC-DS/CDMA; Energy Efficiency; Spectral Efficiency; Game Theory; Dinkelbach.

I. INTRODUCTION

Energy-efficient telecommunications systems is of great importance in terms of design and implementation due to carbon emission reduction and cost. Besides, in wireless communications the transmission power usually is not linearly proportional to the transmitter-receiver distance, which makes cooperative networks often more energy-efficient than non-cooperative networks. In such networks each mobile terminal (MT) communicates with one or multiple relay stations (RS) that forward the MT message to its respective base station (BS). Besides the increase in EE, this sort of networks may also be used to increase spectral efficiency (SE), system throughput or decrease the average transmission power.

MC-DS/CDMA networks are characterized by the division of the total available spectrum into uncorrelated CDMA non-selective sub-channels. This characteristic improves granularity which usually enhances system throughput, capacity, SE and EE as well as lower the average transmission power (ATP). Each one of the sub-channels is interference limited, thus better interference cancellation techniques may be implemented in order to further improve the system. In addition, MC-DS/CDMA networks may carry out adaptive modulation or multiprocessing gain techniques to support different multimedia services increasing the system flexibility from voice service to high data rate services.

1) Related Work: Many studies have been conducted recently aiming to find implementable resource allocation (RA) algorithms for cooperative networks, among them [1]–[6]. RA procedures are directly related to user satisfaction, company profits and environment issues. The work in [1] presents a game theoretic approach for power control and receiver design in cooperative direct sequence (DS)/CDMA networks. A performance analysis for wireless cooperative networks using amplify and forward (AF) protocol is presented in [2] while a method for energy efficiency maximization with minimum transmission rate requeriments is presented in [3]. Meanwhile, in [4] a concave fractional programming approach for EE maximization in orthogonal frequency division multiple access (OFDMA) cooperative networks is presented while in [5] an analysis on EE-SE tradeoff for DS/CDMA networks is offered. Furthermore, in [6] three different distributed solution methods for the EE maximization problem in MC-DS/CDMA cooperative networks are discussed.

2) Contributions: The main contribution in this work is to analyse different algorithms, methods and approaches that can be deployed in resource allocation of the uplink (UL) cooperative MC-DS/CDMA networks. In order to find a good solution/algorithm for power allocation and EE in MC-DS/CDMA cooperative networks, which compromises both performance and computational complexity, this paper extends the work presented in [6] and incorporates two centralized heuristic algorithms to solve the RA problem. All five algorithms/methods are briefly presented and analyzed under the same scenario which consists of a single cell with one fixed relay station, directional antennas and cooperative communications aiming to expand the coverage area without expensive costs for the telecommunications company.

This paper is organized as follows. Section II presents the system model and description; EE and SE, as well as the problem formulation are presented in Section III. Furthermore, Section IV discusses centralized solutions while Section V presents the game theoretic approach. Numerical examples and results are offered in Section VI. Conclusions and future work are addressed in Section VII.

II. SYSTEM DESCRIPTION

On the UL of MC-DS/CDMA cooperative systems each MT communicates with the BS using a RS to forward its message. In this paper we consider a single cell environment with one fixed RS (FRS) as shown in Fig. 1. The complex channel gain for the MT-FRS link is described as $h_i(k)$ where i and k are the MT and subcarrier indexer, respectively. Equivalently, the complex channel gain for the FRS-BS channel is denoted as $g(k)$. Therefore the *power channel gain* vector for the MT-FRS path is:

$$\mathbf{h}(k) = [h_1(k)\, h_2(k)\, \cdots h_U(k)]^\top \qquad k = 1, \ldots N \tag{1}$$

where U is the system loading and N the number of parallel non-overlaping subcarriers. The *power channel gain* vector for the FRS-BS path is:

$$\mathbf{g} = [g(1)\, g(2)\, \cdots\, g(k)\, \cdots\, g(N)] \tag{2}$$

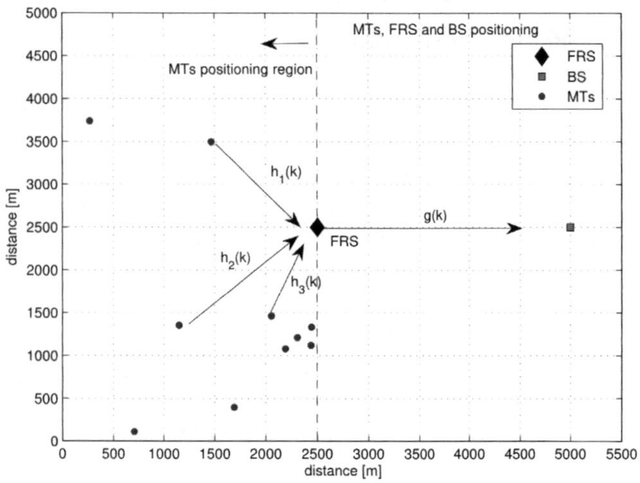

Figure 1. MTs, FRS and BS positioning in a uplink MC-DS/CDMA system with a single fixed-RS.

In cooperative scenarios, the signal received at the relay may go through different procedures before it is forwarded to the next destination. The relay may use amplify-and-forward (AF) protocol, decode-and-forward (DF) protocol or compress-and-forward (CF) protocol. We only consider the AF protocol. Hence, the signal received at the FRS is first normalized by the square root of the average received power and afterwards amplified by the $U \times U$ amplification matrix $\mathbf{A}$ constrained by $\text{tr}(\mathbf{A}\mathbf{A}^H) \leq p_R$ where p_R is the available power at the FRS.

In interference limited multiple access networks an important QoS measure is the signal-interference-plus-noise ratio (SINR) since all users transmit over the same channel at the same time causing multiple access interference (MAI). In a MC-DS/CDMA system, the post-detection SINR, considering the adoption of linear receivers, may be generically expressed for the ith user, kth sub-carrier as [7]:

$$\delta_i(k) = F_i(k) \frac{p_i(k)\mathrm{h}_i(k)\mathrm{g}(k)|\mathbf{d}_i^H \mathbf{A}\mathbf{s}_i(k)|^2}{\mathcal{I}_i(k) + \mathcal{N}_\mathrm{T}(k) + \sigma^2 \mathrm{g}(k)||\mathbf{A}^H \mathbf{d}_i||^2} \qquad (3)$$

where $\mathrm{h}_i(k) = |h_i(k)|^2$ is the *channel power gain* between user i and the single FRS and $\mathrm{g}(k) = |g(k)|^2$ is the *channel power gain* from single FRS to BS, and $\mathbf{d}_i$ is the linear filter at receiver, such as single-user matched filter (MF) or multi-user Decorrelator, minimum mean square error (MMSE) filter and so forth; following the results of [5] only the Decorrelator will be considered herein since it had the best results in terms of complexity-performance trade off. Hence, the Decorrelator filter may be mathematically expressed as:

$$\mathbf{d}_{\mathrm{DEC}} = [\mathbf{d}_1, \ldots, \mathbf{d}_i, \ldots, \mathbf{d}_U] = \mathbf{S}(\mathbf{S}^T\mathbf{S})^{-1} = \mathbf{S}\mathbf{R}^{-1} \qquad (4)$$

where $\mathbf{d}_i$ is the linear filter for the i-th user, $\mathbf{S}$ is the spreading sequence matrix with each column representing an user spreading code and $\mathbf{R}$ is the spreading sequence correlation matrix. Furthermore, the $\mathcal{I}_i(k)$ in (3) is the amplified MAI at the FRS forwarded to the BS:

$$\mathcal{I}_i(k) \;=\; \mathrm{g}(k) \sum_{\substack{j=1 \\ j \neq i}}^{U} p_j(k)\mathrm{h}_j(k)\, |\mathbf{d}_i^H \mathbf{A}\mathbf{s}_j(k)|^2 \qquad (5)$$

and $\mathcal{N}_\mathrm{T}(k)$ is the normalized noise at the BS and treated through the linear multiuser receiver:

$$\mathcal{N}_\mathrm{T}(k) \;=\; \left[\sum_{i=1}^{U} p_i(k)\mathrm{h}_j(k) + \mathrm{F}_i(k)\sigma^2\right] \sigma^2 ||\mathbf{d}_i||^2 \qquad (6)$$

where $p_i(k)$ is the allocated power, associated to the respective users (i) and sub-carrier (k), and σ^2 is the power noise.

III. Energy and Spectral Efficiencies and Problem Formulation

The SE of each user through the N sub-channels can be computed as the number of bits per second that may be transmitted for a single Hertz. Considering a practical approach for the theoretical bound obtained through the Shannon channel capacity equation, the SE of the ith user can be defined as:

$$\mathcal{S}_i = \sum_{k=1}^{N} \log_2\left(1 + \delta_i(k)\right), \; i = 1, \ldots, U \; \left[\frac{\text{bits}}{\text{s} \cdot \text{Hz}}\right] \qquad (7)$$

Finally, the user rate at each sub-channel is given by:

$$r_i(k) = \mathrm{w} \cdot \mathcal{S}_i = \mathrm{w} \log_2\left(1 + \delta_i(k)\right) \quad \left[\frac{\text{bits}}{\text{s}}\right] \qquad (8)$$

In MC-DS/CDMA systems with a single FRS, the EE function for user i can be formulated as [8]:

$$\xi_i = \sum_{k=1}^{N} \frac{r_i(k)\ell_i(k) \cdot f(\delta_i(k))}{\varrho\, p_i(k) + \varrho_\mathrm{R}\, p_\mathrm{R} + p_\mathrm{C} + p_{\mathrm{C_R}}} \quad \left[\frac{\text{bit}}{\text{Joule}}\right], \qquad (9)$$

$\forall i = 1, \ldots, U$, where i and k are the user and sub-channel indexers respectively; $\ell \leq 1$ is the code rate. $p_i(k)$ is the MT transmission power, p_R is the re-transmission power from the FRS to the BS, assumed a fixed and equal power quantity per user overall the subcarriers; p_C and $p_{\mathrm{C_R}}$ are the circuitry power consumption at MT and FRS, respectively; $\varrho > 1$ and $\varrho_\mathrm{R} > 1$ are the power amplifier inefficiency factors at MT and FRS, respectively. The efficiency function $f(\delta_i(k))$ expresses the probability of error-free packet reception. Considering M-QAM square constellation modulations of order $M = M_i(k)$ and Gray coding, the bit error rate is approximately [9], [10]:

$$\mathrm{BER}_i(k) = \frac{2(\sqrt{M}-1)}{\sqrt{M}\log_2 M}\left(1 - \sqrt{\frac{3\delta_i(k)\log_2 M}{2(M-1) + 3\delta_i(k)\log_2 M}}\right) \qquad (10)$$

A. Problem Formulation

To maximize the EE of each user in the MC-DS/CDMA system with a single FRS, the overall EE maximization problem with MT's power constraint is posted as:

$$\begin{aligned} \underset{\mathbf{P} \in \wp}{\text{maximize}} \quad \sum_{i=1}^{U} \xi_i \;&=\; \sum_{i=1}^{U}\sum_{k=1}^{N} \frac{r_i(k)\ell_i(k)f(\delta_i(k))}{\varrho\, p_i(k) + \varrho_\mathrm{R}\, p_\mathrm{R} + p_\mathrm{C} + p_{\mathrm{C_R}}} \\ &\equiv\; \sum_{i=1}^{U} \frac{\sum_{k=1}^{N} \ell_i(k)\,\mathrm{w}\log_2\left[1 + \delta_i(k)\right] \cdot \left(1 - \mathrm{BER}_i(k)\right)}{p_\mathrm{C} + p_{\mathrm{C_R}} + \varrho_\mathrm{R}\, p_\mathrm{R} + \varrho \sum_{k=1}^{N} p_i(k)}, \\ \text{s.t.(C.1)} \quad & \delta_i(k) \geq \delta_{i,\min}(k), \quad \forall\, k, i \end{aligned} \qquad (11)$$

where the total transmit power of the U mobile terminals across N subcarriers must be bounded (and be nonnegative) for any feasible power allocation policy, with the correspondent power allocation matrix described by:

$$\mathbf{P} \in \wp \stackrel{\text{def}}{=} \{[p_i(k)]_{U\times N} \mid 0 \leq \quad p_i(k) \leq P_{\max}\} \qquad (12)$$

where $N \cdot P_{\max}$ represents the maximum total transmit power available at each MT transmitter.

IV. Centralized RA Solutions

Analytical-iterative Dinkelbach method, as well as a heuristic PSO-based and Firefly-based algorithms are explored to solve the RA problem in a centralized way.

A. Dinkelbach Method

The Dinkelbach method is an iterative method to solve quasi-concave problems in a parameterized concave form [11]. The optimization problem in (11) is divided into N subproblems representing the EE problem in each subcarrier k:

$$\begin{aligned} \text{maximize} \quad & \frac{\mathcal{C}(\mathbf{p})}{\mathcal{U}(\mathbf{p})} = \frac{\sum_{i=1}^{U} \ell_i(k)\, \mathrm{w} \log_2\left[1+\delta_i(k)\right]\cdot(1-\mathrm{BER}_i(k))}{p_{\mathrm{C}} + p_{\mathrm{C_R}} + \varrho_{\mathrm{R}}\, p_{\mathrm{R}} + \varrho \sum_{k=1}^{N} p_i(k)} \\ \text{s.t.(C.1)} \quad & \delta_i(k) \geq \delta_{i,\min}(k), \quad \forall\, i \qquad (13) \\ \text{(C.2)} \quad & 0 \geq p_i(k) \geq p_{\max}, \quad \forall\, i \end{aligned}$$

Each subproblem (13) is a quasi-concave problem [6]. The following parametric concave program is associated with the EE maximization problem in each subcarrier [12]:

$$\underset{\mathbf{p}\in\mathcal{X}}{\text{maximize}} \quad \mathcal{C}(\mathbf{p}) - \lambda\mathcal{U}(\mathbf{p}) \qquad (14)$$

where $\mathcal{X} = \{\mathbf{p} \in \mathcal{X} | 0 \leq p_i(k) \leq p_{\max}\ \forall i = 1,\ldots,U\}$. The objective function of the parameterized problem, denoted by $\mathcal{F}(\lambda)$ is a convex, continuous and strictly decreasing function. Without loss of generality, the maximum EE λ^* of the parameterized problem is [12]:

$$\lambda^* = \frac{\mathcal{C}(\mathbf{p}^*)}{\mathcal{U}(\mathbf{p}^*)} = \underset{\mathbf{p}\in\mathcal{X}}{\text{maximize}} \frac{\mathcal{C}(\mathbf{p})}{\mathcal{U}(\mathbf{p})} \qquad (15)$$

which is equivalent to find $\mathcal{F}(\lambda) = 0$. According to [13] the Dinkelbach method is the application of Newton's method to a nonlinear fractional program converging with a super-linear rate. The goal at each iteration of the method is to solve:

$$\mathcal{F}(\lambda_n) = \max_{\mathbf{p}\in\mathcal{X}}\{\mathcal{C}(\mathbf{p} - \lambda_n\mathcal{U}(\mathbf{p})\} \quad @n\text{th iteration.} \qquad (16)$$

Fig. 2 depicts a pseudo-code for Algorithm 1 based on iterative Dinkelbach's method. Moreover, in order to solve problem (16) we have deployed CvX tools [14].

```
Algorithm 1 Dinkelbach's Method
Input:       λ0 satisfying F(λ0) ≥ 0;   tolerance εd
Initialize:  n ← 0,
repeat
    Solve problem (16) with λ = λn to obtain p*n
    λn+1 ← C(p*n) / U(p*n);
    n ← n + 1
until |F(λn)| ≤ εd;
Output: λn; p*n
```

Figure 2. Pseudo-Code for the Dinkelbach's Method

B. Particle Swarm Optimization (PSO)

Created by Kennedy and Eberhart in [15] the PSO algorithm is based on flocks behaviour when searching for food. In this algorithm each possible solution is analogously put as a particle in the swarm and each member of the population has two main attributes: position and velocity. Position itself is the candidate solution to the optimization problem and velocity is the parameter used to move each individual according to the best solution found by him and by the whole group.

In order to deal with unfeasible solutions the implemented algorithm discards any individual which leaves the problem domain or does not satisfy at least one of the problem constraints as in (11). Hence, at each iteration the M individuals move through the search space, being eliminated from the population if they leave the problem domain. At the t-th iteration the PSO updates particle m position through:

$$\mathbf{X}_m[t+1] = \mathbf{X}_m[t] + \mathbf{V}_m[t+1] \qquad (17)$$

where $\mathbf{X}_m[t]$ is the particle m position at iteration t and it is a $U \times N$ non-negative valued real matrix. $\mathbf{V}_i[t+1]$ is the velocity $U \times N$ matrix which can be computed by:

$$\begin{aligned} \mathbf{V}_m[t+1] \quad = \quad & \omega\mathbf{V}_m[t] + c_1\,\mathbf{U}_m^1[t] \circ \left(\mathbf{V}_m^{\text{best}}[t] - \mathbf{V}_m[t]\right) \\ & + c_2\,\mathbf{U}_m^2[t] \circ \left(\mathbf{V}_g^{\text{best}}[t] - \mathbf{V}_m[t]\right) \qquad (18) \end{aligned}$$

where $\circ$ is the Hadamard product, $\mathbf{V}_m^{\text{best}}[t]$ is the best solution found by individual m up to iteration t, $\mathbf{V}_g^{\text{best}}[t]$ is the best solution found by all individuals up to iteration t, c_1 and c_2 are weights for local and global solution candidates, ω is the inertia coefficient, $\mathbf{U}_m^1[t]$ and $\mathbf{U}_m^2[t]$ are random matrices uniformly distributed on the interval $[0, 1]$.

It is important to note that the best solution is stored based on which candidate solution has the best outcome in terms of objective function. The objective function herein for both heuristics is the system effective capacity in (11).

The PSO algorithm is the recurrent computation of equations (17) and (18) and updating process of $\mathbf{V}_i^{\text{best}}$ and $\mathbf{V}_g^{\text{best}}$ up until convergence or when a maximum number of iterations has been reached.

C. Firefly Algorithm (FA)

Another bio-inspired heuristic, the FA was created by Yang in 2008 [16]. It is based on the collective intelligence of fireflies and their light emission patterns. Firefly algorithm dynamics include two main properties of fireflies in some arbitrary environment: the distance between the firefly population individuals and the light intensity of their bioluminescence.

There are different species of fireflies that use their bioluminescence for different purposes. Fireflies attract each other for reproduction purposes and therefore they are more attracted by the most intense flash pattern. Therefore, the link between the firefly behaviour and the optimization problem is that their flash pattern increases its intensity the better the solution represented through the individual of the population which leads the population to improved solutions that yield better objective function outcomes.

To become a useful tool, three basic rules about the individual fireflies are assumed: a) fireflies have no gender definition, hence any firefly can attract any other firefly; b) attractiveness is proportional to the bioluminescence intensity such that less intense flash patterns fireflies are moved on the direction of more intense glints; c) if a particular individual has the most intense flash pattern then it moves randomly in the search universe. Instead of being an intrinsic characteristic to a firefly, the attractiveness is, in fact, a correspondence between firefly i and j which is mathematically defined as [16]:

$$\beta_{ij} = \beta_0 \, e^{-\gamma \, d_{ij}^2} \tag{19}$$

where j attracts i with intensity β_0 and an exponential decay with the distance between them. The parameter β_0 is the base attractiveness at null distance, common for all individuals of the population, and γ is the medium permissiveness or light absorption coefficient; d_{ij} is the Euclidean distance between the fireflies. Hence, at each iteration t, each pair i, j – where firefly j has a larger light intensity than i – performs a move such that i moves in the direction of j according to [16]:

$$\mathbf{X}_i[t+1] = \mathbf{X}_i[t] + \beta_0 \, e^{-\gamma \, d_{ij}^2} \left(\mathbf{X}_j[t] - \mathbf{X}_i[t]\right) + \alpha_f \left(\mathbf{U}_f[t] - 0.5\right) \tag{20}$$

where $\mathbf{X}_i[t]$ is the firefly i position at the t-th iteration and, in this paper, is a $U \times N$ matrix of power allocation, α_f is a random step coefficient parameter and $\mathbf{U}_f[t]$ is a random matrix at iteration t uniformly distributed on the interval $[0, 1]$.

V. Game Theoretic Approach

We have adopted two approaches to solve the optimization problem in (11) in a distributed fashion: a) solving N non-cooperative games aiming to find the best SINR response to a given interference level at each sub-channel and using the Verhulst based distributed power control algorithm (V-DPCA) [17] afterwards; b) considering a non-cooperative game and an average channel gain across N sub-carriers. The problem is solved also in two steps: finding the best SINR response and allocating the same power to all sub-channels using the V-DPCA. Note that in all power control algorithms analyzed herein system users adjust their own transmission power level selfishly.

A. Solving N Non-Coalitional Games

A different game for each sub-channel such that N non-coalitional games must be solved in order to find the best SINR response. The EE maximization game at the k-th subcarrier is:

$$\mathcal{G}(k) \;=\; \left[\mathcal{U}, \{\mathcal{A}_i(k)\}, \{u_i^k\}\right], \quad k = 1, 2, \ldots, N \tag{21}$$

where $\mathcal{U} = \{1, 2, \ldots, U\}$ is the player set, $\{\mathcal{A}_i(k)\} = [0, p_{\max,i}]$ is the strategy set for user i in the kth sub-channel where $p_{\max,i}$ is the maximal resource (transmission power) available at the ith MT; and $\{u_i^k\}$ is the utility function for the ith user at kth sub-carrier; in this case $\{u_i^k\}$ is given by:

$$u_i^k = r_i(k)\ell_i(k)\frac{\left(1 - \text{BER}_i(k)\right)^{V_i(k)}}{\varrho\, p_i(k) + \varrho_{\text{R}}\, p_{\text{R}} + p_{\text{C}} + p_{\text{C}_{\text{R}}}}, \tag{22}$$

with $\text{BER}_i(k)$ defined as Eq. (10). Consider the power allocated to the ith user at the kth sub-channel. The vector:

$$\mathbf{p}_{-i}(k) = [p_1(k), \cdots, p_{i-1}(k), p_{i+1}(k), \cdots, p_U(k)] \tag{23}$$

is the allocated power vector considering all users but user i. Thus, given the power allocated to all except ith user at the kth sub-carrier the best response for user i in a non-coalitional fashion may be expressed as [18]:

$$p_i^*(k) = \arg \max_{p_i(k)} \; u_i^k \left[p_i(k), \mathbf{p}_{-i}(k)\right] \tag{24}$$

Non-coalitional games can be easily solved finding the Nash Equilibrium (NE) of the problem [19]. An NE is a set of strategies such that any unilateral change will not increase the user utility function without decreasing the other players payoffs. Let $\mathbf{p}_{-i}^*(k)$ be the set of optimal strategies for all users but user i. The vector $\mathbf{p}^*(k)$ is a NE if and only if:

$$\forall p_i(k) \neq p_i^*(k) \Rightarrow u_i^k \left[p_i(k), \mathbf{p}_{-i}^*(k)\right] \leq u_i^k \left[p_i^*(k), \mathbf{p}_{-i}^*(k)\right] \tag{25}$$

Note that in the context of distributed energy-efficient power allocation problem the strategy set for each user is $p_i(k) \in [0, P_{\max}]$; thus, it is non-empty, compact and convex. Furthermore, if the utility function is quasi-concave it has been proved in [20] using Glicksberg generalization of the Kakutani fixed point theorem [21] that the non-cooperative game has at least one Nash Equilibrium. As a consequence, distributed energy-efficient power allocation problem under non-cooperative game perspective may be posed as:

$$\begin{aligned} \max_{p_i(k)} \; u_i^k \quad &= \quad r_i(k)\ell_i(k)\frac{\left(1 - \text{BER}_i(k)\right)^{V_i(k)}}{\varrho\, p_i(k) + \varrho_{\text{R}}\, p_{\text{R}} + p_{\text{C}} + p_{\text{C}_{\text{R}}}} \\ \text{s.t.} \quad (\text{C}.1) \quad & \quad 0 \leq p_i(k) \leq P_{\max} \\ (\text{C}.2) \quad & \quad \delta_i(k) \geq \delta_{i,\min}(k), \quad \forall\, k, i \end{aligned} \tag{26}$$

where $\text{BER}_i(k)$ function is defined in Eq. (10).

Since function u_i^k in Eq. (22) depends on both the user allocated power and its SINR from Eq. (3) follows the relation:

$$p_i(k) = \delta_i(k)\frac{\mathcal{I}_i(k) + \mathcal{N}_{\text{T}}(k) + \sigma^2 \mathrm{g}(k)||\mathbf{A}^H \mathbf{d}_i||^2}{F_i(k)\cdot \mathrm{h}_i(k)\mathrm{g}(k)|\mathbf{d}_i^H \mathbf{A}\mathbf{s}_i(k)|^2} = \delta_i(k)\Gamma_i(k) \tag{27}$$

The fact that the power domain is an interval, *i.e.*, $p_i(k) \in [0, p_{\max}]$, and the relation between power and SINR is linear over the optimization window as shown in (27), the SINR domain is also an interval such that $\delta_i(k) \in [0, \delta_{\max}]$, where $\delta_{\max}$ is related to the SINR level when transmitting with the highest power level allowed. So, utility function is rewritten:

$$u_i^k = r_i(k)\ell_i(k)\frac{\left(1 - \text{BER}_i(k)\right)^{V_i(k)}}{\varrho\, \delta_i(k)\Gamma_i(k) + \varrho_{\text{R}}\, p_{\text{R}} + p_{\text{C}} + p_{\text{C}_{\text{R}}}}, \tag{28}$$

Finding the best response strategy for each user is equivalent to maximize the utility function Functions maxima have a null derivative; hence, applying the derivative in (28):

$$\frac{\partial u_i^k}{\partial \delta_i(k)} = 0 \tag{29}$$

Fig. 3 presents the proposed Algorithm 2 for finding the best SINR response, while simultaneously allocating the corresponding transmission power levels for each user i and subcarrier k.

Algorithm 2 Iterative EE-Maximization Algorithm

Input: $\mathbf{p}$, I, ϵ; **Output:** $\mathbf{p}^*$

begin
initialize first population and set $n = 0$;
while $n \leq I$ or $error > \epsilon$
find $\delta_i(k)$, $\forall i = 1, \dots, U$ $k = 1, \dots, N$ through (29)
allocate $p_i(k)$ for all i and k in order to achieve $\delta_i(k)$
calculate $error = ||\mathbf{p}_i[n] - \mathbf{p}_i[n-1]||_2$
$n = n + 1$
end while

$\mathbf{p}$ = initial power vectors;
$\mathbf{p}[n]$ = power vector at the nth iteration;
$\mathbf{p}^*$ = power vector solution;
I = maximum number of iterations;
ϵ = least expected precision;

Figure 3. Pseudo-Code for the Iterative EE-Maximization Algorithm

B. Solving One Non-Coalitional Game (M-DPCA)

As a second approach, the problem is simplified by taking the average channel gain over all N subcarriers. Thus, all variables which had a subcarrier indexer k are now identified by the operator $\bar{\cdot}$, indicating that the variable takes the average value over N subcarriers. Hence, the problem (11) can be re-written as:

$$\underset{\bar{\mathbf{p}} \in \wp}{\text{maximize}} \quad \sum_{i=1}^{U} \bar{\xi}_i = \sum_{i=1}^{U} \frac{\bar{r}_i \bar{\ell}_i f(\bar{\delta}_i)}{\varrho \bar{p}_i + \varrho_R \bar{p}_R + p_C + p_{C_R}}$$
$$= \sum_{i=1}^{U} \frac{\bar{\ell}_i \, w \log_2 \left[1 + \bar{\delta}_i\right] \cdot (1 - \text{BER}_i)^{V_i}}{p_C + p_{C_R} + \varrho_R \bar{p}_R + \varrho \bar{p}_i}, \quad (30)$$
$$\text{s.t.} \quad (\text{C.1}) \quad \bar{p}_i \leq p_{\max,i}, \quad i = 1, \dots, U$$
$$(\text{C.2}) \quad \bar{\delta}_i \geq \bar{\delta}_{i,\min}, \quad i = 1, \dots, U$$

Problem (30) does not have the sub-carrier dimension, thus it is easier to solve when compared to the first approach. To find the best power allocation policy to (30) the same game theoretic approach presented in Section V-A is adopted. Therefore, one may solve this approach through our proposed Algorithm 2 depicted in Fig. 3 in combination with the V-DPCA. This approach will be referred hereafter as M-DPCA.

VI. Numerical Results

Simulations where conducted using MatLab 7.0 Mathworks to establish which are the best parameters for both heuristics. The scenario parameters values used in the simulations are presented in Table I. Before comparing the different methods' performance it is necessary to find the best parameters for both heuristics. Results from 1000 trials with at least 5 different values for each parameters shown that, for FA the best reference light intensity is $\beta_0 = 1$, the best light absorption coefficient is $\gamma = 1$ and the best random step coefficient is $\alpha_f = 10^{-3}$. While for the PSO, the local best and global best coefficients are $c_1 = c_2 = 2$.

The effect of population size for both PSO and FA was analyzed in Fig. 4. The population size and the maximum number of iterations impact was analysed in terms of the average EE obtained for both PSO and FA; also, such heuristic distributed solutions was compared to the centralized solution based on Dinkelbach method (Max EE). As shown, increasing the maximum number of iterations as well as population size leads to better EE results with the only counter effect being the increase on complexity. Furthermore, FA has a significant advantage in terms of achieve EE when compared to the PSO under small population sizes (5 to 10). This gap among each algorithms' solution is reduced when the population size increases and is almost equivalent when it reaches 50 individuals.

TABLE I. Multirate DS/CDMA system parameters

Parameters	Adopted Values
MC-DS/CDMA System	
Noise Power	$P_n = -90$ [dBm]
MT Circuitry Power	$p_c = 0.1$ [W]
Relay Circuitry Power	$p_{c_R} = 0.5$ [W]
Relay Transmission Power	$p_R = 25$ [W]
Power Amplifier Inefficiency	$\varrho = \varrho_R = 2.5$
Codification Rate	$\ell = \frac{3}{4}$
Processing Gain	$F = 128$
Sub-carriers	$N = 16$
Users	$U = 5$
Amplification Matrix	$A = \mathbf{I}_F * (\frac{p_R}{F})$ [1]
Bits per Packet	$V = 1$
Sub-channel Bandwidth	$w = 78$ KHz
Max. power per user	$P_{\max} = 125$ [mW]
# mobile terminals	$U = 5$
cell geometry	rectangular, with $x_{\text{cell}} = 10$Km $y_{\text{cell}} = 5$ Km
mobile term. distrib.	$\sim \mathcal{U}[0.5 * x_{\text{cell}}, y_{\text{cell}}]$
Channel Gain	
path loss	$\propto d^{-2}$
shadowing	uncorrelated log-normal, $\sigma^2 = 6$ dB
fading	Rayleigh
User Types	
User Rates	$r_{i,\min} = [256; 512; 1024]$ [Kbps]
Modulation (For BER purposes)	$M = [4, 16, 64]$
Tolerable BER per class	$[10^{-3}; 10^{-5}; 10^{-8}]$

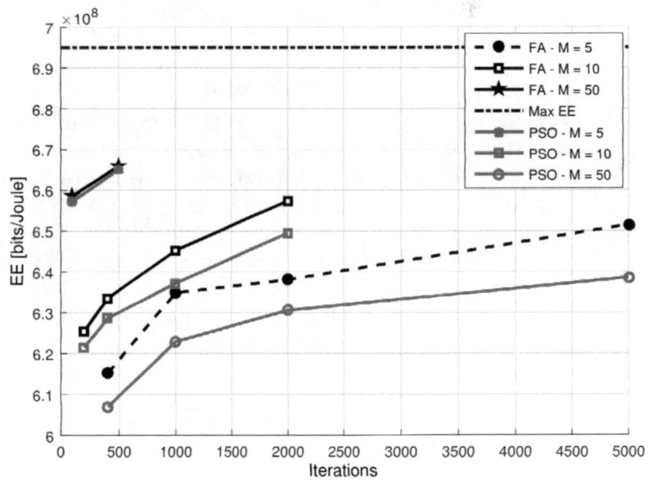

Figure 4. Effect of population size M and maximum number of iterations on the average Energy Efficiency.

For simulation purposes all users have been separated into three different QoS requirement classes. Basically, each class represents one type of multimedia service; thus, users may require low, average or high throughput associated with high, medium and very low maximal tolerable BER, respectively.

To effectively compare the performance of each method one must consider the computational complexity of each method. Some assumptions must be done: a) all algorithms are assumed to execute the same amount of iterations, hence the algorithm with the simplest iteration yield the simplest algorithm of all; b) computational complexity of Dinkelbach's method solution obtained via CvX tool is not considered in the analysis since its complexity cannot be securely obtained; c) number of users in the system is considered $U < N$ and therefore has no impact on the complexity asymptotically.

At each iteration of the V-DPCA algorithm a fixed number of operations are conducted which leads, in asymptotic terms, to a $\mathcal{O}(1)$ complexity. Hence, the M-DPCA approach has a static complexity while the V-DPCA is executed one time at each subcarrier which leads to linear complexity $\mathcal{O}(N)$. It is also easy to show that at each iteration of the PSO algorithm operations are computed for each of the individuals of the population which represents an asymptotic linear dependence of the population size, *i.e.*, $\mathcal{O}(M)$. Finally, the complexity of the FA is directly related to the fact that it must compare every possible pair of fireflies which gives an asymptotic complexity of $\mathcal{O}(M^2)$ where M is the population size. Furthermore, the performance comparison in terms of how close to the optimal solution (on average) each algorithm finds itself is sumarized in Table II. Such results represent the average over a thousand channel realizations and MTs geographical distribution.

TABLE II. AVERAGE EE AND ITERATION COMPLEXITY.

Algorithm	**% of the Optimal EE**	**Complexity**
Dinkelbach Method	100%	-
V-DPCA	57%	$\mathcal{O}(N)$
M-DPCA	96%	$\mathcal{O}(1)$
FA	96%	$\mathcal{O}(M^2)$
PSO	95%	$\mathcal{O}(M)$

N is the number of subcarriers in the system.
M is the population size of the heuristic method.

VII. CONCLUSION

Five different approaches solving the energy-efficient design in MC-DS/CDMA cooperative networks with FRS were analyzed. Also, the algorithms' complexity issues were briefly addressed. Our findings indicate that the best average EE-complexity tradeoff is achieved by the M-DPCA. The M-DPCA algorithm takes into account the average observed interference while performing the power control of the non-cooperative game in a distributed fashion, which is of paramount importance in uplink scenarios. Indeed, such algorithm presented the lowest iteration complexity and achieved similar or better performance results regarding the average EE than centralized solutions, such as the heuristic ones. Another advantage is that it simplifies the interference estimator procedure at the BS side while a low overhead information exchanging between MT and BS is held.

Future works include the problem of the joint resource block and power allocation in the uplink of multi-user multi-cell large scale multiple-input-multiple-output (or massive MIMO) under pilot contamination regime. Since the optimization problem is of mixed-integer nature, we are proposing different quasi-optimal resource allocation algorithms to achieve the better tradeoffs regarding average system spectral efficiency and energy efficiency, all of them supported by a game theoretic framework.

REFERENCES

[1] A. Zappone, S. Buzzi, and E. Jorswieck, "Energy-efficient power control and receiver design in relay-assisted ds/cdma wireless networks via game theory," *IEEE Comm. Letters*, vol. 15, no. 7, pp. 701–703, 2011.

[2] M. Al-Kali, L. Yu, D. Samb, C. Liu, and D. Wang, "Performance analysis for energy efficiency in wireless cooperative relay networks," in *Communication Technology (ICCT), 2012 IEEE 14th International Conference on*, pp. 423–427, Nov 2012.

[3] C. Li, S. H. Song, J. Zhang, and K. Letaief, "Maximizing energy efficiency in wireless networks with a minimum average throughput requirement," in *Wireless Communications and Networking Conference (WCNC), 2012 IEEE*, pp. 1130–1134, April 2012.

[4] K. Cheung, S. Yang, and L. Hanzo, "Achieving maximum energy-efficiency in multi-relay ofdma cellular networks: A fractional programming approach," *Communications, IEEE Transactions on*, vol. 61, no. 7, pp. 2746–2757, July 2013.

[5] A. R. Souza, *et al.* "Energy and spectral efficiencies trade-off with filter optimisation in multiple access interference-aware networks," *Transactions on Emerging Telecommunications Technologies*, 2013. [Online]. Available: http://dx.doi.org/10.1002/ett.2698

[6] L. D. H. Sampaio, Á. R. C. e. Souza, T. Abrão, and P. J. E. Jeszensky, "Game theoretic energy efficiency design in mc-cdma cooperative networks," *IEEE Sensors Journal*, vol. 14, no. 9, pp. 3065–3075, Sept 2014.

[7] S. Buzzi, G. Colavolpe, D. Saturnino, and A. Zappone, "Potential games for energy-efficient power control and subcarrier allocation in uplink multicell ofdma systems," *IEEE Journal of Selected Topics in Signal Processing*, vol. 6, no. 2, pp. 89–103, 2012.

[8] D. J. Goodman and N. B. Mandayan, "Power control for wireless data," *IEEE Personal Communication Magazine*, vol. 7, no. 4, pp. 48–54, 2000.

[9] M. K. Simon and M.-S. Alouini, *Digital Communication over Fading Channels*. Wiley, 2004.

[10] K. Du and N. Swamy, *Wireless Communication Systems: From RF Subsystems to 4G Enabling Technologies*. Cambridge University Press, 2010.

[11] W. Dinkelbach, "On nonlinear fractional programming," *Management Science*, vol. 13, no. 7, pp. 492–498, 1967.

[12] M. Marques, L. D. H. Sampaio, F. Ciriaco, F. R. Durand, and T. Abrão, "Energy efficiency optimization in mpg ds/cdma," in *Simpósio Brasileiro de Telecomunicações 2013 (SBrT13)*, Fortaleza, Brazil, pp. 1–5, 2013.

[13] S. Schaible and T. Ibaraki, "Fractional programming," *European Journal of Operational Research*, vol. 12, no. 4, pp. 325 – 338, 1983.

[14] I. CVX Research, "CVX: Matlab software for disciplined convex programming, version 2.1," http://cvxr.com/cvx, Mar. 2014.

[15] J. Kennedy and R. C. Eberhart, *Swarm Intelligence*, 1st ed. Morgan Kaufmann, 2001.

[16] X.-S. Yang, *Nature-Inspired Metaheuristic Algorithms*. Luniver Press, 2008.

[17] T. J. Gross, T. Abrao, and P. J. E. Jeszensky, "Distributed power control algorithm for multiple access systems based on verhulst model," *International Journal of Electronics and Communications (AEÜ)*, vol. 65, pp. 361–372, 2011.

[18] D. Fudenberg and J. Tirole, *Game Theory*. Cambridge, MA: MIT Press, 1991, translated into Chinesse by Renin University Press, Bejing: China.

[19] G. Scutari, D. P. Palomar, F. Facchinei, and J.-S. Pang, "Convex optimization, game theory, and variational inequality theory," *IEEE Signal Processing Magazine*, pp. 35–49, 2010.

[20] P. J. Reny, "Non-cooperative games (equilibrium existence)," in *The New Palgrave Dictionary of Economics*, S. N. Durlauf and L. E. Blume, Eds. Basingstoke: Palgrave Macmillan, 2008.

[21] I. L. Glicksberg, "A further generalization of the kakutani fixed point theorem, with application to nash equilibrium points," in *Proc. of American Mathematical Society*, vol. 3, no. 1, pp. 170–174, Feb. 1952.

**International Academy, Research,
and Industry Association (IARIA)**
412 Derby Way
Wilmington, DE 19810

ISBN 978-1-5108-3371-5

CURRAN ASSOCIATES INC.
proceedings.com